STUDIES IN WELSH HISTORY

Editors

RALPH A. GRIFFITHS   KENNETH O. MORGAN
GLANMOR WILLIAMS

———

4

THE NORTH WALES QUARRYMEN
1874–1922

Banner of the North Wales Quarrymen's Union

Reproduced from W. J. Parry, *Chwareli a Chwarelwyr* (1897)

THE NORTH WALES QUARRYMEN 1874—1922

by

R. MERFYN JONES

*Published on behalf of the
History and Law Committee
of the Board of Celtic Studies*

CARDIFF
UNIVERSITY OF WALES PRESS
1981

© University of Wales Press, 1981

British Library Cataloguing in Publication Data
Jones, R. Merfyn
  The North Wales Quarrymen, 1874–1922—
  (Studies in Welsh History; vol. 4 ISSN 0141—030X).
  1. Industrial relations—Wales, North—History
  2. Trade-unions—Stone-cutters—Wales, North
  3. Slate—Wales, North
  I. Title   II. University of Wales.
  Board of Celtic Studies   III. Series
  331'.042'2354094291   HD6976.S7/
  ISBN 0–7083–0776–0

Printed in Wales by Qualitex Printing Limited
Cardiff

EDITORS' FOREWORD

Since the Second World War, Welsh history has attracted considerable scholarly attention and enjoyed a vigorous popularity. Not only have the approaches, both traditional and new, to the study of history in general been successfully applied to Wales's past, but the number of scholars engaged in this enterprise has multiplied during these years. These advances have been especially marked in the University of Wales.

In order to make more widely available the conclusions of recent research, much of it of limited accessibility in postgraduate dissertations and theses, the History and Law Committee of the Board of Celtic Studies has inaugurated this new series of monographs, *Studies in Welsh History*. It is anticipated that many of the volumes will have originated in research conducted in the University of Wales or under the auspices of the Board of Celtic Studies. But the series will not exclude significant contributions made by researchers in other Universities and elsewhere. Its primary aim is to serve historical scholarship and to encourage the study of Welsh history.

PREFACE

On a Saturday morning in November 1865, between 1,200 and 1,500 men gathered on the slopes of Mynydd y Cefn above the small town of Bethesda in Caernarvonshire to launch a society which they called *Cymdeithas Undebol Chwarelwyr Cymru* (United Society of Welsh Quarrymen).[1] Although there had been earlier revolts of quarrymen this was the first recorded attempt to organise a trade union for the quarrymen who worked in the small but important slate industry of north-west Wales.[2] The society failed almost as soon as it was started but an idea had been planted and, despite the most strenuous efforts of its opponents, it was not to be uprooted. This book is about the struggle of quarrymen to organise and 'combine' in the slate quarries and mines of north Wales, and particularly in the giant Penrhyn quarries. It was often a battle for survival fought in very distinctive communities, but the struggle witnessed some of the most bitter and dramatic disputes in the history of the British working class.

What follows, therefore, is for the most part concerned with only one strand in the history of the quarrying communities of north Wales: the conflict between men and masters. The book aims at being neither the history of a trade union, though it is restricted to the years of the independent existence of that union, 1874–1922, nor of a group of workers. It attempts rather to supply an account of the central tensions in the slate villages and quarries, tensions which culminated in the desperate pitched battles of the Penrhyn lock-outs of 1896–7 and 1900–3. Events and organisations are mentioned therefore only insofar as they appear to relate to this central theme of conflict. This is an important limitation since there is clearly much more to be said about the people and the movements referred to than appears in these pages.

---

[1] *Yr Herald Cymraeg*, 11 November 1865.
[2] In 1825 some 150 men had struck work in the Penrhyn quarry and 'drove the rest off. The ostensible object of these ill-advised proceedings appears to be an advance in wages.' *North Wales Gazette*, 24 March 1825.

Conflict has a mechanism of its own, and much concerning the particular momentum of events will be related here; but conflict also reveals a great deal else. At the point of struggle a community's strengths and weaknesses become highlighted, as do the ideas and beliefs which lend cohesion and purpose to the efforts of individual men and women. The conflicts in the slate quarries of north Wales helped to shape the area's history; they also expressed much of, and explained much about, the history of that area.

This then is primarily intended to be a contribution to the history of the people of Gwynedd rather than to the history of industrial relations. The national dimension to the quarrymen's history is not ignored but neither is an attempt made to place the Penrhyn disputes in the development of the state's policies toward industrial disputes.[3] This is omitted not because it is considered unimportant but because this book is about something else. It is about the slate quarrymen.

Original sources for the history of the quarrymen are plentiful; in that respect at least they are a fortunate group of workers. The uniqueness and importance of their achievement has rightly attracted many historians and will doubtless continue to do so. The slate quarrymen have by no means been ignored and much concerning their history, and that of their union, has already been published.[4] This book attempts to avoid repeating what is already fairly well known and concentrates instead on those aspects of the slate quarryman's world which have received little critical attention. It attempts also to place the ordinary quarryman, and not his leaders or his employers, at the centre of the stage. A conscious attempt has also been made to use, wherever possible, the actual words of the participants (as recorded in verbatim newspaper reports, evidence to commissions, minutes). Most of these words were originally spoken or written in Welsh and have been translated by the author.

---

[3] The Conciliation Act, 1896, was crucially tested by Lord Penrhyn. See Lord Askwith, *Industrial Problems and Disputes* (London, 1920).
[4] See Bibliography and especially Jean Lindsay, *A History of the North Wales Slate Industry* (Newton Abbot, 1974), and J. Roose Williams, *Quarryman's Champion, the Life and Activities of William John Parry of Coetmor* (Denbigh, 1978).

ACKNOWLEDGEMENTS

A substantially different version of this book was submitted to the Centre for the Study of Social History, University of Warwick, for the degree of Ph.D. and I am indebted to the past and present staff and students at the Centre, and in particular to Edward Thompson, for their advice and criticisms over the years. The original thesis was read by Professor Royden Harrison, Dr. Tony Mason, Dr. Robin Okey and Dr. Cyril Parry. I am indebted to them all for recommending many minor amendments and some major structural changes. The editors of the present series, Dr. Kenneth O. Morgan and Dr. Ralph Griffiths, read drafts of this book with scholarly thoroughness and I am grateful to them for their corrections and suggestions. I owe a special debt of gratitude to Professor Glanmor Williams, who encouraged me to prepare this work for publication and whose careful reading has much improved the text.

Many librarians and archivists have also given me considerable assistance and I am indebted to the Librarians and staffs of the National Library of Wales, Aberystwyth; the British Library Newspaper Collection, Colindale; the Bibliothèque Nationale, Paris; and the libraries of the University College of North Wales, Bangor, the University College of Swansea, the University of Warwick, and the University of Liverpool. Mr. Bryn Parry and the staffs of the Gwynedd Archive Service's offices deserve special mention for their unfailing and patient assistance over many years; they must also be thanked for their conscientiousness in ensuring that so much material relating to the slate industry has been safely stored and catalogued. This book would not have been possible without their efforts or without the permission granted me by the Lady Janet Douglas Pennant to consult previously closed collections of papers relating to the Penrhyn disputes.

A version of Chapter 4 was published in Raphael Samuel (ed.), *Miners, Quarrymen and Saltworkers* (London, 1977), pp. 99–136, and I am grateful to the editor and to Routledge and

Kegan Paul, the publishers, for permission to reproduce some of the material here. A version of Chapter 5 was published in the *Transactions of the Caernarvonshire Historical Society*, Vol. 35 (1974), and I gratefully acknowledge the permission to re-publish given by the Society and the editor of the *Transactions*.

The contents of this book have been discussed with countless colleagues and friends and I am grateful to them all. One friend in particular, my wife Jill Lovecy, has discussed the work with me at every stage. Any errors of fact or eccentricities of interpretation remain my own responsibility.

This book was almost entirely written in Nantlle, Caernarvonshire. In all probability the task would not have been completed without the stimulating support of so many warm friendships made in Nantlle and in neighbouring Talysarn. The book is dedicated, therefore, to the people of that valley who, along with the people of Blaenau Ffestiniog, Bethesda and elsewhere in Gwynedd have, for too long, had to live with the cruel consequences of a dying industry.

R.M.J.

University of Liverpool, 1979

CONTENTS

		Page
PREFACE		vii
ACKNOWLEDGEMENTS		ix
Part 1	The Roots of Conflict	
I	THE SLATE INDUSTRY AND GWYNEDD SOCIETY	1
II	THE QUARRYMEN	17
III	BELIEFS AND ATTITUDES	49
IV	THE QUARRY	72
V	THE UNION, 1874–1900	106
Part 2	Conflict	
VI	DINORWIC AND LLECHWEDD	142
VII	THE FIRST PENRHYN LOCK-OUT	175
VIII	THE PENRHYN LOCK-OUT, 1900–1903	210
IX	REPERCUSSIONS	267
Part 3	Aftermath	
X	THE UNION, 1900–1922	295
XI	'POLITICS OBTAIN HERE'	322
APPENDIX I	Membership of the North Wales Quarrymen's Union, 1874–1925	330
APPENDIX II	The Pennant Lloyd Agreement, 1874	331
APPENDIX III	Some contributions to the N.W.Q.U. Fund, May 1901	332
APPENDIX IV	The Quarrymen's Charter, 1912	333
APPENDIX V	Terms of Amalgamation, N.W.Q.U. and T.G.W.U., 1922	335
APPENDIX VI	Profiles	337
BIBLIOGRAPHY		344
INDEX		351

Part I

The Roots of Conflict

I

THE SLATE INDUSTRY AND GWYNEDD SOCIETY

Wales consists of several regions as well as of a multitude of localities. Gwynedd, comprising the historic counties of Anglesey, Merioneth and Caernarvonshire, is one of the apparently coherent and distinct regions. For much of the nineteenth and early-twentieth centuries the society and economy of Gwynedd were greatly affected by the presence in Caernarvonshire and Merioneth of a small but important extractive industry, the slate industry. Gwynedd was the world's major producer of roofing slate and that had a profound effect on the region's history. The fact that the slate industry was established in the distinctive conditions of Gwynedd had an equally profound effect on the character of the slate industry and of the men who worked in it.[1]

Today Gwynedd is considered a 'peripheral' region within Britain, but the remoteness of the area in the nineteenth century can too easily be exaggerated and thus the history of its people too conveniently interpreted as an example of 'backwardness'. Gwynedd, of course, shared in the undeniable backwardness of much of western Britain until the eighteenth century, but its subsequent modest development, linked in many crucial ways to dramatic economic changes in Lancashire, meant that by the early-nineteenth century it was inextricably tied to the modern British economy and, though a relatively remote region, it could hardly be described as undeveloped. In this process of economic integration the slate industry was the crucial, though, as we shall see, not the only,

[1] Slate was also exploited in France (primarily near Angers in Anjou and Fumay in the Ardennes; slate was also worked in Basse-Bretagne and elsewhere), Belgium (the Bassin d'Herbeumont), Portugal, Italy and Norway. In the United States slate was quarried primarily in Pennsylvania though there were also sizeable deposits in Vermont. T. Nelson Dale et al., *Slate in the U.S.* (1914).

factor. The industrial revolution may have been founded on textiles and powered by steam; but it was roofed with slates skilfully wrenched from the Snowdonia hills.

The development of Gwynedd was closely associated with its few natural geographical advantages: its slate and other resources; its tourist attractions; and its proximity to Lancashire, on the one hand, and to Ireland on the other. By the early-nineteenth century these factors had contributed substantially to the eroding of the historic isolation of the region.

Slate was first exploited on a large scale by Richard Pennant, the hero of the industry's early entrepreneurial phase.[2] Pennant had acquired the Penrhyn estates through his marriage in 1765 when he had taken Anna Susannah Warburton as his wife. Neither Pennant nor his wife had anything other than a geographical interest in the area— Sir Robert Williams, the last 'Welsh' landlord, had died in 1678—until Pennant took over the whole estate in the early 1780s and opened up what were to become the world-famous Penrhyn quarries. Pennant was typical of many entrepreneurs of the time in his audacity and his willingness to invest: by the outbreak of the Napoleonic Wars the independent quarriers who had worked the slate rocks of Caebraichycafn had been bought out and transformed into wage labourers; nearby Crown lands had been leased and appropriated in a way which was to scandalise local opinion for a century or more; the narrow paths leading from the quarries had become roads; Port Penrhyn harbour had been built, and a start made on a model village to house the increasing number of workers. Before the depression of the 1790s, Pennant was employing 400 men; by the 1820s, 900; by the middle of the nineteenth century almost 2,000 were being employed in his quarries.

[2] Richard Pennant (1737?–1808), was succeeded in Penrhyn by a grandson of his sister, George Hay Dawkins (1763–1840), who assumed the name Pennant. Dawkins was responsible for the building of Penrhyn Castle. On his death the estate passed to his son-in-law, Edward Gordon Douglas (1800–86), who also assumed the name of Pennant and was created Baron Penrhyn of Llandegai in 1866. He was succeeded by his son, the second Baron Penrhyn, George Sholto Douglas Pennant (1836–1907), who was in turn succeeded by his son Edward Sholto Douglas-Pennant (1864–1927). In 1951 much of the estate was conveyed to the National Trust.

Penrhyn set the pace and it was not long before the other slate-quarrying districts were compelled to follow. In 1787 a partnership started to work Dinorwic in a serious way on a lease from the landowner Assheton-Smith, and in 1809 Smith took over the main responsibility himself. In the Nantlle valley and the Ffestiniog district, the other two major slate-producing areas, the development of the industry was somewhat different. Ffestiniog was opened up by the Lancashire adventurers, Turner and the Cassons, and the industry later developed by English capitalists such as the Holland and Greaves families and by numerous speculatory companies. In the Nantlle valley the pattern was similar, although there was more involvement of local businessmen. To compete with Penrhyn and Dinorwic, however, similar measures had to be taken, and the familiar pattern of heavy investment in exploratory work and the development of transport links, such as the Portmadoc-Ffestiniog Railway opened in 1836, and port facilities followed. Portmadoc, Caernarfon, Port Dinorwic (Felinheli) and Port Penrhyn (Bangor) all owed their importance as shipping centres to the slate industry.

Whereas the Dinorwic quarries drew upon the local landed wealth of Assheton-Smith, much of the rest of the initial capital invested in the industry came from outside the region, primarily from Lancashire. Richard Pennant's ancestors might have had roots in Flintshire but Richard Pennant, like his father before him, was quintessentially a Liverpool merchant, one of that city's particular breed of merchant princes grown wealthy on the slave trade and on that most primitive of systems of capital accumulation, the West Indian plantation system. From 1768 to 1780, and again from 1784 to 1790, he was Member of Parliament for Liverpool. In 1783 he became Baron Penrhyn of Penrhyn; but the 'Penrhyn' referred to in his title was not his estate in Caernarvonshire but a place in County Louth in Ireland: roots, along with peerages, had become commodities.

Other English businessmen to become involved in the slate industry included Samuel Holland, William Turner, and Thomas and William Casson. Holland was the son of a Liverpool merchant already involved in north Wales mining

enterprises who came to Blaenau Ffestiniog in 1821 at the age
of eighteen and stayed to open up the Rhiwbryfdir slate mine,
eventually becoming Liberal M.P. for the county of Merioneth.[3]
William Turner, who acquired very extensive interests in slate
quarries and mines throughout north-west Wales, came
originally from Seathwaite in Lancashire where his father was
already involved in slate quarrying; the Cassons were from
Cumberland. Later in the century, another Lancashire man,
William Darbishire, became actively involved in quarrying in
the Nantlle valley and other prominent names in the industry,
such as Greaves, Robinson, and, later, Kellow, testify to the
English origins of most of the slate owners, many of them
bringing with them capital already accumulated in endeavours
elsewhere. Some investment in the industry came as finance
capital, much of it from London and siphoned through a
variety of companies. Perhaps the most dramatic example of
this kind of intervention was the involvement in the 1820s
of Nathan Meyer Rothschild and his Royal Cambrian
Company and Welsh Slate and Copper Mining Company.[4]

Economically, therefore, the slate industry integrated Gwynedd into the mainstream of the British economy. This was not
an industry restricted by the limited capital immediately
available within the region but, on the contrary, one which
attracted capital and personnel from distant and metropolitan
centres.

The slate industry itself transformed the infrastructure of
Gwynedd, particularly by developing improved transport
links and port facilities, but other factors were also important
in these changes. Most significant, perhaps, was Gwynedd's importance as a bridge-head to Ireland. Following the act of
Union of 1801, this link came to be crucially important to the
British state, an importance symbolised by the Menai Suspension Bridge, designed by Telford and opened in 1827, and
built with funds allocated by Parliament. The linked improve-

---

[3] Samuel Holland (1803–92), Liberal M.P. for Merioneth, 1870–85.
[4] This brief sketch of the industry's economic history relies in large part
upon David Dylan Pritchard's excellent articles in the *Quarry Managers' Journal*,
July 1942 to October 1946. See also A. H. Dodd, *The Industrial Revolution in North
Wales* (Cardiff, 1951), pp. 203–22; Jean Lindsay, *A History of the North Wales
Slate Industry* (Newton Abbot, 1974); Tom Davies, 'The Arfon Quarries', *Planet*,
30 January 1976, pp. 7–22.

ment of what subsequently became the A5 route from Holyhead to London opened up some of the most mountainous terrain in Wales, while the coastal route was also greatly improved. The expectation that the Irish trade would run through Llŷn and not Anglesey also resulted in improvements in the south of the region.

The railway link to Holyhead via Chester was opened in 1848 and meant that from that date parts of Gwynedd were directly connected to the main British rail system. A network of branch lines and quarry railways connected much of the rest of Gwynedd to that link, with the Cambrian Coast line opened in 1867 and the main London and North Western line reaching to Blaenau Ffestiniog in 1879.[5]

Before the advent of the railway, coastal shipping had supplied excellent transport links, particularly with Liverpool. By the 1820s three or four Liverpool steamers were providing a daily summer service to the Menai Straits.[6] By 1850 the steamers were offering a service from Portmadoc to Liverpool. The schooners of Portmadoc, built locally and manned by local crews, were meanwhile sailing regularly to northern Europe, North America and the Mediterranean.[7]

Gwynedd, then, was not as remote as has sometimes been assumed. Even the genteel tourism of the late-eighteenth century had had an important effect, resulting in the building of large new hotels, such as Beddgelert's Goat Hotel between 1800 and 1802, in previously isolated mountain or seaside villages.[8] The arrival of the railway led to the Gwynedd coast being rapidly developed and to the building of small but popular seaside resorts; by 1856 Llandudno, on the north coast of Caernarvonshire, had room for 8,000 visitors in its carefully-planned accommodation.[9]

Gwynedd's economic development was not stunted or backward as a result of the constraints of the region's own

[5] Port Penrhyn was linked to the general railway system in 1848, Port Dinorwic and Caernarvon in 1852 and Portmadoc in 1867. The Holyhead–Chester link was complete in 1850.

[6] *Gore's Directory* (Liverpool, 1850); A. H. Dodd, *A History of Caernarvonshire, 1289–1900* (Caernarfon, 1968), p. 277.

[7] H. Hughes, *Immortal Sails* (London, 1946).

[8] D. E. Jenkins, *Beddgelert: Its Facts, Fairies and Folk-lore* (Portmadoc, 1899), p. 44.

[9] A. H. Dodd, *Hist. of Caerns.*, p. 273.

scarce economic resources. On the contrary, the region attracted the attention of many enterprising outsiders who energetically (and on the whole successfully) exploited the region's potential. The intervention of these men had profound social consequences which we shall note later, and their economic success meant that, during the first half of the nineteenth century, Gwynedd's historic isolation and backwardness were breached and the area became locked into the economic mechanism of the world's first industrial society. One of the most dramatic symbols of this process of modernisation was the achievement of William A. Madocks, a radical lawyer who invested £160,000 in draining the Traeth Mawr in south-east Caernarvonshire, a project finally completed by 1814. He went on to design and build what he called his 'borough' of Tremadoc and later the harbour of Portmadoc, which was to be so important in the export of slate. In Tremadoc he also built a woollen mill installed with modern machinery. His improving energy and audacity were matched only by Richard Pennant's.[10]

The industrial revolution in Gwynedd may have been incomplete and initiated by outsiders, but it occurred early and had a profound impact on the region. One of the most important effects was the growth in population in the most developed parts of the region, particularly in Caernarvonshire and north Merioneth. Much of the land of Merioneth and Caernarvonshire is mountainous, rocky and acid, and inhospitable for human settlement. The population of Gwynedd in the nineteenth century, however, was much higher than that in some other parts of Wales. The total population in 1891 was 224,530 or 13 per cent of the total population of Wales and Monmouthshire.[11]

That this population was associated with economic development is clearly shown by the imbalance exhibited within Gwynedd between the population levels in rural Anglesey and those in 'developed' Caernarvonshire. Anglesey had experi-

[10] William Alexander Madocks (1773–1828), Radical M.P. for Boston, 1802–18, and Chippenham, 1820–26. See E. Beazley, *Madocks and the Wonder of Wales* (London, 1967).

[11] These and the following population statistics are from the relevant *Census Returns*; they all have to be treated with caution since the registered county totals rarely apply to the geographical limits of any one county.

enced its limited industrial development in the copper boom of the eighteenth and early-nineteenth centuries, when its copper resources had been of crucial importance to the developing industrial economies of north-west England and of the Swansea area. By the nineteenth century, however, its economy had reverted to its agricultural base and its population growth remained small throughout that century. Between 1801 and 1891 the population of the Anglesey registration district, which excluded the more developed south of the county, grew only from 25,692 to 34,219, a rise of 33 per cent. Caernarvonshire and southern Anglesey in the same period experienced a growth in population of 173 per cent—to become, with a total population in 1891 of 126,000, the third most populous county in Wales.

The picture of Gwynedd's patchy, but nevertheless impressive, economic development outlined above is confirmed by an analysis of two of the available printed tax returns which give an indication of the geographical distribution of wealth within Britain in the financial years 1859–60 and 1879–80.[12] Tax returns are notoriously unreliable sources but they do offer some notion of comparative levels of wealth. Such a survey highlights the central importance of the slate industry in the Gwynedd economy and also the relative value of the Gwynedd economy within Wales.[13]

The total sums assessed for tax purposes in Gwynedd are not impressive, but an investigation of Schedule D returns (which assessed taxable profits arising from business, industry and the professions) produces more striking conclusions. In comparing the Schedule D returns for the Welsh counties (barring Monmouthshire), the importance of Caernarvonshire and Merioneth becomes apparent. Caernarvonshire and its boroughs were second only to Glamorgan and its boroughs in the amount of property and profits assessed in Wales in 1879–80 under Schedule D. Even more startling are the returns for sparsely-populated Merioneth which are similar to those of Carmarthenshire, which boasted twice Merioneth's population.

---

[12] *Property and Income Tax*, P.P., 1860 (546), xxxix, pt. 2; *Parliamentary Constituencies (Population)*, P.P., 1882 (149), lii. See W. D. Rubinstein, 'Wealth, Elites and Class Structure in Britain', *Past and Present*, No. 76 (1977), 109.
[13] For a guide to the nineteenth-century tax system, see J. C. Stamp, *British Incomes and Property* (London, 1916).

Until 1867–8 profits arising from mines, quarries and several other industrial sectors were anomalously assessed under Schedule A and not Schedule D. These Schedule A returns for every parish in Britain were published in a Parliamentary Paper of 1860. The economic map of Britain which emerges from an analysis of these returns clearly shows the slate industry's virtual monopoly of industrial capacity in Gwynedd and also indicates the importance of the slate industry in the mid-Victorian Welsh economy.

The gross assessed income arising from the stone and slate quarries of Caernarvonshire and Merioneth in 1859–60 amounted to £155,620, a sum which compares impressively with the £185,680 derived from mines in Glamorgan and the mere £20,162 from the mines of Carmarthenshire. These figures pre-date the phenomenal expansion of the south Wales coal industry from the 1860s onwards but they also pre-date the boom in the slate industry in the 1860s and early 1870s.[14]

However inadequate these assessments might be, they confirm that Gwynedd, and particularly Caernarvonshire, in the second half of the nineteenth century, was not as poor or as rural as is often assumed. On the contrary, they indicate a society in which the capitalist organisation of industry was extensive and well-established at a relatively early date.

The extraction and manufacture of slate was by far the most important industry but there were other industries as well. The dolerite quarries or 'settsworks' of Penmaenmawr, Trefor, Llithfaen and elsewhere employed some 1,500 men by 1891. Transport was itself a significant industry in the area; the railways employed many, but more important was shipping with over three and a half thousand men from the region employed as seamen in 1891, a thousand or so of them being away at sea at any one time. There were also small shipbuilding, fishing and woollen industries. As in Britain generally, the largest single group of employees was that of domestic servants, the largest sector was agriculture, with over 20,000 people involved in a variety of capacities, about half of them employed as agricultural labourers.

---

[14] There are many problems involved in comparing different industries: coal mines, for example, were assessed for profits over a five-year period. See J. C. Stamp, op. cit., p. 223.

The slate industry, employing between 11,000 and 14,000 men depending on trade conditions, was, however, the dominant sector of the local economy, producing 58 per cent of all the wealth accruing from the business, industry and professions of the region in 1859, and claiming 26 per cent of the gross annual value of all business, industry, transport, and all lands and messuages in the same year. In other words, one quarter of the assessed value of all Gwynedd property and profits was concentrated in the slate industry. Even more dramatic, however, was the concentration of ownership within the slate industry: for almost half of all slate quarrymen were employed by just two giant concerns which dominated the industry and its fortunes, the Dinorwic quarries, owned by the Assheton-Smith family, and the Penrhyn quarries, owned by the family which was the crucial element in Gwynedd society in the nineteenth century: the actively political Pennant—later Douglas Pennant—family, of Penrhyn Castle, whose assessed profits from the slate industry amounted to 45 per cent of the total.

The slate industry included two quite different types of owner. On the one hand were the aristocratic Penrhyn and Assheton-Smith families, on the other the entrepreneurial adventurers who owned much of the industry in the Nantlle district and in Blaenau Ffestiniog. This division, expressed in the separate employers' associations that prevailed until the First World War, had many dimensions, including a political one (Lord Penrhyn was Tory M.P. for Caernarvonshire, Samuel Holland the Liberal M.P. for Merioneth) and its effects permeated to the rock face; but its importance should not conceal the fact that by any estimation the most important and powerful men in the industry were Lord Penrhyn and Mr. Assheton-Smith, together with their respective managements. The production of Dinorwic and Penrhyn was crucial to the industry and through their pricing policies these two quarries effectively controlled the slate market and, to a considerable degree, affected the overall fortunes of the smaller concerns.

Had their power and wealth been based on their industrial strength alone, Penrhyn and Assheton-Smith's influence on the industry and hence on the development of Gwynedd would have been formidable. Their central importance in the economy and the class structure and culture of Gwynedd becomes even more visible when one considers their other interests, for these two families controlled not only a significant section of the industry of Gwynedd, but also much of its land.

The ownership of land in Gwynedd, and particularly in Anglesey and Caernarvonshire, was in the late-nineteenth century concentrated in fewer hands than anywhere else in England and Wales, and this gave landlordism a quite particular importance in Gwynedd society. In Caernarvonshire in 1887 only 4.2 per cent of the holdings, 4.6 per cent of the acreage, were owned by the occupier; this was the lowest rate of farm owner-occupation in Wales; in Cardiganshire, in contrast, which had the highest level of owner-occupation, 21 per cent of holdings were owned by the men who farmed them. The average for Wales as a whole was 10.5 per cent, twice the level for Gwynedd; in England 16.1 per cent of holdings were owner-occupied.[15]

Not only was almost all the land in Gwynedd owned by landlords, but the concentration of landholding amongst a few large landlords was also more marked than anywhere else in Wales. Only in Glamorgan did the great landowners approach the concentration of ownership exhibited in Gwynedd and no other county came near to the exceptionally high concentration in Caernarvonshire. In that county in 1873 the landlords who owned estates of 3,000 acres or more, with annual rentals of £3,000 or over, owned 67 per cent of the acreage, a level of concentration twice as intensive as that in Carmarthenshire, Cardigan or Brecon; in Anglesey the great landlords owned 58 per cent of the acreage. If rental rather than acreage is considered, the particular concentration of land ownership in Gwynedd, as compared with the rest of Wales, is even more marked, with the large landowners claiming 48 per cent of the total rental in Anglesey and 44 per cent in Merioneth.

Percentages can blunt the issue; put starkly, the figures mean that in the last quarter of the nineteenth century, for

[15] *Return for 1872–3* (of Every Owner of Land in England and Wales), P.P., 1874 (c. 1097), lxxii, pts. 1–2; John Bateman, *The Great Landowners of Great Britain and Ireland* (4th edn., London, 1883); Brian Ll. James, 'The Great Land-owners of Wales', *The National Library of Wales Journal*, XIV (1965–66), 301–20; *Agricultural Returns*, 1887.

which period reliable figures are available, almost half of Caernarvonshire was owned by five families, whilst over three-quarters of the county was owned by just thirty-five families, the other quarter being distributed between the other 100,000 or so inhabitants. Moreover, only 6 per cent of the households in the county owned any land at all that was bigger than a garden.

In late-nineteenth-century Britain, and particularly perhaps in nineteenth-century Wales, it is extremely difficult to distinguish between commercial, landed and industrial wealth. The financial empire run from Penrhyn Castle is particularly difficult to categorize. For Lord Penrhyn owned not only one of the two largest slate quarries, but was also the largest land-owner in Gwynedd with an estate—most of it in Caernarvon-shire, but some of it also in England—which in 1883 extended to 50,000 acres, his annual rental in the same year being £71,000, £63,000 of it from his Caernarvonshire property. He was the third largest landlord in Wales; only Sir Watkin Williams-Wynn and the earl of Cawdor owned more land. He was also the third richest, as only those coal and urban property-owning giants, the marquess of Bute and Lord Tredegar, enjoyed larger rent rolls. His estates alone, therefore, made Lord Penrhyn one of the wealthiest men in Wales and put him in the very highest bracket of British landowners. He lived in appropriate style in the enormous castle designed by Thomas Hopper and built between 1827 and 1837 for George Hay Dawkins Pennant. But the greater part of his income came from his slate quarries and not from his landed acres. The 2,500 men he employed in Bethesda produced for him an income at least twice as large as his rentals; in 1899 his profits from the Penrhyn quarries amounted to £133,000.[16] Yet his whole empire had originally been made possible by a commercial fortune based on trade with the West Indies and subsequently much of his income was invested in financial and commercial speculation

[16] Gwynedd Archive Service (hereafter GAS), Caernarvon, Penrhyn Quarry Letter book, 7 January 1899. The Penrhyn family was also integrated into the British aristocracy through marriage. The second Baron Penrhyn's daughter Kathleen was married to Viscount Falmouth, his other daughter to Sir Cuthbert Quilter, Liberal Unionist M.P. for Sudbury. His sister Caroline was married to Baron Magheramorne and his sister Eva to Lieut. Gen. Lord William F. E. Seymour, brother of the marquis of Hertford. *Who's Who 1902* (London, 1902). In 1896 it was claimed that the Penrhyn estate had grown to 72,000 acres. *R.C. on Land*, Appendix X.

elsewhere. Merchant capital, landed capital, industrial capital: whichever way it is approached, the Penrhyn fortune can be seen to have been firmly embedded in the structure and mechanics of nineteenth-century British capitalism. It cannot be dismissed as an anachronistic fiefdom set in some remote corner. Further, as we shall see, the behaviour of the Penrhyns, particularly of George Sholto Douglas Pennant, the second Lord Penrhyn and the first in the line to inherit directly from his father, displayed many of the characteristics of both aristocrat and industrialist.

The third largest landowner in Gwynedd, following Lord Penrhyn and Sir Watkin Williams-Wynn, was Assheton-Smith of the Vaynol estate, whose acreage amounted to 34,000. Assheton-Smith, however, like Lord Penrhyn, derived the major part of his income not from his £42,000 annual rental but from the Dinorwic slate quarries.

There were other, more modest, landowners who were also involved in the slate industry: the Oakeleys of Tanybwlch and Lord Newborough of Glynllifon, for example, were both deeply involved in the exploitation of slate, as were the Ormesby-Gores. Land and slate were as intermingled financially as they were in the earth.

What emerges most strikingly from this survey is the degree to which economic dominance in Gwynedd, whether based on land, commercial inheritance, or slate, was concentrated not only into a few but into the same hands. A few dozen families controlled virtually the whole economy of Gwynedd, be it agricultural or industrial, and two of these families, the Assheton-Smiths and the Penrhyn family, owned a massive share of the total, effectively sharing between them half the slate industry of Gwynedd and a quarter of the land of Caernarvonshire. Any analysis of the class structure of late-nineteenth-century Gwynedd must start with that fact for, if we accept E. P. Thompson's definition of class as a relationship and not a thing, then it was to the fact of the economic might of Penrhyn and Vaynol that everyone else in Gwynedd had to relate.

Before we can examine the way the relationships between the various classes in Gwynedd shifted and changed, we must look briefly at the state of the other classes in the late-nineteenth century, for they are not without their own power and significance. What is strikingly lacking in nineteenth-century Gwynedd society, as indeed in much of Wales, is a fully formed middle class. The reason for the failure of a business, manufacturing middle class to emerge in Gwynedd is obvious: there was no real opportunity for it to do so.

Slate was an extractive industry restricted to the winning, splitting, dressing and subsequent transportation of slates; it was not an industry that spawned small manufacturing ancillaries that could lay the basis for the development of a prosperous middle class. In the case of Gwynedd, the largest slate-masters owned the land, the quarries, the rail lines to the sea, the ports and indeed some of the ships which exported the slate; in some cases they even owned foundries which manufactured the tools and machines needed in their quarries. There was, of course, room for local initiative to assert itself and profit; there were some notable Welsh quarry owners, and many others participated in profitable slate-quarrying and shipping ventures. But room for expansion was extremely limited by the sheer scale of resources available to the major concerns.

The weakness of the indigenous Gwynedd middle class was therefore based on its inability to achieve a solid base in the local economy. It is important to note that this did not result from its weakness in numbers. On the contrary, Gwynedd had a significant number of men involved in small business and trading and in the professions. Who else was to employ the army of domestic servants resident in the region? They did not all work for the local gentry and the slate-masters, and in nineteenth-century Britain one crucial symbol of class differentiation was the employment of a domestic servant.

Particularly important in Gwynedd society and politics, as we shall see, were the professional, educated middle class: the 147 lawyers, of whom David Lloyd George was one, the 159 doctors, the 54 accountants, the 606 male teachers and lecturers (and 894 female teachers), and above all, perhaps, the 381 Nonconformist ministers, recorded in the census of 1891. These professional middle classes and their business colleagues were of especial importance in the small towns in which they practised: Dolgellau in Merioneth; Holyhead and

Llangefni in Anglesey; Portmadoc, but above all Caernarfon and Bangor, in Caernarvonshire.

This Gwynedd middle class was swollen by a considerable number of English immigrants; we have already noted their presence in the slate industry, but they were also to be found in many other spheres of activity, particularly in the growing tourist trade of the latter half of the nineteenth century. Retired professional people and those with private means expanded this middle-class presence, especially in such coastal resorts as Llandudno, Cricieth and Harlech.[17]

Let us now turn briefly to the rest of the population of Gwynedd, a section of whom is the primary concern of this book. By the end of the nineteenth century at least 50,000 men and women were employed in various sorts of manual work in the three counties of the region, the largest concentrations of labouring men being, as we have seen, in agriculture and in slate quarrying and mining. The slate quarrymen as a labour force were created in the closing decades of the eighteenth century and during the early-nineteenth century.

The early establishment of the industry involved the deliberate creation of a force of wage labourers: Richard Pennant could not exploit slate rock; he could only exploit the workers who quarried it. The materials used were the ones familiar to the far-sighted adventurers of British capitalism— the use of the law, particularly of Enclosure Acts; the use, when necessary, of the soldiery; and, perhaps most important of all, the ruthless use of sheer economic power. To state the problem simply: if slate was to be quarried extensively then tenant farmers and others had to be cleared from the area and simultaneously transformed from small farmers and/or independent small-time quarriers into a group of 'free' labourers with nothing to sell but their labour power and no one to sell it to but the quarry owners. This process was not easy. Men and women resented and physically opposed the degradation which capitalism required and there was much resistance to

---

[17] The population of Llandudno leapt by 53 per cent in the decade after 1881, while the population of most of Gwynedd remained static: *Census Returns*, 1891. For a fascinating account of Harlech's development, see L. Lloyd, 'Harlech and Ardudwy, 1880–1930', *Journal of the Merioneth Historical and Record Society* (1977), 16–26.

the process, particularly in Dinorwic and in the Cilgwyn area of Nantlle.[18] Capitalism triumphed, though it also created a resilient tradition of bitterness and loss which was to last for generations, a tradition which was nourished by the fact that the law clearly need have little to do with justice and that much of the land which the new masters of Gwynedd were clearing and developing had previously been Crown or common land. Capitalism in Gwynedd therefore created a 'modern' industry, roads, ports and towns; it also created a working class.

Two important features characterised this working class. In the first place, it was locally recruited and therefore Welsh-speaking; second, it was destined, as an organised force, always to be a minority of the region's population. There was no significant, let alone mass, immigration of workers from other areas into Gwynedd. Despite its proximity to Ireland, even Anglesey had a very low level of Irish immigration, whereas Merioneth, with thirty-six Irish-born males in the county in 1891, had the lowest level of Irish immigration in Britain. English or south Walian workers were no more common. This meant that the Gwynedd working class was culturally homogeneous with little reason to learn English in order to communicate with English-speaking immigrants. Throughout its existence the North Wales Quarrymen's Union held all its meetings and wrote all its minutes and accounts exclusively in the Welsh language.[19]

To sum up: the concentration of wealth in Gwynedd was remarkable, as indeed was the composition of that wealth. The landlord quarry-owners were immensely wealthy, far, far richer than any local businessmen; their mock castles, surrounded by enormous protective walls, symbolised their very real economic power. Until the 1880s—in some localities even later—they also exercised political power. The slate industry, and consequently Gwynedd, was therefore dominated by a very small group of immensely wealthy families. This left little room for an indigenous business or industrial class to develop a sound economic base. Such men were effectively excluded from the

---

[18] As late as 1845 the Cilgwyn quarries were re-possessed by local quarrymen 'who appropriate the produce to their own use'. *Caernarvon and Denbigh Herald*, 22 March 1845.
[19] See Chapter 3.

ownership of land and from the massive profits of the slate industry. The substantial wealth created in nineteenth-century Gwynedd was enjoyed by a very few families who were almost entirely English. The local small businessmen were stung into a radical fury by this exclusion. The Welsh radical onslaught which they unleashed against the *status quo*, an onslaught which led to the great political battles of the second half of the nineteenth century between radical Liberalism, closely associated with Welsh culture and nonconformity, and the conservative power of landlordism, and which formed the political context of the slate quarrymen's struggles, was fuelled by this exclusion.

II

THE QUARRYMEN

Slate quarrying was an economically important but nevertheless small industry. Between the 1870s, when the industry reached a peak, and the end of the century, the number of men labouring in the quarries fluctuated between 11,000 and 14,000. Despite its small size, however, it was an industry which had a profound effect upon the mountainous counties of Merioneth and Caernarvonshire. The quarrymen and their families created distinctive communities which were remarkable for many reasons: the intensity of their allegiance to nonconformity, the radical edge to their politics, the importance of their contribution to Welsh culture, their multifarious organisations, ranging from Sick Clubs to Football Clubs and Silver Bands. This chapter will be mainly concerned with another aspect of these communities in the nineteenth century: the physical conditions in which the quarrymen were obliged to live.

These conditions varied, of course, from the stonewall-strewn slopes of the Cilgwyn and the threaded terraces of Tanygrisiau, to Lord Penrhyn's 'model village' in Llandegai. But while the differences between these areas have always to be borne in mind certain general comments can still be usefully made.

I. AN INDUSTRIAL COMMUNITY

The quarrymen lived in small and sometimes isolated villages and townships but they were settlements that bore indelibly the stamp of industry, and many of the beliefs and actions of the quarrymen stemmed from the conditions imposed upon, and created by, a group of industrial workers concentrated in their villages in a rural and mountainous setting.

The first point to note is that these were industrial villages which owed their size, and in most cases their very existence, to the slate industry. And despite the backdrop of mountainous grandeur, they shared many of the conditions of industrial communities elsewhere. W. J. Gruffydd, who was born in the quarrying village of Bethel, commented angrily in his autobiography that

> the Rhondda and Dowlais are talked of by us as dreadful examples of the lack of concern of public authorities in the last century, but even the people of the Rhondda would be shocked if they could come on a visit to the villages of Arfon . . . all the arrangements for health, water, cleansing and planning are more primitive and barbaric than in any slums I know of.[1]

There was, of course, a difference in scale between the choked, crammed valleys of south Wales and the scattered townships and villages of the slate industry, but many of the problems associated with industrialisation were as oppressive and intolerable in the quarrying villages under the shadows of the slate tips as they were elsewhere; on a smaller scale, but equally ferocious in their effects on the people who had to live with them. For despite the fact that north Wales had long been a popular tourist area the slate villages perched on the very mountains the tourist came to see had no picturesque flourishes, only terraced streets, squatting chapels and the artificial and growing mountains of slate waste which overhung it all: 'shapeless, monotonous villages—grey and drab', as one historian has called them.[2] Even the official guide to Bethesda, amidst descriptions of spectacular mountain scenery, had to admit that 'the main street is not attractive'.[3] Bethesda was no more unattractive than Blaenau Ffestiniog or Penrhyndeudraeth in Merioneth, Penygroes and Talysarn in Dyffryn Nantlle, or Llanberis and Ebenezer. Even the smaller quarrying communities such as Nantlle are marked distinctly as slate villages by their squashed terraces, the brooding chapel and the acres of slate waste rising from the back gardens to the skyline. These were industrial villages housing an industrial community.

But it was an industrial community which had by no means lost all contact with the land. Many quarrymen and their

---

[1] W. J. Gruffydd, *Hen Atgofion* (Denbigh, 2nd ed., 1942), p. 84. W. J. Gruffydd was one of the leading literary figures of twentieth-century Wales.
[2] Dodd, *The Industrial Revolution*, p. 203.
[3] *Bethesda—The Official Guide* (1938).

families still held a very close relationship with farming either by having laboured at some time in the fields, having relatives still farming or by having small farms themselves. 'Attendance poor', reported the headmaster of the Tregarth National Infant School in July 1901, 'owing to children going to hay making'.[4]

In 1892 the manager of the New Welsh Slate Company in Blaenau Ffestiniog also complained that

> in the summer, for instance in hay harvest, a good many go away so that our men are rather more irregular in the hay harvest.[5]

The farmer's calendar was, therefore, to some extent the quarryman's also and a good number of hands skilled in gauging rock and wielding chisel and mallet could also perform with a long scythe in one of the bands that on July mornings would, standing in line, swathe their way through hilly hay fields. Many quarrymen had relatives who had farms or smallholdings and many lived with parents or other relatives on small plots of land.[6]

A substantial number of quarrymen were also cottagers, renting and farming small plots of land: 'a great many of them keep small farms', remarked a witness before the Quarry Committee of Inquiry of 1893, referring to the Dyffryn Nantlle area;[7] 'some come from a distance and have farms', commented a quarry manager to the Royal Commission on Labour when referring to quarrymen working in Blaenau Ffestiniog.[8] In

[4] GAS, Tregarth National School Log Book, 8 July 1901.

[5] *Royal Commission on Labour*, Minutes of Evidence, Group A II, 1892, xxxvi, 19 January 1892, question 9449.

[6] Robert Griffith, for example, aged 30 in 1871, lived on his uncle's 15-acre holding in the Nantlle valley while he himself worked in the quarries; his neighbour Robert Hughes was also a quarryman living on his brother's 40-acre farm, Pentrebach. *Census Returns* (1871), County of Caernarvon, Parish of Llanwnda, District No. 27.

[7] *Report by the Quarry Committee of Inquiry*, Parliamentary Papers, C-7237, 1893–4, lxxiii, p. 195.

[8] *Royal Commission on Labour*, Minutes of Evidence, Group A II, 1892, question 9410. Some of those referred to must have been from the parish of Llanfrothen, an area of scattered agricultural holdings some miles from a major quarry where, as early as 1841, almost half the men were employed in the slate quarries and lived in cottages with some land; by the end of the century most of the men of the parish earned their living in the quarries but they also maintained their holdings. With improved transport to Blaenau Ffestiniog later in the century and the establishment of the quarrying hamlet of Croesor, the number of quarrymen increased. *Census Returns* (1841), County of Merioneth, Parish of Llanfrothen. A local historian, Ioan Brothen, himself a quarryman, wrote in 1906 that 'the majority of the men

Bethesda one observer noted in 1893 that 'some have actually realized the Chamberlain idea—three acres and a cow', an observation borne out by the existence of 168 rented cottages on the Penrhyn estate in Bethesda, mostly inhabited by quarrymen, and 'with land sufficient to keep a cow'.[9] The quarryman-cottager's life was one of ceaseless labour, tending the rocks by day and the small fields at every other opportunity; a farmer from Llanfihangel-y-Pennant recalled in 1893 how

> in my father's time I worked at the quarries, and used to hand over the whole of my wages to my father to assist him to live and to pay the rent and rates . . . in the summer months I used to work upon the farm after returning from the quarry until it was too dark to work.[10]

Money from the quarry must, therefore, have helped many a family to remain on the land: 'the farmers about Ffestiniog are not the same as farmers in other parts of the country', explained William Cadwaladar Williams of Tanygrisiau to the Royal Commission on Land in 1893, for

> they get assistance in certain parts of the year in the quarries to pay their ways, and amongst many of the small farmers I think they work in the quarries to be able to pay rent for these farms. If it had not been for the quarries they could not live on the farm.[11]

The impoverished agriculture of the Snowdonia hills was therefore able to sustain a level of population higher than any income from the land could provide, because of the money earned in the quarries by farmers and their sons.

It is unlikely, however, that the situation was seen in this way; it appears, rather, that quarrymen with a piece of land

work in the various slate quarries. Many who work in them also hold a cottage and they work on their cottages every opportunity they can get such as Saturday afternoons, the end of the [quarry] month and in the summer months in the evenings after a day at work.' GAS, Z/M/522, Ioan Brothen, 'Hanes Plwyf Llanfrothen'.

  [9] J. Owen Jones, 'Quarrying at Bethesda', *Wales*, I (1894), 167; *Royal Commission on Labour*, Minutes of Evidence, question 16,846. According to E. A. Young, manager of the Penrhyn quarries, many quarrymen also had, 'certain rights on the mountains for grazing according to the amount of rent, they are allowed to graze so many sheep or ponies on the mountain free'.

  [10] *Royal Commission on Land in Wales and Mon.*, First Report 1894, xxxvi, p. 431, evidence of Cadwaladr Roberts.

  [11] Ibid., evidence of Cadwaladar Williams, 10,072.

to farm saw this as a welcome additional source of income to their main employment in the quarries.[12] The fierce attachment of men to land they have 'mixed their labour with' should not, of course, be underestimated and those forced off their farms into the quarry villages often smarted with bitterness. But notwithstanding such forcibly-disinherited farmers, it would appear that in the areas where the quarryman-cottager was common he thought of himself as a quarryman rather than as a small farmer. To some extent, of course, this reflected the extremely small size of many of the holdings: slate quarrymen in Abergynolwyn in southern Merioneth, for example, rented holdings as small as three or even two acres in size.[13] In census returns tenant farmers who also worked in slate quarries tended to declare their occupation as 'quarryman' and very rarely added details about any land held. Ioan Brothen explains how deeply this consciousness had gone in his own quarry-cottager area in 1906:

> very few boys born in the parish work on the land—their attraction, the majority of them, is toward the quarries, and therefore we must get men and boys from Caernarvonshire and elsewhere to farm the old parish.[14]

In a slightly more uncertain position were those men who worked as labourers in the larger quarries, staying in 'barracks' during the working week and returning home to rural villages on Saturday afternoon. Many of these men came from Anglesey and the largest contingent worked in Dinorwic; some of them eventually settled in the quarry villages but many more continued to live the life of migrant workers, seeing their families only on Sundays and spending the rest of a comfortless week in appalling conditions in the barracks. These Anglesey

[12] The situation varied, depending upon local circumstances. Writing of Bethesda, one observer commented that the quarryman's 'hereditary love of the land has not been lost amid the sunless caverns of Snowdonia. A cottage and a piece of land seem necessary to his happiness and ambition, and to the latter he devotes his leisure hours with meritorous assiduity.' A. G. Bradley, *Highways and Byways in North Wales* (London, 1919), p. 258.

[13] *Royal Commission on Labour*, The Agricultural Labourer, Vol. 2, Wales, Appendix C., p. 107. In Caernarvonshire in 1885 there were 4,756 holdings under 50 acres and only 5 over 500 acres (D. Ll. Thomas, *The Welsh Land Commission*, [1896]).

[14] Ioan Brothen, op. cit.

men were the objects of some antagonism in the quarrying villages. W. J. Gruffydd testifies that

> there was a strange prejudice in Arfon years ago against Anglesey people; they were considered a famished primitive people rushing for their lives to the quarries.[15]

They were derided as 'foreigners' and labelled, because of their rural background and habits, as 'moch Sir Fôn'; other rural workers were referred to as the 'me-mes', i.e. sheep.[16] Such expressions suggest a conscious differentiation made by the people of the quarrying areas between themselves and the surrounding rural population, a differentiation accentuated by craft differences in the quarries. By the last quarter of the nineteenth century immigration into the quarrying towns had slowed down and the slate craft had become the possession of those already resident in them; there was no constant stream of rural labourers into the quarrying areas. D. Lleufer Thomas noted this fact and suggested an explanation to the Royal Commission on Labour in 1893:

> The slate quarries of North Wales do not seem to drain the agricultural population . . . exhaustively, one probable reason . . . apart from the small dimensions of the industry, is that those who are engaged at the chief quarries form a kind of hereditary guild of skilled workmen, into which it would be difficult for an agricultural labourer to be admitted.[17]

For, despite the strong connection with the land which a minority of quarrymen had, the majority of quarrymen and their families, living in the terraced streets of their villages, had no direct connection with agriculture. 'Have most of the men . . . farms or allotments?', a Ffestiniog quarry manager was asked by a Labour commissioner in 1892. 'Not in our district', he replied, 'the bulk of them live in the town of

---

[15] W. J. Gruffydd, op. cit., p. 30.

[16] 'Anglesey pigs'; Emyr Jones, *Canrif y Chwarelwr* (Denbigh, 1964), p. 41. The differences between the agricultural and industrial populations of the parish of Beddgelert were commented upon in 1899: 'Miners, quarrymen, and artisans form a class of very different characteristics. Their mode of life is different . . . They are not always so shrewd as the farmers, but nearly always more enlightened. They are progressive, and most unselfish in their efforts for social, educational, and religious improvements.' D. E. Jenkins, op. cit., p. 11.

[17] *Royal Commission on Labour*, Summary Report by D. Lleufer Thomas.

Blaenau.'[18] And referring to that town, a doctor commented three years later that 'we have really very few in this neighbourhood outside the quarrymen'.[19]

Many quarrymen, of course, had sizeable gardens, conscientiously cultivated; in Abergynolwyn a three-acre field was split up into thirty-five gardening plots for the use of quarrymen.[20] Again, many a long garden had a *cwt mochyn* (a pig sty) at the end furthest from the house.[21] But gardening and pig-keeping do not amount to agriculture and many houses had no gardens at all. As the Inspector of Mines reported in 1876, quarrymen 'generally live in places where the luxury of a garden cannot be bought at any price'.[22] Animal husbandry must, for many, have meant the careful breeding of poultry, pigeons or show rabbits and little more.[23]

Immigration into the slate villages came almost entirely from within the three counties of Gwynedd. Of 49,149 people in Merioneth in 1901, 46,231 (94 per cent), had been born within Wales and 36,807 (75 per cent), within the county of Merioneth itself. The picture was similar in Caernarvonshire. A minority of the 659 people who lived in the village of Nantlle in 1871 had been born within the boundaries of the parish of Llandwrog within which the village stood; but 548 of them had been born within Caernarvonshire. Of the 111 born outside the county, 50 had come from Anglesey (chiefly to work the copper mines in nearby Drws-y-Coed) and fifteen

---

[18] *Royal Commission on Labour*, evidence of Nathaniel F. Roberts, 9410.

[19] *Report of the Departmental Committee upon Merionethshire Slate Mines*, 1895, evidence of Dr. R. D. Evans, 1704.

[20] *Royal Commission on Labour*, The Agricultural Labourer, Appendix C, evidence of Hugh Roberts, p. 107.

[21] In 1894 an observer noted the particular wealth of Bethesda gardens; 'it is not often that one meets with gardens so neatly and carefully done,—with their rows of gooseberry trees, the currant trees along the garden walls, an apple tree here and there, the short rows of beans and peas, and the beds of lettuces, radishes, onions and cress, and the cabbage, cauliflowers, and turnips in their seasons'. J. Owen Jones, op. cit., p. 167.

[22] *Report of Inspector of Mines*, 1875 (1876 xxiii), 292.

[23] The Nantlle Vale Annual Show, held in Penygroes, catered for both normal agricultural pursuits and the small-scale gardening and pet-breeding popular with quarrymen; in 1904, apart from the usual agricultural classifications of horses, cattle and farm produce, there were also 22 classes of poultry to be judged, 17 classes of dogs, 9 classes of pigeons, 7 of cage birds and a competition for rabbits; for the horticultural contest there were 70 separate classes. The show also had slate-splitting (3 classes) and sett-making (2 classes) competitions. GAS Dorothea 1655, Nantlle Vale Annual Show, *List of Prizes*, 20 August 1904.

from Merioneth. Only thirty-two had been born outside Wales and they consisted mainly of quarry owners, engineers and their families. As the village grew in the 1860s, many quarrymen and their families moved into the new terraces from the immediate locality; more moved in from parishes slightly farther away but very few came from outside north-west Wales.[24]

There is little evidence of much movement of quarrymen from one quarrying village to another after mid-century.[25] There was, however, a significant movement of Caernarvonshire quarrymen to the Corris area in south Merioneth in the 1840s.[26]

Many men, however, travelled significant distances to work. The quarries of Blaenau Ffestiniog, for example, drew some of their labour from as far away as Dyffryn Ardudwy, Cricieth and Portmadoc, while a considerable number travelled daily by train from Penrhyndeudraeth, Trawsfynydd, Dolwyddelan and elsewhere.[27] The Dinorwic quarries near Llanberis employed men from over sixty villages and hamlets in

[24] Of 659 people, 548 had been born in Caernarvonshire, of whom 229 had been born in the parish of Llandwrog and 319 outside the parish. Of the 32 born outside Wales, 14 were from Liverpool, 4 from other parts of Lancashire, 5 from Ireland, 2 from Salop, 2 from Staffordshire and one each from Cornwall, Cheshire, Gloucestershire, London and the Isle of Man.

[25] This does not mean that there was not a degree of movement out of or between the quarrying districts. Emigration was always a significant feature of these communities and some men certainly did move in and out of the slate villages: John Ellis Roberts of Tanygrisiau, a slatemaker for forty years, had worked both in Caernarfon and in Ffestiniog; David W. Jones of Penrhyndeudraeth had worked 'off and on' in Cwmorthin mine for 13 years, moved away to work in coal mining for 5 or 6 years and then returned to Cwmorthin for another 13 years; John Roberts of Wesley Street, Blaenau Ffestiniog, a rockman and miner for 20 years had worked in gold and coal mines before returning to the Oakeley. Many other quarrymen moved from one quarry to another within a particular district: William Cadwaladar Williams of Newmarket Square, Blaenau Ffestiniog, had worked in Upper Oakeley, Wrysgan and Cwmorthin, while David Jones of Manod Road had worked 'in a great many quarries in this district'. (*Report* . . . *Merionethshire Slate Mines*, evidence 1249, 3169, 3419, 1143, 3282.) The tendency was, however, for quarrymen to stay for long periods in the one quarry.

[26] Morris Griffith, for example, aged 33 in 1851, had been born in Llanbeblig near Caernarfon, Hugh Hughes came from Llanllechid (Bethesda) and Ellis Williams from Llandwrog (Nantlle); they all moved to work in the quarries near Corris, married local women and settled there. See also the evidence of Meyrick Roberts, manager of Bryneglwys quarry, that the slatemakers in the Abergynolwyn-Corris area came originally from Llanllyfni (*Report* . . . *Merionethshire Mines*, evidence of M. Roberts, 4276).

[27] In 1895, 177 men travelled to Blaenau Ffestiniog daily from Penrhyndeudraeth, 25 came from Minffordd, 20 from Portmadoc and some from Tanybwlch (*Report* . . . *Merionethshire Mines*, evidence of Dr. R. D. Evans, 1648).

Caernarvonshire and Anglesey (though the bulk of the labour force, and almost all the skilled quarrymen, lived in the immediate vicinity of the quarries).[28]

The slate-quarrying industry therefore extended its influence farther than the villages clustered round the quarries themselves. The rural areas of Llŷn and Anglesey, in particular, felt the pull of the influence of the quarries, and, as we have seen, Anglesey witnessed a weekly exodus of men heading for the quarries of Caernarvonshire, their neat white satchels full of food for the coming week.

The quarrymen, therefore, can be seen to have had a peculiarly close connection with the land, but one which should not be overestimated. None of the quarry towns was very large; almost all of their inhabitants came to them from the immediate hinterland; many quarrymen had a direct interest in small-scale agriculture, either by renting small-holdings themselves, or by living on their parents' holding. But this only applied to a minority; for the majority of quarrymen, apart perhaps for an occasional evening in the hay harvest, agriculture was no part of their livelihood; that was gained in the rocks of the quarry or mine and their lives were lived in the terraced streets of their industrial villages.

II. HOUSING

In the Ffestiniog Local Board District in 1895 there were 2,110 houses of a rateable value of £9 a year or under and occupied almost entirely by quarrymen. A quarter of these homes were owner-occupied. There were also 265 houses of a rateable value of over £9, a high proportion of which were also occupied by quarrymen.[29] In Llanberis the majority of houses seem to have been built by quarrymen themselves or bought by them from local builders, though ground rent continued to be paid to the two main landlords in the area.[30] In the Bethesda area, also, the houses, some of them built by the quarrymen, were on

[28] GAS, DQ 1560, p. 213.
[29] Report . . . Merionethshire Mines, Evidence of Henry Percy Maybury, surveyor of Ffestiniog Local Board.
[30] G. Tecwyn Parry, Llanberis. Ei Hanes, Ei Phobl, Ei Phethau (Caernarfon, 1908), pp. 26, 114, 120.

land owned by the Penrhyn or Cefnfaes estates to which ground rent was due; a high percentage of the houses also belonged directly to one or other of the estates, with 1,600 of the men employed at the Penrhyn quarries living on the Penrhyn estate.[31] In the village of Abergynolwyn, much farther to the south, 'nearly all the village' belonged to the Bryneglwys Quarry Company, according to the quarry's manager in 1893.[32]

The ground rent charged and the implications of the leasehold system in general caused considerable resentment amongst the quarrymen. D. G. Williams of Blaenau Ffestiniog, for example, who paid 15s. ground rent, felt in 1885 that he was being overcharged by 14s. 6d., since 'before the house was built [the land] would not keep a hen alive'.[33] In 1892 the North Wales Quarrymen's Union attacked the Penrhyn quarry manager's evidence to the Royal Commission on Labour in the same vein. What, they asked, was

> the value of the boggy and rocky land on which . . . [the houses] are built before these poor quarrymen put their labour, and their hard earned money, and their life-blood in them?

And, moreover, it was added that the 'poor boggy mountain land . . . was common land in the recollection of some old inhabitants'.[34]

It was, however, the other implications of the leasehold system, particularly the fact that when the lease was up the whole property reverted to the landlord, which agitated the quarrymen. Writing on the situation in Llanberis, the Reverend G. Tecwyn Parry condemned

> the oppression of paying £120 ground rent and then when the lease comes to an end the landlord claims everything as his own property—and there is all his labour in vain for him and his family, gone to enrich the landlord.[35]

---

[31] *Report . . . Quarry Committee*, evidence of Hugh H. Davies, 2092; *Royal Commission on Labour*, evidence of E. A. Young, 16, 844. The estate's housing stock consisted of 390 leasehold houses with a garden and an average rental of £1 per annum, 540 houses with gardens at a rent of £3 10s. 0d. per annum and 168 houses with land sufficient to keep a cow at £6. Ibid., 16845–16846.

[32] *Report . . . Merionethshire Mines*, evidence of M. Roberts, 4261.

[33] *Cambrian News*, 28 August 1885.

[34] W. J. Parry, *The Penrhyn Lock-Out* (London, 1901), p. 61.

[35] G. Tecwyn Parry, op. cit., p. 120. In Bethesda the quarrymen claimed that of the 1,100 houses on Lord Penrhyn's estate, he had 'not built 60 of these. The remainder are the result of the labour and investment of his workmen, who in

It was a system which affected tenant farmer as well as quarry-man and its harsh logic was graphically outlined by Lloyd George in 1903 when, assuming the landlord's voice for dramatic effect, he explained

> when you have built your house, it does not belong to you. Part of it will belong to me, and that part will grow year by year. I will have a few stones this year, and the stones will grow year by year, and I will take your house piece by piece. When you are an old man half of it will belong to me, and when you are dead it will pass to my son, and not to yours.[36]

Money to buy or build a house was generally borrowed from one of the many building societies (there were over twenty in Bethesda in 1865) and was then paid back on a monthly basis.[37] Given this system it was hardly surprising that the quarrymen were enthusiastic campaigners for a change in the land laws.

Accounts of the condition of the housing tend to differ but it would appear that the situation improved somewhat after the late 1870s. Writing in 1875, the Inspector of Mines was harsh in his condemnation of living conditions in Blaenau Ffestiniog:

> the dwellings are overcrowded and badly ventilated, and the sleeping accommodation has been so deficient that instances have been common of the same beds having been slept in night and day without intermission by successive occupants. Rent is consequently high, and a cottage is often let in portions to several families who each pay for their rooms as much as would secure them a neat cottage and good garden in many parts of the Principality. The villages in which the miners live are in a filthy state, and the water used is not fit for culinary purposes. These conditions bring about the invariable result. Typhoid and other fevers are always present, and occasionally break out with extreme virulence.[38]

this manner return to him their hard earned wages, besides vastly increasing the value of his property and adding materially to his rent roll.' Parry, op. cit., p. 61.

[36] D. Lloyd George, 'Trusts and Monopolies' (speech in Newcastle, 4 April 1903), printed in *Better Times* (London, 1910).

[37] *Yr Herald Cymraeg*, 9 December 1865; G. Tecwyn Parry, op. cit., p. 26.

[38] *Report of H.M. Inspector of Mines for North Wales, and Isle of Man District No. 9*, 1875, p. 384.

These were still boom years in the slate industry with new people moving into the quarry towns in search of employment and before facilities were adequate. In the 'eighties and 'nineties the situation seems to have improved with a steep drop in cases of typhoid and typhus in Blaenau Ffestiniog as between 1865–1874 and 1880–1890.[39]

The situation remained very unsatisfactory, however, with overcrowding and damp as the main afflictions. Dr. Evan Roberts of Penygroes explained in 1893 that 'in some places the houses are very small . . . there are not sufficient bedrooms very often, and they sleep three in a bed very often'.[40] Dampness was a particular problem, especially as north-west Wales experiences very heavy rainfall.[41] A doctor in Blaenau Ffestiniog complained that 'our houses are faulty . . . no provision to prevent the evaporation of underground water . . . no system of drainage'. By the 1890s improvements were being made and while, in Blaenau Ffestiniog, there remained in 1893 a 'few deficient houses belonging to employers that should have been condemned long ago', the sanitation had greatly improved with the houses having water or pail closets, the latter removed fortnightly, and slop drains fixed with properly tapped gullies; ashes and other refuse were also collected fortnightly and nearly every house had pure water piped to the houses, though a few still had wells.

Conditions in the quarry barracks continued to be bad, however, and showed little improvement by the end of the century. Some 350 men lived in barracks in the Ffestiniog area in 1893 and although the Local Board had intervened to cut down the number of men in each cubicle from six to four, it was generally agreed that the barracks, particularly those at

[39] In 1865–74 the percentage of deaths from typhus and typhoid was 12.6 per annum; in the 1880s this fell to 1.3 per cent, a drop largely explained by the piping of fresh water to the town from the new reservoir at Llyn Morwynion *Report . . . Merionethshire Mines*, evidence of Dr. Richard Jones, 111.

[40] *Report . . . Quarry Committee of Inquiry*, evidence of Dr. E. Roberts, 102. William Gadlys Williams, a 40-year-old quarryman, described his own house (with which he also had 'not quite three acres of land') as having 'two rooms on the ground floor, and those above have very little headroom'; one bedroom was two square yards, the other three and the ceiling sloped up from 2 ft. off the floor to a height of 6 ft. In this house lived a family of seven, which included William Williams's father and brother. See evidence of William Gadlys Williams, 928–950.

[41] Blaenau Ffestiniog has almost 100 inches of rain per annum.

the Rhosydd mine high up above Tanygrisiau, 'required considerable improvements'.[42]

Conditions at the barracks had been complained of by the Inspector of Mines in 1886, for there were in Rhosydd

> scarcely 200 cubic feet of space per man in rooms used for sleeping, taking meals and keeping provisions and coal . . . the men were nearly all sleeping two in a bed, and some of the rooms were dark, with a bad floor and an indifferent roof.[43]

Conditions at the Oakeley quarry barracks appear to have been much better with each man having his own sleeping room. But in 1892 the Inspector of Mines again devoted a lengthy section of his report to the unsatisfactory conditions in some of the barracks:

> On more than one occasion I have said that the barracks in which some of the miners in my district have to spend the greater part of each week do not give the accommodation which, in my opinion, a respectable working man may fairly expect to receive; and I regret that owners of mines, who are ready to risk thousands of pounds in mineral adventures, do not realize the advisability of setting apart a small fraction of their capital for making their men more comfortable. I visited a mine where barracks were in the course of construction last year and I was surprised that the owner of the mine could ask men to put up with such housing. The inside walls were unplastered, and sleeping bunks were being fixed in the big room side by side without any intervening space. The passage at the end of the building, not partitioned off from the sleeping quarters, was destined to be the eating and living room. As the bunks were fixtures it was difficult to clean the space under them properly. The whole arrangements showed a great disregard of comfort and of the requirements of sanitary science.[44]

---

[42] *Report . . . Merionethshire Mines*, evidence of Dr. R. Jones, 54, 70; evidence of Dr. R. D. Evans, 1649; evidence of H. P. Maybury, 4198, 4202.

[43] *Report of Inspector of Mines, 1886*. His warnings as to the roof, an ironic comment on a building at a slate mine, were proved to be well founded five years later in November 1890, when a storm ripped off the roof during the night and the men, half-naked and clutching their beds, had to flee in what a local newspaper called a 'miraculous escape'. *Y Rhedegydd*, 15 November 1890.

[44] *Report Inspector of Mines*, 1892, p. 406.

In such accommodation, for which they paid between 1½*d*. and 3*d*. a week, hundreds of quarrymen spent their non-working hours from Monday morning to Saturday afternoon. Some came from distant rural areas but others were forced to live in barracks because the mines or quarries at which they worked were so isolated. Perched on a gale-swept ridge between Cwm Cwmorthin, leading to Blaenau Ffestiniog five miles away, and Cwm Croesor, leading down to Llanfrothen four miles in the opposite direction, life for the 200 workers at the Rhosydd mine must have been bleak and uncomfortable indeed, working and sleeping at over 1,400 feet and washing in the mountain streams.[45]

As we have seen, there were many who travelled long distances to and from their work; on a Monday morning Anglesey workers at the Dinorwic quarry would have to rise at 3 a.m. and walk to the ferry at Moel-y-Don (it was about an hour's walk from Brynsiencyn, an area whence many quarrymen came). After crossing the Menai Straits there was another walk to the station before catching a train up to the quarry, arriving at 6.15 a.m. and then, after depositing their week's supplies at the barracks, going straight to their labours.[46] Conditions were hardly better for over 200 men who travelled to Blaenau Ffestiniog on the narrow-gauge railway: 'May not the Ffestiniog Railway be to the quarryman a sort of pneumonia trap?', a doctor was asked. 'Undoubtedly', he replied.[47]

Another doctor complained that many men had 'really exhausted their muscular energy before they go to their day's work' because of the long journeys many of them had to undertake. Such men, he claimed, were 'in a state of semi-starvation until they partake of their so-called dinner at mid-day'. On

[45] *Report . . . Merionethshire Mines*, evidence of H. P. Maybury, 4209, 4247. Conditions at barracks in the Ffestiniog area were attacked again by the Inspector of Mines in 1900. See also M. J. T. Lewis, J. H. Denton, *Rhosydd Slate Quarry* (Shrewsbury, 1974).
[46] Emyr Jones, op. cit., p. 41.
[47] They travelled sixteen to a carriage, 10 ft. 7 ins. long by 4 ft. 9 ins. wide. Not only were they, in the words of the report of the 1895 Departmental Committee upon Merionethshire Slate Mines, 'much overcrowded', but they were also open to wind and rain as the carriages were open behind their necks. *Report . . . Merionethshire Mines*, evidence of Dr. R. D. Evans, 1648; evidence of Dr. R. Jones, 91.

the return journey they had to be 'hanging about wet for hours at the station'. All in all, the doctor concluded, these men were 'treated more like animals than human beings'.[48]

III. DIET, DRESS AND HEALTH

The quarryman's diet attracted considerable adverse comment from observers. The poor health of the quarryman was normally attributed to his eating habits: 'In proportion to the wages they get', explained Mr. Frank Turner, the manager of the Glynrhonwy Slate Co. in 1893, 'I think they are the worst fed men of any class in the kingdom'[49]; and his opinion was supported by most of the doctors working in the quarrying areas. Of the doctors who gave evidence to the two commissions of inquiry in the early 'nineties or who contributed to Dr. John William's pamphlet *Peryglon i Iechyd y Chwarelwr* ('Dangers to the health of the quarryman'), only one, Dr. R. D. Evans of Blaenau Ffestiniog, thought that the quarrymen did not live as sparingly as it was normally thought.[50]

The general medical verdict was that the quarrymen drank too much tea and ate very poor food. Heavy tea-drinking appears to have been a particular characteristic of the quarryman; 'tea for breakfast, tea for lunch, tea for tea and tea for supper', complained Dr. Jones of Penygroes; 'they are too fond of tea and coffee at the quarry and never think of taking anything else', echoed the doctor in charge of the Penrhyn quarry hospital. The tea they drank was, moreover, brewed in a particular and, in doctors' eyes, harmful way, for it was the normal

> habit of the quarryman . . . to send a boy about half an hour before the meal time to an eating house, prepared by the owners for their comfort, with tea and sugar and water in

---

[48] Ibid., evidence of Dr. R. D. Evans, 1648. He cited the case of a man walking from his home in Tremadoc to the station in Portmadoc, sitting in the overcrowded and windy conditions of the train on the long journey to Blaenau Ffestiniog and then having to walk again the steep miles to one of the further quarries such as Votty and Bowydd or Cwmorthin.

[49] *Report . . . Quarry Committee*, evidence of Mr. Frank Turner, 570.

[50] *Report . . . Merionethshire Mines*, evidence of Dr. R. D. Evans, 1649. 'I do not think', he said in 1893 of Blaenau Ffestiniog, 'that there is a town in North Wales of its population in which the inhabitants eat so much meat and drink so much milk.' He estimated that 1,800–1,900 gallons of milk and 15 tons of meat were sold in the town every week.

the same kettle which is put on the fire and boiled. It then
stews there half an hour or more before the men come there
to drink it.[51]

This constant drinking of stewed tea was clearly a stimulant
which made up for the scarcity of nourishing food; 'he cannot
work on bread with his meagre supply of butter', explained
Dr. R. H. Mills Roberts, surgeon to the Dinorwic quarries
hospital, 'and [he] therefore endeavours to stimulate himself
by means of tea'.[52]

The rest of the quarryman's diet was poor: a diet typical of
the 'best class' of quarryman, of 'those who take most care of
themselves', consisted of tea, egg and bread-and-butter for
breakfast; tea and bread-and-butter for lunch; bread-and-
butter at teatime; potatoes, sometimes with beef, bacon or
buttermilk on arriving home around 6.30 p.m. and sometimes
porridge or buttermilk or coffee before going to bed at 10; on
Sunday there would be lunch of 'potatoes and meat and some
kind of tart'. It is clear, however, that many quarrymen never
approached such a diet; Thomas Hugh Griffith, a quarryman
at the Penyorsedd quarry in the Nantlle valley, for example,
never had an egg for breakfast but only tea and bread-and-
butter. Dr. Mills Roberts of Dinorwic considered that the
majority of quarrymen ate only tea, bread-and-butter for
breakfast, dinner, tea and supper, and though 'sometimes he
may have in addition a little cheese, potatoes, or bacon . . . this
is the exception'.[53] 'The people here need more food, especially
more nourishing food. They only seem to get meat once a
week; that is to say, on Sunday', protested an English cooking
instructress in Blaenau Ffestiniog.[54] A glaring deficiency in the
diet was the lack of vegetables and of dairy produce; 'they do
not take enough vegetables', complained Dr. Evan Roberts of
Penygroes, while Dr. Mills Roberts complained of how little

[51] Dr. John William, *Peryglon i Iechyd y Chwarelwr* (1891), p. 6; *Report* . . .
Quarry Committee, evidence of Dr. J. William, 267; *Report* . . . *Merionethshire Mines*,
evidence of Dr. Richard Jones, 64.
[52] The alternative was to 'take tea in their cans in the morning . . . leave it
in the cans and drink out of them at intervals throughout the day'. *Report* . . .
Quarry Committee, evidence of Dr. Evan Roberts, 74; evidence of Dr. R. H. Mills
Roberts.
[53] Ibid., evidence of William Gadlys Williams and Hugh Griffith; evidence of
Thomas Hugh Griffith; evidence of Dr. R. H. Mills Roberts.
[54] *Report* . . . *Merionethshire Mines*, evidence of Miss Eleanor H. Russell, 4132.

milk was consumed. In this respect, and in others, the quarryman's diet was compared unfavourably with that of agricultural
workers; 'the agricultural labourer', explained Dr. Roberts,
'eats good coarse flour, which is much more wholesome.
The quarryman on the other hand eats too fine a flour.'[55]
Dr. Jones, also of Penygroes, pointed out that the whitest
bread, preferred by the quarrymen, was not nutritionally the
most desirable.[56] In this respect it is clear that, to some extent
at least, the quarryman's diet was a matter of preference, a
conscious choice of foods preferred to the more wholesome food
of agricultural workers. As Dr. Roberts pointed out,

> they could get plenty of sweet-milk, or butter-milk to drink,
> but they have got into the habit of drinking tea at every meal.
> They have no relish for any liquid but tea. It is tea all day
> long.[57]

To satisfy this demand, a special tea was packaged locally and
marketed under the label *Tê'r Chwarelwr* (The Quarryman's
Tea).[58]

The quarryman's dress was even more distinctive than his
diet: corduroy trousers, hob-nailed boots and flat cap came to
be the distinctive badge of the quarryman in the twentieth
century, but in the nineteenth the quarryman's normal dress
was of white fustian with

> a thick flannel vest, a flannel shirt, generally lined, flannel
> drawers, usually double thickness round the waist, and in
> addition he generally also wears round the waist a flannel belt
> or bandage.[59]

A narrow leather belt also appears to have been popular. In
addition, the nineteenth-century quarryman on his way to
work invariably wore a bowler hat and carried an umbrella.

[55] *Report . . . Quarry Committee*, evidence of Dr. Evan Roberts, 82; evidence of
Dr. Mills Roberts, 737.

[56] Dr. John William, op. cit., p. 7.

[57] *Report . . . Quarry Committee*, evidence of Dr. E. Roberts, 76. Even quarrymen
'who have a cow or two prefer to take tea in their cans in the morning rather
than milk'. Ibid., 74.

[58] Advertised in GAS, Dorothea 1655 (List of Prizes, Nantlle Vale Annual
Show, 1904).

[59] *Report . . . Quarry Committee*, evidence of Dr. R. H. Mills Roberts.

In dress and diet, therefore, the quarryman was distinctively marked as separate from his neighbours. These were to some extent questions of choice. He also carried other, involuntary, badges of his identity, in particular, his ill-health. A Ffestiniog doctor explained in 1893 that, 'we do not meet with very many people in Ffestiniog who are what we call robust'.[60] A Llanberis doctor concurred, for 'their muscular development is very poor and their health is not what it should be'.[61] The main complaints suffered by the men were respiratory diseases, stomach disorders, hernias and haemorrhoids. The haemorrhoids were caused by long hours of sitting on hard, cold surfaces (for the slate-splitters), while hernias were brought on by the very strenuous nature of much of the work; the stomach disorders were attributed to poor diet and in particular to the over-imbibing of tea.[62] Respiratory diseases were the most serious complaint: of 157 male deaths certified by Dr. R. D. Evans of Blaenau Ffestiniog in the period before he gave evidence to the Departmental Committee upon Merionethshire Slate Mines in 1893, 78 of the men had died of some respiratory disease, i.e., almost exactly 50 per cent. Of 129 female deaths, only 31 had been caused in a similar way.[63] Doctors explained this high rate of respiratory disease by pointing to such factors as the wet climate of the area, the dampness of the houses and the poor diet; some pointed to the cold and wet conditions the men often had to work in, and a few suggested that slate dust might be a contributory factor. Dr. Richard Jones of Ffestiniog, thought that slate dust might be 'an irritant—perhaps sets up inflammation which will lead to chronic phthisis'.[64] But the weight of medical opinion suggested poor living conditions rather than occupational hazards as the main cause of poor health; one doctor even suggested that the quarryman's habit of assembling in hundreds to escort the coffin of a neighbour on its final journey was the major cause of disease: 'I have had

---

[60] *Report . . . Merionethshire Mines*, evidence of Dr. R. Roberts, 1115.
[61] *Report . . . Quarry Committee*, evidence of Dr. R. H. Mills Roberts.
[62] Dr. John William, op. cit., *passim*.
[63] *Report . . . Merionethshire Mines*, evidence of Dr. R. D. Evans, 1648.
[64] Ibid., evidence of Dr. R. Jones, 54. But he had no real evidence for this since he did 'not know of anyone who had performed a post-mortem examination of the lung of a quarryman in this district'.

more cases which could be attributable to exposure at funerals than to working at the quarries', he stated.[65]

Figures seem to suggest otherwise. The mean age at death of those registered in Blaenau Ffestiniog in 1883–93 as 'quarriers', that is, those employed in the dressing-sheds where slate dust was most heavy, was 47.9 years; the average age at death for engine-drivers and plate-layers in the quarries—those least exposed to slate dust—was 60.3 years; labourers could expect to live until they were 54.3 years of age, while rockmen and miners could only look forward to a couple more months than the quarriers, 48.1 years. No wonder a witness before the Committee on Merionethshire Mines who remarked that few quarrymen continued after 60 years of age was asked, 'Do they retire or die?'[66] Slate-makers died young; in the New Welsh slate mine in January 1893 the average age of all the workers was 34.4 years; the average age of the slate-makers was 28.7 years; out of 78 of them employed, only 13 were over 40 years of age. And yet the slate-maker's craft was the most skilled in the quarry, the work being less physically exhausting than that of the rockman.[67]

The quarrymen themselves seem to have been in little doubt that slate dust was injurious to their health: 'the men complain of dust', observed Dr. Richard Jones:

> they think that the dust is the cause of their illness, and many of them seem to believe that if they take a drink to wash the dust out of their mouth they improve their condition—say a glass of beer or water.

Some doctors suspected that there might be something in the men's complaint; William Gadlys Williams, a 40-year-old quarryman who had spent thirty years in the industry and spat up slate dust every morning, explained to the Quarry Committee of Inquiry that Dr. Hughes of Waunfawr had confirmed that the dust was injurious to him.[68]

[65] *Report . . . Quarry Committee*, evidence of Dr. Evan Roberts, 38.

[66] *Report . . . Merionethshire Mines*, evidence of Dr. R. Jones, 6–9; 108.

[67] Ibid., Appendix 6, workmen employed at the New Welsh slate mine, January 1893.

[68] Ibid., evidence of Dr. R. Jones, 160. The only consequence of the drink was that the dust 'gets into a state of clay, and clings to the roof of the mouth'. *Report . . . Quarry Committee*, evidence of W. G. Williams, 982. 'The slate dust

But some medical opinion took an opposite view, Dr. R. D. Mills Roberts, surgeon to the Dinorwic quarries and hospital, for example, considered 'this occupation to be very healthy', indeed exceptionally so, 'slate dust', he remarked, 'does not exist at the Dinorwic Quarries to an injurious extent' and he scoffed at the quarryman who 'will not open his windows . . . and fancies that this foul air is healthier than the slate-dust'.[69] Not all doctors went to Dr. Mills Roberts's lengths in portraying slate quarries as second only to health spas in their therapeutic blessings—'the healthiest possible employment', he called it— but few of them drew particular attention to conditions of work as a cause of ill-health; diet, housing and other factors were more generally blamed by the doctors who gave evidence to the two committees of inquiry and who contributed to Dr. John William's pamphlet. Only one doctor, Dr. John Roberts, went on to condemn in highly political language the social and economic conditions which underlay the men's poor health. A remarkable letter which he sent to Dr. John William in January 1890, of which only a section was later published in William's pamphlet, deserves quotation:

> My first impression regarding Welsh quarrymen is that their hard lot produces premature decay and old age—very frequently affecting particular tissues, often causing a general withering. God turns them out a very even lot as babies; look at them above sixty as they pour out of a large quarry, and pray that the Almighty may give them sense and knowledge to understand what has produced the awful change.
> . . . how terribly numerous are the tubercular class of affliction that produces their premature death and how frequently they die when a well fed man would recover. I will not enlarge to you on these points . . . it seems to be their lot to die young of consumptive diseases, while their English masters die of gout and apoplexy, with white hair and rubicund faces above sixty.[70]

get's into one's stomach', stated H. H. Davies to the Quarry Committee of Inquiry. 'How do you know that?', he was asked. 'The doctors say so for one thing', he replied, 'and it tells on the men themselves.' Ibid., evidence of H. H. Davies.
    [69] Ibid., evidence of Dr. Mills Roberts.
    [70] GAS, DQ 2537, letter from John Roberts to John William, 7 January 1890. He went on prudently to advise William that he should 'Disclaim all responsibility for yourself for what I say if you honour me with quotation. It is honestly given to you.'

Working conditions were certainly dismal. Subsequent medical research has confirmed that the quarrymen were entirely correct in their belief that slate dust was harmful, despite the opinions of some of the local doctors. Those working underground were saved the extremes of temperature and weather suffered by open quarrymen (slate heats up and cools down very rapidly) but they often worked in very wet conditions by the light of spluttering candles which emitted 'such a bad smell that they cannot eat at dinner time'.[71] Privies were few and inadequate, as were eating facilities. Those working in the sheds seem to have suffered the most: immobile because of their work, they could not exercise sufficiently to resist the cold and they were, of course, covered in slate dust. Slate quarrying was not as healthy as agricultural work, stated another quarryman, Thomas Hugh Griffith, who had worked in Penyrorsedd quarry for fifty years, 'because there is slate dust.'

'Do you consider quarrying a healthy occupation?', H. H. Davies was asked. His reply was emphatic: 'No, I do not indeed.'[72] He was right: the average age of men not working in the slate mines who died in Blaenau Ffestiniog in 1875 was 67.12 years; the average age of those who had died in the same year and had also laboured in the mines was 37.78 years.[73]

Ill-health was not the only cause of early death; the slate quarries were also extremely hazardous places in which to work. In 1877 the Inspector of Mines responsible for the underground slate mines of north Wales, T. F. Evans, reported that, 'it has not perhaps occurred to the slate mine owners of Wales that their workmen are exposed to greater danger than the coal miners of the U.K.'[74]

This view was supported three years later by his successor, C. Le Neve Foster, who estimated that

> the average death rate from accidents underground is nearly twice as high in the slate mines as in other mines of my

---

[71] *Report . . . Merionethshire Mines*, evidence of Robert Roberts, 3058.
[72] 'After you have been working in one of those huts all day long, are you covered with dust?', H. H. Davies was asked by a member of the 1893 Committee of Inquiry. 'Yes', he replied. 'Everywhere?' 'Yes.' 'One side of the sheds is open?' 'Yes, and they are built very loosely, so that the draught comes through.' *Report . . . Quarry Committee*, evidence of H. H. Davies, 2059, 2062, 2066; evidence of T. H. Griffith, 1388.
[73] *Report of H.M. Inspector of Mines*, 1875.
[74] Ibid., 1877.

district . . . as far as safety is concerned it is better to work
in a colliery than in an underground slate mine.[75]

They remained dangerous a decade later when it was reported
that the proportion of deaths from accidents in slate mining in
north Wales 'is from 1.75 to 2 per thousand against 1 to 1.50
per thousand in metalliferous mines.'[76] The underground mines
had come under the provisions of the various Metalliferous
Mines Regulation Acts of 1872 and 1875 and under the Slate
Mines (Gunpowder) Act in 1882. The dressing sheds of both
open and underground quarries came under the provision of
the various Factory Acts. The open slate quarries, in which the
majority of slate quarrymen worked, remained, however,
outside the scope of any effective legislation. They were lethal
places in which, between 1883 and 1892, out of a workforce
of only some 8,500, 116 men lost their lives in accidents.[77]

The mine-owners had originally opposed the application of
the Mines Acts to slate mining and had only been forced to
accept the Acts' jurisdiction after a court case, Sims v Evans,
in 1874 which had resulted in the ruling that 'a slate quarry,
worked by means of underground workings by levels, is a mine
within the intention of 35 and 36 Vict. c.77.'[78] Inspection of
the mines remained infrequent, however, and the fines imposed
by magistrates upon law-breaking mine-owners were negligible.
The Welsh Slate Company was taken to court by the Inspector
in 1876 for a relatively serious offence, a failure to have a plan
of the mine; they were fined 2s. 6d. by the local bench which,
the Inspector commented ruefully, was 'all slate mine
proprietors'.[79]

The quarrymen often complained about the verdicts of
jurors in inquests on men killed at their work. It was not so

---

[75] Ibid., 1880.
[76] *Royal Commission on Labour*, evidence of N. F. Roberts, 9473.
[77] *Report . . . Quarry Committee*, Caernarvonshire Slate Quarries at work in
1893, Merionethshire Open Slate Quarries.
[78] *Report . . . Inspector of Mines*, 1875, p. 383.
[79] A case brought by the Inspector after two men had been killed in the
Cwmorthin mine was dismissed in 1892. Following an accident in which a young
man had been killed by a runaway wagon in the Maen Offeren mine the company
were prosecuted for not providing manholes along the tramway; found guilty,
they were fined 2s. 6d. with 10s. 9d. costs. *Report . . .Inspector of Mines*, 1876, 1892,
1893. The owners of the Llechwedd mine were fined £1 without costs for a similar
offence in 1885. *Y Gweithiwr*, 23 May 1885.

much prejudice as ignorance which they criticized, for 'the jurymen at inquests . . . are made up of shopkeepers and other tradesmen, who are not familiar with the terms used in the quarry'. There were also complaints of witnesses not being called and of men who did not give full accounts at inquests as 'they fear that if they told the truth it might cause them inconvenience in the quarry'.[80]

In such an unhealthy and dangerous industry the fact that medical services, at least in the larger quarries, were directly linked to places of work was of great significance. There were hospitals at Penrhyn and Dinorwic and also at Llechwedd and Oakeley for injured and sick quarrymen. These had been originally established by the owners but were largely maintained by quarry sick-clubs to which the employees contributed.[81] Other quarries had similar schemes to provide medical care, though they did not support hospitals.

Men normally paid 1s. a week towards the clubs and in return received free medical care, some sums of money weekly during absence from work caused by injury or illness, burial expenses and, in some cases, pensions.[82] During 1889 the Dinorwic Club paid out a total of £584 to 1,634 club members (about half the workforce), a figure which, in itself, indicates the risk to health run by quarrymen; the sums received varied from 3s. to £5 12s. 0d. In addition, thirty-three men, of whom three died, received treatment in the quarry hospital. The resident doctor, then Dr. Hughes, was employed at a wage of £550 per annum.[83] Many men also belonged to various friendly societies, both local and national, which also contributed during illness: the Ffestiniog Friendly Society in 1895 paid 8s. a week for the first six months of illness and 4s. a week from then on.[84]

Given conditions in the industry, independent medical opinion was of some importance. Quarrymen in Blaenau

[80] Report . . . Merionethshire Mines, evidence of O. R. Jones, 1296.

[81] The owners often contributed sizeable sums of money to the sick clubs. Assheton-Smith, for example, gave £50, his 'annual gift', to the Dinorwic Quarry Club in 1889. GAS, DQ 2524, Adroddiad Clwb Chwarelau Dinorwic Am 1889.

[82] Report . . . Merionethshire Mines, evidence of Dr. R. Roberts, 1062.

[83] Adroddiad Clwb Chwarelau Dinorwic Am 1889.

[84] GAS, Z/M/1028/1, Llyfr Cofnodion Cymdeithas Gyfeillgar, 1894–1910, 2 May 1895.

Ffestiniog in the late 1860s had successfully agitated against compulsory membership of quarry sick-clubs as they did not trust doctors appointed by the quarry owners; a workmen's committee was set up which employed its own doctor but some quarries insisted that the men pay their 1s. a month to the 'official' club.[85] The running of the Penrhyn Sick Club was a matter of bitter dispute for a quarter of a century, with accusations of pilfering and mismanagement complicating the issue of control. Assheton-Smith and his manager, W. W. Vivian, clearly had decisive control over the Dinorwic Club, on whose committee they both sat. The 'independence' of doctors is a difficult quality to define, particularly when they were employed and had been chosen by wilful and powerful men. The 'cause of death' registered by doctors could, for example, affect compensation and other claims. At least one Dinorwic quarryman who had died as a result of injuries received at work was officially registered as having died of 'syncope'.[86]

A comparison of the two commissions which investigated the quarryman's health in the early 1890s reveals a somewhat more critical awareness of the problems in the comments of doctors before the committee on Merionethshire slate mines than in the subsequent investigation of the open slate quarries of Caernarvonshire; an awareness which might have owed something to the lack of quarry owners' monopoly-control of medical care in Blaenau Ffestiniog.

It has been noted earlier how Dr. Mills Roberts of Dinorwic testified to the healthy nature of slate quarrying. A question mark must remain over the sincerity of his remarks in the light of a letter he wrote to the Dinorwic manager, W. W. Vivian, in November 1893, presumably when he was preparing the evidence he was to submit before the committee of inquiry:

[85] *Y Genedl Gymreig*, 19 August 1885.

[86] Robert Roberts of Cwm-y-Glo was a 74-year-old patient in the Dinorwic quarry hospital who was declared to have 'died suddenly of syncope' on 24 February 1892; he had in fact entered the hospital on 12 January with 'all ribs on left side fractured, also collar bone, three ribs on right side fractured. Laceration of right kidney; laceration of left lung, pneumonia suspected.' These were injuries received whilst at his work. We do not know the circumstances of his accident as the official report prepared by the management was brief to the point of being useless; a slip which 'explains cause of accident' reads as follows: 'He was splitting a block of slate when a portion of it fell upon him. He was taken to the Hospital, and subsequently died of syncope, 24 February. Widower Aged 74.' GAS, DQ 2540, 21 November 1893, 12 January 1892.

My visit to Caernarvon is not of much service. Respiratory diseases among women being 449, among males not quarrymen 375; against 506 quarrymen. So that is best left alone.

Referring to these figures, he adds, 'I hope you will sit on them'.[87] The question of the control of doctors was not a central one for the quarrymen but it was a continuing source of complaint.

IV. WOMEN

Another reason for the quarryman's ill-health which was advanced during the nineteenth century was the inadequate care he was supposed to have received from his wife. There is much evidence which is hostile to the women of the quarrying districts and which judges them harshly. Oral evidence in other areas teaches us to be wary of such comment but, in the absence of written evidence to the contrary, a certain pattern can be discerned in the existing testimony.

Little is known about the quarryman's wife and daughter and what follows is a very brief and impressionistic sketch, which reflects the restrictions imposed by the scarce and impressionistic evidence immediately available. Slate quarrying was a male industry and as far as is known no woman worked in a slate quarry in any capacity, certainly not after the early period of capitalisation and development of the industry. Moreover, since slate quarrying was the only major source of employment in the quarrying areas, women who stayed at home found difficulty in gaining any employment at all. Thus, of 2,289 women over ten years of age in Bethesda in 1901, 83 per cent were not in employment; of the 381 who were at work, 141 were domestic servants and 117 tailoresses.

The alternative to work was marriage; 78 per cent of women at work in Bethesda were unmarried and of the remainder a number were widowed, and since work was scarce marriage tended to be early.[88] Several commentators on the slate communities note this tendency: 'the general rule', according to

---

[87] GAS, DQ 2539, letter from Dr. Mills Roberts to W. W. Vivian, 12 November 1893.
[88] *Census Returns*, Bethesda U.D., 1901.

Dr. Evan Roberts of Penygroes, 'is that they marry very young'.[89]

The women of the quarrying villages, excluded from most forms of employment and confined to the house, developed a way of life which attracted considerable censure from observers. In 1875 the Inspector of Mines was harsh in his criticisms of the quarryman's wife:

> The wives lack thrift, know nothing of cooking, and spend a large proportion of their husbands' earnings in the purchase of gaudy finery for which they are seldom free from debt. The men therefore fare badly . . . their homes are as comfortless as slovenliness can make them.[90]

Miss Winifred A. Ellis, a cooking instructress for the Merioneth County Council, was also critical of what she considered to be the extravagance and profligacy of women in the quarry towns, comparing their interest in gay finery very unfavourably with the more stolid tastes of the farmer's wife. She was also scathing about their cooking skills, complaining that they preferred to make 'pancakes swimming in butter than a proper dinner' and that they would gossip all day and then open a tin when their husbands arrived home from work.[91]

It is difficult to estimate how accurately these generalized judgements applied to women in the quarrying towns in the nineteenth century, for they surely involve the weighty prejudices of the observers. The popular image of the quarryman's wife, however, did always involve some element of such criticisms. The character of Leusa in T. Rowland Hughes's novel *William Jones* is a cruel caricature of the lazy and extravagant quarryman's wife.[92]

The criticisms become peculiarly clear in comparisons between the women of quarrying families and the women on

[89] *Report . . . Quarry Committee*, evidence of Dr. E. Roberts, 243. His opinion was echoed by Dr. Mills Roberts of Dinorwic who complained that men married before they were twenty and the women even younger. And in Blaenau Ffestiniog a local newspaper condemned the practice of 'inexperienced children' getting married resulting in 'children bringing up children' in the town. U.C.N.W., Coetmor MSS., 44, n.d.

[90] *Report of Inspector of Mines*, 1875.

[91] *Report . . . Merionethshire Mines*, evidence of Miss W. A. Ellis, 4752–77.

[92] T. Rowland Hughes, *William Jones* (1944). Leusa should be contrasted with the character of the quarryman-cottager's wife in Kate Roberts, *Traed Mewn Cyffion* (Aberystwyth, 1936).

the surrounding farms.[93] On the land women played an important role in production and preparation, while in the terraces of the slate towns women's work was almost exclusively domestic. In such circumstances an interest in appearances, both of themselves and of their houses, was to be expected. An obsession with cleanliness and the collection of 'best' furniture and ornaments, often carried to apparently self-defeating ends, came to be the hallmark of the 'idle, frivolous, senseless girls'. There was the statutory piano and they had

> become mad on furniture. They must get a grandfather clock as large as Goliath's coffin and worth eight guineas; an eight guinea glass cupboard full of trinkets; an eight guinea dresser moaning under the weight of crockery, as well as of china dogs, cats, and soldiers and in between them all there is no room for the quarryman to turn.[94]

Tiny parlours filled to overflowing with gleaming possessions, places to look at, not to sit in, except perhaps over a tin of salmon when the rare relative visited—these were the creations and preserves of women denied employment.

V. BEHAVIOUR

Infertile for agriculture, the soil of the quarrying areas sprouted voluntary organisations, cultural, sporting, political and religious; so many of them that one doctor complained that a cause of the quarryman's poor health was his rushing off every evening to attend some committee or other. Apart from the Friendly and Benefit Societies which flourished, there were trade unions, Liberal organisations, innumerable chapels, choirs, bands, football and billiards clubs.[95]

The most extensive and demanding organisations were the chapels, which dominated behaviour outside of the mere act of worship in the same way as their gaunt shapes overshadowed

[93] For an account of women's work on the land in late-nineteenth-century Wales, see David Jenkins, *The Agricultural Community in South West Wales* (Cardiff, 1971).

[94] U.C.N.W., Coetmor MSS., 44, 'Sefyllfa Naturiol a Moesol Isel y Chwarelwyr fel Dosbarth' (*Y Faner*, n.d.), p. 9.

[95] Particularly well known bands were the Royal Oakeley Silver Band, the Royal Vaynol Brass Band (Band Llanrug), and the Nantlle Vale Silver Band; there were also bands in Bethesda, Moeltryfan, Waunfawr, Llanberis and Deiniolen.

the terraced streets. They watched everthing and shaped much and their influence was pervasive. The chapel's embrace was intense and not restricted to Sundays: the weekly timetable for one Bethesda chapel in 1900 ran as follows:

Sunday at	9 a.m.	Prayer meeting for the young.
	10 a.m.	Sermon.
	2 p.m.	Sunday School.
	5 p.m.	Singing meeting.
	6 p.m.	Sermon.
Monday	—	Prayer meeting.
Tuesday	—	Church (organisational meeting)
Wednesday	—	Five Study Meetings.
		Literary Society.
Thursday	—	Four Study Classes.
Friday	—	Band of Hope.[96]

When asked in February 1907 by one of the commissioners investigating the Church in Wales whether the chapel formed all the quarryman's interest, the Rev. D. H. Williams, who had spent several years ministering to the Congregationalists of the quarrying town of Ebenezer (Deiniolen), replied, 'Practically all his interest'. 'There is no theatre or concert room?', pursued the commissioner. 'Absolutely nothing.' 'The chapel supplies all his wants?' 'Yes, and if a concert is got up it is, as a rule, got up by one of the chapel choirs.'[97] The chapels did not supply all the quarryman's wants by any means, but their presence was central to the life and structure of slate-quarrying communities: a complex network of allegiances and a powerful organisational framework, nonconformity came to hold a position of quite particular importance.

This was true of much of Wales, of course, but in the quarry villages denominational allegiances seem to have been particularly strong. The Rev. Ellis James Jones pointed out to the 1907 Commission that there were, in the rural areas of Caernarvonshire, large numbers of farm servants and some farmers who adhered to, but were not actually members of, chapel congre-

[96] *Adroddiad Eglwys a Chynulleidfa, Jerusalem M.C. Bethesda*, 1900.
[97] *Royal Commission on the Church of England and other religious bodies in Wales and Monmouthshire*, 1910, evidence of Rev. D. H. Williams, 6815–7355.

gations, while 'in the quarry districts you often find the case different, and the population generally are church members'.[98]

The censorious eye of nonconformity deeply affected behaviour and observers were unanimous in their high regard for the respectability of the quarryman. 'The Queen may be proud to rule over such a body of men', commented an English traveller in 1869:

> not your street corner loungers and pickpockets and burglars and blacklegs; but honest fellows with good furniture at home, mostly some small savings in the bank, the children at school and best suits for Sundays.[99]

A Welsh commentator estimated that the quarrymen were morally superior to the coal miners of south Wales, though not to the lead miners of Cardiganshire, while a nonconformist minister asked in 1878

> What class of men, taking the great majority of them, will be found more respectful towards the word of God and the ministry of the gospel? what class more well disposed toward good works? and what class with so many total abstainers [than the quarrymen]?[100]

After visiting north Wales in 1874, Lord Chief Justice Cockburn was profuse in his congratulations to the inhabitants for 'an absence of offences of the graver and more serious character'. Commenting on his remarks, a local paper noted that the workers did

> not delight in cock-fighting, dog-fighting, pugilism, kicking, biting, and other such brutal pleasures. Even in the more refined pleasures of horse racing and betting they take no interest. But to literary competitive meetings and to concerts they go by the thousands. Their world may be very narrow but it is a quiet one.[101]

By the 1890s, however, football and billiards were both popular in the quarrying areas, much to the fury of many of

---

[98] Ibid., evidence of Rev. E. J. Jones, 35365–35863.
[99] K. K., *Wales and its People* (Wrexham, 1869), p. 47.
[100] Ceredig, *Y Dosbarth Gweithiol yng Nghymru* (Carmarthen 1866), pp. 68–72; R. Ellis, 'Adgofion am Ddiwygiad Beddgelert', in J. O. Jones, *Cofiant a Gweithiau y Parch Robert Ellis* (Caernarfon, 1883).
[101] *Caernarvon and Denbigh Herald*, 8 August 1874.

the more puritanical nonconformists, and by the end of the century there were well-established football clubs in Blaenau Ffestiniog, Nantlle Vale, Llanberis and Bethesda, and the clubs in Portmadoc, Caernarfon and Bangor also owed much to the enthusiastic backing of quarrymen.[102]

What little crime there was, was dominated by drunkenness; accurate statistics are difficult to come by but those available tend to confirm the comments of observers as to the rarity of serious offences. Crime was largely confined to charges of drunkenness. Of 96 people charged in Bethesda police station between 1884 and 1888, only 23 were quarrymen; of the 23, 14 were charged with drunkenness.[103] This was not a record to arouse much concern amongst the guardians of the ethic of respectability, except, perhaps, for the high percentage of drunkenness offences in a community that liked to regard itself as abstemious.

Temperance and total abstinence were part of the ideology of the chapel and were important influences on the quarrymen, but they should not be over-estimated: public houses were stacked cheek-to-jowl along the length of the high streets of Bethesda and Blaenau Ffestiniog and there is plenty of evidence that they enjoyed a buoyant trade.

A correspondent to the *Herald Cymraeg* in 1865 complained of drinking in Blaenau Ffestiniog, where 'Wherever I happened to go, they were lying in the ditches, along the side of the roads, in all directions'. In Llanllyfni, another quarrying village near Penygroes, he complained of singing in the public houses on a Sunday and of a fist-fight, watched by a large crowd, which disturbed the sermon in a nearby Calvinistic Methodist chapel.[104] The Rev. Robert Ellis, a champion of the moral quarryman, also complained in 1878 that 'drunkenness and unruly behaviour have recently increased greatly amidst this class of men'. He estimated, however, that the percentage of unruly drunkards in the population was 'hardly six or seven per cent'.[105]

---

[102] See, for example, letters to *Yr Herald Cymraeg*, 14 July 1896; 28 July 1896, discussing the relative immorality of dominoes and football. See also GAS, DQ 2594, Llanberis Football Club, *Balance Sheet*, 1902, 1903.
[103] GAS, Police papers, Bethesda Charges Book, 1885–1948.
[104] *Yr Herald Cymraeg*, 27 May 1865.
[105] R. Ellis., op. cit.

It is difficult to know how he arrived at such an estimate; whatever gauge was to hand for him will evade any present-day assessor, but the proportion of the total who were the drinkers is not to be overlooked. They were certainly not overlooked at the time, inviting both the censure and the 'blind eye' of the chapels, which allowed the rear seats to be vacant for the 'rebels' to slip in, unnoticed, during the service. The young in particular were warned from joining those who

> paraded idly back and forth along the streets, lounging about by shop windows and public-houses, chattering and fooling about . . . spending their money . . . on expensive clothes and useless habits . . . drinking, smoking, chewing tobacco, playing billiards, bagatelle, cards, dominoes, and fighting of all sorts, from the thoughtless animal to the man.[106]

Here are hints of the 'condition of the working class' in less puritan and less isolated parts of Britain, stalking the streets in a way foreign and frightening to rural and respectable onlookers. Whatever the percentage involved—and puritan paranoia would have exaggerated where local patriotism deflated—the nonconformist monolith had its underbelly, defined in drink, which it needed, as much to embrace as to keep at a distance.[107]

These, then, were some of the main features of the quarrymen's communities; industrial dungeons in the hills, they were also Welsh communities. Their inhabitants lived their lives almost entirely through the Welsh language; only a few had even a rudimentary knowledge of *yr iaith fain* (English). As we shall see in the next chapter, this is a crucial dimension to the quarryman's world, for the quarryman's language was one of the most important elements in the character of his community.

The quarryman carried many identifying marks: some he bore with pride, some involuntarily. As we have seen, he could be recognised by, amongst other things, his diet, health and his relationship to his farming neighbour. There were also other

---

[106] U.C.N.W., Coetmor MSS. 44; Un o Honoch, *Y Faner*, 2 September.
[107] Drink was the main challenge to respectability, but there were also dark suggestions of prostitution; three prostitutes were charged in Caernarfon in 1887 and one in Merioneth, and a correspondent to *Llais y Wlad*, 18 September 1874, rather improbably accused a Bethesda house of being of ill-repute.

features of this identity: culture, work, trade unionism, politics. But it is important to realize the particularity of the quarryman's experience, not only in his aspirations and achievements, and his endurance, but in a more difficult sense also, in a certain style which reflected considerations of himself and his evaluation of others. It was an identity as multi-faceted as a fly's eye but which could also be reduced to simple expressions. Thus, quarrymen from Penrhyndeudraeth, arriving home by train from their day's work in the mines of Blaenau,

> would, on emerging from the train at their home station, immediately begin to run or trot downhill towards the town, and about a quarter of a mile of roadway would be filled with running men, thinning out as groups would turn from the the main group in order, still trotting, to take the nearest side streets to their respective homes.[108]

Or consider how the children in quarrying areas emulated, with admiration and a sense of the inevitability of their own futures, the quirks and concerns of their elders. Looking back in 1936, Thomas Phillips remembered his childhood in the Llanberis district before the turn of the century, when

> the children of 'Refail newydd' used to copy the quarryman . . . the image idol of the quarryman was of the air they breathed . . . They had their little quarry, they copied their fathers in the craft, they owned their hammers and their gimlets; they went from time to time to the quarry.[109]

These, and many others, were customs which marked out some men as quarrymen.

---

[108] Moses Kellow, 'Autobiography', *Quarry Manager's Journal*, January 1944, p. 300.
[109] Thomas Phillips, *Bro Deiniol* (Bala, 1936), p. 37.

III

BELIEFS AND ATTITUDES

I. POLITICS

The emergence and persistence of a tradition of political radicalism in Wales, and the importance of cultural factors in that tradition, are subjects which have attracted considerable attention. It is not intended to rehearse the arguments concerning the development of a Welsh politics in the mid-nineteenth century here but rather to investigate some aspects of the political behaviour of the slate quarrymen and to consider especially those factors which reflect a concern for specifically Welsh issues.[1]

The quarrymen lived in an area where radical Liberalism achieved great success. In few other areas in Britain was the dominance of the Liberal Party in electoral politics to be so complete and the performance of the Conservative Party to be so ineffective. Of the eighty-one electoral contests held in the five (later four) constituencies of Gwynedd from the appearance of something approaching a popular democracy in the election of 1885 until 1945, the Conservatives won only two contests.[2] In the election for the first Merioneth County Council in 1889 the Conservatives won nine seats and the Liberals thirty-three.[3] In the rocky soil of Gwynedd the Welsh radical tradition not only flourished but ran riot, and two of the most notable figures in Welsh politics, Tom Ellis, who rose from a small tenant farm to the Liberal hierarchy, and David Lloyd George

---

[1] See, in particular, Kenneth O. Morgan, *Wales in British Politics* (3rd ed., Cardiff, 1980); Cyril Parry, *The Radical Tradition in Welsh Politics* (Hull, 1970); Kevin R. Cox, 'Geography, Social Contexts and Voting Behaviour in Wales, 1861–1951', in E. Allardt & S. Rokkan (eds.), *Mass Politics* (New York, 1970), 117–59. For Gwynedd politics, see the survey by Ieuan Gwynedd Jones, 'Merioneth politics in mid-nineteenth century: the politics of a rural economy', *Journal of the Merioneth Historical and Record Society*, IV, 273–334.

[2] F. W. S. Craig, *British Parliamentary Election Results, 1918–49* (Glasgow, 1969); idem., *British Parliamentary Election Results, 1885–1918* (London, 1974). The Conservatives won Caernarvon Boroughs in 1885 and again in 1945.

[3] *The Cambrian News*, 20 January 1889.

were both members for Gwynedd constituencies.[4]

It is hardly necessary to stress the importance of this radical tradition but it might be worthwhile to point to its limitations. A mere description of the area's radicalism can disguise as much as it can reveal, for although the battle over the political terrain was ferocious and often brilliantly orchestrated (serving as a sound enough training-ground for a Lloyd George) and despite the political victories, no amount of propaganda could hide the economic impotence of Conservatism's radical adversaries when faced with the wealth and economic control of landlordism.

The Liberal objective was simple and clear: to achieve, through the ballot box, control of the political levers of power and to use that power to undermine the authority of the landlord class. In order to win the political struggle, an anti-Tory alliance of professional men, ministers of religion, tenant farmers and workers needed to be, and was, constructed.[5] That alliance did not appear fully formed and automatically radical from the womb of the Tory past; on the contrary, it had to be fought for and enforced. Nowhere was this process clearer than in the case of the Penrhyn quarrymen.

By the last quarter of the nineteenth century the slate-quarrying areas were a bastion both of the Welsh language and also of a Welsh culture dominated by nonconformity and Liberalism. But until 1874 the Penrhyn quarrymen were also firmly controlled politically by Penrhyn Castle; those who admitted their radicalism could expect very short shrift. In 1865 the *Cymdeithas Undebol Chwarelwyr Cymru* had been meekly dissolved when Penrhyn had declared that he would not tolerate any attempt 'to form a species of Trade Union among the quarrymen', and that any such attempt would force him to close the quarry and he 'would only reopen it and his cottages to those men who declare themselves averse to any such scheme'.[6]

---

[4] Thomas Edward Ellis (1859–99), M.P. for Merioneth, 1886–99, Liberal chief whip, 1894–95. See N. Masterman, *The Forerunner: the Dilemmas of Tom Ellis* (Llandybie, 1972). David Lloyd George (1863–1945), M.P. for Caernarvon Boroughs, 1890–1945.

[5] Of the 33 Liberal county councillors elected in Merioneth in 1889, four were nonconformist ministers, whereas the remainder were farmers, businessmen and professional men. Of the nine Conservative councillors, five were 'esquires' and two were 'gentlemen'. *The Cambrian News*, 20 January 1889.

[6] W. J. Parry, *The Penrhyn Lock-Out* (London, 1901), p. 6.

The effectiveness of Penrhyn's control over the men was again demonstrated in the 1868 general election. The year of Welsh political emancipation, 1868 was not a glorious one in the history of Bethesda. With a trebled electorate the hold of the Penrhyn family over the Caernarvonshire parliamentary seat was challenged and broken by a Liberal, Thomas Love Jones-Parry. He won the seat with 1,963 votes against the 1,815 votes of Lord Penrhyn's son, George Sholto Douglas Pennant.[7] In Bangor and Bethesda, however, areas under direct Penrhyn influence, Pennant had a majority. In Bethesda the number of Liberal votes was particularly small, 47 out of a total of 359, and this despite the enthusiastic pro-Jones-Parry meetings held in the town before the election.[8]

Those brave enough to be public Liberals in Penrhyn's domain were soon made to pay the price. Following the pattern of victimisation and eviction set by the Tory landlords of west Wales, fighting to retain their political control, Penrhyn sacked and intimidated many prominent Liberals. In 1870 he purged his quarries of agitators, dismissing 'over 80 quarrymen, most of them among the best men in the quarry in character and work . . . without any reason being given'.[9]

Condemned by the Welsh press, this action was accepted by the Penrhyn quarrymen, who held an apparently well-attended meeting in June 1870 to 'protest against the slur cast upon the respected stewards and the generous and kind proprietor'.[10] They resented especially the words of a local radical columnist who had castigated them as 'white slaves'.[11] On the contrary, the men protested, the sackings had been perfectly justified by the downward turn in the slate trade and even one of the dismissed men maintained that this was so and that he was no

---

[7] The Penrhyn family had won the Caernarvonshire parliamentary seat in 1841; the first Baron Penrhyn sat for the constituency from that date until his elevation to the House of Lords in 1866; the seat was lost to the Liberals in 1868, was recaptured in 1874 but lost again in 1880. Lord Penrhyn was also an influential member of Caernarvonshire County Council. See Frank Price Jones, 'Gwleidyddiaeth Sir Gaernarfon yn y Bedwaredd Ganrif ar Bymtheg', *Transactions of the Caernarvonshire Historical Society* (*TCHS*), 26 (1965), 75–106.

[8] Frank Price Jones, op. cit., p. 94.

[9] W. J. Parry, op. cit., p. 7.

[10] *Caernarvon and Denbigh Herald*, 30 July 1870.

[11] U.C.N.W., Coetmor MSS. No. 46, p. 8, 'Bethesda and its prospects', by Vox Caban Coch, paper and date unknown.

radical, and had helped with the plans for a union (in 1865) against his own will. Such was Penrhyn's power.

In 1874 Pennant comfortably regained his seat, for despite the Ballot Act which had come into operation since its passage in 1872 the fear of victimisation and a genuine sense of obligation toward their master demanded a vote, not necessarily for Toryism, but for the Penrhyn family. Even prominent nonconformist figures such as 'Tanymarian'[12] (Rev. Edward Stephen) and a host of deacons sat on Penrhyn's platform and spoke on his behalf.[13]

The Liberal Welsh press was furious and lashed out at the subservience of the quarrymen. The perceptive *Herald Cymraeg* columnist on Bethesda affairs, wrote:

> Does Wales know, I wonder, that the workers of Chwarel y Cae are slaves, perfect slaves? Ever since the election of 1868 they slip further every year into the hold of servility, until most of them have by now lost the last grain of independence . . . they will have to be squeezed almost to death before they will shout.[14]

Despite the election result, the early months of 1874 saw a consciousness stirring. '*Y mae swn ym mrig y morwydd*',[15] noticed the editor of the *Herald Cymraeg* in the first week of April; before the end of the month a trade union for the slate quarrymen had been formed; by the end of the year both Penrhyn and Dinorwic had experienced major disputes, and it was clear that this union was not going to go away.

The struggle for trade unionism was inseparable from, though not, as we shall see, synonymous with, the challenge of Welsh radical Liberalism. The quarrymen were the only significant and potentially organizable group of workers in Gwynedd, and their support was essential for Liberalism's well-being. The quarrymen themselves, moreover, were natural candidates for radicalism, as subsequent years were to show, but first the power of Penrhyn Castle and the Vaynol had to be broken,

---

[12] F. Price Jones, op. cit., p. 98.
[13] *Yr Herald Cymraeg*, 20 March 1874.
[14] Ibid.
[15] Ibid., 3 April 1874. "the sound of a going in the tops of the mulberry trees, (that then thou shalt bestir thyself)", Samuel II, 5, 24.

and with that power the silvered manacles of their paternalism.[16]

Those manacles were sundered in 1874 by the North Wales Quarrymen's Union, which in that year challenged both the Castle and the Vaynol and won. In 1880 Douglas Pennant lost his seat and Arfon with William Jones as M.P. rapidly became an impregnable Liberal stronghold. But there had been nothing automatic about that allegiance; on the contrary, the Welsh radical tradition in the Penrhyn quarries had had to be created and then fought for. Its victory, although sweeping, was never complete. Partly through conscious policy and partly because of the economic development of the region, Gwynedd came to be effectively two societies, culturally and religiously defined, with their respective élites struggling for control of the local state.

On the one hand was the Liberal consensus. On the other, ranged behind the power and wealth of the Castle, was Tory Gwynedd, claiming the allegiance of the remaining gentry and of a significant proportion of the middle class, much of it Welsh in speech, and drawing strength also from the already growing number of middle-class English immigrants who clustered in particular in the seaside towns and in the constituency of Caernarvon Boroughs. It was here that Liberalism with its army of quarry workers and tenant farmers was most stoutly resisted. Caernarvon Boroughs, consisting of the towns of Caernarfon, Bangor, Conwy, Cricieth, Nefyn and Pwllheli, was a marginal seat when David Lloyd George won it with a majority of eighteen in a by-election in 1890; ten years later, after three more elections, the Liberal majority was still slim. Lloyd George was an exceptional Member of Parliament who eventually made the seat securely his own, but whenever a Conservative candidate fought the seat (and the Conservatives did not fight in 1918, 1922 or 1924) their vote never fell lower than a quarter of the electorate; in most of the contests it was considerably higher. And in 1945, following the vacation of the seat by Lloyd George, it again returned (though admittedly in an unusual four-party contest) a Conservative M.P. The Tory

---

[16] Penrhyn's paternalism, like that of some of the other quarry owners, went to considerable lengths; for example, he built a quarry hospital and provided pensions for widows of quarrymen killed at work; he also offered light work or pensions to those who had given him long service.

leadership consisted of landlords, ably supported by Anglican clergy and hoteliers, but there were also influential lawyers and doctors as well as small businessmen, merchants and sea-captains who supported the Castle. This 'loyalist' middle class was ideologically excluded from being Welsh by the definitions of radicalism. But it did not disappear.

Neither did that small section of the working class, almost entirely Welsh-speaking, which supported the Tory cause; on the contrary, it returned to the stage with a vengeance in June 1901 when, as blackleg labour, it made sure of Penrhyn's final victory.

Politically, this Tory society was removed from power in Gwynedd as Liberals claimed the parliamentary representation and in due course controlled the new county councils and urban district councils. In 1900 the Bethesda U.D.C. felt secure enough in its radicalism to follow Blaenau Ffestiniog's example and determined to transact its business henceforth entirely in the Welsh language.[17] The Tories were not, however, removed entirely from the local state; not only did Lord Penrhyn himself join the Caernarvonshire County Council, there to sit with his bitterest adversaries in an extraordinary demonstration of aristocratic political militancy, but essential parts of the local state, crucially the police and the magistracy, evaded direct Liberal control. During the Penrhyn lock-out the magistrates of Bangor defied every elected authority in Gwynedd and called out the cavalry; during the same dispute the County's Standing Joint Police Committee denounced the behaviour of its own police force, but it could not control it.[18]

Even more crucially, the radical Liberals never replaced their opponents as the wielders of economic power in Gwynedd; economic decline and change saw in the twentieth century the

---

[17] GAS, Caernarfon, Bethesda Urban District Minute Book, 13 July 1900. For the Ffestiniog U.D.C., see Ernest Jones, *Senedd Stiniog: Hanes Cyngor Dinesig Ffestiniog, 1895–1974* (Blaenau Ffestiniog, n.d.). For an interesting account of political change at a local level, see Peter Ellis Jones, 'The Bangor Local Board of Health, 1850–83', *Transactions of the Caernarvonshire Historical Society*, No. 37 (1976), 87–132.

[18] See Chapter 7 and the discussion about the absence of Welsh Liberal J.P.s in Coetmor, 45, p. 16 and *passim*. Of the nine Conservative county councillors in Merioneth in 1889, seven were magistrates, including amongst their number the chairman of Quarter Sessions; of the 33 Liberal councillors only six were magistrates.

erosion of the enormous landed fortunes of the nineteenth, but the local economy was not taken over; rather did it disintegrate.[19]

II. THE WELSH DIMENSION

The Welsh language, and the culture it expressed, though a permanent factor in Gwynedd's social and political life, was rarely, if ever, an issue in political struggles. The inter-relationship between language, class and politics was neither static nor automatic. On the contrary, it offers major problems of interpretation. By concentrating here on the cultural consciousness of the quarrymen it is hoped that some of that complex relationship will become more apparent. The problem is compounded by the inexactitudes of the self-images of the propagandists of Welsh culture and by the rhetoric which nourished those images. To detach the reality from the claims is not easy, for in a quite profound sense the Welsh radical tradition, and the cultural apparatus which sustained it, was a genuinely ideological construct.

The programme of late-nineteenth century Welsh Liberalism was built around land reform and disestablishment. The cement which held the political alliance together was Welsh culture and its institutions, and this culture and these institutions came to be thought of as synonymous with nonconformity and radical Liberalism. During the 1880s and 1890s the middle-class non-conformist élite, through the agencies of chapel and press, re-defined the idea of Wales in its own image, deftly excluding its opponents and sometimes also its supporters. The myth of the *gwerin*, of a classless or one-class Welsh democracy, was its main ideological achievement. The quarrymen came to bask in the glory of that myth, but came also at times to test its limits.

A sense of nationality was rarely carried as a banner by the quarrymen or by any other group of workers in Wales, but nevertheless the significance of such a consciousness can hardly

[19] For an interpretation of the decline of the landed estates of Wales, see John Davies, 'The End of the Great Estates and the rise of freehold farming in Wales', *Welsh History Review*, 7, 186–213. The Vaynol estate flowered somewhat in the inter-war period; the frippery is preserved in Cecil Beaton, *Diaries* (2 vols., London, 1961, 1965).

be doubted. It was part of their identity, worn, like their working clothes, unquestioningly, almost unconsciously. The roots of their consciousness lay in that social and cultural tradition, that profound condition which makes the history of Welsh society so apparently similar and yet so tantalisingly different from the history of England.[20]

Threaded crucially into the pattern was the astonishingly resilient Welsh language. The slate-quarrying areas were situated in one of the areas where the Welsh language was at its strongest. The first census to enquire about respondents' language found in 1891 that 54 per cent of the people of Wales and Monmouthshire spoke Welsh; 30 per cent of them spoke only Welsh. In Gwynedd, however, 69 per cent of the total population over two years of age spoke only Welsh, a total of 147,836 people. A further 47,554 were bilingual and 9 per cent, 19,657 persons, spoke only English.[21]

The slate-quarrying communities themselves were even more emphatically Welsh in speech. 'Welsh', commented an observer of the quarrying township of Bethesda in 1911, 'is the language of the home, the street, the quarry, the farm and the sanctuary.'[22] Of a total population of 28,000 in the registration district of Ffestiniog in 1891, 4,200 were bilingual, some 700 spoke only English and 21,500 were monoglot Welsh speakers. A decade later, in the Bethesda Urban District, 1,500 males over the age of three could only speak the Welsh language, 700 had some command of both languages and only 12 men were monoglot English speakers.[23] The incidence of bilingualism amongst women was slightly higher; this was one of the many effects of the fact that domestic service, often in well-off English-speaking homes, was the only possible paid occupation for women. These census figures are not altogether reliable; officials suspected that there were many capable of speaking English who claimed that they could not out of a stubborn instinct to defend the position of the Welsh language. This may be a feature of present-day censuses in Wales but there is little evidence to suggest that

[20] For a historical discussion of these themes, see Glanmor Williams, *Religion, Education and Nationality in Wales* (Cardiff, 1979).
[21] *Census Returns*, Division IX, Monmouthshire and Wales, Language spoken, 1891.
[22] D. J. Williams, *The Borough Guide to Bethesda* (1911).
[23] *Census Returns*, 1891, 1901.

it was also a common nineteenth-century ploy. The opposite—
people with only a very basic grasp of the English vocabulary
flattering themselves by officially claiming bilingualism—
would have been more likely.

The slate-quarrying area, therefore, was a bastion of the
Welsh language in which those who were able to speak English
were a minority and those unable to speak Welsh were in a very
small minority indeed. It is not therefore surprising that the
quarrymen acquired a reputation for developing a high level
of Welsh culture and several of Wales's leading poets and
writers had their roots in the hard soil of these districts: R.
Williams Parry, one of Wales's best modern poets; Kate
Roberts, an outstanding novelist and short-story writer, to
name only two. If not always a rich culture, it was a lively one
and it was pursued with a rare enthusiasm. Important *eisteddfodau* were held regularly in the quarry towns, and quarries
and mines often held their own smaller *eisteddfodau*. The quarry
itself was, in fact, an important cultural centre where much
music was made and innumerable verses were composed.
There has been a certain mythologising about the cultural
attainments of the quarrymen and a rather idealistic picture has
tended to be painted of scrubbed, starched, hard-working men
discussing Ruskin in their lunch hour, writing poetry in the
evenings and singing on Sundays with naturally perfect voices.
Few, if any, achieved such perfection but it is true that the
quarrymen generally had an obsession with involved discussions, a talent for dry, anecdotal humour (as well as for
buffoonery and practical jokes), and a huge appetite for a diet
of alliteration, rhymes and *cynghanedd*.

Central to the quarryman's cultural pursuits was the *caban*,
the lunchtime canteen which was also the union office, debating
chamber and the scene of a permanent test of literary skill. The
caban had strict rules of behaviour and often had a very formal
structure of chairman, secretary, etc. It was a unique creation
of the quarryman: *eisteddfod* and friendly society and trade
union office all rolled into one; it was, in effect, the quarryman's
canteen, where sections of the men gathered for their lunch
breaks. But the *caban* was much more than a mere canteen, for
it was also organised for educational, cultural and, at times,
agitational activity. The level of such activity clearly varied

enormously, but the *caban* was an impressive institution. Many a *caban* was a forum for humour, politics, trade unionism, poetry and a thousand different word games: some *cabannau* held regular *eisteddfodau*, many on a monthly basis, where the men, in their working clothes, would compete in poetry, prose and recitation.

The minute book of one *caban* survives: that of Sinc y Mynydd in the Llechwedd mine, and it gives a compelling picture of self-activity and organisation.[24] Discussions and competitions were organised daily, grievances were aired and money-raising concerts arranged for injured or ill colleagues or their families; order was kept by a chairman (known as the sergeant) and minutes kept by a secretary. All took place in a damp, dark tunnel by the light of spluttering candles and over jamjars of stewed tea in snatched lunch hours.

The Sinc y Mynydd programme for October 1902 included Owen Morris talking about his holidays, a mental arithmetic contest, a competition to sing the words of '*O Fryniau Caersalem*' to the tune of Crug-y-bar, a lecture on the topic 'How much greater is a man than a sheep', discussion on the Education Act and the need to oppose it, a solo-singing competition, a competition to read aloud a piece which had not been punctuated, a spelling contest, a contest to create Welsh words, a general knowledge quiz, recitation of a précis of the poem *Dafydd Brenin Israel* (this lasted a whole week), a quiz on Biblical knowledge, a competition to name places which all began with the same letter, a debate on whether ministers of religion should be appointed for life or for a certain term of office, a competition to interpret the meaning of a particular poem, and a lecture on vanity. In July, apart from debating 'whether a wife is a choice or a necessity', the *caban* also held contests to write an *englyn* to 'The Jumper', to recite a poem after only having read it twice and to scan the poem '*Y Don*'. However modest such cultural pursuits were, they produced a certain mental agility, a high level of literacy and ensured that the quarrymen were steeped in the genuinely popular aspects of Welsh culture.

[24] U.C.N.W. MS. 5440, Llyfr Cofnodion hen giniawdy Sinc y Mynydd, Llechwedd, 14 February 1902–15 April 1904.

The quarrymen were also avid readers of a host of small, local Welsh weekly newspapers. Two such papers, *Y Werin* produced by radical Liberals, and *Y Chwarelwr Cymreig* controlled by Lord Penrhyn's Tory interest, were aimed exclusively at the quarryman, while a host of other papers carried many columns on quarrying affairs and news from the quarrying areas. 'The quarrymen', said a witness to the Royal Commission on the Church of England in Wales in 1907, 'I should think, form the majority of the subscribers to the *Geninen, Y Dysgedydd, Drysorfa, Y Genedl, Yr Herald Gymraeg, Gwalia, Y Goleuad, Y Werin, Yr Eco Cymraeg.*'[25] The secular amongst these papers, moreover, though carrying a great deal of local news, took a much wider interest in politics and international affairs and usually sported a poets' corner and carried short stories, etc. The papers were also, of course, aflame with fiery anti-landlordism and other radical and often nationalistic comment.

The quarrymen were therefore very much influenced by the mainstream of Welsh culture and they made a contribution well beyond their numbers to that culture. They were also workers in what was virtually a Welsh industry. The slate-producing area of Britain was confined to the western coast and extended with certain breaks from Argyllshire via Cumberland to Cornwall, with outcrops also in Pembrokeshire; but during the nineteenth century, with the development of large-scale operations in north Wales, this area came to overshadow completely the other slate-producing districts and in 1882 north Wales was producing 93 per cent of Britain's slate.[26] Not surprisingly, the industry came to see itself purely as a Welsh industry. This heightened the quarryman's consciousness of being Welsh; there were few fellow slate quarrymen in England with whom he could identify. When they came to found their union, therefore, it was never envisaged as being anything other than a Welsh organisation. In 1865 there was a first abortive effort to set up *Cymdeithas Undebol Chwarelwyr Cymru* (United Society of Welsh Quarrymen) and when a

---

[25] *Royal Commission on the Church of England and other religious bodies in Wales and Monmouthshire*, 1910; evidence of Rev. D. H. Williams, 6815–7355.
[26] D. Dylan Pritchard, 'The Expansionist Phase in the History of the Welsh Slate Industry', p. 78.

successful organisation was launched in 1874 it was called the
North Wales Quarrymen's Union. The union never seems to
have made any serious attempt to unite with slate quarrymen
elsewhere in Britain.[27]

The quarry craft itself was Welsh; apart from the sales
nomenclature of the slates themselves, the vocabulary of the
work, the technical glossary thrown up by the skill and the
difficulties of working slate, was completely Welsh or integrated
into Welsh.[28] This led many quarrymen to disqualify Englishmen altogether from ever being able to understand the tasks
involved. 'Some would argue,' explained Dewi Peris in his
winning essay in the Bethesda Eisteddfod of 1875, 'that there
is in the Welsh, more than in any other nation, a particular
suitability, an innate genius, to treat slate.'[29] Dewi himself
disagreed with such a view but as we shall see later there were
many who upheld it.[30] Since almost all quarrymen were themselves Welsh these remarks were invariably aimed at the
English managers of many quarries who were consistently
condemned and attacked for their lack of understanding of
the immense complexity of the quarrying craft. When English
workmen were, once, introduced in 1876 into a Welsh slate
quarry there was an uncharacteristically violent flare-up. But
it was in relations with managers that anti-English venom came
to the surface. 'We seem to live', wrote an anonymous
Caernarfon pamphleteer in 1895, 'to do the bidding of aliens.
As landlordism imposes upon us Scotch agents and game-
keepers, so capitalism places over us English managers and
gangers, who out-herod Herod in their arrogance toward
native workmen.'[31]

And while some quarry companies had Welsh shareholders
and most employed Welsh under-managers and agents (and

---

[27] This is in sharp contrast to the organisation of north Wales's other major
group of quarrymen, the dolerite workers; they were not ignored by the Settmakers' Union, an organisation based as securely in the Aberdeen area of
Scotland as the N.W.Q.U. was in north Wales. There were, in 1903, 13 branches
of the Settmakers' Union in north-west Wales with a membership of 1,025 (out
of a total of 3,274); see *Settmakers' and Stoneworkers' Journal*, January 1903.

[28] See Emyr Jones, 'Termau'r Chwarel a'u Hystyrau', *Canrif y Chwarelwr*
(Denbigh, 1964), pp. 123–62.

[29] Dewi Peris, 'Chwarelyddiaeth', *Y Geninen*, XIII (1895), 273–74.

[30] See Chapter IV, p. 78.

[31] Celt, *Cymru Fydd Gymru Rydd* (Caernarfon, 1895), p. 5.

there were a few Welsh proprietors of some small quarries), the ownership and overall management of the larger quarries were largely in English hands. As we have seen, it was the names of English families like Assheton-Smith, Penrhyn, Holland, Greaves and Darbishire that dominated the industry. Resentment, rather than anger, was the nineteenth-century reaction to such a state of affairs, especially amongst the Welsh business class which felt that it had missed the biggest opportunity that was ever liable to come its way, or anybody else's way, in the barren mountainous terrain of Snowdonia.[32] It was with a growing and keen frustration that such men watched English adventurers make huge fortunes from the mountains. John O. Griffith, not himself a quarryman but nevertheless an early official of the N.W.Q.U., argued eloquently for a more aggressive Welsh intervention in the industry. 'While we are dozing,' he wrote in 1864,

> hosts of foreigners are pouring in . . . and they have already taken into their possession most, and I fear, the best of the slate beds. Dear fellow countrymen, we kept hold of our old mountains from the beginning and they have been our safe refuge in the days of our affliction and our tribulations; do we then have to give them up now in the day of our success and of our strength?[33]

In 1864 his plea was already too late. The hostility of the quarrymen toward managers and owners came, therefore, to have a strongly anti-English flavour directed at first at the arrogance of some quarry managements but growing in time into a general awareness that the mountains themselves, and therefore the quarries too, were stolen property.

A Ffestiniog quarryman, savouring the freedom of speech that came with retirement, exclaimed in 1926 that

> the blood boils in the veins with a just anger when one thinks of the brutality and the slavery that the worker had to suffer in his own country from the hand of a foreign company.[34]

[32] See, for example, Morgan Richards, *Slate Quarrying and How to make it Profitable* (Bangor, 1876?), 86–99.
[33] J. O. Griffith, *Traethawd Ymarferol ar Lechfeini Sir Gaernarfon* (Tremadoc, 1883), p. 7.
[34] Hugh Lloyd, *Hunangofiant Rybelwyr* (Caernarfon, 1926), p. 17.

It was not surprising, therefore, that industrial relations in the quarries were often soured by the clash of cultures. The quarrymen's openly displayed feeling that they understood slate quarrying far better than any English manager could ever hope to do, and their constant criticisms of managerial decisions led some managers to give up altogether and hand over effective control to the men; others were goaded to fury, and to the paranoia of men surrounded by a work force whom they literally did not understand, and who did not understand them. 'The smallest thing', wrote the exasperated manager of the Penrhyn quarry in 1900, 'seems to irritate these Welshmen . . . these Welshmen are so ignorant and so childish that there is no arguing with them.'[35] Squabbles over the credentials of different interpreters were constant features of negotiations; neither side trusted the other's nominee and the men were always suspicious of any double meaning in the only too supple and slippery English language.

It was not only at work that cultural consciousness was apparent; it was there also in the other concerns of the community. As we have seen, the quarrymen were themselves deeply religious, spawning chapels and vestries at an astonishingly high rate. Within 3 miles of the centre of Bethesda there were 29 places of worship, 22 of them nonconformist.[36] Seating accommodation for worshippers in fact exceeded the total population of the town by over 1,500.[37]

The chapel was much more than a place of worship; it was also an organiser and an identity, the focus and the expression of the community's values. In the Nantlle valley in 1906 a wave of strikes in the quarries of the valley was organised by the chapels rather than by the union lodge[38] and the strike in Llechwedd in 1893 was sustained not so much by union support as by chapel collections throughout north Wales and the Welsh community in Liverpool. Welsh nonconformity was acutely conscious of its Welshness. Calvinistic Methodism was a Welsh denomination which, by the late-nineteenth century, was

[35] GAS, Penrhyn Quarry Letter Book, 28 November 1900, 11 December 1900.
[36] *Baner ac Amserau Cymru*, 11 December 1872.
[37] *Royal Commission on Church of England in Wales*, evidence of Rev. E. J. Jones, 35365.
[38] *Yr Herald Cymraeg*, 3 July 1906.

clearly aware of its national identity. Other denominations, especially the Congregationalists, were also conscious of their standing as Welsh institutions. The particular nature of Welsh religion was never stressed so much as in the great religious revivals that swept the country periodically, but always seemed to run out of enthusiasm at the English border. The last great revival of 1904–5 bore the unmistakable signs of a Welsh phenomenon. Nonconformity gave to Wales a self-confidence and security which also often engendered self-righteousness and a generally smug belief that Wales was the most faithfully religious corner in the whole world.

During the 1904–5 revival echoes of a belief in the special mission of the Welsh people could at times be heard, especially in the uneven voice of the revivalist Evan Roberts: while Wales was not to conquer the world with power, or with armies, she was to achieve something far more important; 'the young men of Wales', it was prophesied at one revivalist meeting, 'are to lead the way in the salvation of the world'.[39] And there were many during the amazing winter of 1904–5 who thought that God had indeed chosen the Welsh people to be his especial agents.

The very names of so many slate-quarrying villages— Bethesda, Bethel, Ebenezer, Nebo, Carmel, Cesarea and Nazareth—bear testimony to their faith: the villages grew around their chapels. Bethesda, an English observer noted in the early-twentieth century, was 'the headquarters . . . of Caernarvonshire nonconformity'; its chapels were massive and their hold intense.[40]

Making its ritualistic challenge to the nonconformist presence was the 'alien church' of Anglicanism, conscious of the strength of its wealthy English patrons. (Lord Penrhyn gave generously to the building and renovating of Anglican churches throughout north Wales.) This is not the place to describe the battle for the disestablishment of the Church in Wales but it was a major political issue in late-nineteenth century Wales and nowhere was it fought so doggedly and consistently as in the quarrying areas. The church was scorned, its parsons characterised at best

---

[39] Awstin, *The Religious Revival in Wales* (Cardiff, 1904), p. 26.
[40] A. G. Bradley, *Highways and Byways in North Wales* (London, 1919), p. 257.

as lazy, ignorant and drunken, at worst as tyrants forcing their church and their dogmas on a hard-pressed people. Its followers were a minority in the slate-quarrying districts: while some 4,000 people attended nonconformist chapels on a Sunday evening in Bethesda in December 1872, it was reported that the Anglican whips could get only some 500 into their church aisles.[41] The quarrymen were enthusiasts for disestablishment, a question which itself reflected a national consciousness amongst Welsh religionists,

For a group of industrial workers, the majority of them living in the streets of the quarry villages, the quarrymen were, as we have seen, also enthusiastic land reformers. Land was another question which raised the issue of nationality and which was nourished as much by hostility toward an anglicized squirearchy as by any actual injustices in the land system.

The cry for land was a strident one. 'We as workers', read a resolution adopted by the N.W.Q.U. in 1884,

> must come to own land, land is the raw material from which wealth is created, and without land our life and pleasure, our freedom and honour will be left to the tender mercies of others.[42]

As we have seen, the quarrymen themselves took more than a holiday interest in agriculture. Many of the sins of landlordism, moreover, particularly the leasehold system, applied equally to the inhabitants of the villages as to the occupants of farm cottages. And in some areas the tenant farmer's landlord was also the quarrymen's employer; Lord Penrhyn and Mr. Assheton-Smith, as we have seen, owned, as well as their quarries, two of the biggest estates in Wales.

But the land question was more than a list of grievances: it held an emotional charge, a bitterness which owed much to the feeling that the land of Wales was owned by an alien English aristocracy. And the land, moreover, was universally believed to have been common land not long before. As E. Morgan Humphreys, a radical north Walian journalist, wrote in the *Socialist Review* in 1909,

---

[41] *Baner ac Amserau Cymru*, 11 December 1872.
[42] U.C.N.W., Coetmor 46, p. 5.

The question upon which the average Welshman will most readily adopt Socialistic views is that of the land, and that is, I have no hesitation in saying, because he knows that under the old Welsh law every individual had an interest in the land, and he regards the right as having been filched from him by English invaders.[43]

And for the quarrymen, the return of the mountains to the people meant also the return of the quarries.

Temperance, the other powerful aspect of the quarryman's political credo, was not so exclusively linked to Welsh conditions though, with the passing of the 1881 Sunday Closing Act which applied to Wales, it did see an important legislative admission that Welsh issues deserved special consideration and action. To this Liberal programme the nationalists of *Cymru Fydd*, the Young Wales movement of the 1880s and 1890s, added the muddled but nevertheless powerful demand for Home Rule for Wales. The quarrymen were distinctly sympathetic to such ideas and the suggestion of a separate Parliament for Wales was warmly applauded by the 1886 Annual Conference of the N.W.Q.U. Not surprisingly, Home Rule for Ireland was also a popular demand and the Irish campaigner Michael Davitt received a friendly reception when he addressed a notorious meeting of quarrymen in Blaenau Ffestiniog in February 1886.[44] The newly-formed North Wales Property Defence Association, presided over by Lord Penrhyn, viewed Davitt's visit with consternation and was terrified at the prospect of the importation of what were called 'Irish methods' into Wales, although the only episode which even started to fulfil these fears was the so-called tithe war of 1886–9.[45]

The demand for Welsh political representation was most dramatically voiced by the quarrymen during the 1885 election in Merionethshire which followed the retirement of the sitting Liberal member. Henry Robertson, the new Liberal candidate

[43] E. Morgan Humphreys, 'Socialism and Welsh Nationality', *The Socialist Review*, October 1909, p. 118.

[44] Frank Owen, *Tempestuous Journey* (London, 1954), p. 46.

[45] A correspondent to a local Welsh paper wrote in horror of the men who 'wish to Irishise "The old land of the hills" . . . do you wish to see', he asked, 'the land of song turned into a hellish bonfire by the admirers of O'Donovan Rossa?' Coetmor 46, p. 15.

and a wealthy industrialist and landowner with extensive interests in north-east Wales, had been nominated by the Liberal party caucus some three years earlier, i.e. before the 1884 Reform Bill.

At that time only a few Ffestiniog quarrymen had been enfranchised; by 1885 it was estimated that over 2,000 of them had the vote.[46] The political debut of these quarrymen was an angry one as they objected strongly to the choice of Robertson as Liberal candidate and demanded that he be removed. But his removal was not intended to make room for a radical candidate, but rather for a Welsh one. At the first meeting held to discuss the issue, D. G. Williams, chairman of the Ffestiniog lodge of the N.W.Q.U., and vice-chairman of the union itself, insisted that 'as a Welshman I wish to see Wales governed by Welshmen'.[47] This, and the question of loyalty to the Liberal machine, was to be the keynote of the election. The quarrymen chose as their man an Anglesey barrister and small entrepreneur called Morgan Lloyd whose actual politics were hardly distinguishable from Robertson's. As the Aberystwyth *Cambrian News* correctly commented,

> Mr. Morgan Lloyd never has been an advanced Liberal, and is not an advanced Liberal now . . . he is, in fact, a small, vain person.[48]

It is difficult to disagree with this verdict. Lloyd tried to put on a radical face over the land question but in reality his position was, while perhaps more eloquent, certainly no more advanced than Robertson's. Both men were landowners and if Robertson was a large one, Lloyd was accused of being a hard one. The election was fought almost exclusively on the Welsh question. 'It would be wrong of us as a nation to cast away our own children and honour a stranger', cried D. G. Williams at a meeting in Harlech.[49] 'The unionists [i.e. trade unionists] want a Welshman and if they cannot have a Welsh Liberal

---

[46] *Cambrian News*, 21 August 1885; see also *The Times*, 10 December 1885. For an account of the election, see R. Emyr Price, 'Lloyd George and Merioneth Politics, 1885–1886—A Failure to Effect a Breakthrough', *Journal of the Merioneth Historical and Record Society*, VII (1973–76), 292–307.
[47] *Cambrian News*, 21 August 1885.
[48] Ibid., 11 September 1885.
[49] Ibid.

they will have a Welshman who is not a Liberal', commented the *Cambrian News* sadly.[50]

Not only Welsh representation but also Welsh independence was a theme. 'Welshmen', said Lloyd, 'can manage their own affairs without the intervention of the few Englishmen who live in Wales . . . I am ready to fight the battle for Welsh independence'.[51] Later he called for a Welsh party in Parliament on the Irish model and demanded that 'Every member for Wales ought to be able to speak the Welsh language'.[52] In response Robertson endeavoured to play up his own Scottish background which made him 'familiar with the wants and aspirations of the Celtic Races'.[53] (It is doubtful what effect this had on electors who had suffered as much, if not more, at the hands of Scottish agents as of English landlords.)

In 1885, therefore, the Merionethshire quarrymen showed their willingness to go it alone in the battle for a nationalist political identity and to break with the Liberal machine. In this they were supported loudly by the young and radical Lloyd George. To the other past and future leaders of the national movement, however, this strategy was anathema. Michael D. Jones, the lion of the nationalist movement for decades past, declared himself for Robertson, whom he was sure would 'work for Wales'. Tom Ellis, despite his own nationalist position, did likewise.[54] Robertson won the election with 3,700 votes and the Conservative, Wynne, came second with just over 2,000 votes. Lloyd received just under 2,000. It was generally agreed that virtually all Lloyd's votes came from one group, the quarrymen of Ffestiniog and the surrounding districts. His election committee, composed almost entirely of quarrymen, debated for some time whether to go it alone or to rejoin the Liberals. There were plans to form a 'Political Union of the Welsh Nation', but they never materialised.[55] With a more reliable candidate than Lloyd something might have come of it, but with a permanent rural majority in the county under the control of the Liberal machine the quarrymen

[50] Ibid., 28 August 1885.
[51] Ibid., 11 September 1885.
[52] Ibid., 25 September 1885.
[53] Ibid., 20 November 1885.
[54] Ibid., 11 September 1885.
[55] *Y Genedl Gymreig*, 9 December 1885.

had not much choice but to return to the fold. But first they thanked Lloyd 'for his efforts on behalf of the workers'.[56]

Robertson, however, was not an M.P. for very long. He resigned from the Liberal Party in 1886 and was replaced as M.P. by Tom Ellis, a Welsh and nonconformist radical who soon won the allegiance of the quarrymen.

As the *Cambrian News* had feared, the election had fostered a spirit of opposition between the industrial and agricultural classes of Merionethshire, for the quarrymen had on this occasion pushed their nationalism much further than the rural voters were willing to go. And yet, even in this incident, the situation was far from clear cut. Nationalism was used by the quarrymen's leaders more as a weapon against the old Liberal party caucus than as a cause in itself. The vocabulary of the election was that of nationalism and yet its meaning surely pointed to an active group of workers resentful and suspicious of the Whiggish pretensions of their leaders and striking out for a new kind of Liberalism.[57] It was not long, in fact, before a more predictable political vocabulary was being used and labourism rather than nationalism came to be the quarrymen's quarrel with the Liberal machine.

Quarrymen came increasingly to talk not of Welsh representation but of working-class representation. By the early nineties such talk was widespread. 'Why must we be oppressed by those who already profit from us?' asked a Dinorwic quarryman in 1892; he went on to call for a united front of quarrymen to demand parliamentary representatives 'who understand our needs and feel for us and are ready to do all they can to exalt us as a working class'.[58]

The previous year there had been moves to get workers on to the Board of Guardians in Caernarfon. 'The members of the board', ran a complaint, 'own their mansions, their homes, their oxen and their wines. They are surrounded by luxury. What do they know about living on 12s. a week with a family

---

[56] Ibid., 16 December 1885.

[57] A correspondent to the *Cambrian News* explained why the quarrymen were exasperated: 'Confound your political machinery . . . we voted for a Welsh Radical by a vast majority, and we have nominated an English Whig by our delegates . . . a man we have never seen and know nothing of, to act for us in the most momentous circumstances of life.' *Cambrian News*, 11 September 1885.

[58] *Y Genedl Gymreig*, 9 December 1891.

of 9 or 10?'[59] And in the county council elections of 1892 a few candidates were put up in Blaenau Ffestiniog under a labour label and others stood earlier as test candidates (including Morgan Lloyd's most doughty champion, D. G. Williams), though all were defeated.[60] These were only very tentative first steps toward no more than a Lib-Labism, and yet they were definite signs that the political articulation of class consciousness was astir among the quarrymen.

The Penrhyn lock-out of 1900–3 brought an increasing awareness of class identification to the quarrymen, but it would be wrong to see the latter quarter of the nineteenth century as a period when the quarrymen were asked to choose between class and country and were able to make a decisive choice for the former. There were, after all, eloquent voices which had raised the possibility of a fusion of class and nationalist aims.

Lloyd George had set up in 1888 his short-lived *Udgorn Rhyddid* (Trumpet of Freedom) which, in his own words, was intended to be a 'thoroughly nationalist and socialist paper'. [61] R. J. Derfel, a prominent Welsh poet, member of the S.D.F. and later of the Fabian Society, argued concretely in the 1880s for a socialist and independent Wales.[62] W. J. Parry, for many years general secretary and president of the N.W.Q.U., flirted in the 1890s with a plan to set up a new political organisation with nationalist and labourist aims. And as we have seen, the quarrymen of Ffestiniog toyed in 1885 with the idea of setting up a Political Union of the Welsh Nation. Finally, as late as 1918, R. T. Jones, general secretary of the N.W.Q.U., stood for Parliament on a 'labour and nationalist platform'.

A national outlook did not evaporate, therefore, with a growing class consciousness; on the contrary they for a while seemed as if to co-exist. Even at the height of the Penrhyn lock-out, W. W. Jones, the president of the N.W.Q.U., was able to claim the struggle as 'the battle for nationalism',[63] as the clash

---

[59] Ibid., 21 October 1891.
[60] Ibid., 24 February 1892, 9 March 1892.
[61] Frank Owen, op. cit., p. 51.
[62] D. Gwenallt Jones, *Detholiad o Ryddiaith Gymraeg R. J. Derfel*, I, (Denbigh, 1945), 9–60. Derfel's influence on Welsh politics was not, however, very great. He was probably more influential in socialist circles in Manchester, where he lived.
[63] *Yr Herald Cymraeg*, 18 February 1902.

of the values and the people of Wales with English tyranny. And yet, in real political terms, these attempts to fuse a nationalist programme with the quarrymen's consciousness were no more than gestures.

Herein lies the problem of Welsh nationality, the problem of why a nationalist movement with working-class support did not emerge at least in north-west Wales in the late-nineteenth century. In part it was the weakness of will and muddled policies of the middle-class Home Rulers of Cymru Fydd which ensured that no such movement would be built. For despite all their rhetoric, they demonstrated quite clearly that, unlike some of the quarrymen, they were unwilling to break with the Liberal Party—indeed, were incapable of doing so.

Perhaps even more than this failure of leadership, there was something in the nature of the Welsh working-class community itself, and in the way it viewed its Welshness, which prevented such a movement from emerging. The quarrymen were steeped in Welshness and in a consciousness of their nationality; at work, in prayer, in pleasure and in politics, this consciousness informed their activities and their beliefs. Yet that national consciousness never became a nationalist movement because the politics of that nationality were aimed essentially at preserving control of the Welsh community itself and rarely, if ever, at challenging the English power-system outside. For while, as we have seen, the land agitation aimed to limit the power of landlordism and of quarry owners in Wales, what was really striking about this and other agitations was its readiness to admit the legitimacy of English power and ownership. For the Welsh middle class, of course, which sought to replace that power, things were different, but for the quarrymen it was not so much the *English* power-system which drove them to fury, but rather any attempts by that system to interfere with the values of their own communities. That is why disestablishment was such a burning issue; for Anglicanism was a thorn in the side of the community, penetrating such vital questions as education and burial places. The crucial borderline for the slate-quarrying community ran through the quarry. Here the integrity of the community faced its gravest risk, and here a curious pattern emerged in the great strikes of 1874, 1885, 1896–7 and 1900–3. For these battles were essentially about the control of work; the right of the masters to own was rarely challenged, but their right to manage, to interfere in an essential part of the community's identity, certainly was. The quarrymen manned the defences of their community, but only for its right to live within the greater and different society outside. It was here that nationality was so powerful, for all struggles were interpreted as offering a choice of one community or another. It was the consciousness of belonging which often made the struggle so bitter. Those who rejected a part of the community's identity (be it by their Anglicanism or their 'blacklegging'), and thus threatened the whole, were forced out of their right to a nationality. Referring to 'blacklegs' in one of the quarry disputes, the quarrymen were recommended not only to scorn and to revile them but also

> not to allow one of them, or any of their sons, to marry a Welsh woman. Let their descendants be forever foreigners to our land and to our language.[64]

Despite such rhetoric a fully developed nationalism could not grow from such limited, closed and essentially defensive ideas of nationality.

[64] U.C.N.W., Coetmor 45.

IV

THE QUARRY

The two largest slate quarries in the world were Penrhyn and Dinorwic; the world's largest slate mine was the Oakeley in Blaenau Ffestiniog. The Penrhyn quarries employed some 2,800 men who, with gunpowder, and crowbar, hammer and chisel, and skill, blasted and coaxed the slate from the mountain. Its galleries varied in height from 36 to 66 feet (with an average of 54 feet), in breadth from wide platforms of 45 feet to narrow ledges no wider than 6 feet.[1] When levering blocks from the face men would hang over the precipitous and shattered sides with a hemp rope looped around them. Every hour a bell rang out to signal them to shelter; one minute later on the signal of another bell fuses would be lit all over the quarry; following the roar of rock shattering in the explosions, four minutes later another bell would ring summoning them back to work. The slabs loosened by the blast had to be prised from the face and pushed in trucks running along rails to the head of the gallery, where they were lowered down an incline to the great sheds below. There they were sawn and dressed, and split into slates and then taken down Penrhyn's own railway to Port Penrhyn, whence they went to roof the industrial centres of England and the world.

Working hours were determined largely by the weather and the seasons, the working day lengthening with the coming of summer.[2] All worked the same hours but wages depended on which category of work was executed. The quarrymen proper, making up just over 50 per cent of the work force, organised

[1] *Report Quarry Committee of Inquiry* (1893), Appendix III, p. 47. See also William Jones, M.P., *Hansard Parliamentary Debates*, vol. cxviii, 5 March 1903, p. 1651.

[2] 'In a full week, exclusive of mealtimes, about 46 per cent of the total number of Men and Boys worked 52 hours, 36 per cent from 54¼ to 57 hours, 17 per cent about 50 hours; and of the remainder, some worked 46 to 49 (miners) hours and others about 58½ hours. The full time worked at open quarries would be reduced by bad weather and short days in winter.' These figures are averages covering all of north Wales' quarries. *Return of Rates of Wages in Mines and Quarries in the U.K. with Report 1890–91*, lxxviii, 667–8. The figures apply to 1 October 1886.

themselves into crews consisting normally of three or four men, each crew coming to a separate working agreement with the management.

The other main occupational groups in the quarries were 'bad-rockmen' and 'rubbish men'. The bad-rockmen worked usually in crews of three, taking a bargain which, unlike that of the quarrymen proper, would be of bad-rock, that is of rock from which no slates could be worked. The agreement worked out with the management would give them a sum per ton for removing the bad rock. The rubbish men were divided into two groups, those who cleared the rubbish (waste rock) from the galleries where the quarrymen's bargains lay, and those who were responsible for building the giant tips of waste rock which were built around the quarry. They were paid by the ton or by the yard of materials removed.

Also at work in the quarry were the *rybelwrs*, boys who were in the first stage of learning the craft, whose job was to wander along the galleries offering assistance whenever there was need for an extra hand. Sometimes they would be given an extra slab of rock to split for which they would be paid by the crew. From this stage the *rybelwr* could hope to become a journeyman and then a quarryman proper, though many men found themselves stuck at this stage for their whole working lives.

The quarry also employed a number of time-workers, such as weighers, hauliers, brakesmen, stationary enginemen, locomotive engine drivers, engineers, blacksmiths, saw sharpeners, carpenters, platelayers, storekeepers, timekeepers and general labourers, but their total number was small.[3]

The quarrymen proper formed the élite group of the quarry, for though they did not earn considerably more than the bad-rockmen, their status was always treated with respect. Although there was no apprenticeship in slate quarrying in the nineteenth century, and a man became a quarryman through his skill and his connections in a fairly informal way, a quarryman was conscious of his superior skill and status, and relations with other workers were sometimes strained, exacerbated by the fact that the quarrymen usually lived together in the quarry village while lower grades often came from outside the

[3] Ibid.; these 13 groups of workers added up to only 9.7 per cent of the total work force.

immediate area. The North Wales Quarrymen's Union, however, was an industrial union open to all those employed in slate quarries; and wage claims, while respecting differentials, were almost always made on behalf of all the workers. In Penrhyn in 1874, in fact, the quarrymen went so far as to put in a claim, along with their own, on behalf of the journeymen who were employed by themselves, and not by the quarry-owner. This fairly amicable relationship between quarry workers was reflected in the relatively small difference in wages between the higher grades. Only the labourers, particularly those from the surrounding agricultural areas, were omitted from the consensus; their lives were not staked in the quarries and they knew of other ways to earn a living.

Slate-quarrying was not only heavy and difficult work, it was also highly skilled. As the correspondent of the *Pall Mall Gazette* noted in 1885,

> slate quarrying is not a matter of mere manual labour but an art which years of patient practice will hardly require . . . a slate-splitter is like a poet . . . and contends with the poet on an equal footing at the National Eisteddfod where slate-splitting, music and poetry are stock subjects of rivalry.[4]

In the normal crew of quarrymen there would be two rockmen, a splitter and a dresser; the crew might also employ one or two journeymen, young men or boys learning the craft. The rockmen worked on the face itself and were primarily responsible for the first stage of drilling holes for and then placing the explosive charges and then, with a crowbar, levering off the giant slabs loosened by the blast, this being executed while hanging over the rock-face with a rope (or a chain in wet conditions) looped around their thighs. The huge slabs were then split into manageable sizes before being sent to the sheds, where the blocks were sawn before the splitters split them with hammer and chisels into slates, which were then dressed to various sizes.

In the slate mines of Merionethshire a man was usually expected to master either the underground, rock-face skills or the splitting and dressing processes of the sheds; in the open

---

[4] U.C.N.W., Coetmor 46, p. 30.

quarries of Caernarvonshire, however, while each member of a crew had his special responsibilities, each was also expected to be able to carry out all the processes, to follow the rock from the face to the finished slate. For what was vital to the quarryman's work was not so much his skill at using various tools and explosives, but rather his understanding of the nature of the particular face of rock he was dealing with. Thus, a rockman, before laying his charge, had to know exactly how big a slab he wanted bringing down and which way it would fall; too big or too small a charge, placed in the wrong place, could shatter rather than loosen the rock or could make the winning of further slabs more difficult. As a Ffestiniog rockman pointed out in 1893, being a technically good workman was not the point; 'to bore a hole is one thing, but to know where to put it is quite a different matter'.[5] The splitter, the real aristocrat of the quarry craft, had to be able to tell at a glance what size and quality slate he could coax out of a particular block. It was this understanding of the rock which gave the quarryman's craft such a mystique; looking at the rock and recognizing the 'posts, crychs, bends, sparry veins, faults, joints and hardened rock',[6] which would affect the work was perhaps the most important part of the quarryman's skill.

This acquaintance with the rock was, moreover, bred of a lifetime of familiarity. There was no defined apprenticeship in the industry, and different men took very different periods to learn; some could never learn and 'some learn in two what others would not in twenty-two years'.[7] What was important was an early start; 'they must begin young', declared the manager of the New Welsh Slate Company, 'to understand the rock, to thoroughly work it. A man does not take to slate rock unless he is brought up to it.'[8] This was particularly true of the above-ground slate-splitter; one quarryman had 'never known of anyone who learnt slate making after 17 or 18'.[9]

The rockmen, on the other hand, often learnt their skills later, though it was generally agreed that 'it requires a man

[5] *Report on Merionethshire Mines*, 2477.
[6] D. C. Davies, *A Treatise on Slate and Slate Quarrying* (London, 1880), p. 118.
[7] *Report on Merionethshire Mines*, 2473.
[8] *Royal Commission on Labour*, Minutes of Evidence, Group A 11 (1892), question No. 9387.
[9] *Report on Merionethshire Mines*, 905.

to be working for four or five years before he can be considered a good practical rock man', and one rockman of thirty-three years' experience considered that he had 'been at it long enough and I am learning even now'.[10] Ideally a rockman should have spent some years as a slate maker before going on to the face, not because the particular techniques of the sheds would be very useful to him but rather because he could thus learn the 'nature and proclivities of the slate'.[11]

With such an emphasis on growing up with the rock, it was generally agreed by many outside commentators, as well as by all quarrymen, that no one really understood slate-quarrying except slate-quarrymen. Morgan Richards warned that

> let a man be in a quarry ever so long and let him pay all the attention possible to his duties, yet, if not brought up a quarryman, he can never properly and thoroughly understand quarrying.[12]

And a quarry manager confessed in the *Mining Journal* in 1865 that

> I have read the best German, American, English authors on geology, and I have not seen one single passage in any one of their works that can help, assist or enlighten a quarryman in any one of his operations. It is all very well to talk of things, and compile large volumes, but bring these great authorities face to face with Nature or to a slate quarry and I will be bold enough to affirm that I can point to more than one hard working Welshman that will shame the best of them.

Another correspondent to the *Mining Journal* three years later, having dismissed the claims of engineers and surveyors to any knowledge of quarrying, went on to remind solicitors, geologists and Oxonians that they had yet to learn that 'a simple quarryman has more real knowledge of slate quarries than they will acquire in a lifetime'. Geologists were dismissed in the same breath as retired soldiers, and a Doctor Bower went so far as to declare that 'an honest quarryman knows more of the appearance of the genuine laminating features, for every working purpose, than all the members of the Geological

[10] Ibid., 1596; 3117.
[11] Ibid., 1977.
[12] M. Richards, *Slate Quarrying . . . Profitable*, p. 29.

Society put together'. With the introduction of more complex machinery and electricity into some of the quarries toward the end of the century, engineering and technical expertise was not so easily frowned on.[13]

Members of higher management in the larger quarries were not often skilled quarrymen and a considerable number, even of those of local origin, had risen to their positions through the quarry office rather than the rock-face or the splitter's stool. Their competence to manage at all was therefore viewed with some contempt by most quarrymen. 'The agents with whom I have been working', a Ffestiniog quarryman told a committee of inquiry in 1893, 'are as incompetent as a child three years old.'[14] The annual conference of the N.W.Q.U. regularly accused the various managers of 'gross mismanagement' and incompetence, a charge which was also forcefully made at Dinorwic in 1885, when the men passed a vote of no confidence in the management; John Davies, the resident manager, who had worked at the quarry for forty years and had been manager for eleven, and was heartily detested, had his claims to proficiency dismissed by the men with the comment that his first twenty-nine years had only given him 'experience in figures and nothing more', while during the following eleven years Mr. Davies's opportunities to gain experience in slate quarrying consisted mainly of 'a daily walk from his house to the various offices in the works'. As to the qualifications of the haughty principal manager of the quarry, the Hon. W. W. Vivian, a man of some business experience, the men pointed out that

> an extensive experience in a Manchester Mercantile House would qualify a man for a managership of a slate quarry just as much as a knowledge of farming would qualify a young man to be the captain of a ship.[15]

Managers should, it was held by the men, either be skilled men themselves or have passed an examination in 'practical quarrying' (which presumably only a skilled quarryman could do). Business expertise did not impress them; what they considered essential was skill at the job.

[13] *Mining Journal*, 22 April 1865; 11 January 1868.
[14] *Report on Merionethshire Mines*, 2677.
[15] *Caernarvon and Denbigh Herald*, 23 January 1886.

Their distrust of management was, as we have seen earlier, deepened by the inability of many managers to speak Welsh.[16] John Williams, a quarryman, recalled in 1942 how an English manager visiting his quarry saw a man smoking, and asked 'Do you allow this idleness?'; the accompanying agent explained that the man was, in fact, studying the rock as well as smoking. This episode, concluded Williams, proved that 'it is not possible to work a quarry in English'.[17] A hundred years earlier in the 1840s, a David Jones had sung

> Os bydd eisiau cael swyddogion,
> Danfon ffwrdd a wneir yn union,
> Un ai Gwyddel, Sais neu Scotsman,
> Sydd mewn swyddau braidd ymhobman.
>
> Mewn gweithfeydd sydd yma'n Nghymru,
> Gwelir Saeson yn busnesu;
> Rhaid cael Cymry i dorri'r garreg,
> Nid yw'r graig yn deall Saesneg.[18]

'The English element', Robert Parry had explained to the annual conference of the Union in May 1882, 'does great harm to the success of the quarrymen'.[19] Few present would not have nodded in agreement. There was, moreover, as we have seen, an institution present at the point of production which exemplified in the workplace the cultural identity of the quarrymen: the *caban*.

What was significant about the *cabannau* was not only the cultural activity that took place in them but the fact that this activity took place in the quarry itself. In the *caban* the quarryman was asserting his separateness from the culture of his masters; in the *caban* he was for a while in a context that was beyond their control. It was not so much an explicit

---

[16] Some words were originally English, e.g. *rybelwrs* had began as 'rubbelers', and some English terms were used, e.g., the classification of slate sizes according to the noble hierarchy (duchesses, etc.); but most quarry words were Welsh; for a glossary see, Emyr Jones, *Canrif y Chwarelwr* (Denbigh, 1964).

[17] John Williams, 'Atgofion Chwarelwr', *Y Llenor*, Winter 1942, 129–35.

[18] British Museum, *Welsh Songs, etc., 1767–1870*. No. 69. ('If officials are needed, They are at once sent for from afar, Either Irishman, English or Scots Are in jobs almost everywhere. In works here in Wales, Englishmen can be seen interfering, You must get Welshmen to break the stone, For the rock does not understand English.')

[19] *Y Genedl Gymreig*, 24 May 1882.

challenge to the masters' control, though it could be that also, but rather it placed itself outside that control.

The quarrymen therefore were the masters of an immensely complicated and delicate craft, a craft which they well knew only they could exercise. They had no doubt but that they were in all respects 'the best class of workmen in the United Kingdom'[20] a description they often appropriated. The very 'attitudes' of managements and agents caused them much pain and were as much in dispute as wages and conditions.[21] The agents who were recruited from amongst the quarrymen themselves were considered to be insufferably arrogant and rude, refusing to acknowledge the quarryman's morality and skill.[22] The kind of taunt they had to suffer was retold in April 1882: a quarryman explained to a manager that he could not face his creditors because of his low wages, a plea to which the manager replied by advising him that if he could not face them he should 'walk towards them backwards'.[23] Such a comment, and many worse, cut their pride like a knife. An elegy for such an under-manager expressed the resentment; there was nothing to rejoice in except his unpopularity!

> Oes faith ddi-broffit dreuliodd hwn
> Gan chwyddo rhif gormeswyr
> Ac yma mae ci arch a'i fedd
> Ond ple y mae'r galarwyr?[24]

The degree of supervision varied considerably from quarry to quarry, for slate quarrying itself entailed a great many supervisable processes, and a degree of what could be called 'policing' activity had been a feature of the industry since the early decades of the century (checking, for example, such important details as whether the men were actually producing as many slates as they said they were). Large-scale quarrying, however, called for more extensive organisation and its effective management needed a considerable array of skills,

---

[20] See, for example, *The Lock-Out at the Dinorwic Quarries* (Caernarfon, 1885), p. 1.
[21] See Parry, op. cit., 172–73.
[22] See *Yr Herald Cymraeg*, 5 February 1901.
[23] *Y Genedl Gymreig*, 5 April 1882.
[24] Ibid. 'A long and profitless life he spent swelling the number of oppressors. And here are his coffin and grave, But where are all the mourners?'

pre-eminently in engineering, and not only a practical knowledge of actually working the rock. Quarrying had to be carefully organised and planned in advance, and one authority lamented that plans could not be laid to last for a hundred, or even two hundred, years.[25] The reason is fairly obvious; a rapid concentration on one section of the quarry would soon bring higher parts crashing down; areas which could be long unprofitable to work would still have to be cleared in the long-term interest; rubbish tips had to be placed in parts which would not in the future be needed for quarrying. The continuing difficulty for both management and men was that a long-term plan was not always apparent and the short-term attractions of profitability were always tempting; when a period of reorganisation was finally forced on the working of a quarry each side accused the other of having sacrificed the long-term interests of the quarry for easy money.

The Penrhyn management claimed in 1885 that the men had hitherto controlled the organisation of the quarry by insisting on working only good rock, leaving the unproductive rock to be cleared at some future date when it would be absolutely necessary, and expensive, to remove such rubbish before normal work could resume. Without 'proper supervision, many a bargain may be spoilt through over-anxiety of the men to make good wages',[26] complained the manager of the Aberllefenni quarry in 1893; and a quarry was not much more than a collection of bargains.

The men, of course, hotly denied that there was ever such an intention in their work, complaining bitterly that all the difficulties were due to incompetent management. Managers were 'too keen to make big profits', complained Dewi Peris in 1875, and consequently quarried too deep into the mountain-side without clearing the tops of the galleries, thus causing both danger and trouble for the future.[27]

Most of the charges (for example, that it was more profitable for quarrymen working very low poundages to throw away good slate as rubbish, and to be paid by the ton for it, than actually to make slates out of it) were normally proven, an

[25] Dewi Peris, 'Chwarelyddiaeth', *Y Geninen*, vol. XIV (January 1896), p. 52.
[26] *Report on Merionethshire Mines*, 4500.
[27] Dewi Peris, op. cit., July 1896.

indictment of managerial policies. But the men's defence briefs were not so convincing; there was probably some considerable truth in the management's charges of short-sighted working by the men. It is, however, difficult to establish the truth, for most of the arguments vied with each other in drama rather than in detail. The Dinorwic quarry, the locked-out men of 1885 claimed, would 'completely fall in' if the existing manager continued in control, a prophecy which subsequent years did not fulfil.

To the new men in control of the larger quarries in the 1880s and 1890s, to the new Lord Penrhyn himself, and to men like his manager E. A. Young and the Dinorwic manager W. W. Vivian, it was obvious that to pursue the industry profitably it would be necessary to break the independence and the control of the men, and if they overstated the degree of that control there is no reason why it should be underestimated. The crucial underpinning to the men's relative independence was the bargain system, the effects of which were profound for both men and masters.

The bargain system was central to the method of working and to the identity and individuality of the quarryman. It was a system which in its different forms was known in other extractive industries, and in the slate industry in other countries, though perhaps in no other did it survive on such a scale into the twentieth century.[28] The problem with which the system was supposed to deal was the one posed by the tremendous unevenness in the nature of the rock worked in one part of a quarry compared with another. Thus, one man's stretch of rock might be buckled or the slate imperfect while another's would be finely grained and easily worked; moreover as it was quarried, the nature of the rock was constantly changing. Any wages system which merely remunerated men for the number of slates produced was therefore clearly inoperable. The

[28] Caernarvonshire copper mines knew the system in the eighteenth century and the Cornish tribute system was similar; slate quarries in Anjou and in the Bassin d'Herbeumont in Belgium were also worked on similar lines; in Belgium there was a *contrat de travail* between *sociétés* of four or five men and the employer. E. Savoy, 'Ardoisier du Bassin d'Herbeumont Belgique', *Les Ouvriers des Deux Mondes* (Paris, 1905), pp. 180–82; in Anjou, 'la plupart des ouvriers d'à bas et d'à haut travaillent au marchandage', M. Poperen, *Un Siècle de Luttes au Pays de l'Ardoise* (Anjou, 1972), p. 34.

bargaining system meant that each crew of four or five quarrymen would negotiate a monthly contract with the management,
the terms of which depended on the assessed ease or difficulty
of extracting slates from the face in question; depending on the
bargain settled monthly, the men were paid a sum of 'poundage'
per pound's worth of slates produced. Men working on intrac-
table rock would be paid a high poundage, compensating for
the low yield or poor quality of the slates produced; those
quarrying good rock received a low poundage.

Theoretically, therefore, the bargaining system recognised
each quarryman, or at least each crew of quarrymen, as an
independent contractor who could argue about the terms of
the contract before coming to an agreement. The traditional
independence of the quarrymen was thus formalised into a
wages' system. It need not, and usually did not, work, but it
maintained, and indeed encouraged, the feeling among the
quarrymen that they were equals in some sense with the quarry
owners. In practice, of course, the bargain was rarely equal;
it could not be. The men usually had to accept the terms
offered by the setting steward, for if they refused they were
simply out of a job. The haggling on setting days, however,
continued and formal compromises were still arranged and
occasionally a crew could convince a steward that his assessment
of the rock was mistaken. In good times, indeed, in the smaller
quarries the system could become one of genuine bargaining
again with the crews holding out for a higher poundage and
the management, eager to meet the demands of the market,
yielding readily. But in the larger enterprises any element of
free bargaining had long since passed. What remained—a wages'
system which reminded the men constantly of their equal and
independent position but at the same time treated them like
wage slaves—was a persistent source of friction. In the Penrhyn
strike of August 1865,

> the common complaint was that the manager always deter-
> mined the price, and that therefore the men had no choice
> but to either accept his offer or turn their backs on the works
> and go to seek work elsewhere, this is considered by them to
> be the greatest oppression.[29]

[29] *Yr Herald Cymraeg*, 12 August 1865.

In Dinorwic the situation had degenerated so much by 1885 that the men were not even allowed to state their case during the bargain-setting, but merely to accept the steward's ruling; they appealed in that year that a bargain taker 'should be allowed to advance his reasons when he considered the offered terms of the manager unreasonable and insufficient'.[30]

This break-down of the bargaining system was a crucial factor in collective action though it has been argued that this kind of wages' system might also encourage an individualistic, anti-union sentiment in the work force.[31] Such attitudes, as we shall see later, were certainly prevalent among a large section of slate quarrymen, but an inoperative bargaining system was also a powerful force in the creation of a collective consciousness. For as a wages' system which had lost its genuine bargaining element, it invited a collective response while at the same time stressing and encouraging not necessarily an individualistic, but certainly an independent, spirit among men: a combination which could produce a willingness to indulge in a collective struggle.

As a reporter from the *Pall Mall Gazette* noted in 1885,

> there exists in the system upon which the quarry is worked a permanent source of difference, i.e. the bargaining system.[32]

In some of the more inefficiently managed quarries the system could be manipulated by the men to their own advantage; they could deliberately hold back output, pleading hidden complications in the rock, thus pushing the poundage up. They could then either enjoy good wages for less work, or, after winning a high poundage at the beginning of the month the rock could miraculously improve, the slates would come off *fel menyn* (like butter) and the month's wages could be considerably higher than the setting steward had anticipated. An inexperienced agent could therefore be 'in their hands and they know how to handle him'.[33] The opportunity for this kind

---

[30] *The Lock-Out at the Dinorwic Quarries*, p. 5.

[31] See D. Dylan Pritchard, 'Trade Unionism', *Quarry Manager's Journal* (January 1945); for a discussion of this problem in another industry, J. G. Rule, 'The tribute system and the weakness of trade unionism in the Cornish mines', *Bulletin of Society for the Study of Labour History* (Autumn 1970).

[32] U.C.N.W., Coetmor 46, p. 30 (n.d.).

[33] M. Richards, op. cit., p. 19.

of anti-managerial action which the bargaining system afforded, coupled with its essential imprecision (bargain-setting time was known as 'The Guess' by the Penrhyn quarrymen), meant that the setting stewards were hostile and suspicious and that most quarrymen at one time or another suffered from a sense of grievance. Every month the system invited distrust and hostility and the result was continuous friction between men and management.

The system was jealously guarded by the quarrymen. In 1876 the defence of the bargain system lead to a riot at the Hafod y Wern quarry in Betws Garmon; when the management tried to introduce a scheme of payment by the hour, the men walked out, were sacked and then replaced by Cornish blacklegs. This roused the quarrymen of a wide area to fury, and a large body of between 500 and 1,000 men marched to Hafod y Wern, many of them, it seems, from the Nantlle quarries some miles away. The men marched into the quarry, scattering the Cornishmen and assaulting the agent and engineer, the latter having been 'knocked down with a stone and brutally kicked, was, it is stated, dragged some distance on a wagon, and pitched out upon a heap of iron pipes'.[34] The men remained in control of the quarry for an hour, leaving before the police could arrive from Caernarfon.

Quarrymen were not often moved to take such action and the incident shows how much they treasured the bargain system and how determined they were to protect it, not just in their own quarry but wherever slate was worked. The union had nothing officially to do with the incident, following which sixteen men were fined £5 each;[35] only one of them was a union member, and the union roundly condemned the behaviour of the men. In the defence of the bargain system, however, the union, too, was determined and in December 1877 the union council, for the first and only time during the nineteenth century, itself called a strike. The scene was the small quarry of Rhos in Capel Curig, where the management tried to introduce new regulations which the union felt to be 'destructive of the principle of contract which has worked so

---

[34] See Caernarvonshire Record Office, *Bulletin*, 1970, p. 16.
[35] Ibid.

well in slate quarries';[36] the strike involved very few men but lasted for two and a half years and it cost the young union £1,100 to sustain. Such was the readiness of slate-quarrymen to prevent any breach in the bargain system.

The real threat to the bargain system was not, however, to come, in the nineteenth century, from payments-by-the-hour schemes but from another variant of 'contract' work. In May 1879 the Penrhyn quarry committee decided for the first time to look at an issue which was to preoccupy it for twenty years, namely, to 'investigate the case of those who had taken "contracts" '.[37] Though a bargain was, in a sense, a contract, and that term was frequently used to describe it, the form of contract which had now come to the committee's notice was quite different and posed a real threat to the bargain system. The new contract system was one under which parts of the quarry were sub-contracted to men who then themselves employed a gang to do the work; under such a system a quarryman was not himself a contractor but was merely the employee of one. It is not clear how he was to be paid by the contractor, presumably by a piece-work system, but howsoever the wages were paid, a part of what would previously have been the quarryman's reward now went into the middleman's pocket. But far more important than this financial consideration was the assault on the independence of the quarryman implicit in this contract system, for under contract a man worked not for himself in his own style but for a wage and under the direct instruction of a contractor.

By March 1881 there were twenty-six contracts in the Penrhyn quarry and the main victims were boys. The choice of boys as the labour force for this system was in itself an interesting one, suggesting, as it does, that quarrymen of any experience were loth to lose their former status but also, perhaps, pointing to a management strategy of trying to breed a new generation of workmen unused to the freedoms of the bargain system and trained to accept the indignities of contract work. The boys working under contract in November 1884 complained bitterly that they were 'not allowed the same amount as boys in

[36] N.L.W., W. J. Parry MSS. (4), 87360, 29 December 1877.
[37] GAS, M/622/11, 19 May 1879.

general', and they felt that 'they are bound to carry out that which is ordered that they do by their masters whether or not it is right or wrong'.[38]

The contract system was consistently opposed and the threat of its further extension was a central underlying cause of the 1896–7 lock-out in Penrhyn, for it was 'believed to be the cause of great injustice to a large number of quarrymen'.[39] In 1900, in fact, hatred of the contractors once again led quarrymen to violence and it was the assaulting of two contractors which led directly to the 1900–3 lock-out.[40]

The bargaining system was defended not merely for the good wages it could bring with effective organisation, though that was not to be overlooked, but also, and more important, because of the style of working it allowed; for the very organisation of their work gave to quarrymen a considerable degree of independence and control over their labour. Once a bargain had been settled the crew could work it as it deemed best. As Robert Parry, one of the leaders of the Penrhyn men in 1874, explained:

> contracts should be let according to the nature of the work, and after that is done no further meddling with the industry of the contractors should be tolerated in any way.[41]

And twenty years later a Ffestiniog rockman was adamant that

> When they let me a bargain I do not want them to interfere with me in my work until I have finished my contract.[42]

So strong was this feeling that it was generally considered that a bargain—that is, an actual place in the quarry rather than the settlement—was in a sense the property of those who worked it, not just for the month of any agreement's life, but for good. Morgan Richards advised managers that

> the customary or prescriptive right of a crew to their bargain is so sacred and well established that no wise manager wishing to be at peace with his men, will venture to interfere with it.[43]

[38] GAS, Cofnodydd Penderfyniadau Pwyllgor y Gwaith, Caebraichycafn, 14 November 1884.
[39] Parry, op. cit., p. 74.
[40] See ibid., 172–73 and below pp. 000.
[41] *Caernarvon and Denbigh Herald*, 15 August 1874.
[42] *Report on Merionethshire Mines*, 1186.
[43] Richards, op. cit., p. 30.

Disputes over the manning and location of bargains were therefore not uncommon, managers attempting to arrange the working of the quarry as they saw fit and quarrymen protecting their rights in the bargain. Such a system was not one that suited the employers, for a degree of mobility, moving crews from bargain to bargain depending on their abilities and the demands of the rock, would have been to their advantage. Joseph Kellow, a quarry engineer with 'twenty six years of practical experience', complained bitterly in 1868 of this practice of one crew staying permanently on the same bargain; the best bargains, he argued, should be given to the best crews and the poorer crews should be moved if their bargain improved, but

> unfortunately it is the rule for each party to retake the same bargain (regardless of their general fitness) at the monthly letting, however much it may militate against the employer.[44]

Such a system did not encourage close supervision. Each crew worked its bargain in its own way, advice was not sought and interference coldly received. This tradition also militated against adequate safety supervision as well as work discipline, for though the union in the 1890s was calling for government inspection, there still existed a residue of resentment amongst many of the men against any such interference. A bargain, in all its aspects, was the responsibility of the crew concerned and it was up to them to ensure that it was safe.

Supervision was also discouraged by the fact that, as the men were working a kind of piece-work, it was in their interest as well as that of the employers to work as hard as possible. Indeed, there were complaints that it drove men to work too hard. On the other hand, it also meant that the pace of work was to some extent determined by the men themselves, and in the boom of the 1870s it was apparently a

> great and constant complaint . . . that quarrymen do not work as they ought to do the first and second week in every month.[45]

[44] Joseph Kellow, *The Slate Trade in North Wales*, *Mining Journal* reprint, 1868, p. 9.

[45] Richards, op. cit., p. 71.

The work itself was therefore largely out of the management's control, though the situation varied considerably from quarry to quarry, some claiming to inspect each bargain daily, others not really inspecting them at all. Supervision was not made any easier by the huge scale of some of the workings and by the remoteness of others. William Jones M.P. claimed in the House of Commons that the Penrhyn quarry was 'four miles long, three wide and nearly a mile deep',[46] which is an exaggeration but it seemed that big. Even in the more efficient quarries, supervision was not at all tight compared with factory production; in 1886 there were 19 foremen and 40 slate inspectors in the open quarries keeping an eye on the work of over 6,000 men.[47] In the smaller and more remote mines supervision and management of any kind seem, in the 1860s and 1870s, to have been virtually absent. When H.M. Inspector of Mines came to investigate conditions in the Merionethshire slate mines for the first time in 1875, he encountered considerable difficulty because he could rarely find, on his visits to the mines, the managers or agents in charge of them. It was in some consternation that he complained in his report about this startling absence of management, for 'it is manifest that an idea prevails that a mine is able to manage itself'.[48] In a great many mines this indeed seems to have been the case; a correspondent to the *Mining Journal* in 1865 listed twenty-two Welsh slate quarries and mines, some of them quite substantial, which showed a profit and

> are all worked under the command of a quarryman with a clerk, without even a secretary, no engineers, no directors, not even an office.[49]

The nature of employment at the quarries sustained this independence of the men. Not only, as we have seen, were the bargain takers in a sense sub-contractors themselves employing journeymen, but the *rybelwrs* were also relatively free of managerial control (though not of managerial vindictiveness), wandering as they did around the quarry in search of someone

[46] William Jones, House of Commons, *Hansard Parliamentary Debates* vol. cxviii (4th Series), 5 March 1903, p. 1651.
[47] *Return of Wages in Mines and Quarries*, p. 667.
[48] *Report of H.M. Inspector of Mines* (1875), p. 385.
[49] *Mining Journal*, 15 April 1865.

to assist, a kindly soul to help them out, or an unfulfilled debt. These men, and the journeymen, worked in reality for the quarrymen themselves rather than for the quarry-owners, though they were also attached to, and policed by, the quarry officials to whom they sold their slates. It was a system, as one can imagine, which could rapidly get out of the control of the management, especially a management not familiar with the men, their language or their ways.

Not only the actual work of slate-quarrying but also the hours and days worked were only tenuously controlled by the management, and until the 1880s the men seem to have established a relatively free and easy system of working hours, treating them more as guide lines than as imperatives. This is not to say that working hours were ever short but attempts to regularise them, especially to extend them into the hours of darkness before dawn and after dusk, do not seem to have been particularly successful. Thus, even in the mines, where under-ground work made considerations of day-light irrelevant, the managers encountered considerable difficulty and resentment in their attempts to enforce a pre-dawn start to the working day in winter; thus, a rockman explained in 1893 how he might ignore the whistle and 'follow the day'.[50] Draconian disci-plinary measures intended to regularise hours of working were an essential part of the employers' offensive in the 1880s and 1890s.

Equally disturbing for them were the disruptive effects of quarrymen taking unofficial days off. In 1878 this had become such a problem in Penrhyn that a new code of discipline, causing much opposition, had to be introduced. The manager intended a system of fines for late-comers to work and to have, as the *Caernarvon and Denbigh Herald* explained,

> Some arrangement by which what are called 'extraordinary holidays' shall not exceed a certain number of days during the year. The latter is a matter respecting which the managers wish more particularly to have an understanding with the men for as many as 150, we are told, have frequently an-nounced their intention of going away for an excursion for a day, thus causing inevitably a considerable stoppage of work.

[50] *Report on Merionethshire Mines*, 3140.

We have heard it stated that as many as 2,300 days have been lost to the proprietor in one month, the workmen taking holidays in this way.[51]

Despite rules and regulations, the problem was not easily solved and in June 1889 the 2,323 men employed at Penrhyn lost between them 5,789¾ working days.[52]

There seem also to have been some 'official' unofficial holidays accepted by the community but not by the quarry management, such as Ascension Thursday, which was taken as a holiday by Penrhyn quarrymen. It was said that a serious accident was bound to take place if the men worked on that day and

in order to strengthen this belief it has been ensured that accidents have happened every time there has been an attempt to break the holiday.[53]

Not only the seasonal demands of smallholdings but also social demands such as funerals, often attended by hundreds of men, and fairs could, and did, claim priority for time which would otherwise have been the quarry's. The right to take the day off if he considered it necessary was held by the quarryman to be a fundamental one, so it is not surprising that the question of regularity of hours, and of days worked, loomed as a central issue in most of the major disputes in the industry. The demand that the men obtain permission from the manager before absenting themselves from their work was considered by them to be a monstrous imposition. 'The permission paper', in the opinion of the locked-out men of Dinorwic in 1885, 'places us on the same ground as the black slaves in the South of America used to be on.'[54] This defence of the freedom to decide within limits when one worked might have reflected the rural patterns which still exercised an influence over some quarrymen, but this influence should not be exaggerated;[55] the crucial factor was the bargain system.

---

[51] *Caernarvon and Denbigh Herald*, 12 January 1878.
[52] GAS, 55/27, Penrhyn Quarry Wages Book, June 1889.
[53] *Y Genedl Gymreig*, 24 May 1882.
[54] Ibid., 5 August 1885.
[55] Slate quarrymen in other countries were also known for their independence at work; in Anjou, 'Le fendeur (slate splitter) organise son travail à sa guise, il commence et termine sa journée aux heures qui lui conviennent', whereas in the Bassin d'Herbeumont in Belgium 'L'organisation du travail d'abord est telle que l'ouvrier conserve une grande indépendence.' See M. Poperen, op. cit., p. 64; Émile Savoy, op. cit., p. 181.

The bargain system imposed its own pattern of wage negotiation in which power and personalities often mattered more than skill or hard work, for the only way that the quarrymen could hope to improve their month-to-month bargains and thus their wages was in some way to influence the setting agent or the higher management which appointed him. For, within wide limits, the setting steward by his assessment of the rock could give excellent wages or pitiful ones, and variation in wages could be immense. In Penrhyn in 1865, for example, a well-paid quarryman earned 22s. 10d. a week, while one less fortunate bargain taker earned only 6s. 10d.[56] This kind of difference can be partly explained by distinctions of skill, labour and the nature of the rock, but in a functioning bargain and poundage system the partiality of the setting agent might also be central.

The agents could be influenced in two ways, individually or collectively. The individual method created a widespread system of bribery and flattery by which the individual crews hoped to grease, or buy, their way into the favour of the management and thus easy bargains, good rock or high poundage. The other way, attempted less frequently but with more dramatic consequences, was collectively to pressurise the management or even attempt at times to remove the existing management altogether and replace it by one more favourable to the men. Both methods could be effective and both pursued a similar goal—higher wages. As Henry Jones of the Alexandra lodge told the N.W.Q.U. annual conference in May 1882:

> there is a particular likeness between the brave and manly Union man and the cowardly and flattering *cynffonwr*. Both want good recognition for their labour. Both struggle, not in the same way perhaps, but equally energetic, for more of the gold than the silver. They are one in their aim but they separate on the methods used to achieve it.[57]

He went on to uphold the union method of collective struggle and to condemn the man for whom 'the general voice is quite meaningless . . . the centre point of all his impulses is himself'.

[56] *Yr Herald Cymraeg*, 12 August 1865.
[57] *Y Genedl Gymreig*, 24 May 1882.

Such men were not uncommon in the slate quarries of the nineteenth century, and the bribery and flattery system which they worked remained as long as the bargaining system itself. Robert Parry, the first quarryman president of the N.W.Q.U., explained that

> when once a workman felt that an interest was being taken in him greater than his position as workman claimed, there soon would set in a system of peace offerings, and once this began it would, like that of Israel's sins, demand sacrifices every morning and every evening and never be satisfied.[58]

The sacrifices were of bacon, beer and self-respect. The bribery system could only operate satisfactorily for a minority, a minority which invited the severest moral censure, and the hatred and bitterness which existed between them and the union party is a central part of the story of the quarries, for the division was hardened by differing allegiances in religion and politics.

This hatred is, perhaps, best summed up by the very term with which the union men lashed their opponents, *cynffonwyr*. Literally it translates as 'flatterers' but *cynffon* is also the Welsh for 'tail': the *cynffonwyr* had grown tails and thus betrayed their animal natures. As a Penrhyn striker explained in 1901, they were

> creatures of a man's shape with tails, yet they were not men. If Prof. Darwin were living in Bethesda now he would not have to go far to find something to prove his point that man is descended from the ape.[59]

The derision expressed an intensity of hatred which even affected the local Liberal press. One paper wrote that they knew of

> no class crueller, more loathsome, sicker, dirtier or more dangerous to live or work with than the *cynffonwyr* of our quarries.

After much more abuse underlining the inhuman nature of the *cynffonwyr*, the paper recommended the quarrymen of Penrhyn

---

[58] *Caernarvon and Denbigh Herald*, 28 May 1881.
[59] *Yr Herald Cymraeg*, 6 August 1901.

and Dinorwic and all other quarries afflicted by such creatures to

1. not accept them into your houses,
2. put your hand on your lips in their presence,
3. let them and their property be accursed things to you.[60]

For those others who chose collective struggle and the self-sacrifice and threat of repression it invited, the greatest success was the Penrhyn strike of 1874 and the agreement which came from it. The mechanics of that dispute are revealing.[61] The men initially made a demand for a 'standard' wage of 30s. a week for all skilled quarrymen. Penrhyn replied that he could not agree to this but that he would, as a concession to the men, raise the 'making price' of slates, i.e., the price paid to the quarrymen for the slates they produced. In a properly functioning system this would have been acceptable to the men, but they rejected the offer because, though generous, it really did not amount to much if the management persisted in their low-wage policies. For wages could still be kept down despite the rise in prices by the agent offsetting the rise by cutting down on the poundage. The men therefore replied that, 'owing to our distrust of the management we are compelled to decline the offer as it now stands'. Management, therefore, became the central issue of the dispute. 'Grant us our demands as they were laid before you at first', the men asked, 'or a change in the chief manager.'[62]

As the dispute proceeded, the men came to see a formula which might effectively grant them both demands, an agreement on a 'standard' of wages and the appointment of a 'supreme manager' who would oversee the quarry managers and to whom appeal could be made in cases of unfair treatment or unduly low wages. The men even recommended the man for the job, Mr. Pennant Lloyd, the Penrhyn estate agent; they also recommended as a second acting chief manager Mr. T. H. Owen, who would keep a further watch on the exising management.

Given such changes in the structure of management, they were willing to modify their earlier demands for 30s. a week

[60] U.C.N.W., Coetmor MSS. 45 (n.d.).
[61] See Parry, op. cit., 7-24.
[62] Ibid., p. 12., p. 16.

'minimum standard' for quarrymen. Their new plan differentiated crucially between bargains set on the men's terms and those taken by men 'compelled by the manager to work on his price'. In cases of the first type, the bargain was to stand whatever the resulting wages; in cases of the second, however, when the crew

> fail to realise proper wages on that taking, and they have worked honestly the whole month, that the wages of quarrymen (bargain takers working slate) in such a case, and in such a case only be made up to 28/– per week.

This was to ensure that managerial control of wages was kept to an absolute minimum. The men's demands were eventually granted in substance; the test was to be their implementation and the men's suspicions of the managers were well founded, for when they returned to work they found that the agents were simply ignoring the agreement. The men, therefore, came out a second time and an arbitration board studied their complaints against the management; out of 19 cases brought forward, 17 were sustained and a mass-meeting of the men decided that they would

> return to our work under the agreement come to with Mr. Pennant Lloyd and to take lettings from others than the present managers.[63]

The three managers J. Francis, R. Morris and O. P. Jones, were forced to resign and a new chief manager was appointed.

A struggle for improved wages thus became a struggle to limit the power of management, to check its control of the bargaining system. And the battle ended not only with the new structure of management brought about by the appointment of a supreme manager acceptable to the men, but also with a built-in counter to the setting agents' previous ability to force bargain agreements on unwilling crews. And a managerial clique that had been in power for forty years was swept out of the quarry and a quarry committee was elected by the men to investigate 'all complaints about letting'.[64]

[63] Ibid.
[64] Ibid.

This committee was able to maintain an effective pressure on the managers. It worked very much like a shop stewards' committee in that it consisted of the elected representatives of the galleries in the quarry, though there was also an executive committee which met regularly. In later years it was vehemently denied that the committee had been a union body, and its defenders insisted that it had been open to receive complaints from all workers employed in the quarry, irrespective of union membership. Receive complaints from all quarrymen they did, but they certainly did not act on any except those coming from union members, and crew No. 158 from Sebastopol Gallery was not alone in having its complaint on wages rejected in November 1881 with the comment that 'the case was thrown out because they were not union members'.[65]

The committee dealt with a wide range of questions and took up with the managers matters relating to the location and manning of bargains, disciplinary offences against quarry rules, craft questions, disputes between crews, costs payable to the quarry and, above all, questions of wages and poundage. It is difficult to assess how much power the committee actually exerted, but acting as it did as a watch-dog on conditions in the quarry, ready to press on management all issues it considered of importance, between 1874 and 1885 it certainly prevented the management from having a free rein in the works and from introducing any major new regulations or reorganisation. The number of cases actually taken up was not very great, but this might well reflect an unpreparedness on the part of the managers to carry out unpopular measures which would invite the committee's attention. Of 41 cases taken up between 1881 and 1884, only 4 were definitely settled in the management's favour, while a good many ended in verbal compromises, and 16 were definitely settled in the men's favour; of these 41 cases, 26 concerned wages in some way.

The quarry committee, while certainly a union committee, being in effect the Penrhyn lodge of the N.W.Q.U., was democratic and sensitive to all the happenings in the quarry,

[65] GAS, Cofnodydd Penderfyniadau Pwyllgor y Gwaith, Caebraichycafn, 25 November 1881.

concerning itself at times even with such mundane matters normally referred to the management as controlling petty thefts. When a complaint about the theft of slates was received from the Red Lion Gallery in August 1881, the committee did not inform any authority either in the quarry or outside, but decided rather that

> the representatives of the place where there is complaint about the thieves meet together in order to arrange something to meet it.[66]

The committee had authority, and could enforce discipline in the quarry as well as face up to management every time it departed from the Pennant Lloyd agreement or tried to push through any unheralded change.

The management, and Lord Penrhyn himself, came to make many charges of interference and even of intimidation against the committee, but what angered them most was the effect the committee was having on wages, pressing every case in which they thought the men were not being given their due; 'the worst part of it is', complained E. A. Young, the manager of the Penrhyn quarries,

> the Committee has endeavoured to interfere with the bargain setting, which virtually means managing the quarry . . . interference such as I mean is practically intolerable . . . it means pressure on the management in their favour.[67]

Herein lay the strength of the committee and the threat of union organisation to the owners in general; the combining of an individualised wages' system with a collective consciousness created a situation difficult for the management to control; for the whole power of the quarrymen, organised in the committee, could be brought to bear not on a general wages front but on any individual bargain about which there was complaint. In such a situation the bargaining strength of the men was much enhanced, for a crew no longer confronted the agents alone but rather in the knowledge, and with the threat, that the whole weight of the work force could be swung to their side if the agents failed to set to the required standard. In such a situation

[66] GAS, M/622/11, 18 August 1881.
[67] Parry, op. cit., p. 109.

the committee was indeed a severe limitation on the power of the management. And when men and management held different interpretations of fundamental rights and obligations, then this limitation could be exercised with subtlety as well as determination. In defence of the right to work, for example, quarrymen exhibited an array of tactics.

By the end of the nineteenth century, slate-quarrymen were not often given to wandering; once they settled in one area they tended to stay. This parochial attachment was, of course, cemented by homes and gardens and pensions, but their attitude to the place of work was also important. Men grew to belong to certain quarries and would rarely move. Morgan Richards commented that a

> Bethesda quarryman . . . would almost rather live on bread and water at Bethesda, were that necessary, than go to Nantlle or Ffestiniog where perhaps he would earn more and live better.[68]

Once established, a family would expect employment for its sons at the quarry, for kinship ties were important determinants in recruitment: of 45 applicants for work in the Penrhyn quarry in 1896, 39 had fathers already at work there, 4 had brothers, 1 an uncle and 1 a grandfather.[69] Apart from rejecting unfit or quite unsuitable boys, the management's ability freely to choose recruits was therefore somewhat limited. Indeed, in some quarries the situation appears to have been so much under the men's control that it was claimed that rockmen were 'taken on without any reference at all to management'.[70]

The quarry, therefore, was expected to give continuing employment to the sons of the community, and though the men accepted that depression limited the scope for such employment they would not tolerate any attempt to recruit skilled labour from outside their number. One of the underlying causes of the Dinorwic lock-out was the resentment felt by the men towards the attempt by the management to recruit 'children of others who were not tenants, nor children of old workmen'.[71] It was a resentment inflamed by the suspicion

---

[68] Richards, op. cit., p. 49.
[69] GAS, Penrhyn Quarry Letter Book, 11 June 1896.
[70] Report on Merionethshire Mines, p. 316.
[71] The Lock-Out at the Dinorwic Quarries.

that recruits were being chosen for their political and religious allegiances.

The quarrymen also rejected the idea that an immediate reduction in the labour force was the right reaction to depression. They accepted, as they had to, that some unemployment was inevitable, but they maintained firmly that 'as it is the worker who brings in the true profit to all works he should be the last to suffer',[72] and they fought determinedly to uphold this principle. In the Penrhyn quarries the initial reaction of the men to the management's proposal for redundancies in November 1878 was total opposition to any sackings, and they expressed their willingness to bargain away other rights in order to maintain the right of all to work. They passed a resolution which pointedly expressed their concern 'that we as workmen make an appeal to be allowed to suffer together', and asked on 'what grounds can they meet us without turning anyone away from the works?'[73]

The management was sensitive to the feelings of the men and proposed a scrupulous plan for 'turning away from the end of the book', and dismissing only those who had come recently to the quarry, and lived furthest away. Such a scheme, coupled with protection for skilled men was, in fact, accepted by the quarry committee, but was rejected by the men as a whole, who still opposed all redundancies though these must by then have appeared inevitable.

Other tactics were also employed and enforced to beat the effects of redundancy. In February 1879 the committee called for 'compelling crews in which there are only two partners to take an additional partner'.[74] It is not clear whether the initiative for short-time working, four days a week, came from the men or the management. Both sides could benefit from such a scheme, the men because it was a means of keeping more of them at work and the management by being saved the misfortune of turning away a number of skilled men who could not be easily replaced when the trade revived. Whoever was responsible for introducing it in May 1879, the quarry com-

[72] *Y Genedl Gymreig*, 2 February 1882.
[73] GAS, M/622/11, Copy, minutes of the Quarry Committee, 19 November 1878; 21 November 1878.
[74] Ibid., 17 February 1879.

mittee was certainly involved in enforcing it. In January 1880 they held meetings throughout the quarry 'to set forth the voice of the works namely disapproving of those who worked on Fridays and Saturdays', and in December 1879 they had talked severely of 'the harm to the general body of workmen that some persons come to the works six days instead of four'. It seems, however, that some men persisted in working full-time and were allowed to do so, which would suggest that the committee was more interested than the management in the protection of employment offered by short-time working, and in March 1881 it had to call again for all the men to work 'but four days a week unless unavoidable circumstances arise in the work'. [75]

Work-sharing by short-time working was therefore one method used by the organised quarrymen in Penrhyn to cushion the effects of unemployment. Another tactic which one might have expected would have been output control, with the workforce disciplining itself to produce less and thereby preventing over-production and redundancies. Short-time working itself was, of course, one way of doing this; the deliberate slowing down of work could have been another. There is no mention in the committee minutes of any such practice, but the quarry management seems to have been in little doubt that something like this was going on and blamed an otherwise inexplicable drop of 600 tons of manufactured slate in September 1879 on the men's 'unconcern'. [76]

Employment itself, therefore, was something which was expected from the quarry and during a severe depression extreme measures would be adopted to try to ensure the highest possible employment. To a certain extent managements and quarry-owners respected this basic function, but the men's defensive actions drove an irritated Morgan Richards to lecture them on the laws of the economy:

> the working class should pay more attention to the governing laws of trade than they do at the moment . . . the worker is naturally slow to believe in and realise the disadvantages and difficulties of quarry owners when the market is low and unsettled, but if he had to sell his produce himself he would

[75] Ibid., 14 January 1880; 29 December 1879; 25 March 1881.
[76] Ibid., 8 September 1879.

soon come to understand the effects of the law of 'supply and demand' on the value of labour.[77]

Quite so; but the quarryman was not a quarry-owner and however much his union leaders might appear to acquiesce in the theories of supply and demand he himself found no difficulty in interfering with the 'natural Law' and defending his right to a job.

The quarry was expected to be sensitive to needs other than its own and to respect the men's independence. The men expected respect, too, for their status and their skill, because they had a high sense of the dignity of that skill and of the respect which it deserved; and they considered that it deserved better than the bullying of ignorant managers and agents. As the president of the N.W.Q.U. explained in 1901,

> if Mr. Young (the manager of the Penrhyn quarries) thinks that he can work the quarry on the same principles of government as dockwork or brickwork, he is greatly mistaken.[78]

Quarrymen expected and demanded something better— expected, in fact, 'to be treated like men'.[79] On the foundation of the bargain system had been built a whole structure of customs and attitudes and beliefs which added up to the only definition of a quarryman which most of the men would find acceptable.

Gazing out in the early 1880s from the turrets of his father's cyclopean revivalist folly, Penrhyn Castle, the future Lord Penrhyn may often have wondered about how much control he really had over his quarries. They produced the profits regularly and generously enough, but the 2,500 men at work there had virtually all spent their entire working lives among the galleries and sheds there; they knew infinitely more about the place than did he or any of his managers, and their skills, the source of his wealth, were a mystery to him. They spoke a foreign language, worshipped in nonconformist chapels, and had voted against him when he stood for Parliament. In 1874 they had unseated the whole management and set up their North Wales Quarrymen's Union, with the assistance of

[77] *Y Genedl Gymreig*, 12 January 1882.
[78] *Yr Herald Cymraeg*, 24 December 1901.
[79] *Daily News*, 8 January 1901.

prominent radicals, and a quarry committee, which pounced
on his present management whenever it acted contrary to the
quarrymen's wishes. His charities no longer bought allegiance.
He was unsure what the men were doing much of the time and
they seemed to be coming and going as they pleased. Their
independence made them an uncontrollable work force,
unwilling to obey the capricious demands of a by-now disturbed
market.

For W. W. Vivian, trained in Manchester business, the rules
which he was trying to impose on the Dinorwic men seemed
exceedingly reasonable and sensible; real factory rules, he
claimed, were much harsher. 'If the men', he charged with
some exasperation,

> will take the trouble to get a copy of factory rules, or of those
> in use in any real business company, they will at once see
> the great leniency of the new rules.[80]

The Dinorwic quarrymen, however, would accept nothing
that smelt of factory discipline without a fight, and they
resisted for five months the attempt to bring

> the works under the same rules as the works in England, that
> is the factories, a thing which is quite impossible and the
> attempt to do so betrays a lack of experience and common
> sense. Because to bring such a big, wide and open works such
> as this under the strict rules of the factories is lunacy.[81]

That would mean 'the best class of Welsh workmen being
trodden upon as mere slaves'.[82] For them slavery and factory
discipline were synonymous.

We can only guess at the masters' strategy, but it seems
fairly certain that they intended to pursue a two-pronged
policy: the bargain system, on which so much else depended,
could not be dropped at will because its hold and its demands
were too extensive; hence an attempt was made, on the one
hand, to minimise the effects of the system while, on the other,
gradually to introduce an altogether new wages' system. The
rules and regulations which pinched the quarrymen so hard

[80] *Caernarvon and Denbigh Herald*, 30 January 1886.
[81] *Y Genedl Gymreig*, 29 July 1885.
[82] *The Lock-Out at the Dinorwic Quarries*, p. 7.

were the means to achieve the former aim, while the latter was to be attained by the extension of the contract system.[83] We have already noted the attempt to introduce boys into contract work in the early 1880s and there was a strong suspicion by the end of the century that Penrhyn's long-term aim was to re-create completely his skilled work force, to bring up a whole generation of quarrymen in a disciplined fashion.[84]

Commenting on the Dinorwic lock-out of 1885–6, a reporter noted that the dispute was not a matter of wages: it was

> simply a matter of sentiment; whether the quarry should be worked under one set of rules or another set of rules and whether the men or the managers shall be permitted to regulate the business.[85]

The question was nicely stated; the quarrymen did not claim that the quarries were theirs and they were always extremely respectful towards the rights of the owners, but what they did assume was that they had the right to regulate the way they were worked, the right to have some control over their own working lives. This was an assumption, rarely a claim; the men were usually adamant in their denials that they wished in any way to interfere in the 'rightful' concerns of their employers. Rule 2 of the union caught the contradiction: the union's aim was to,

> resist any infringements that may be attempted by employers upon the established rights and privileges of the quarrymen of North Wales . . . it is not intended that this Union is in any way to interfere in the management in any works.[86]

Protecting their 'established rights and privileges' usually entailed a degree of 'interference' in the management which the quarry-owners found unpalatable. And at times such

---

[83] Tightening regulations also meant tightening the grip of the overlookers: 'the over-anxiety on the quarryman's part to split blocks into slates during the winter is solely due to the want of energy on the part of the officials to stop them doing so'. Letter from H. P. Meares, 8 December 1899: GAS, Copy Memo Book of Quarry Manager, Penrhyn, PQ 295.

[84] *Yr Herald Cymraeg*, 19 November 1901.

[85] *Pall Mall Gazette* (U.N.C.W. Coetmor MSS. 46, p. 30, n.d.)

[86] Richards, op. cit., p. 140.

interference was admitted and its rationale eloquently articulated. R. Jones, a Dinorwic quarryman, explained to a mass meeting in 1885:

> there were some who denied the rights of the workmen to have a voice in the management of the works, and that that was the privilege of the master, who had invested his money, his capital, in the quarries . . . this was partly true, but when the master was not careful in his selection of proper agents, the workmen under such circumstances had a right to raise their voices and object because the appointment of incompetent managers endangered their lives. If the argument that the master, because he invested his capital, had the right to appoint the managers, was logic, then for the very same reason, the workmen ought to have a voice in their appointment. What were the workmen's labour and their lives, but their capital? How many workmen had lost their capital in the Dinorwic Quarries, and how many orphans and widows were there in the neighbourhood of Llanberis who had seen their capital brought home in pieces upon a bier. These facts . . . justified their present action in raising their voices against the incompetence of the head manager.[87]

Such feelings were not often expressed, but the quarrymen did feel that they had invested their labour and their lives in the quarries, and that they therefore had a stake in the way they were run. This consciousness did, at times, find explicitly political articulation. The nationalisation of the quarries seems to have been discussed by Nantlle quarrymen in the early 1890s, and in 1886 a delegate from Penmachno had declared, to the approval of the N.W.Q.U. annual conference, that if the masters could not work the quarries without losing money, then

> should they not be forced to sell their works and mines for reasonable royalties and let the working class try their hand?[88]

But such schemes made little headway. More popular was the ideal of co-operative quarries, and two attempts were made to launch such ventures: in 1880 the N.W.Q.U. invested £2,000 in a co-operative quarry and one of the results of the 1900–3

---

[87] *Caernarvon and Denbigh Herald*, 2 January 1886.
[88] *Y Genedl Gymreig*, 26 May 1886.

lock-out was the setting up of another trade-union-backed co-operative quarry. The nationalisation of the land on which the quarries stood and the other schemes for land reform were also, as we have seen, popular notions, for if the ownership of the quarries, of the productive units, was not in dispute, the ownership of the mountains in nineteenth-century Wales certainly was. 'Do not go back to Egypt my people', a speaker urged a mass meeting of Dinorwic quarrymen in 1885, 'demand the Elidir again . . .'[89] Dinorwic was the quarry, the Elidir was the mountain itself.

As we have seen, the slate-quarrymen fought consciously as members of a well-defined community with its own values and aims, and this perspective should not be lost; but it needs to be emphasised that the fact that it required only a translation of terms to turn the struggle against Anglicanism into an industrial battle—for the enemy, an alien squirearchy, remained the same—should not detract from the fact that north Wales at this time witnessed disputes which were, for the men involved, essentially about work, about how and when it should be done and about how much should be paid for it. For the activist Welsh middle-class radicals, usually the publicists of the quarrymen's struggles, the perspective was different and they consistently used the strikes and lock-outs of the quarries in their own continuing campaign against landlordism and the Anglican Church. For them, caught between a suspicion of the quarrymen and an enduring hatred of landlordism, the battles in the quarries were seen invariably as blows for religious and political emancipation rather than as battles for freedom at work.

The quarrymen themselves were prone to use extravagant language and an Old-Testament turn of phrase; and people who speak in the language of the pulpit, in moral absolutes, in terms of justice and basic human rights and principles, as the quarrymen consistently did when discussing their industrial relations, do invite misunderstanding. But whatever such words might mean to us, they seemed to them appropriate terms for the concrete realities of their own working lives; the least we should do is to take them at their word. The nature of the work men

<hr>

[89] Ibid., 16 December 1885.

and women must do, a central experience in the lives of the vast majority, might well deserve such a vocabulary. The principles for which the quarrymen fought were intimately connected with their working lives, with working hours and holidays, with wages' systems, with work discipline, rates for the job and managerial prerogatives. They were no less noble principles for that. For the quarrymen sensed accurately enough that what was at stake was fundamental: 'we have been told,' wrote the Dinorwic Quarrymen's Committee in 1885, 'that we are too independent'. Their reply was: 'we must fight like men or fall lower than men'.[90]

[90] *Y Genedl Gymreig*, 16 December 1885.

V

THE UNION 1874–1900

Slate-quarrymen in different parts of north Wales had widely different experiences of trade union struggle, ranging from the relative quiescence of the Oakeley workforce to the combativeness of the Penrhyn men. Internationally, also, it is difficult to generalize about slate-quarrymen's levels of struggle: the Scots quarrymen of Ballachulish were involved in one long and bitter dispute, but otherwise the slate-quarrymen of Britain, other than those of north Wales, had no record of militancy.[1]

In Brittany and Belgium, similarly, the slate-workers had little tradition of organisation, but on the other hand the Angevin slate-workers were amongst the most militant and class-conscious of all French workers; they were enthusiastic supporters of anarchist and anarcho-syndicalist ideas and between 1900 and 1913 they were involved in almost constant clashes with their employers.[2] Welsh quarrymen did not share the Anjou exuberance when it came to revolutionary theory, but their record of struggle and sacrifice is equally noteworthy; in particular they fought as determinedly as any other section of British workers in defence of the 'right of combination', their right to organise themselves into the North Wales Quarrymen's Union.

The North Wales Quarrymen's Union, established in 1874, was not to be in the nineteenth century an altogether successful organisation. It served, of course, to a significant extent, to defend and advance its members' interests on numerous occasions, but the enduring impression left by its history in this period is one of weakness, ineffectiveness and tragic defeat. Apart from a few brief months in 1878 the union never succeeded in organising more than 8,000 of the 14,000 or so quarrymen labouring in the slate quarries and mines of the

---

[1] The strike in Ballachulish in 1903 concerned the quarrymen's right to hire their own doctors. *Slate Trade Gazette*, 1903, 9, pp. 111, 213.
[2] See M. Poperen, op. cit.

area; for many years the number organised was hardly a third of that total, and on more than one occasion the union came perilously close to extinction.

Following the years of boom which lasted until 1879 and which witnessed the union's enjoyment of some heady success, steady growth and encouraging consolidation, the slate industry entered a long period of depression, not significantly relieved until the late 1890s, which had a seriously damaging effect upon the union. The major battles of the post-1880 period, the five-month lock-out in Dinorwic in 1885, the Llechwedd dispute of 1893, and the Penrhyn lock-outs of 1896–7 and 1900–3, all ended in, at best, unsatisfactory compromise or, at worst, in total defeat. While membership fluctuated greatly from year to year, the overall picture was one of constant decline: from an average of 7,667 members for the five years from 1875, the union fell to an average of 4,376 in the five years from 1880 and declined even further to 3,469 for the nineties and 2,995 for the first decade of the twentieth century.[3] Membership slumped dramatically in the only too bitter aftermath of the struggles of 1893, 1897 and 1903. When the union affiliated to the General Federation of Trade Unions in 1899 it had fewer than a thousand members.[4]

The N.W.Q.U. was not, of course, alone in being a weak trade union. One is struck by the resilience which the organisation at times displayed: it did after all survive despite all its difficulties and defeats, and the quarrymen themselves fought some of the most determined battles in trade union history to defend their right to organise. Yet the union failed to organise the majority of slate quarrymen and failed, moreover, to hold for any length of time many of those whom it did organise. Many possible reasons for this failure suggest themselves: the depression itself was a major factor, but there were other weaknesses, in the nature of the industry, the structure of the union and the policies of its leaders, which the depressed state of the industry only served to expose. This chapter is particu-

[3] For N.W.Q.U. membership figures see Appendix 1; *Annual Report on Trade Unions*; N.W.Q.U. Conference Reports and N.W.Q.U. Minute Books (1874–80 in N.L.W. MS. 8736, and 1880 onwards in GAS, N.W.Q.U. MSS.).
[4] N.W.Q.U. Minute Book, September 1899.

larly concerned to locate and understand those factors underlying the union's weaknesses.

The N.W.Q.U. played an important and often dramatic
part in the history of Gwynedd in the last quarter of the
nineteenth century; had it been a stronger and healthier
organisation, then tragedy and defeat might not so often have
had to be the bitter harvest reaped by the quarrymen's
courage.

The picture, and the possibilities, were not always
depressing: the quarrymen formed a small workforce, culturally homogeneous and not riven by strict craft hostilities,
and they were in a potentially powerful position to influence
the world production of slate. Above all, the N.W.Q.U.'s birth
had been successful beyond all reasonable expectation; after
only a few months of existence two of Wales's most powerful
men lay smitten by its efforts. This was a victory the impact
of which can hardly be overestimated; as a contemporary
observer of the quarrying industry commented:

> Mr. Assheton Smith and Lord Penrhyn, the noble proprietors
> of these quarries, suffered a defeat that North Wales had never
> seen its equal in any connection, or under any circumstances
> whatever.[5]

And what had happened had indeed been momentous. The
North Wales Quarrymen's Union had evolved during the
early months of 1874. There had been a growing sense of
frustration and anger in Penrhyn and Dinorwic for some
months and Dinorwic was especially agitated—serious discussion had taken place there about forming a union in
January and in February there had been an energetic and
successful campaign by the men to prevent a retired school-
master being made manager of the quarry.[6] The general
election took the steam out of the movement temporarily
though it added to the general air of excitement.[7] A new
consciousness was discernibly stirring by early April and in
that month consultations were held between a group of

---

[5] Morgan Richards, *Slate Quarrying . . . Profitable*, pp. 135–6.
[6] W. J. Parry, op. cit., p. 7; *Yr Herald Cymraeg*, 6 March 1874.
[7] The election witnessed, as in 1868, a fairly solid Tory vote from Bethesda
and Llanberis quarrymen.

Dinorwic activists and some 'friends of the quarrymen' with the aim of establishing a union.[8] On 27 April, in the Queen's Hotel, Caernarfon, these talks reached fruition and the North Wales Quarrymen's Union was launched.

It was immediately in trouble for, with uncharacteristic unity, quarry proprietors and managers determined to stamp out this new development. The storm broke in early June in the Glynrhonwy quarry near Llanberis when the manager, Mr. Wallace Cragg, forbade 120 union men the right to work until they disowned the N.W.Q.U.[9] To his astonishment the men stood solid, and Cragg surrendered after a short struggle, passing on the responsibility for breaking the union to the altogether weightier figure of Mr. Assheton-Smith, owner of Dinorwic. The Dinorwic men were in no mood for compromise, angry as they were about wages and particularly about the low payment for essential but non-productive clearing work.[10] Nevertheless, Assheton-Smith went ahead with his plans, and at the June bargain setting, when the crews of quarrymen came to negotiate the rates for the coming month, each man was asked to choose between his union and his work. Most men had already collected their tools in expectation of the question and their verdict was overwhelming: 11 quarrymen denied their union, 2,200 stood by it.[11] They were locked out for five weeks but stayed resolute and achieved a substantial victory.[12]

The excitement in Dinorwic soon spread to the Penrhyn quarries near Bethesda. It was now Lord Penrhyn's turn to test his power against that of the newcomer. The outcome was to be the quarrymen's biggest victory. As in most industrial disputes, the issues were complicated, and while the final breach came over the question of support for the locked-out men in Dinorwic—Lord Penrhyn forbade the collecting of funds on threat of closing the quarry—this only served to inflame an already tense situation. The Penrhyn men had worked out a series of demands concerning wages, conditions

[8] Parry, op. cit., p. 7.
[9] *Yr Herald Cymraeg*, 12 June 1874.
[10] Ibid.
[11] *C(aernarvon) & D(enbigh) Herald*, 20 June 1874.
[12] Though they did allow the management to interfere somewhat with their union rules. *C. & D. Herald*, 20 June 1874.

and the management of the quarry, and these they now presented to Lord Penrhyn. Their basic demand was for a 'standard' of wages (of 30s. a week for quarrymen, 27s. for bad-rockmen, etc.) 'when they were unable to do it on the contract and allowed what they can do over and above this', a sort of minimum wage.[13]

After a bitterly-fought and widely-publicised battle, the men won most of their demands in the Pennant Lloyd Agreement, and they returned to work on 17 September. The calm did not last long, however, for the management of the quarry simply ignored the conditions laid down in the agreement concerning the standard of wages and the men turned on their heels almost as soon as they had arrived and walked out again. The union proved beyond any doubt that the agreement was being flouted by the management and made it clear that they were not prepared to work under the existing régime in the quarry. Consequently, the three senior managers of the Penrhyn quarries were forced to resign and a new manager, more amenable to the men, was appointed in their place.[14] The victory, against one of the richest and most powerful men in the realm who had himself set out to destroy the union, was complete. A 'minimum' standard, long hoped for, had been achieved, a hated management clique which had dominated the running of the quarry for half a century had been unceremoniously swept out of office, and, perhaps most important of all, a committee of the men had been recognised to negotiate on their behalf.

These events had an electrifying effect on the quarrymen generally and the victories were to be a powerful spur to organisation for many years to come. The union had proved itself as a power in the land and its ranks swelled accordingly. By July the union had 4,843 members, almost all at Dinorwic and Penrhyn; by the end of October, as the message spread to other areas, the number had grown to 5,700; three months later it was up by another thousand, and by May 1875 the total had reached 7,196. The lodges of the union already established by the time the first conference was held in May

13 N.L.W. MS. 8738 (Llyfr Penderfyniadau Perthynol i gangen Undeb Chwarelwyr Gogledd Cymru, Dosbarth Cae-Braich-y-Cafn), 24 July 1874.
14 For a fuller account of the dispute, see W. J. Parry, op. cit., pp. 7–34.

1875 were No. 1 Dinorwic, No. 2 Caebraichycafn (Penrhyn quarries), No. 3 Ffestiniog, No. 4 Nantlle, No. 5 Corris and Abergynolwyn, No. 6 Llanberis (for quarries other than Dinorwic), No. 7 Port Bangor and Port Dinorwic (the docks which exported the slates), No. 8 Bethesda (for quarries other than Penrhyn), No. 9 Moeltryfan and No. 10 Waunfawr.[15] An eleventh, Rhos and Dolwyddelan, was recognised in 1878.[16]

These lodges covered virtually all the major quarrying areas, and in the months following the 1874 victories the union's influence was felt throughout the industry, in quarries large and small. According to that perceptive observer of the slate industry, Morgan Richards, 'the name of the union became a "terror" to the owners', and in quarry after quarry to whisper its name was sure to bring concessions.[17] Wages rose throughout the industry and the selling price of slates had to be re-adjusted three times to make up for the wage rises[18]—an unprecedented action as price lists were always set at the beginning of the year and were valid for the coming twelve months. The insistent pressure from the union went so far as to affect the only common prices policy achieved by the quarrelsome quarry-owners when, in 1875, at the request of the Merioneth owners, the otherwise headstrong Dinorwic and Penrhyn quarry managements agreed not to increase their prices as this would fan 'the flame of disquietude raging among the men' and encourage them to strike.[19] The officials of the N.W.Q.U. assessed in May 1876 that 'more by upwards of £150,000 has been paid in wages during last year in the slate quarries of North Wales than in any other year'.[20]

The union also had some successes in reducing the excessive hours of work, a serious grievance for men who often had to walk miles over stony mountain paths before they started their

---

[15] Report of First Annual Conference, *C. & D. Herald*, 29 May 1875.
[16] Report of Fourth Annual Conference, *C. & D. Herald*, 29 May 1878. Further lodges were to be set up: e.g., Penmachno, Penrhyndeudraeth, Maentwrog in 1896; Trawsfynydd in 1897.
[17] M. Richards, op. cit., p. 138.
[18] Ibid.
[19] D. Dylan Pritchard, 'Aspects of the Slate Industry in the Expansionist Period, Part vi', *Quarry Managers' Journal* (August 1944), p. 71.
[20] *C. & D. Herald*, 27 May 1876.

labours.[21] Campaigns on the question were launched with some success in Dinorwic and Ffestiniog, and a two-week strike on the hours question in the Penyrorsedd quarry in Nantlle brought a satisfactory settlement.[22]

The three years 1875–7, with the union growing in strength and the owners eager to settle in order to satisfy a booming market, did not witness many serious strikes. There was a dispute at the Welsh Slate Company's Rhiw quarry in early 1875, a 'disagreement' at Pantdreiniog quarry in Bethesda in December 1876, and a short strike at Cwmeiddew, Corris, in May 1877.[23] The only serious incidents occurred when there was a threat from quarry-owners to the wages' system of the industry, the 'bargain' system. As we have seen, such a threat led to a riotous response in the Hafod y Wern quarry in Betws Garmon in May 1876 and to a two-year strike at the small Rhos quarry in Capel Curig which broke out in December 1877. The young union had had a most auspicious start, but its success was not to last.

The history of trade unionism in general consistently and eloquently testifies to the fact that few agencies are as corrosive of union membership and success as economic depression and its consequences: unemployment, low wages and short-time working. The depression which affected the slate industry from the late 1870s until the late 1890s was no exception.

In May 1878 the union had a membership of 8,368 and the funds amounted to 'a handsome sum of £6,977'.[24] The delegates at the 1878 Conference felt well satisfied with their achievements; the union appeared to be on solid enough ground. The viability of the structure they had built was, however, soon to be severely tested. In his address to the 1878 annual conference of the union, W. J. Parry warned against a possible downturn in the slate trade and a resulting reduction in wages; the trade, he pointed out, was 'always fluctuating' and it would be as well to be prepared. In fact, a prolonged depression was already setting in, the slate industry's long 'expansionist phase' was

[22] Ibid., 22 April 1876; C. & D. Herald, 26 May 1877.
[21] Hours were as long as eleven hours a day in Ffestiniog: N.W.Q.U. Minute Book, 22 March 1876.
[23] N.W.Q.U. Minute Books, January–February 1875; 30 December 1876; 5 May 1877.
[24] Ibid., 4 May 1878; C. & D. Herald, May 1878.

over, and the N.W.Q.U. was never again in the nineteenth
century to have as many members as it did in that May of
1878.[25]

The effects of the downturn were aggravated by the sudden-
ness of the change in the industry's fortunes. 'The slate trade',
wrote W. J. Parry in 1879, 'has during the last six months gone
into, if not through, one of the most sudden and strange panics
that has ever occurred.'[26] For the N.W.Q.U. the depression
was a severe blow. Within three months of its peak of over
8,000 members, membership had fallen to 6,776.[27] The owners
lost no time in cutting wages and attempting to reduce
drastically their labour costs. In November 1878 the union
council recommended that skilled quarrymen, bad-rockmen
and miners accept the reductions in the making price of slates
made by the masters; in May 1879 the Penrhyn quarry
committee accepted a reduction of 2s. 6d. in the 'average
standard' of 27s. 6d. stipulated by the 1874 Pennant Lloyd
agreement, and also went onto a four-day week.[28]

The quarrymen did not accept these changes calmly and
there were strikes in numerous quarries, including Cook and
Ddol, the Goodman and Cambrian quarries, Glynrhonwy Isaf,
Chwarel Braich (Rhostryfan), Pantdreiniog, Cilgwyn, Penyrorsedd, Cefn Du (Waunfawr) and Alexandra. On the whole,
however, the men were forced to accept the worsening situation
without struggle. The depression turned out to be not a mere
'fluctuation' as W. J. Parry had prophesied, but a serious and
prolonged recession which only improved slowly in the late
nineties. So bad was its impact upon the union that in 1880,
only six years after the N.W.Q.U.'s successful launching, a local
newspaper commented that

> the union has apparently fallen into a state of lethargy and
> but for the anniversaries some might think that the institution
> that the men formed for their mutual protection has ceased
> to exist.[29]

[25] 'The expansionist phase' was defined by D. Dylan Pritchard, the pioneer
economic historian of the slate industry, as the period from 1790 to 1877.
[26] C. & D. Herald, 25 January 1879 (letter from W. J. Parry).
[27] N.W.Q.U. Minute Book, 31 August 1878.
[28] C. & D. Herald, 24 May 1879.
[29] Ibid., 29 May 1880.

The union, in fact, still had over 5,500 members at this time, but the frailty of its construction was becoming increasingly exposed. The most obvious weakness was in the great variation in the union's strength as between different areas, particularly the difference between, on the one hand, the lodges in Penrhyn and Dinorwic and, on the other, the ones in Dyffryn Nantlle, Ffestiniog and Corris.

The areas of union strength were Bethesda and Llanberis. Significant inroads were to be made in the Blaenau Ffestiniog district, but the Nantlle and Corris areas, while supporting small lodges, were for many years, to all intents and purposes, largely unaffected by union influence: the union's 1887–91 Roll Book shows only 56 members in the whole Nantlle valley where some 1,500 quarrymen laboured, and there were only 24 men in lodge No. 5 representing Corris and Bryneglwys.[30] Even in the heyday of the union this geographical difference had been apparent. In 1877 ten out of every eleven men in Penrhyn were union members, in Dinorwic seven out of every eight; in Corris there were three non-unionists to every member, in the Nantlle valley the union men were outnumbered four to one, and in the Ffestiniog district by twelve to one.[31] The situation in Ffestiniog was to improve considerably, but the mass of the membership was to remain largely based in the two lodges of Penrhyn and Dinorwic. This was partly due to the fact that it was in these quarries that the union had been born and that it was here that it had achieved most. The victories in Penrhyn and Dinorwic in 1874 had convincingly and clearly demonstrated to the men of those quarries the value of collective action. In other areas, however, the value of union membership was not so obvious, the point of joining not so apparent; as John Owens of Corris pointed out to the 1877 Conference of the union, 'conviction cannot be brought home to some people unless they are directly gainers by the union'.[32] What there was to gain from union membership was by no means as clear to quarrymen outside the Llanberis and Bethesda areas as it was to those who had already experienced the power and benefit of combination.

[30] GAS, N.W.Q.U. MSS., Union Roll Book, 1887–91.
[31] M. Richards, op. cit., p. 144.
[32] C. & D. Herald, 26 May 1877.

There were other differences, both in patterns of ownership and methods of working, between the areas which also affected union development. The union's long and energetic campaign to bring the quarries under government safety regulations, for example, and to appoint an Inspector for slate quarries did not have the same appeal to the workers in the underground slate mines of Merioneth who had, since the legal decision of 1875, come under the jurisdiction of the various Metalliferous Mines Regulation Acts, as it did to the workers in the 'open' quarries of Caernarvonshire, whose conditions of work cried out for legal regulation.

It has been suggested that the very geography of the industry, the distribution of the slate vein and the opportunities offered— and taken—to work it, was itself a major cause of weak organisation,[33] that in particular the difficulties of communication imposed by mountainous terrain accounted for a degree of local chauvinism in the various quarrying communities which discouraged the development of a consciousness of common identity amongst quarrymen of different areas. This argument carries some weight. The quarrying communities were relatively stable by the end of the nineteenth century and, as has been noted, there was a marked disinclination on the part of quarrymen to move from one area to another. On the other hand, the slate industry had a remarkably homogeneous working force supporting many organisations, including energetic religious ones, which seemed to overcome the problems of isolation easily enough. The industry was concentrated into one small and relatively compact corner of Wales; the union's headquarters were in Caernarfon, situated within a few miles of most of the important quarrying centres. Despite difficult terrain, therefore, the union never faced on anything like the same scale the communication problems which many national unions encountered and which, for example, affected in particularly acute form the stone and granite quarrymen of north Wales who, when they became members of the Settmakers' Union, had to deal with union headquarters in distant Aberdeen. In 1903 one-third of the Settmakers' Union's

[33] See D. Dylan Pritchard, 'Trade Unionism', *Quarry Managers' Journal* (January 1945), p. 303; C. Parry, 'The North Wales Quarrymen's Union', and J. Lindsay, 'Background to Unionism', *Chwareli a Chwarelwyr* (Caernarfon, 1974).

members worked in the stone quarries of north Wales, but the union was Scottish-based.[34]

The fact that almost 90 per cent of Britain's slate was produced in this compact area, moreover, gave the union, which never attempted (or needed) to recruit in slate quarries elsewhere in Britain, a potentially very powerful bargaining position. A relatively small workforce could drastically affect the production of what was then an important commodity. This enviable position compares well with workers in many other industries, particularly coal mining, who when organised regionally were always in a precarious bargaining situation as they could not affect production in other coalfields.

The location and distribution of the quarries did, nevertheless, present problems and proved formidable obstacles to effective trade unionism. The main problem lay in the huge variation in scale between the different enterprises. In the early 1890s there were some sixty quarries and mines being worked for slate in north Wales, employing between them 13,500 men;[35] almost exactly half of those quarrymen worked in just three quarries, the giant concerns of Penrhyn near Bethesda (2,500 men), Dinorwic in Llanberis (2,590 men) and the Oakeley slate mine in Blaenau Ffestiniog (1,652 men).[36] 3,000 more worked in seven moderately-sized quarries and the remaining 4,000 men were scattered in fifty small workings, 700 of them in quarries employing fewer than 24 men. Two quarries indeed 'employed' only one man. In a mountainous region the problems of communication confronting the union were obvious and it is not, therefore, surprising that the strenth of the organisation always lay in the two biggest quarries; of 5,355 members in the late 1880s, over 3,000 were concentrated in lodges Nos. 1 and 2, Dinorwic and Penrhyn.[37]

Size alone does not appear to have been always a deciding factor, however. The union's position in the giant Oakeley mine was weak, with only 13 per cent of the men unionized, while in the same year (1887) the moderately sized New Welsh Slate Company's Cwmorthin mine employing 290 men had 60 per

[34] *Settmakers' and Stoneworkers' Journal*, January 1903.
[35] At least a further 21 workings had closed down during the previous decade.
[36] *Report of the Quarry Committee of Inquiry*, 1893-4; *Report of the Departmental Committee on Merionethshire Slate Mines*, 1895, Appendix 5.
[37] Union Roll Book, 1887-91.

cent of its workforce unionized.[38] And some of the smaller and
moderately-sized quarries sometimes displayed an impressive
degree of militancy: the two dozen men at the Rhos quarry
in Capel Curig stayed out for over two years in 1877–9,
Moeltryfan saw disputes in 1892, 1896, 1899 and 1906, men in
Brynhafodywern near Bethesda stopped work in 1879, 1881,
1883 and 1886.[39]

Neither was remoteness a guarantee against union influence.
Rhosydd quarry, which employed fewer than 200 men, was
1,500 feet above sea level and over four miles up the slopes of
the Moelwynion from Blaenau Ffestiniog. Much of its workforce was drawn from small villages in the Llanfrothen area
and most of them stayed in barracks at the quarry from Monday
to Saturday; and yet over a quarter of the Rhosydd men were
union members and there was a fortnight's strike at the quarry
in October 1886.

The semi-rural setting of the industry presented other
problems. In many of the quarries there was always a sizeable
minority of labourers who were not domiciled near their place
of work, but travelled in to work from nearby rural areas. In
some quarries these men, some of whom stayed in barracks
near their work throughout the week to return home on
Saturdays, formed a definite group who did not identify with
the body of quarrymen as such and took little interest in the
affairs of the union. This was particularly true of the Anglesey
labourers at work in the Dinorwic quarry, who were bitterly
criticized by a union man in 1890 for 'being too cowardly, not
enough manhood in them to demand their rights'.[40]

Many quarrymen were themselves small-holders and cottagers and one historian has commented that this led them
to 'follow a life style which stressed a rugged individualism
rather than mutual dependence'.[41] This is a question which
should be treated with caution, however, for there is little
evidence to suggest that quarrymen who lived on small-
holdings were necessarily any less loyal to their union than
those who did not. Indeed, to the contrary; the Moeltryfan

[38] Ibid.
[39] N.W.Q.U. Minute Books.
[40] GAS, DQ. Llyfr Cofnodion Cyfrinfa Rhif 1. Dinorwic, 19 February 1890.
[41] C. Parry, op. cit., p. 33.

quarry, for example, which appears to have employed a high percentage of cottagers,[42] also witnessed a series of industrial clashes in the 1890s and again in 1906; the only major dispute in Blaenau Ffestiniog took place in 1893 in the Llechwedd quarry, a mine which was well known as an employer of workers from outside the town of Blaenau itself and, therefore, also with a good number of cottagers at work.[43]

There were other differences within the workforce; in particular there was a degree of craft jealousy and exclusiveness. What is surprising in the history of the N.W.Q.U. is how little this fact affected its development. As the depression deepened in the 1880s the skilled quarrymen became increasingly jealous of their status and attempts were made to limit the number of those recognised as properly skilled. Various plans for establishing an apprenticeship system and of limiting entry into the craft were discussed, but little came of them. But the resentment between the various grades in the quarrying industry was real enough: a delegate from Nantlle at the N.W.Q.U.'s 1882 conference complained bitterly that 'the craft at the present time is too open to all classes to come in . . . each and every beast should be prevented from entering', and the *rybelwrs* and other grades often felt that they were unjustly treated by the skilled quarrymen.[44] More serious was the often-expressed division between those who actually worked the rock in some way and those sundry other skilled men employed in the quarries—blacksmiths, carpenters, pattern makers, engine drivers, etc. These men felt quite separate from the mass of quarrymen and were consistently to be found at work during disputes though this had no great effect as their total number was low.

What is striking is that despite these strains the N.W.Q.U. did not fall victim to any serious divisions between its skilled and unskilled membership. Unusual for a trade union in its time, it was, in effect, an industrial union open to all workers employed in the slate industry irrespective of craft. Even the

---

[42] David Thomas, *Diolch am Gael Byw* (Liverpool, 1968), p. 22.
[43] *Departmental Committee upon Merionethshire Slate Mines*, 1895, evidence of Owen Rowland Jones, 1359.
[44] *Y Genedl Gymreig*, 24 May 1882. See also *Y Werin*, 17 June 1893 and Hugh Lloyd, *Hunangofiant Rybelwr* (Caernarfon, 1926).

dockers who loaded the finished slate onto ships in Portdinorwic and Port Penrhyn were eligible for membership and had their own lodges; the Dinorwic lodge of the union represented eight different groups in the quarry;[45] the Penrhyn lodge negotiated on behalf of platelayers and stonemasons amongst others, and in 1874 the lodge had demanded an increase for the journeymen whom the men themselves employed.[46] This relative unity amongst different sections of quarrymen, therefore, when compared with relations in many other industries, could have supplied the union with a solid enough base.

Another aspect of work relations in the quarrying industry which, it has been suggested, may have militated against trade-union consciousness was the 'bargaining' system whereby wages were determined. But as has been argued earlier the individualistic tendencies inherent in the system should not be overestimated. By the late-nineteenth century the system was no more than a formality in many quarries and any genuine element of bargaining between men and master had largely disappeared. Increasingly the men were forced to accept the setting price of the management and this resented fact raised, often in an urgent form, the need for a standardised minimum applicable to all bargain-takers which would serve to defend the men when the poundage agreed was low and the rock proved difficult to work. As we have seen such a demand was a consistent feature of industrial relations in the quarries and the system thus served to unite the men. The bargain system, moreover, by its monthly haggling, invited continuous disagreement and bad feeling between the men and managements. Few men did not at some time or another labour under a sense of grievance at being cheated at the monthly bargain setting.

The Pennant Lloyd Agreement won by the Penrhyn men in 1874 was a clear demonstration of the benefits which could be brought by a standardised agreement on wages to underlie the bargain system itself. The operation of the agreement from 1874 to 1885 showed even more clearly the effectiveness of trade unionism when operating within the bargain system. It was that effectiveness in influencing wages and defending the

[45] GAS, DQ. Llyfr Cofnodion . . . Dinorwic, 5 June 1891.
[46] N.L.W., MS. 8738, 3 August 1874, 24 July 1874.

financial interests of individual crews in dispute which undoubtedly lay behind Lord Penrhyn's decision to withdraw
recognition from the union committee in 1885.[47] When it
operated as an at least fairly equal arrangement between men
and master the bargain system probably was a disincentive to
trade unionism and the influence of the system's competitive-
ness and individualism lingered long in the quarries; when the
system was breaking down, however, as it clearly was in the
last quarter of the nineteenth century, then its debilitating
influence on trade unionism waned and the system could at
times become a positive encouragement to collective action.
The inevitable corruption which it bred, as men tried to
influence the setting agents to give them a good price, was,
however, long to remain a source of bitterness and division
between quarrymen.

It was not only via the wages system that the quarry owners
made their mark on the growth of the union. Their power and
their paternalism were also very relevant factors. Paternalism
laid a heavy restraining hand upon any move for changing the
relationship between men and master. Lord Penrhyn and Mr.
Assheton-Smith, in particular, controlled well-organised
machines for dispensing their benevolent patronage, and even
in the less 'feudal' atmosphere of Blaenau Ffestiniog some of
the quarry owners made regular paternalistic gestures: seven
trainfuls of Oakeley quarrymen and their families, for example,
were entertained in Llandudno in September 1890 at their
master's expense.[48]

But this influence again should not be over-estimated; it
was that selective use of managerial patronage that came close
to bribery and corruption which was the potent divisive force in
the Penrhyn quarries rather than the general air of lordly
largesse. And while the quarrymen were, at least until the
struggle of 1900–3, always fastidiously careful not to offend the
quarry owners personally, as opposed to the managers, their
relationship to at least one owner had been bravely stated in
1874 in an explicit rejection of the paternalistic system: 'we are
perfectly willing', said the Penrhyn men's representatives in

---

[47] For a fuller exposition of this argument, see Chapter IV.
[48] *Y Rhedegydd*, 20 September 1890.

that year, 'that his lordship should keep his charities to himself—if those in any way interfere with him in his giving us proper wages'.[49] It was in these tones that combination came to challenge paternalism.

An interesting case-study in paternalism is offered by the Cwmorthin quarry near Tanygrisiau. This quarry was famous for its enlightened management, which provided housing for some of its employees, gave generous allowances to the widows of men killed at work and even instituted a profit-sharing scheme.[50] And yet it had one of the worst industrial relations records of any quarry in north Wales.

Paternalism, of course, was a preservative for wealth and power and it was the exercise of this power in rather cruder forms which was to block the union consistently. Victimisation was only too often the lot of any radical or trade unionist in the slate quarries, not only in the well-known cases of Dinorwic and Penrhyn, but also in other areas—the Llechwedd dispute of 1893 was the result of barefaced victimisation, and five members of the union committee had been summarily sacked in Blaenau Ffestiniog in 1891.[51] It was in Penrhyn that the ruthless rooting-out of radicals was most vicious, and examples of such action are legion, especially in 1870 and again in the years following the 1896–7 lock-out, when Lord Penrhyn showed his contempt for the agreement he had just signed by claiming that his promise of no victimisation in no way interfered with his 'right to dismiss whomsoever I wish from the quarry without giving any reason', a 'right' which he freely exercised.[52]

The union's problem in facing up to such power was cruelly simple: compared with the wealth of some of the quarry owners the union would always appear weak. Slate quarrying was, on the whole, a profitable industry, and in the larger quarries it could be hugely profitable. It was estimated by the *Mining Journal* in 1859 that the 2,500 men working in the Penrhyn quarries created £100,000 annual net profit for Lord Penrhyn, while the 2,000 men in Dinorwic created £70,000 a

[49] Parry, op. cit., p. 13.
[50] Lindsay, op. cit., p. 15.
[51] *Y Rhedegydd*, 28 February 1891.
[52] Parry, op. cit., p. 170.

year for their employer.[53] A few private individuals, commented the *Mining Journal*, had 'amassed colossal fortunes'. This trend was to continue; in 1894 another trade journal quoted the figure of £100,000 annual profit for Lord Penrhyn, 'one of the richest men in the Welsh principality', and in 1898, just before the major Penrhyn struggle broke out, Lord Penrhyn reaped a record £133,000 profit.[54]

The power and ruthlessness of some of the quarry owners therefore were a tremendous obstacle for a small union. But even here the picture was not all black, for a major weakness of the quarry owners was their persistent and signal failure to combine on an industry-wide basis. Only once, shortly after the union had been born in 1874, did the owners demonstrate a united willingness to combat the union. Then, in a famous meeting at the Royal Hotel, Caernarfon, nineteen quarry owners and managers met to kill the union in the bud. They agreed that 'every quarry proprietor in North Wales should refuse to employ any man who is ascertained to be a member of the union'.[55] The union, as we have seen, braved that storm and won decisive victories. From then on the owners showed little interest in another combined onslaught on the union. The owners quarelled over trade matters and over politics, there being strong Tory and Liberal factions. The competitive price-war that raged in the industry militated against unity, while a few quarry owners, such as Messrs. Robinson and Darbishire from the Nantlle valley, were, at times, openly sympathetic to the N.W.Q.U.

Repression and victimisation were dangerous weapons for the owners, effective in the short term but building up a store of bitterness and resentment for future battles: 'Give the screw another turn', warned a correspondent from Bethesda in April 1874, 'and the people here will shout. And you look out for the consequences.'[56] A timely warning which Lord Penrhyn was time and again to ignore. It was no accident that the N.W.Q.U. was strongest in precisely those quarries where the owners were

---

[53] *Mining Journal*, 10 September 1859, p. 639.
[54] *Our Gazette* (National Association of Slate Merchants and Slaters), October 1894, p. 2. GAS, Penrhyn Quarry MS. 496, see letter from E. A. Young to Lord Penrhyn, 7 January 1899.
[55] Parry, op. cit., p. 7.
[56] *Yr Herald Cymraeg*, 24 April 1874.

richest and the repression of trade unionists most ruthless, a point which the Liberal and ever-perceptive Morgan Richards noted with some satisfaction.[57]

Another factor which sapped the potential strength of the N.W.Q.U. was the existence and strength of other organisations which catered for the quarryman's needs. The extensive control of, and energy displayed by, some of the quarrymen's own institutions made it difficult for the union to carve out an area for its own specialised functions. The union's failure to develop an adequate welfare scheme, despite regular debates on the issue over twenty-five years, was at least partly the result of the existence in the quarrying districts both of flourishing Friendly Societies and of quarry-organised sick clubs, medical schemes and hospitals. The Independent Order of Oddfellows was established in Bethesda in 1837; on Ascension Day 1845, 500 members from five local lodges paraded colourfully through the town, to be followed by 300 members of the three lodges of the True Ivorites. The Ogwen Benefit Society, a local organisation, also took part in the processions.[58] In 1865 the town supported over twenty Building Societies, a Savings Bank, Insurance Schemes, five different Friendly Societies and the Caerllwyngrydd Lending Society.[59] The competition from such well-organised societies made it difficult for the union to intervene with its own benefit schemes.

The Quarry Sick Clubs and other funds, contributory schemes the control of which was often cause for heated dispute, were also well organised and many sick quarrymen relied heavily on them. John Edwards, a quarryman from Ffestiniog, for example, drew about equally from the Oddfellows and the Quarry Fund during the various weeks and months of illness and unemployment which regularly afflicted his 50 years as a quarryman.[60] Even in the field of emigration, which was an important part of union policy in the early 1880s, the N.W.Q.U. found it difficult to compete with other agencies, and though over 250 quarrymen emigrated under its aegis from 1879 to

[57] M. Richards, op. cit., p. 144.
[58] C. & D. Herald, 10 May 1845.
[59] Yr Herald Cymraeg, 9 December 1865.
[60] U.C.N.W. MS. 2390 (Llyfr Cownt John Edwards Ffestiniog.) He drew, e.g., £1 18s. 4d. from the Quarry Fund and £1 3s. 0d. from the Oddfellows in July 1889.

1881, this was a relatively small percentage of the total number emigrating.[61]

More serious was the union's failure in many areas to establish itself as the men's representative in negotiations with the masters. In Penrhyn after 1885 this was a direct result of managerial intransigence, but in other districts it was simply a result of other, sometimes ad hoc, organisations doing the job. The successful hours campaign in Blaenau Ffestiniog in 1882, for example, was waged and organised by a committee which does not appear to have had any direct links with the union, and D. G. Williams, the most active and prominent union figure in Ffestiniog in those years, was not himself a member of the committee though he did play an effective role in the campaign.[62] In many other quarries non-unionists were as active as members in pushing for improvements.

Even more striking was the organisational role of nonconformist chapels during these years. The chapels weakened trade unionism not because of any hostility toward the N.W.Q.U. but rather because they themselves carried out some of the social and organisational roles in the community which could otherwise have fallen to the union. During the bitter 1893 strike in the Llechwedd slate mine, for example, fund-raising was automatically seen by the strike committee as the function of the chapels and circulars were sent to chapels in north Wales and Liverpool and local ministers dispatched to propagandise on the men's behalf.[63] And in the Nantlle valley in July 1906 a meeting of quarrymen took the decision that the prevailing difficult situation in the quarries should not be discussed by the union lodges, but that the question should rather be taken to the chapels.[64]

Many factors within the situation in which the N.W.Q.U. had to operate can be seen, therefore, to have conspired against strong trade-union organisation; the prevailingly depressed state of the slate industry and the hostility of quarry owners, in particular, being powerful deterrents to combination. And yet, as we have seen, none of the factors mentioned above

[61] N.W.Q.U. Minute Books.
[62] *Y Genedl Gymreig*, 15 March 1882.
[63] U.C.N.W., MS. 5911. Rhan o gofnodion am Streic y Llechwedd, Blaenau Ffestiniog, 11, 21 July 1893; 2 August 1893.
[64] *Yr Herald Cymraeg*, 3 July 1906.

seem adequate in themselves to explain the union's lack of success; and the situation was often contradictory—the very brakes on union development sometimes encouraged that development at the same time. It was not just the objective situation which was unfavourable for the union, though, as we have seen, the conditions were always inclement and often harsh, but the union's own structure, policies and leadership also contributed to its mediocre performance. From here on we shall be concerned with those internal problems which afflicted the union and stunted its growth.

The local organisational structure of the union left much to be desired, for apart from lodges No. 1 and No. 2 in Dinorwic and Penrhyn, the branches were geographical rather than workplace based. Many of the weaknesses of the union in Ffestiniog and Nantlle stemmed from this form of organisation. The Dinorwic and Penrhyn lodges worked effectively as grievance committees consisting of delegates elected from the various districts of each quarry. Based firmly in the workplace, these lodges thus had immediate day-to-day relationships with problems in the quarries and were in a position to organise and intervene directly in them. The Ffestiniog lodge, on the other hand, worked on a different pattern and had members in at least twelve different quarries. The lodge itself was, therefore, in no position to intervene directly and consistently in the working situation in each quarry, and this was a major weakness in its make-up. In Penrhyn the union drew its strength until 1885 from the relative effectiveness of the lodge in defending the men's interests through regular negotiations with management.

Such effectiveness could not be achieved easily in a lodge covering many quarries or, indeed, as with the Penrhyn-deudraeth lodge, consisting of men who lived in one village but who worked in quarries elsewhere. It is not clear how exactly the lodges did operate in Ffestiniog and Nantlle, but there is little evidence of effective co-ordinated action affecting the various quarries represented by these lodges. The relative weakness of the geographically-based branches in comparison with the workplace-based ones makes too marked a contrast for one not to conclude that the divorce between the union lodge as such and the organisation in the quarry itself, consequent upon geographical organisation, had a seriously debilitating effect upon the union's growth. The suggestion was made on the N.W.Q.U.'s committee in June 1892 that the Nantlle area, where the situation was, as usual, 'very flat', should adopt a system of separate lodges in each of the quarries, but no action was taken along these lines.[65]

One of the enduring strengths of most trade unions in this period was their extensive benefit schemes. The N.W.Q.U. failed to develop such a scheme partly, as has been mentioned, because of the already well-rooted existence of Friendly Societies and other welfare organisations, but partly also as a result of the union's insufficiently centralised structure. The benefits question had been raised as early as October 1875[66] and in 1877 the General Secretary, W. J. Williams, proposed a 'Scheme of Relief for Old and Disabled Members', 6d. contributed per member per quarter would have given 3s. a week to old and disabled members. The scheme was not well received. J. O. Griffith, a founder-member of the union, considered that 'it ran contrary to the functions of the union. The object of the union's formation was to protect the quarry-men while at their work, and not to support those of them unable to work.' It was also pointed out that 'very few quarry-men reach old age'. The matter was postponed for discussion at the lodges, a procedure to be followed many times later. A scheme put forward by Bethesda lodge which would have made it possible for the payment of unemployed members was turned down in 1879, as was a scheme proposed by Nantlle lodge in 1881 and 1883, to help the old, the infirm and the injured; the same scheme was referred back to the lodges again in 1884. It was a very cautious plan which offered nothing until a member had paid his dues regularly for ten years, but it was still not acceptable. A plan was accepted in 1885, but its implementation was not successful, and the question continued to be discussed and grumbled about in the union for another twenty years.[67]

---

[65] N.W.Q.U. Minute Book, June 1892.
[66] Ibid., October 1875.
[67] C. & D. Herald, 26 May 1877; 7 June 1879. N.W.Q.U. Minute Book, 27 August 1881; Y Genedl Gymreig, 30 May 1883, 14 May 1884, 20 May 1885.

The union was not indifferent to the welfare of out-of-work members. In the twelve months prior to May 1880 it had collected over £900 'to assist and alleviate the sufferings of members discharged'.[68] But this money had been collected informally and was in no way connected with the union's funds. The only way in which these funds were used for the immediate financial relief of members was in the event of a lock-out or strike. This assistance was, of course, of tremendous value during the struggles fought by the quarrymen, especially in Penrhyn and Dinorwic, but for the many quarrymen working in quarries which had never experienced significant strike action the promise that the union would pay them in case of such action was a fact of no great consequence. Most quarries in north Wales experienced no strikes or lock-outs in the nineteenth century, and though over 25 quarries did have reported disputes during these years many of these were of brief duration or involved only a section of the workforce. The failure of the N.W.Q.U. to develop a comprehensive benefits scheme, therefore, meant that the financial support offered by the union to its members seemed inconsequential or irrelevant to a good many quarrymen. It also made it difficult for the union to hold on to members. Trade union benefit schemes demanded uninterrupted membership and regular dues payment; the threat to the member's right to receive benefits was thus a great incentive to conscientious membership. Lacking such a scheme, N.W.Q.U. members often allowed their membership to lapse until trouble loomed again on the horizon.

This failure to develop a benefits scheme was in part a reflection of the lack of decisive leadership from the union's executive committee and from its officials. The union rarely acted as a united force and there was never a real attempt at a unified industrial policy. This reflected the already-mentioned sense of district parochialism which was so strong among the quarrymen, but it also, to a significant extent, reflected the nervousness and indecision of the union's leadership, for even when districts were eager to move together the leadership was not forthcoming. The most dramatic example of this was the

[68] *C. & D. Herald*, 29 May 1880.

new consciousness stirring the quarrymen in the early 1890s. The slate market was improving, while the owners maintained their iron intransigence. In February 1892, with union membership close to 5,000 again, the union's executive decided that the time had come for 'all the quarries to move by making a claim for a rise on 5s. a day in the wages'.[69] A bond was circulated pledging the signatory to the claim; over 6,500 quarrymen, including close on 2,000 men in each of the three main districts, Dinorwic, Penrhyn and Ffestiniog, signed the bond and the stage seemed set for a united move. The claim was submitted in May and, as was only to be expected, the reaction of the individual owners was a firm negative; Vivian, the manager of Dinorwic, called the claim 'childish' and refused to countenance it. Only John Robinson of Talysarn was sympathetic.[70]

The union decided in June to ballot the men; the ballot paper asked whether

> in the face of the refusal of the masters to meet the claim for a rise in the standard of wages . . . you are in favour of moving forward to secure (the claim) even as far as a strike, if that be necessary.

The members' reply was unequivocal with 79 per cent in favour of going ahead even if it meant a strike. The eleven lodges balloted each showed a majority for going forward, a total of 5,781 as against 1,534 who wanted the matter delayed.[71] The union, however, continued to delay and showed itself quite unwilling to carry out its members' wishes and decided instead to push for the claim to go to two arbitrators, Sir John Gorst, M.P., and Thomas Burt, M.P. In July the union wrote to the quarry owners expressing their fear that a confrontation between workers and masters might take place, 'a confrontation which we do not wish to see if it can in any way be avoided'.[72] The masters predictably refused arbitration, and the union committee failed to agree to any move other than to 'urge the workers to not step as far as going on strike at the moment'.[73] The earlier unity now began to wilt and many lodge represen-

[69] N.W.Q.U. Minute Book, 6 April 1892.
[70] Ibid., 11 June 1892.
[71] Ibid., 25 June 1892.
[72] Ibid., 13 July 1892.
[73] Ibid., 5 August 1892

tatives expressed doubts about the whole idea; the union decided to shelve any notion of action and chose instead to gather more precise information about members' wages, a campaign that met with a poor response. In November the union sanctioned a separately-negotiated agreement in Ffestiniog which fell below the 5s. a day demand. By March 1893 and throughout the spring of that year the lodges were again pushing for action, but again with little response from the union.

The Llanberis lodge delegate expressed the feelings of his members: 'they are asking what the Council of the Union are going to do. They are ready to move. Some are deciding to leave from the union if we do not go forward'; a similar feeling was expressed by the delegate from Alexandra.[74] But little was done and the union continued to dissuade the men from taking strike action.[75] After eighteen frustrating months, the movement for wages became lost in the bitter battle in the Llechwedd mine over a victimisation issue in July 1893.

The union's failure to mobilize its members effectively had a drastic result, and membership fell from 4,346 in 1893 to 1,652 in 1894. Disillusion within the union was widespread. In Dinorwic

> the union is shrinking in membership, and it is of no practical use at all as it is at the moment, all the friends feel very eager for a re-organisation and to start again on better foundations in the future.[76]

This was by no means the first call from within the union for a change in its structure. In April 1890 a ballot was held in Dinorwic on the future of the union when the result had been as follows:

Join with an English Union.	206
Change the Union's Rules.	254
Local Union.	363
Undecided.	58
For the old union.	72
Others.	105.[77]

---

[74] Ibid., 11 March 1893.
[75] In July 1893, for example, they urged the Glynrhonwy men to go once more to their master before taking strike action. Ibid., 1 July 1893.
[76] GAS, Llyfr Cofnodion . . . Dinorwic, 23 August 1093.
[77] Ibid., 3 April 1890.

In a further ballot the same month, 579 voted for a change in the rules and 124 for a break-away local union.

This lack of support for the union was the product of several factors. The move towards 'Home Rule' for the districts had always been a strong one, but, as can be seen from these ballot results, it was not the only challenge to the structure of the union, a fact most eloquently shown by the astonishing number of Dinorwic quarrymen eager to join an unspecified English union, probably the Lancashire Miners' Federation.[78] Another factor was the increasing frustration as the masters remained hostile and intransigent. No meaningful collective bargaining had existed between men and masters since the employers' successful and ruthless offensive in 1885, when recognition had been removed from the men's most powerful organisation to date, the Penrhyn quarry committee, and the Dinorwic men had been locked out and humiliated. Unable to fulfil this function, it was inevitable that frustration and disillusion with the union should follow; what is surprising is that the union managed to retain any followers at all during these bleak years. The nervousness and extreme moderation of the leaders became a cause of disillusion and a real threat to the union's effectiveness. A despondent lodge secretary in Dinorwic in 1890 noted that they had 'lost everything by trying to grasp nothing'.[79] The union's inactivity, partly a consequence of the employers' strength, but reinforced by the beliefs and characters of the union's leadership, called into question for many quarrymen the reason for its existence.

The union's policies were based on a strict adherence to the rules of a market economy: 'approval and acceptance of laissez-faire', it has been pointed out, 'provided a basic theme in the

---

[78] Ponc Wyllt, Dinorwic, wanted to join the Miners' Union, so that we can 'be one united army in defence as well as in attack'. Ibid., 24 January 1890. Sixty men voted to join the Miners' Union in yet another ballot in February 1890. Ibid., 7 February 1890. In March 1890 the Secretary of the N.W.Q.U. wrote to the Lancashire Miners' Federation enquiring about the possibilities of a merger. The Lancashire secretary Thomas Ashton suggested they apply to the North Wales Miners. This matter was not, however, discussed by the N.W.Q.U. executive. Lancashire Miners' Federation, Committee Meeting Minutes, 18 March 1890. I am indebted to John B. Smethurst for this reference.

[79] Ibid., 24 January 1890.

union's attitude on all matters'.[80] This was clearly demonstrated in the union's reaction to the advent of the depression in the late 1870s. In the face of wage reductions, the union argued against any resistance to 'fair' reductions in wages and urged the men not to be 'defiant' in their behaviour; W. J. Parry advised the men to 'Be Respectful to their Superiors' as well as 'Faithful to each other' and the union made every effort to avoid conflict.[81] The union's answer to the crisis was 'forbearance' and an emigration scheme, and despite a wave of small disputes in 1878 and four strikes in the first months of 1880, Robert Parry, the union's new president, could credibly compliment his members for

> the great virtue of forbearance had been signally manifested on the part of the quarrymen . . . 'forbearance' not in the sense it was used towards slaves but forbearance arising out of sincere submission to circumstances and things.[82]

In the face of the depression the union was in no position to put up a real fight and, afraid of seeing its funds spent on bitter and unwinnable strikes, the leaders counselled submission. In this way, they hoped, they could win the scarce but precious 'respect' of the masters and thus salvage something from a sorry period. This was not the only decision that could have been made, and many a N.W.Q.U. member chose otherwise, but it was the only one consistent with the laissez-faire liberalism of the leadership; their policies were securely anchored in the ideological bed-rock of the free activity of market forces.

In any confrontation with the quarry owners, the union's counsel was for peace and patience. This was the theory of co-operation between labour and capital propagated by the founding leaders of the union, pre-eminently by W. J. Parry. It was a theory of labour which insisted upon the right of labour to a 'fair' share of the wealth it created but which was also careful not to make 'unreasonable' demands on capital. A belief in the noble qualities of work—and in the respect due to the workman—was also a belief in the sanctity of private property and the proper respect due to gentlemen. It was an

---

[80] C. Parry, op. cit., p. 37.
[81] N.W.Q.U. Minute Book, 30 September 1878.
[82] C. & D. Herald, 29 May 1880.

ideology well expressed by Robert Parry in his 1881
presidential address:

> It was true that capital was a great power, but it might be
> asked whether it was a self dependent or a dependent power.
> Time need not be wasted to reply to the question. Capital
> was as dependent upon labour as labour was upon capital.
> The one was absolutely necessary to the other.[83]

In this co-operative situation the role of the union was 'not to
separate the workman from the capital, but to regulate the
relation between the two'. The union was seen as a force for
mediation and moderation, disowning the undisciplined within
its own ranks and attempting to curb the overbearing power of
haughty quarry owners.

With the onset of the depression, therefore, the union saw it
as one of its main tasks to control its members. In 1876 the
union had been hard pressed to disassociate itself from the
'riot' in the Hafod y Wern quarry, Betws Garmon, when
several hundred Nantlle quarrymen had terrified Cornish
workers at the quarry. This incident was energetically
condemned by the N.W.Q.U., which claimed that 'not a single
officer connected with the union was aware that such proceedings on the part of the men were to take place, otherwise,
depend upon it, they would have interfered'.[84] And, indeed,
only one of the fifteen quarrymen subsequently charged turned
out to be a union member.

This nervousness about action by their members characterised
the union throughout. In June 1878 they castigated the quarrymen in the Pantdreiniog quarry for taking unauthorised action
which impinged upon managerial prerogatives, and in August
1891 they successfully urged caution on the quarrymen of
Penrhyn who were eager for determined action.[85]

The union's rules had been framed in such a way as to
exercise the greatest possible central control over the strike
weapon. Rule nine insisted that

> no Lodge in any district of the union shall cause or counsel its
> members to strike work without first dispatching a general

[83] Ibid., 28 May 1881.
[84] Ibid., May 1876. See also N.W.Q.U. Minute Book, 19 May 1876.
[85] N.W.Q.U. Minute Book, 29 June 1878, 8 August 1891.

statement to the Executive Council, reporting the facts and matters under dispute with the employers of the district. The Executive shall then depute one or more of its members to the place where the dispute is pending, to investigate the matter at issue, who will bring back a faithful report to the Council. The Council shall then decide whether the members of the union in the district shall leave work or not.[86]

Any lodge not observing this procedure could 'lose the protection of the union'. This rule, however, was hardly effective and the only strictly 'official' strike in the slate industry throughout the nineteenth century was the one called in the small quarry of Rhos in Capel Curig in December 1877.[87] On every other occasion the union had to accept the decision of the local lodge; this was especially true in the industry's major disputes at Dinorwic 1885, Llechwedd 1893, and Penrhyn 1896–7, 1900–3, where the union only became involved sometime after the disputes had already started.

Embarrassed by industrial conflict, the union leaders envisaged their major role as being that of a pressure-group acting on behalf of the quarrymen in a wider sphere. This was particularly true following the return to the active leadership of the union in 1884 of W. J. Parry, the union's first general secretary. Parry led the union away from its previously largely abstentionist political role and developed for it an energetic sectionalist campaign on the question of an inspectorate for slate quarries. From then on the union was to press in Parliament for particular demands with relevance to the slate industry. As W. J. Parry explained in 1885, 'we do not wish for anyone to look at the union as the instrument of a political party . . . but at the same time we are for the union to be felt in the political world'. Parry steered the union into an active political role which he saw as being an important force in Gwynedd politics, for in order to win their demands the quarrymen had to ensure that they were sympathetically represented; 'you must', Parry emphasised, 'insist on men who will sympathise with you and will do something for you'. In giving this advice the political effects of the 1884 Reform Act

[86] M. Richards, op. cit., p. 140.
[87] N.W.Q.U. Minute Book, 29 December, 1877.

were uppermost in his mind and he congratulated the quarrymen for 'coming into possession of the right to use their voice
in the choice of those men who in the future will legislate on
their behalf. This is a priceless acquisition.'[88]

The union continued to steer clear of explicitly stating a
political allegiance, although the point of Parry's words must
have been obvious to all. The union, in fact, although energetic
in its denials of political bias, was never shy about making
political statements. In 1878 the union council agreed to
organise a petition calling for the appointment of J.P.s who
were 'in sympathy with the working class';[89] in 1883 they sent
a deputation to lobby Gladstone on electoral reform;[90] in 1886
the union urged further colonisation in a petition to Parliament;
in 1887 they condemned the opening of museums on the
Sabbath; in 1888 they sent a delegate to a Free-Trade conference.[91] Nevertheless, the union's major campaigns were on
sectionalist issues of direct relevance to the slate quarries
though even these led them into more openly political stances:
in March 1894, for example, the union condemned in no
uncertain terms both the House of Lords and local Members
of Parliament for the peers' action in removing a crucial clause
from an act to defend workmen's interests.[92]

The union also campaigned on the dire economic condition
of the slate industry, blaming the continuing depression in trade
on the total lack of co-operation displayed by the quarry
owners, most disturbing being the cut-throat cutting of prices
as the masters competed for a share of the shrunken market.
The union also accused the masters of a lack of drive, of failing
to build up new export markets in the colonies and elsewhere.
The advice met with some sympathy from smaller quarries
facing difficulties as a result of the policies of the large concerns,
but was ignored by the major owners in the industry. A letter
from W. J. Parry to all the owners in 1884 had a limited success
in that it did at least result in the owners meeting to discuss
pricing-policies, but the union itself was not invited, being

[88] *Y Genedl Gymreig*, 20 May 1885.
[89] N.W.Q.U. Minute Book, 23 March 1878.
[90] Ibid., 29 December 1883, this move had been strongly opposed by the
Penrhyn Lodge (see GAS, Penrhyn Lodge Minute Book, 21 December 1883).
[91] N.W.Q.U. Minute Book, 8 May 1886, 24 September 1887, 3 March 1888.
[92] Ibid., 3 March 1894.

reminded that the state of the market and the price of slates were a question for the owners and not for the union.[93] This was a view that the union's leadership refused to accept and they were consistently free with their advice on economic and managerial questions. Parry himself was probably the most intelligent and well-informed commentator on the state of the slate trade in the country, and it was to their subsequent cost that the owners consistently chose not to heed his advice.

The N.W.Q.U., therefore, was a largely campaigning union rather than one deeply involved in developing structures of collective bargaining or conducting an aggressive industrial policy. This reflected not only the difficult conditions of the industry but also the marked predilection of the union's leadership. The union had an interesting leadership characterised above all by the fact that the moving spirits were not themselves quarrymen. The union's president for the first couple of years was John Lloyd Jones, an 'extensive quarry proprietor in the Nantlle Valley', the general secretary was W. J. Parry of Bethesda, a radical tradesman, and other early members were schoolteachers and journalists, W. J. Williams (later to become general secretary), J. O. Griffith (Ioan Arfon), J. J. Hughes and W. E. Williams.[94] The Caernarfon bank manager, Hugh Pugh, and Ffestiniog surgeon, David Thomas, also played prominent roles in the first meetings. Some of these were to drop out as the union grew, but W. J. Williams and W. J. Parry were to continue to play leading roles in the union until the late 1890s.

W. J. Williams took over as general secretary in June 1876 and remained in substantial control of the union until his resignation in 1897. W. J. Parry served the union in many roles, first as general secretary, then as president, trustee and adviser until he, too, resigned in July 1898.[95] The only two quarrymen to play prominent roles in the early days of the

[93] Ibid., 28 June 1884; *Y Genedl Gymreig*, 20 May 1885.
[94] *C. & D. Herald*, 26 September 1874. Morgan Richards, another business man, appears to have been the president for the first few months.
[95] William John Parry (1842–1927) was a prominent Liberal as well as leader of the N.W.Q.U.; chairman of Caernarvonshire County Council, 1892–3; editor, *Y Werin* 1885–88; an author and journalist, his books included *Caebraichycafn: yr Ymdrafodaeth* (1875); *Chwareli a Chwarelwyr* (1897); *The Penrhyn Lock-Out, Statement and Appeal* (1901); *The Cry of the People* (1906). See J. Roose Williams, *Quarryman's Champion, The Life and Activities of William John Parry of Coetmor* (Denbigh, 1978).

union were the two Robert Parrys—Robert Parry, Ceunant, elected vice-president in 1875 and president in 1880, and Robert Parry of the Caebraichycafn (Penrhyn) lodge, elected vice-president in 1880.

The predominant influence in the councils of the union, therefore, was that of Gwynedd's extremely active radical middle class and some, at least, of the union's policies sprang from that fact. Whatever the issue at stake, the union's propaganda was always the authentic, outraged voice of a frustrated, articulate, nonconformist middle class struggling, as always, against the power and control of Anglican, Tory, land-owning quarry owners. To a very large extent, of course, they were expressing the anger of a good many quarrymen; there was no sign until the end of the century of the future fissure between Labour and Liberal. They were the political leadership of Gwynedd radicalism and radical quarrymen were, by and large, happy to follow their lead. This meant, however, that the N.W.Q.U. failed to give sufficient priority to the need for a positive industrial policy and the development of effective collective-bargaining structures. Trade unionism is essentially about bargaining, and while intransigent owners, in some instances, made this a virtual impossibility, this was by no means true of all quarries. The union never fully grasped this fact and made no real attempt to develop strong organisation where it really mattered, at the point of production. Only in the Penrhyn quarries was there anything approaching tight trade-union organisation, and this was often admitted shamefacedly by the union (and later downrightly denied). Trade unionism was conceived of as a statement of belief, a stand, rather than as a method of collective bargaining. Seen as a matter of preference rather than as an obligation, membership of the union was inevitably to remain low.

This situation caused strains within the N.W.Q.U. as well as disillusion with it. Not even the energetic and able W. J. Parry escaped without some criticism from within the union for his over-ready tendency to compromise in order to end conflict. His role in arriving at the unsatisfactory settlement to the Dinorwic lock-out in 1886 attracted some criticism and the union council was moved to pass a vote of confidence in him in order to dispel some 'unsubstantiated fables' being spread about his role in the dispute.[96] More serious was his disagreement with the Penrhyn strike committee during the 1896–7 dispute, which eventually led to his severing of connections with the union's new leaders.

It was W. J. Williams, rather than W. J. Parry, however, who was the greatest subject of dispute within the union. Born in Bethesda in 1839, Williams did spend some time as a quarry worker when a boy, but he returned to full-time education, spent some time in the Normal College and qualified as a teacher, becoming headmaster of the British School in Bethel. He later became a chartered accountant. He held several posts with the Caernarfon council and was for a time secretary of the local Liberal Association.[97] Elected general secretary in 1877, he moved the union's headquarters to his own office in 1878 and divided his time between union work and his own business and political interests. There was an unsuccessful attempt to remove him in 1884, when delegates to the union's conference from Waunfawr and Ffestiniog proposed that the 'secretary should be chosen from amongst the quarrymen themselves'.[98] He was criticised for his lack of activity during the Dinorwic lock-out when he was more active in supporting the Liberal Party during the election than in assisting the locked-out quarrymen.[99] Two years later, fairly detailed charges of inefficiency and mismanagement were brought against him on the union council, particularly serious being the fact that he had represented local businessmen in cases against quarrymen. He was ordered to stop this practice and also to put up a sign on his office door indicating that the room was the union's headquarters as well as being an accountant's office.

Following the failure of the wages campaign of 1892–3, Williams came under increasing pressure and there is no question that the campaign to elect a full-time organiser for the union which gathered momentum in the early 1890s was a reflection of the increasing suspicion with which Williams was viewed. The final breach came in 1897 following the end

[96] GAS, Llyfr Cofnodion . . . Dinorwic, 20 January 1888; N.W.Q.U. Minute Book, 20 February 1886. See also pp. 156–57.
[97] U.C.N.W. Coetmor MS. 44, p. 50.
[98] Y Genedl Gymreig, 14 May 1884.
[99] This and other charges were levelled against him in June 1887, N.W.Q.U. Minute Book, 4 June 1887.

of the Penrhyn dispute; the Penrhyn leaders claimed that
Williams had undermined and effectively sabotaged the men's
negotiations, and a bitter struggle ensued to remove him.[100]
A new post of financial secretary was created and its purpose,
'to uproot an old official', was clearly understood. Williams
refused to work with any new officer and resigned.[101] Elected
as financial secretary was the tough and able spokesman from
Bethesda, W. H. Williams.[102]

W. J. Williams had never committed himself totally to the
union. He was always deeply involved in his other concerns
and there is no question that the union suffered from his
indifferent generalship. For not only did he fail to pursue the
union's interests as energetically as he could have, but his
presence was in some instances an actual hindrance to recruitment. In Dinorwic, in particular, there was widespread
hostility towards him and it was reported as early as 1893 that
some men were refusing to join the union until he was
removed.[103]

It was not until the late 1890s, therefore, that the N.W.Q.U.
developed an able and energetic quarryman as their leader.
In the early 1880s the two Robert Parrys had exerted an
influence, but their period of office had not been particularly
successful and was later to be criticised by W. J. Parry when,
in 1884, he was once again recalled to instil into the union some
direction and energy. Referring to the previous four years of
stagnation, Parry made a forceful attack during the 1885
conference on indifference and inactivity: 'the principles of
union and brotherhood are good in themselves', he declared,
'but useless if practical use is not made of them. They are
beautiful to look at, but their value is in their practice. The
principled inactive unionist is worth nothing to society'[104]—a
pointed critique of a philosophy of unionism which had gained

---

[100] The charges were detailed in 'Statement by W. H. Williams', etc., N.L.W.
D. R. Daniel MS. 2496.
[101] N.W.Q.U. Minute Book, 28 August 1897, 25 September 1897.
[102] W. H. Williams, 1848–1917, financial secretary N.W.Q.U., a formidable
quarrymen's leader from the Penrhyn quarries. E. M. Humphreys, 'W. H.
Williams', *Gwŷr Enwog Gynt* (1950), pp. 113–23; John Williams, 'Rynys, *Braslun
Buddugol o William H. Williams, Arafon* (1896); see also pp. 204–209.
[103] GAS, Llyfr Cofnodion . . . Dinorwic, 24 September 1893.
[104] *Y Genedl Gymreig*, 20 May 1885.

much currency in the N.W.Q.U. Parry's own recipe for action was an invigorated sectionalist Parliamentary campaign.

In 1874 the 'friends of the quarrymen', who had come to the men's assistance in founding and staffing their union, gave as the reason for their intervention the prevailing fear of victimisation amongst the quarrymen, a fear well-based on the experiences of previous years. This was a valid reason, but it leaves unanswered the question of why no significant trade-union leader, other than Robert Parry, who died at the relatively young age of 43 in 1884, rose from the ranks of the quarrymen to lead the union until very nearly the end of the century.[105] Victimisation and the fear of it cannot be a sufficient reason, if only because not all quarrymen were in the desperate plight of the Dinorwic and Penrhyn men. More significantly, many quarrymen did play prominent roles in the union as annual presidents and vice-presidents, roles that exposed them to all the dangers of victimisation but allowed them little continuing influence over the development of the union. There were many individual quarrymen, moreover, who demonstrated many times their willingness to risk and suffer victimisation for the sake of trade unionism in their own quarries—why not, therefore, for position and influence in the union itself?

For almost a quarter of a century the quarrymen allowed their union's course to be steered largely by men who were not themselves quarrymen and who had political and business interests outside the union. These leaders were able and articulate exponents of radical Welsh Liberalism and they drew their policies and their attitudes from that radicalism rather than from any trade-union tradition of collective bargaining and regulated workplace relations. The union for them was another and important part of the general struggle of the people against landlordism and Anglicanism; the union's successes and failures were judged in relation to this general context rather than strictly in the light of the union's day-to-day effectiveness on the ground. Thus the union persistently interpreted the major battles in the quarries as being struggles for political and religious emancipation when in truth most of

---

[105] Robert Parry, 1841–84, 'a deep philosopher and a faithful and hard working deacon' from Ceunant, Llanrug. *Y Genedl Gymreig*, 9 January 1884.

the struggles, while indeed being blows for freedom and against autocracy, were also firmly rooted in the level of wages and the nature of working conditions in the quarries.

It was the union's consistent failure to develop a united industrial policy, linking its campaigning efforts to the day-to-day conflicts in the quarries which above all reflected the influence of its middle-class leaders. For W. J. Parry and W.J. Williams the battle must have often seemed a battle of words to be fought not with industrial action but with acid newspaper articles and eloquent testimony to commissions and committees. Parry was himself a master propagandist, marshalling his facts, his arguments and his emotional appeals in an often brilliant fashion. Trade-union negotiation, however, is not just a matter of arguments; it involves also the threat and the use of industrial power as a bargaining counter. The N.W.Q.U.'s leadership never bargained with the threat of action as a weapon. With one minor exception, the union never called or even threatened to call a strike. The campaign for higher wages, which seemed as if it might unite all the quarrymen in the early 1890s, was abandoned in favour of a move to collect more information about existing wage-rates in order to construct a more conclusive case for the men. Not one of the major disputes in the industry was called or organised by the union itself; it was the individual lodges, forced by conditions in their quarries, who invariably initiated and strove to control the action.

This was not, of course, a reflection on the leadership alone; it also to a large measure reflected the consciousness of the quarrymen themselves. Despite the often-expressed complaints within the union, the majority of members were willing to support the policies of the dominant leaders until the mid-nineties. For they, too, were adherents of much the same radical Liberalism, with all that credo's cultural associations, as their leaders, and they shared with them similar views on the co-operation of labour and capital. It was not so much these 'moderate' beliefs which weakened the N.W.Q.U.; until the growth of new unionism in the late 1880s these were the commonly-held beliefs of most trade unionists throughout Britain. The weakness of the N.W.Q.U. lay in the fact that these moderate, conciliatory policies went hand in hand with a failure to grasp fully the importance of effective trade-union organisation at the base. The union never even fully distinguished between members and non-members, a failure which did not encourage quarrymen to join. It was with pride that the union claimed that it represented non-unionists in negotiations. The lodges tried with varying degrees of success to sort out this confusion, but the union itself never stressed sufficiently the need for all quarrymen to join the union, not just as a matter of principle, but as the only sure guarantee of effective bargaining.

The union's relative inactivity and ineffectiveness on the bargaining front and its failure to define adequately membership of a trade union inevitably led to some disillusion and made it even more difficult to recruit new members. 'We are presently under a wave of failure', reported the Penrhyn lodge in 1889, 'would it not be better to give up the union? Many of those who are paying are very soft, many of those who will not pay say that they are as good trade unionists as we are.'[106]

The history of any group of workers is not synonymous with the history of their trade union. This is peculiarly true of the quarrymen. There was, in the last quarter of the nineteenth century, a section of the quarrymen, a sizeable minority, who were committed trade unionists; there was also a smaller but still significant minority who were as bitterly opposed to the union. What is striking is that the majority of quarrymen, ready on occasion to struggle valiantly for what they considered to be their rights, paid only a lukewarm allegiance to the N.W.Q.U.; they were prepared, at times, to join the organisation, but on the whole they viewed the union with indifference and at times with grave suspicion. Much of the reason for this lay in the nature of the industry and the attitudes of men and masters, but some of the blame must also rest with the N.W.Q.U. itself, with its structure, and with the character and policies of its leadership.

---

[106] N.W.Q.U. Minute Book, 27 April 1889.

Part 2
Conflict
VI
DINORWIC AND LLECHWEDD

I. THE DINORWIC LOCK-OUT 1885–6

By the mid-nineteenth century the Dinorwic quarries near Llanberis were a vast and profitable enterprise, the second largest slate quarry in the world and soon to become the largest; only the Penrhyn quarry, gouging into the mountain from the northern side was at that time bigger. In 1859, 2,000 men were employed and it was estimated that the quarry produced some £70,000 annual profit for its owner.[1] By 1885 the quarry employed 2,700 men who produced 90,000 tons of slate annually. The men were drawn from over sixty towns and hamlets in Caernarvonshire and Anglesey, though the great majority, and almost all of the skilled quarrymen, lived in the villages and hamlets that had grown up around the quarry.[2] Many of the labourers who travelled long distances to their work, particularly those from Anglesey, stayed throughout the week in 'barracks' near their work and returned home only for Saturday afternoons and Sundays. The owner of the quarries in 1885 was George William Duff Assheton-Smith, who had inherited the Vaynol estates from his uncle, the second Thomas Assheton-Smith, on his coming of age in 1869.[3] On his estate, covering 36,000 acres and worth an annual rental of some £25,000, lived 1,800 tenants.[4]

---

[1] *Mining Journal*, 10 September 1859.
[2] GAS, DQ. 1560. Of a total of 783 men working in the Garret Department of Dinorwic in 1902, over half came from Ebenezer (now Deiniolen), Dinorwic and Clwtybont. Fewer than 150 men came from over 10 miles' distance, of whom 50 were from Anglesey; of these only 8 were skilled quarrymen. 506 of the 589 skilled men in the department lived in the immediate vicinity of the quarry.
[3] When he had also assumed the name Assheton-Smith.
[4] J. E. Vincent, *The Land Question in North Wales* (London, 1896), p. 273. Bateman, op cit., quotes a rental figure of £42,000. See p. 12.

The dispute which broke out in the quarry in October 1885 was an eventful and important one. Just as the earlier victory of the Dinorwic men in 1874 had been a harbinger of success for the North Wales Quarrymen's Union, so the dispute of 1885 introduced long, desolate years of managerial aggression and bitter defeats for the slate-quarrymen. The famous drama that was later to unfold in the Penrhyn disputes of 1896–7 and 1900–3 followed a remarkably similar course to the events of 1885 in Dinorwic.

The dispute took place against a disturbed background: the general election of November 1885, riots of the unemployed in London in February 1886, and in north Wales general agitation over the land question leading to disturbances over the payment of tithes, and a violent labour dispute in the Llanddulas limestone quarries. North Wales figured so prominently in these agitations that the Dinorwic dispute itself attracted considerable and excited discussion. H. H. Hyndman of the Social Democratic Federation visited the area in January 1886 and wrote a long and uncharacteristically detailed account of his visit in the S.D.F.'s *Justice*, in which he expressed the somewhat premature hope that

> we shall be able to organise social-democracy through the District. The ideas are already spreading despite the Nationalism of the people.[5]

Following the lock-out of 1874, which had witnessed the birth of the North Wales Quarrymen's Union, industrial relations at Dinorwic were fairly relaxed, with few major issues cropping up to disturb either master or men. The depression of the late seventies, however, hit hard and the last two months of 1878 witnessed a general wage reduction of 20 per cent and before the end of the year short-time, four- and three-day working, was in operation. In January 1879, 200 men were dismissed and another 100 were turned away in March; wages were cut again three times during the year and in January 1880 the price for working third-quality slate was reduced and a new rule introduced insisting that a quarryman's

[5] *Justice*, 23 January 1886.

count of slates amount to hundreds rather than to the half-hundreds which had been customary.

The men accepted these blows without protest, realising that bad times brought bad wages, but they were perturbed when their efforts to negotiate on dismissals in January 1879 were brusquely swept aside by their employer. Since 1874 Assheton-Smith had always received delegations from the men, treating them courteously and often acceding to their requests. Times had changed, however, and in 1879 the master replied that 'Mr. Assheton-Smith did not intend seeing a deputation on the application of the men, as he cannot see that any benefit could be derived from it'. In 1880 things were to get worse, for in that year there was a change in the management of the quarry and the mellow Colonel Wyatt was replaced by the stricter John Davies, soon to be accompanied by the strongly anti-union Hon. W. W. Vivian; 'with the change of medium', complained the men, 'came also a change in everything'.[6]

The new management was accused of introducing a régime of favouritism and partiality at the quarry, and it continually infuriated local opinion by its political and religious sympathies. Following the general election of 1880, known Tory voters and supporters were rewarded and it was claimed that they were paid a bonus of £1 monthly for their services;[7] even more important, it was also suggested that they were granted the best bargains in the quarry and were more likely to be appointed to minor supervisory jobs. The fact that it seemed as if favour and not skill had earned them these positions enraged the majority of quarrymen, for 'nothing could be more irritating to the best feelings of an honest workman'. Feelings were further embittered as it became apparent that the custom of a son's following his father into the quarry was being interrupted by the introduction of what looked suspiciously like an informal religious and political test, and some of the boys entering the quarry were strangers to the area but, it was alleged, with loyalist fathers. It is impossible to gauge how

[6] *The Lock-Out at the Dinorwic Quarries* (Caernarfon), 1885, signed by the Lock-Out Committee.

[7] There certainly was bribery in the quarry: the Dinorwic Quarry papers contain an undated list of 15 men 'who received the £1. 0. 0. Mr. Assheton Smith for defending him'. Of the 15, 10 were Anglicans, 5 Nonconformists.

widespread this practice had become and it is difficult to believe that it was true of very many new workers, but in the depression and unemployment of the 1880s even a handful of recruits chosen in this way would have been seen by the quarrymen as a grave threat to their families; it was also a serious undermining of the relationship which had previously existed between men and master in Dinorwic. When Assheton-Smith was approached about this state of affairs in 1881 he made it clear that he still considered it to be 'his first duty to give preference to the children of his own tenants'; this duty, the men claimed, was persistently ignored by the quarry managers. Relationships deteriorated rapidly in the quarry and a dispute over the Employers' Liability Act in 1881 embittered them further. Assheton-Smith, along with Lord Penrhyn, immediately demanded that the men should contract out of the law, for he saw it as a slight on the good intentions of the employer and an interference in his freedom of action (contracting out legally was in fact impossible; what was aimed at was a promise from the men that they would not back up or initiate any prosecutions under the law). The men's almost unanimous decision in January 1881 was to remain under the protection of the act. The managers retaliated by threatening to dismember the various welfare services offered by the quarry: by removing their support from the Workmen's Benefit Club, closing the quarry hospital and letting the doctor's residence to someone else, and by discontinuing the payment of pensions.

The men replied by reaffirming their desire to remain under the act, though compromising considerably on the implications of so doing. By setting up an arbitration board which would judge cases, they hoped to avoid recourse to the law itself and to the courts; moreover, they were ready to contribute themselves to the fund for injured persons. Assheton-Smith would have nothing to do with such a scheme, pointing out that either they worked under the act or they did not; there was no possibility of compromise. The men pleaded for the whole matter to go to arbitration, but the only response of the management was to return the bank and cheque books of the Benefit Club to its quarryman secretary. The men yielded, claiming that they did not wish to 'endanger the good feeling that had existed between them and Mr. Assheton-Smith', perhaps more accurately that they did not wish to endanger the fruits of his paternalism, and they signed an agreement contracting themselves out of the law on 1 March 1881.

Encouraged by its victory, the management continued in its attempt to reorganise the working relations at the quarry, and things had come to such a pass that in June 1882 the men appealed that they be allowed to explain their opposition to a manager's setting evaluation of a bargain. The men sent a deputation representing the whole works to see John Davies, the works manager, to raise the question, but he refused to allow more than two of them to speak and informed them that no deputations would be received in future and that all communications were to be in writing. The rudeness with which the deputation was treated, even more than the manager's ruling on further deputations, soured relationships considerably, for the men felt that they had been 'insulted through their representatives'. [8]

Until 1882 the managers had been tightening existing customs and regulations as far as they could; now they started to introduce new rules which were eventually to lead to the explosion of October 1885. In this they were acting in step with most of the employers in the industry.

In an overwhelmingly labour-intensive industry, the effort to maintain profit levels in a declining market led not only to a cutting of wages but also to a confrontation with the customs and agreements which underlay wages. Compared with Penrhyn, production at Dinorwic appeared to be more expensive: in the early 'eighties production at Penrhyn was almost 40 tons per employee per year; in Dinorwic production was under 32 tons per employee. [9] W. W. Vivian, the new general manager of the quarry and a man with wide experience of business affairs, was not impressed with such a state of affairs. He determined that the men's customs would have to be altered and also that the labour force at the quarry would have to be drastically reduced. The months previous to the dispute were dominated by the attack on customs; the other aim, of reducing the work-force, did not become apparent until

---

[8] This account is taken largely from *The Lock-Out at the Dinorwic Quarries*.
[9] In 1882 the 2,757 men at Dinorwic produced 87,429 tons of slate; in Penrhyn in the same year 2,809 men produced 116,116 tons.

well into the dispute itself.[10] At the end of 1882 a number of verbal bye-laws and working rules were introduced which the quarrymen considered 'unnecessary and oppressive',[11] but they led to no major incidents. The situation in fact seemed to be easing and a proposed protest by the men against the continuing favouritism in the works was pre-empted in August 1884 when the management summoned a deputation to inform them that all such favouritism and discrimination would be discontinued in the future, and that the 'workmen from then on would be looked at quite apart from their religious and political beliefs'.[12] All were now to be subjected equally to the stringent new rules that were being introduced and enforced. It was on this issue, rather than on the question of religious and political discrimination, that the storm was to break. Religion and politics, however, had ensured that relationships in the quarry were as tense and bitter as they could be and the record of the management in the five years previous to the lock-out ensured that it was distrusted and hated by a large body of the quarrymen.

Part of the accepted rhythm of the quarry month had always been the day off at its end, but in early 1885 the men working in the Steam Mills section of the quarry, most of whom were bargain takers, were refused this customary full holiday and were forced to work until 10 a.m. on that day, an imposition which caused much disquiet.[13] Then, in July, came the first clash arising initially out of a relatively minor incident: Davies, the resident manager, saw a few men, perhaps ten, leaving their work early and climbing up from their workplace to the top of one of the tips, where they stood for a while waiting for the final hooter to sound.[14] When Davies attempted to find out from their workmates who these men were he received no response and all the men pleaded ignorance of the

---

[10] Vivian's aims were revealed years later in a letter to Lord Penrhyn, 10 November 1902, in which he disclosed that as a result of the closure of the quarry, 'I was enabled . . . to carry out my scheme as to reorganising the Quarries, staff etc., and to start the Dinorwic Quarries afresh in 1886 under entirely changed conditions, regulations and staff.' GAS, DQ. 2054.

[11] *The Lock-Out*, p. 6.

[12] GAS, Cofnodydd Penderfyniadau Pwyllgor y Gwaith Caebraichycafn, 5 September 1884.

[13] *The Lock-Out*, p. 6.

[14] *Y Genedl Gymreig*, 29 July 1885.

early departures. Furious at this attitude, Davies suspended the whole gallery of fifty-three men for eight days.[15]

When, the next day, it became known in the quarry that this punishment was being carried out and that the men had been suspended, the whole of the upper section of the quarry ceased working and marched down to hold a meeting, where they were joined by all the other workmen. The meeting was an angry one, the main topic being the management's policy of 'restricting the freedom of the worker by introducing endless petty rules'.[16] The men complained not only of the rules themselves but also of the uncertainty they produced, for the managers were experimenting by introducing rules one day and modifying them or repealing them the next. The men's case was that the 'over exactness in petty, worthless and arbitrary rules, and those being made by ignorant and inexperienced men, being constantly changed and transgressing old customs which have been in force in the quarry for years is certainly intolerable'.[17] After the meeting the men went back to their work, but their spontaneous and united action had been an impressive warning to the managers, and the dispirited unionists in Penrhyn marvelled at the spirit being shown in Dinorwic, and were envious of the absence of the bitter rivalry among the men which was characteristic of their situation.[18]

Vivian, the principal manager, though warning that any further mass-meetings during working hours would not be tolerated, in fact accepted the case that the suspension of the fifty-three had been a mistake and he admitted that Davies had made 'an error of judgement'.[19] The suspended men, however, were only allowed a day's pay in lieu of their eight-day absence, a payment which infuriated the men for 'if they were entitled to one day's wage they were certainly entitled to eight'.[20] The fact that Vivian had admitted the management's error led the radical press to hail the events as a victory for the quarrymen; but as a letter from a Dinorwic quarryman in the *Genedl Gymreig* reminded them, 'the general oppression in the

[15] *The Lock-Out*, p. 6.
[16] *Y Genedl Gymreig*, 29 July 1885.
[17] Ibid.
[18] Ibid., 5 August 1885.
[19] *The Lock-Out*, p. 6.
[20] Ibid.

form of strict and repressive rules, insulting to any man who holds that he is a man' still remained.[21] The writer complained that the negotiating committee had failed to bring their agreement to a mass-meeting which, he claimed, would have sent them back for something more substantial. Such was the atmosphere in the quarry that it must have been obvious that it would need only one more incident to lead to a real clash, which could not now be long averted.

That incident happened in October and the scene was again the Steam Mills.[22] The men there, goaded already by having their monthly holiday curtailed, were informed ten minutes before they were due to stop working that they were to continue until noon, thereby cutting their leisure time by another two hours. The men objected and, claiming that they understood that the ruling was to apply in any case to the following month, left their work at 10 a.m. The men claimed that they had been granted permission to leave by the resident manager, something which he hotly denied. The men were suspended for a week for leaving their work early and all the appeals made to the managers were rejected; in consequence, the whole body of quarrymen gathered together on 12 October to protest again at what they considered a grave injustice. They were refused permission to meet in the quarry and so marched some miles to another spot to hold their meeting. They returned to work the next day and there was relative calm for ten days until the management, on 23 October, posted a notice in the quarry which read:

Notice to all Men and Boys employed at the Dinorwic Quarries.
Inasmuch as a mass meeting was held during work hours on Monday afternoon, the 12th October instant, in defiance of an order made in July last when you were cautioned that such a meeting, if held during work hours, would not be tolerated,
        Notice is hereby given,
That your services will not be required after Saturday, the 31st October instant; and that all barrack furniture, tools,

[21] *Y Genedl Gymreig*, 19 August 1885.
[22] *The Lock-Out*, p. 6.

velocipedes, materials, and other effects, belonging to you
must be removed before twelve o'clock at noon on Saturday,
the 31st October instant . . .[23]

There was no doubt that the lock-out had been engineered
by the managers. Their exact motives are not clear, but a
major aim must have been to force the men to accept with less
protestation the far-reaching new regulations that were being
introduced; to show finally and unmistakably who held the
whip hand. The men, however, were also determined not to
accept the reorganisation without some resistance, and
spontaneous demonstrations, such as the two one-day walk-outs
that had already occurred, might well have persisted and
grown into strike action. For the men were irreconcilably
opposed to some of the rules, considering them to strike at
their fundamental rights as quarrymen. The rules they most
objected to were those which restricted their liberties; it was
not, for example, permissible to sell any newspapers in the
quarry nor to organise any sort of collection without the
permission of the manager.[24] In particular, the men objected
to those regulations which curtailed or interfered with their
spare time. As bargain-takers (and 2,100 of the 2,700 involved
were bargain-takers[25]) they believed it to be their right to
determine, within limits, when they were to work and that if
a man had a pressing engagement to meet or task to perform
outside the quarry then he had the right to leave; the need to
earn proper wages, and to satisfy his partners, would, it was
thought, impose a sufficient discipline. The management,
however, had introduced a rule which insisted that if a man
was to be away from the quarry he had to receive permission
from the overlooker for short absences and from the manager
if he was to be away for more than a day. This must have
seemed fairly reasonable to them and, indeed, even the *Genedl
Gymreig*, extremely sympathetic as it was to the men's case,
considered it fair.[26] To the quarrymen, however, it was an
intolerable invasion of their freedom and dignity. One period
of persistent absence from work which the management was

[23] Ibid., pp. 6, 7.
[24] *Y Genedl Gymreig*, 4 November 1885.
[25] *The Lock-Out*, p. 4.
[26] *Y Genedl Gymreig*, 19 August 1885.

specifically keen to discourage was the annual hay harvest. They accepted that a man had a right to stay at home to gather his own hay and even that his neighbour had the right to assist him, but they refused to allow men to go to work in the harvest of others apart from their immediate neighbours. This was an attempt to prevent men, many of whom did not themselves have any land, from spending too much time away from the quarry and travelling round the country to work in the hay. How common this practice had been we do not know, but it must have been fairly widespread for this was the rule, above all others, to which the men objected most. It was, in fact, a patently absurd and unfair rule based on an ignorance of local conditions, for friendship and kinship ties, rather than just neighbourliness, were the main criteria for such work in an area like this; thus, a man would surely wish to help his own quarry partner in the harvest even though he lived some distance away, while he might not at all feel so compelled to help at a smallholding adjoining his own home, which might in any case be in a village. To make matters worse, the definition of neighbourliness originally adopted by the management was one based on parish boundaries, which made the case of a man with the boundary running between his home and his friend's farm an obviously unjust one. *Y Genedl Gymreig* pounced on these anomalies[27] and reported at some length (in a style typical of much Welsh radical journalism of the period) the hypothetical case of the quarryman who was forced to stay at home and watch his poor, widowed mother struggle on the other side of the lake to get her few precious loads of hay gathered before the approaching cloudburst washed them away.

It was not so much these particulars which infuriated the men, however, but the attack on their freedom implicit in them; for, as we have seen, it was part of their definition of a quarryman that he was able to regulate his own working life within what they considered to be the palpably obvious bounds of common sense.[28] Even so, had the management been one which they could have trusted, the men might well have

[27] Ibid., 29 July 1885.
[28] Ibid.

acceded to the rule; Vivian and Davies, however, were not men they trusted and they feared that to ask permission of them would have often brought the answer 'No'. That was why the meeting of 12 October had passed a motion of no confidence in the managers and why the men were to call for their removal.

The lock-out continued through November with no significant moves from either side and with numerous appeals to the men to avoid the public houses,[29] to behave in a manner deserving of the honour accorded the quarrymen,[30] and to remain united; many hymns were sung and prayer meetings sought guidance from above.[31] The union as such had played a very small role in the whole matter, though one of its vice-presidents, Griffith Griffiths, originally of Portmadoc, was also a member of the eight-man strike committee. Now, however, the men turned to their union for relief; it is not known exactly what percentage of the men were fully-paid-up members of the union but the initial payments made would suggest that there were some 1,400 members eligible to receive lock-out pay of 10s. a week, i.e., just over half of the men involved.[32] Others may have been members but were not eligible. The question of relief immediately brought a serious problem and the threat of dissension, as those who were not members of the union looked enviously at those receiving lock-out pay. A mass-meeting in early November urged the union members to share their money with others[33] and this did indeed happen, but the matter was to cause further dispute in early February 1886.[34]

Support came from many quarters. At the beginning of December, Nantlle quarrymen declared their solidarity at a large meeting[35] and in the following week a meeting of Bethesda shopkeepers and merchants also pledged their support;[36] at a well-attended meeting in Caernarfon, a local watchmaker

[29] Ibid., 4 November 1885.
[30] Ibid., 11 November 1885.
[31] Ibid., 4 November 1885.
[32] GAS, N.W.Q.U., Minute Book, 26 December 1885. £1,427 was paid out per fortnight; the full rate of lock-out pay was 10s. a member.
[33] Y Genedl Gymreig, 4 November 1885.
[34] C. & D. Herald, 6 February 1886; see also GAS, DQ. 2275.
[35] Y Genedl Gymreig, 16 December 1885.
[36] Ibid., 23 December 1885.

promised that 'while a loaf remained in Caernarfon it would be shared with the quarrymen',[37] and £230 was raised further to emphasise the point. Collections were also made in the rich Welsh chapels of Liverpool,[38] whose members saw the struggle as one for religious freedom.[39]

The union's funds, slowly built up since 1874, were being drained and on 23 January[40] the union council urgently discussed a plan for levying union members, a plan which the lodges rejected in favour of collections.[41] In February, payments to Dinorwic had to be discontinued,[42] and by March, the union's coffers were quite empty.[43]

By early December, the managers had decided that the men had learnt their lesson and were ready to accept defeat; on 9 December a list of rules, including all those to which the men had originally objected, was formulated by Vivian and publicised. They were to be accepted by all those seeking work at the quarry, which would reopen to take men on again on Monday, 15 December. A mass-meeting of all the men decided not to return under the rules nor indeed under the existing management,[44] but it was with some apprehension that they approached the morning of the fifteenth, for though there had not until then been many willing to blackleg (those that had, had had their names published in *Y Werin*),[45] there had been rumours that a substantial body was now willing to restart work on the employer's terms and to attend the quarry on Monday morning. Consequently, preparations were made and 15 December was to be a memorable day in the history of Dinorwic.

Early on Monday morning a large crowd of quarrymen and their wives gathered on the road to the quarry, many of the men armed with cudgels;[46] they were there to guard against anyone who might have wished to work that morning and,

[37] *C. & D. Herald*, 2 January 1886.
[38] Ibid., 16 January 1886.
[39] *Pall Mall Gazette*, n.d. (U.C.N.W., Coetmor MSS., 46, p. 30).
[40] N.W.Q.U. Minute Book, 23 January 1886.
[41] Ibid., 30 January 1886; see also Caebraichycafn Minute Book, 27 January 1886.
[42] *C. & D. Herald*, 13 February 1886.
[43] N.W.Q.U., Minute Book, 13 March 1886.
[44] *Y Genedl Gymreig*, 16 December 1885.
[45] Ibid., 11 November 1885.
[46] There are two reports of the incident in *Y Genedl Gymreig*, 16 December 1885.

had their picket been successful, they might well have all gone home later in the day without any disturbance. By coincidence, however, Monday the 15th was also the day on which Assheton-Smith had recalled the silver instruments worth £400 which he had given to the 'Royal Vaynol Silver Band', or Band Llanrug as it was commonly known.[47] On their way to return the precious instruments to a room in the quarry, the band struck up a tune and marched together past the picketing crowd. Emboldened by the music, the crowd fell in behind and a great body of men, women and children marched into the quarry, where Vivian and the other managers were waiting to take on workmen. With the crowd completely surrounding the office, as they had done before in February 1874, the bandmaster Mr. Tidswell went in to offer up the instruments, only to be told by a rather annoyed Mr. Vivian that he had had no intention of recalling the instruments at all. Sensing their strength, the crowd decided to exercise their power, and a note was handed to the police sergeant who had appeared on the scene to the effect that if Vivian and Davies did not leave the quarry in ten minutes they would have to take the consequences. Davies appeared in a few minutes and agreed to leave if the crowd would part to let them through. This was done and the manager and his assistants walked through the hooting and jeering crowd, into a railway truck which carried them off to Port-dinorwic. The crowd then decided that they would give a similar notice to the few men who were continuing to work in the quarry; these men were not quarrymen but carpenters, blacksmiths, a pattern maker, a fitter, an engine driver and, somehow, a sailor. A note was again handed to the police sergeant, who seems to have been quite willing to act as the crowd's emissary, and within a few minutes the men fled, though two of them continued to receive the attentions of a section of the crowd who followed them back to the village and to the doors of the police station where they had gone to seek refuge.

During the whole episode no actual violence had been used at all and once they had ensured that the quarry was deserted the crowd marched off again; nor did their adventure show

[47] Emyr Jones, op. cit., p. 33.

any signs of previous planning; it happened spontaneously out of the meeting of the band and the picket. What had been done was not, however, without significance; never before (or since) had the whole management of a major quarry been driven out of its own premises. Despite the seriousness of the incident, there seem to have been no immediate repercussions, and no arrests or summonses followed the incident. The unfortunate Mr. Tidswell, however, who had been receiving £10 a month from Assheton-Smith for training the Llanrug Band, was relieved of his post and returned to England.[48]

There were other incidents following the attempt to re-open the quarry: the telephone wire connecting the quarry with Portdinorwic was cut; a haystack was set on fire and another damaged by pouring water into it; some of the few who attempted to work had the doors of their homes tied up so that they could not get out, and others were pelted with turf and stones.[49] Such incidents drew forth a sharp rebuke from the men's committee, and a mass-meeting in the New Year condemned 'the work of some people in damaging the property of Assheton-Smith Esq.'.[50]

These incidents, and the fact that the men were no longer technically locked out but were themselves refusing to work under a particular management, brought a new spirit to the struggle. Owen Jones, Ebenezer, told a meeting on the 15th: 'Today the battle starts. We have been on the defensive but now we are on the offensive.'[51] Another speaker pleaded with the meeting: 'Do not go back to Egypt my people. . . you will destroy the slate works of creation if you give way.'[52] The men determined that 'as a class of workers we refuse completely and resolutely to work under such rules and managers'.

In the new year the men offered to put the whole matter before an arbiter, but Assheton-Smith would have nothing to do with such a scheme at this time; he also refused blankly to receive the men's committee as a deputation, though he

[48] Ibid.
[49] GAS, DQ. 2,276.
[50] Ibid., 2,286.
[51] *Y Genedl Gymreig*, 16 December 1885.
[52] Ibid.

dropped a hint that he might receive another representative to speak for them.[53]

At this time there was also a bitter and well-publicised strike at the Llysfaen limestone quarry in Llanddulas,[54] which, though some distance away from Dinorwic, nevertheless held certain parallels with the slate-quarrymen's struggle. Following disturbances in Llanddulas, when blacklegs were three times taken to the quarry and were three times repelled, 60 policemen and over 100 military were moved into the area. Fears now spread that the troops were also to come to Dinorwic to allow the re-opening of the quarry, and the proposal was in fact discussed by the magistrates.[55] Many and fiery were the speeches made in anticipation of such an act, 'instead of speaking to them with words', it was asked, was Vivian now going to 'speak to them with bullets; instead of writing to them with pen, ink and paper, some said he was going to write on their bodies with swords'.[56] Despite regular crowds meeting each train to Llanberis in the expectation of the arrival of the 'red-coats' the troops did not appear and the day set for a second re-opening of the quarry, 11 January, passed without incident and without one of the 1,200 men promised by the managers turning up for work.[57]

During January a rather mysterious but significant development took place when it became known that W. J. Parry, the president of the N.W.Q.U., had been in private contact with Vivian. Parry first approached Vivian by letter on 5 December 1885; 'I have been connected with the Quarrymen of North Wales for the last twenty years', he wrote, 'and I can claim that I have done all in my power, by words and deeds to foster a kindly feeling between master and men.'[58] They corresponded, and met in great secrecy, throughout the dispute and, though Vivian insisted that the two men were conducting no more than friendly and private interviews, there is no doubt that

---

[53] *C. & D. Herald*, 2 January 1886.
[54] *Y Genedl Gymreig*, 30 December 1885.
[55] *C. & D. Herald*, 2 January 1886.
[56] Ibid.
[57] Ibid., 16 January 1886.
[58] GAS, DQ. 1,905. Letter from W. J. Parry to Hon. W. W. Vivian, 5 December 1885. The two men exchanged 35 letters concerning the dispute and met at least five times, once in London, twice in Chester and twice in Portdinorwic.

Parry himself tried energetically to agree to terms with Vivian which he could get the men to accept. He was himself far from enthusiastic about the men's actions and he made this quite clear to Vivian. When he finally did secure what he considered to be realistic proposals for the termination of the dispute in mid-January the strike committee rejected them and they were later turned down by a mass-meeting. These proposals called for an admission by the men that they had acted improperly in holding their meeting on 12 October and also called on them to withdraw the vote of no confidence in the management which had been passed at that meeting.[59] They also contained a number of vague promises as to the future fairness and practical experience of the future management, but they made it obvious that all the disputed rules were to stand, albeit to be interpreted leniently, and that not all the men would get their jobs back at the end of the dispute. In reply the men drew up their own counter-proposals, which demanded that

1. All the men at the Dinorwic Quarries shall work under practical experienced men.
2. All the workmen should be governed by, and give obedience to, fair and reasonable rules.
3. Every workman will be acknowledged as such on his own merits, independently of all political and religious connections.
4. As the men were locked out in a body they shall be allowed to resume work also in a body instead of applying individually.
5. A signed agreement shall be reached between master and men on these questions.[60]

Following this rejection of his peace plan, relations between Parry and the strike committee became increasingly difficult; he complained to Vivian on 25 January that he could not 'approve of the stand they have taken and trust it will not influence you and Mr. Assheton-Smith against them. I have done my best, I can assure you, and I believe I have the support of the best amongst the men as well as amongst the general public.'[61]

[59] *C. & D. Herald,* 23 January 1886, p. 7.
[60] Ibid.
[61] GAS, DQ.1,905, Letter from W. J. Parry to W. W. Vivian, 25 January 1886.

Two days later he was again at pains to explain that the rejection of the terms by the men was not his fault. 'I am doing my best to prove myself worthy of the confidence you have placed in me,' he wrote, but 'you know the kind of men I have to deal with.'[62]

It now became apparent that the kernel of the men's case was the removal of John Davies from the management and his replacement by a 'practical' man, that is, a man who had some experience of actually working slate rock. Davies had been connected with the Dinorwic quarries for some 30 years as an office worker and had been an under-manager for eleven but the men claimed that as he had no practical experience he had no right to run a slate quarry on which depended their livelihood and indeed their lives.[63]

To this accusation Vivian retorted that the men did not really object to Davies's competence but to the stringency with which he applied the quarry rules and that their main objection was to the rules themselves which, he claimed, insisted on their doing a fair day's work.[64] The men conceded the point but parried that only an incompetent manager would dream of introducing such rules in the first place, for they displayed a total ignorance of the demands of the work. As an example, they took the need to work the rock before dawn on a hot summer's day, a necessary act which would be prevented by any rules on working hours which did not allow the men themselves to decide.[65] The men's case was that the rules themselves were impracticable and unfair and proved the lack of experience of the managers, but that they would agree to work under them if the manager were a practical man, that is, a man who would interpret the rules in a lenient and sensible way, and John Davies, they felt, was not such a man.

Their other demand, which assumed greater importance as the end of the dispute grew nearer, was that the quarry accept back all those who had worked there in October. It became apparent, however, that this was not to be allowed and that the lock-out had been the opportunity taken, or perhaps

---

[62] Ibid., 27 January 1886.
[63] C. & D. Herald, 23 January 1886, p. 4.
[64] Ibid., 30 January 1886.
[65] Ibid., 23 January 1886.

engineered, by the management for a thorough re-organisation of work within the quarry, a re-organisation which would leave some 300 men without employment. This was made clear by Vivian when he confided in Parry that before October he was employing more men than he needed and warned, 'I intend altering this'.[66]

Towards the end of January, a body calling itself the Non-Unionists Association appeared and sent letters to the press, signed by ten Dinorwic quarrymen claiming that it represented men quite willing to work but for the 'intimidation and violence shown'; the letter emphasised that the members of the association, while not opposed to the men's stand, were quite unable, because they were not union members, to carry on, as they were on 'the verge of actual want'.[67] Such a group, though originating amongst a few, could have been influential in splitting the union from the non-union men, though there is no record of their growing as an 'association'. It must, however, have been with developments such as these foremost in their mind and with a growing consciousness that the union fund could not sustain them for much longer that on 11 February the committee members approached Mr. John Robinson, the owner of the Talysarn quarry in the Nantlle valley, to intercede with Vivian on their behalf. Robinson seems to have been greatly respected by the quarrymen, despite the fact that he was, unlike some other Nantlle quarry-masters, an Anglican.[68] He had earlier impressed the men by making a gift of coal to them in January.[69]

Robinson had several interviews with Vivian and reported to the committee, advising them to re-apply for work.[70] He convinced them that the reorganisation of the quarry, though entailing a short-term reduction in labour, would eventually lead to an expanded work-force. He also promised that the work would henceforth be carried out fairly and that no one would be victimised for his politics, religion or role during the lock-out, and that the works would be managed by 'able,

[66] GAS, DQ. 1,905, Vivian to Parry, 15 February 1886.
[67] C. & D. Herald, 30 January 1886.
[68] Ibid., 20 February 1886.
[69] Ibid., 30 January 1886.
[70] Ibid., 20 February 1886.

practical, men'. The committee accepted these proposals on the morning of Saturday, 13 February, and put them to a mass-meeting in the afternoon. The meeting was far from satisfied with the proposals, and bitterness was felt that as many as 300 of them would not be allowed work. There was some interruption of the chairman and one man moved that motions should be put by the meeting and not by the committee; another shouted 'what have we gained after fighting for fifteen weeks?', to which another replied: 'nothing at all'.

An attempt to adjourn the final decision was made but it was overruled by the platform, and after some bitter argument the men finally agreed unanimously to return to work; but it is clear that there were still many among the quarrymen who were bitterly dissatisfied with the verdict. 'You know the difficulties and opposition I had to contend with', wrote Parry to Vivian following the men's final decision, 'and the step had to be taken suddenly and got through quickly.'[71]

The men marched from the meeting to the quarry offices in a body some two miles long, but no amount of gestures of solidarity could hide the fact that the quarrymen of Dinorwic had suffered a major defeat; although the men had been out for fifteen weeks, the rules still remained, the managers still remained, and the quarry had been reorganised and the labour force reduced substantially. It is difficult even to accept the committee's judgement of the affair that they should not 'cry victory but rather rejoice at having won an honourable peace'.[72]

When the list of those not receiving work was finally made public the men held another mass-meeting that was angrier than the first.[73] There was much criticism of the seemingly arbitrary way in which men had been refused work and it was without enthusiasm that the meeting voted for a realistic motion which declared that 'we as workmen are of the opinion that the wisest course we can adopt under the present circumstances is to return to work under the terms offered, although such terms are not all that we desire'. The motion was initially voted for by only half the meeting and some young men tried

[71] GAS, DQ. 1,905, Parry to Vivian, 15 February 1886.
[72] *C. & D. Herald*, 20 February 1886.
[73] Ibid., 27 February 1886.

unsuccessfully to move an adjournment; peace was counselled, however, even by some men who had themselves lost their jobs, and the whole meeting finally acquiesced in the defeat.

'True, they have been beaten, it is useless to assert the contrary as some do; but it is equally true that they have not been disgraced.'[74] Such was the judgement of the *North Wales Observer and Express* on the final result of the Dinorwic lock-out. The dispute left the men demoralised and divided, with confused and contradictory feelings toward their union. They had suffered considerable hardship and had not only gained nothing but had also witnessed a commitment somewhat less than total to their cause on the part of the president of their union. This, and the fact that the general secretary of the union, W. J. Williams, had played virtually no part in organising the dispute left a bitter residue of distrust toward the N.W.Q.U. amongst many of the men.[75]

The dispute introduced to north Wales a new style of business management which was determined to wrench from the quarrymen that control of wages and production which they still retained. W. W. Vivian in Dinorwic was soon joined by E. A. Young as manager of Penrhyn; both were men from outside the slate industry whose training had been in the harsh world of business, a training which did not make them sympathetic to 'inefficient' customs and practices.[76] Vivian was clearly in charge throughout the Dinorwic dispute and Assheton-Smith himself played only a minor role. This was partly because Smith was severely embarrassed during the course of the dispute by a court case in which he was being sued for shooting a beater while hunting, a case tailor-made for the jibes of the Welsh radical press,[77] but it is also clear that Smith had no stomach for, and less understanding of, the unpleasantness in his quarries which distracted him from his many hobbies.[78] He even went so far as to organise, at his own theatre in the Vaynol, a theatrical performance in which he

[74] *North Wales Observer and Express*, 19 February 1886.
[75] GAS, Llyfr Cofnodion Cangen Dinorwic, 20 January 1888; 29 April 1887; N.W.Q.U., Minute Book, 4 June 1887.
[76] Young had been a London accountant who had previously been 'entrusted with winding up many big limited liability concerns' (DQ. 2,290).
[77] GAS, DQ. 2,282.
[78] Other than shooting, Assheton-Smith also delighted in yachting and fishing and took an interest in the theatre and his private menagerie.

himself starred, 'the receipts from which are to swell the fund
for the persons suffering from the effect of the strike at his slate
quarries'. Vivian was not a man given to behaviour of this
sort, and during the years following the quarrymen's defeat
in 1886 he was quick to drive home his advantage.[79] He
continued to allow regular deputations to visit him with
grievances, though his reactions were invariably inflexible and
at times ruthless. For instance, in July 1892 Thomas Parry, a
member of a deputation to meet Vivian, was summarily
dismissed because he was accused of leaking incorrect information to the press about the meeting.[80] Information in this, as
in other disciplinary cases, was elicited from informers in
various parts of the quarry.[81] An earlier victim had been Owen
Williams of Portdinorwic, an articulate and energetic Liberal
who, until his dismissal at a moment's notice in 1889, had been
employed all his working life as a barrow-man on the Portdinorwic quay.[82] No reason for his dismissal was given but
Vivian's lawyers, in a privately-drafted document, explained
that he was held to have been one of the agitators responsible
for the 1885 dispute and that 'in consequence of information
lately conveyed privately to Mr. Vivian he considered it
desirable in order to maintain discipline and to avoid the
possibility of unpleasantness in the future to dispense with this
man's services, which he did on a pay day'.[83] Of many such
'desirable' actions did the defeat of 1886 consist.

II. THE LLECHWEDD DISPUTE, BLAENAU FFESTINIOG, 1893

In the late-nineteenth century Blaenau Ffestiniog in Merioneth
was a town renowned more for its political radicalism than for
its trade-union militancy. With a population of over 11,000 in

---

[79] A hint of the difference in attitude between Smith and Vivian is to be
found in Vivian's letter to Lord Penrhyn, November 1902: 'previous to 1886 I
found a so-called Quarry Committee in existence, some had been (more or less)
recognised by Mr. Assheton Smith and his representatives. On my taking charge
of the Quarries this so called committee and self clashed.' Vivian's conduct
during negotiations with deputations of the men was markedly different when
Assheton-Smith was present (DQ. 2,332, 2,356).

[80] DQ. 2,339–43; the information leaked, whether by Parry or not, was in
any case fairly innocuous.

[81] See, for example, DQ. 2,336, a letter from M. Jones to W. W. Vivian,
7 June 1892; DQ. 2,317, a letter from John Williams to W. W. Vivian, n.d.

[82] See Owen Williams's eloquent letters to W. W. Vivian (DQ. 2,302–06).

[83] DQ. 2,311, The Hon. W. W. Vivian and Owen Williams, *Case*.

1891, the Ffestiniog Urban District constituted the biggest of the slate-quarry towns,[84] and although remote and in mountainous country, strung out as it was along the rocky head of the Vale of Ffestiniog, 700 feet above sea level, it was well connected by rail links.

It was here that the Irish land reformer, Michael Davitt, had come to a rousing welcome in February 1886; and it was the quarrymen of this district who had pushed their radicalism so far as to split the Merioneth Liberal Party in the election of 1885 by putting up their own independent Liberal candidate. In 1895 they had forced A. M. Dunlop, the general manager of the Oakeley quarries, to resign as chairman of the U.D.C. because of his inability to speak Welsh;[85] and as early as 1892 candidates were put up in local elections under a 'labour' designation.[86]

This combativeness flourished in a political atmosphere considerably freer than that of the other main slate centres of Bethesda and Llanberis. Unlike those areas, Blaenau Ffestiniog was not a one-quarry town; the largest quarry in the area, the giant Oakeley mine employing in 1891 over 1,600 men, was only half the size of the Dinorwic or Penrhyn quarries; and there were several moderately-sized quarries in the vicinity, the larger of which were Llechwedd, Votty and Bowydd, and Maenofferen.[87] The people of Ffestiniog, therefore, owed allegiance to no one master and the number of quarries meant that men could—and did—move from one to another. There were, moreover, political divisions amongst the masters, most obviously between the Tory Oakeleys and the Liberal Greaves brothers, owners of the Llechwedd mine. The Tory cause, well-established in the shadow of Penrhyn and Vaynol influence, was hardly rooted at all in Blaenau; the balance sheet of the local Conservative and Unionist Club for 1899 tells a sorry tale, with few individual subscribers other than nine publicans, two

[84] Ffestiniog Urban District had a population of 11,073 in 1891, 11,435 in 1901. *Census Report*, 1901.
[85] *Our Gazette* (Nat. Assoc. of Slate Merchants and Slaters), February 1895, p. 32. A M. Dunlop had originally been a Tory, fighting Merioneth in 1880; however he became a Liberal (ibid., February 1896, pp. 98–99).
[86] *Y Genedl Gymreig*, 24 February 1892, 9 March 1892.
[87] *Slate Trade Gazette*, Vol. VIII, p. 229. Other quarries in Ffestiniog employing over 100 men in 1893 were Cwmorthin, Graig Ddu, Diphwys Casson (Lord), Rhosydd, Wrysgan.

vicars and the Oakeley family; we are 'often at a disadvantage', reported the committee, 'having only the working class to carry on the work'.[88]

Trade unionism had been established in the town since 1874, but the North Wales Quarrymen's Union had not flourished. There had been a reasonably effective campaign to reduce hours in 1882,[89] but apart from this there were few attempts at concerted action by all the quarries represented on the Ffestiniog Lodge. There had been disputes in the area: the Rhosydd mine witnessed a strike in October 1886 and there was a dispute in Graig Ddu in the same month.[90] The Cwmorthin mine above Tanygrisiau was the scene of various clashes in the 'eighties and early 'nineties,[91] while labourers in the Votty and Bowydd mine stopped work in April 1885.[92] But these had been minor skirmishes indeed compared with the 1874 and 1885 battles at Penrhyn and Dinorwic.

The Llechwedd stoppage of 1893 was by far the most important dispute in the town in the nineteenth century. The quarries negotiated on their own behalf rather than through the union lodge; in 1887 there were 876 union members in twelve quarries in Ffestiniog out of a total number of over 3,200 quarrymen.[93] The Oakeley quarry had a relatively low percentage of men organised, but there was a committee of quarrymen conducting some kind of regular negotiations from the late 1880s.[94] In Llechwedd each *caban* in the quarry sent representatives to a general committee.[95]

The main problem confronting the union in the area was the number of different quarries in the lodge, each with different

---

[88] Lord Penrhyn also contributed £5. GAS, Tanybwlch, D/U2/21.

[89] It is not clear what real control the N.W.Q.U. as such had over this campaign.

[90] N.W.Q.U., Minute Book, 30 October 1886.

[91] There were clashes in Cwmorthin in 1882, 1883, 1885, 1890 and 1891.

[92] GAS, Z/DAG, 1 Votty and Bowydd Papers, 16 April 1885.

[93] N.W.Q.U., *Roll Book*, 1887–91; N.W.Q.U., *Cash Book*. In 1897, after much fluctuation, membership rose to 928 before dropping drastically in 1899 and rising again in 1902.

[94] Richard Griffiths of Ffestiniog claimed in 1903 that 'a standing committee of members elected annually' and with power to appoint deputations had existed in the Oakeley for 15 years past and that the committee had 'not failed to settle a dispute so much as once during that time'. *Slate Trade Gazette*, Vol. IX, p. 45.

[95] In December 1902, Ciniawdy Sink y Mynydd sent a delegate to the general committee to argue for an increase in wages (U.C.N.W. MS. 5440, Rhagfyr 1902).

procedures and customs.[96] The number of quarries competing for labour also gave the quarrymen an obvious answer to local dissatisfaction. 'I do not value my employment so much as that', said Robert Roberts, a rockman in the New Welsh Slate quarry in 1895, 'if I cannot get work in one place I can get it in another.'[97] Such an answer was not so meaningful to men in Dinorwic or Penrhyn, who were forced to stay in one quarry and fight.

By the early 'nineties Blaenau was sharing in the general air of excitement which an apparent quickening of the market had brought to the quarrymen. In 1892 the men working in the area had voted by 1,526 to 248 in favour of moving towards a strike for an improvement in wages to 5s. a day.[98] In November of that year, however, they disappointed their fellow unionists by accepting something less than this sum.[99]

In Llechwedd the situation remained tense even after the November settlement, which had raised wages by 2s. to 27s. a week,[100] and there were threatened walk-outs twice early in 1893. Of the 486 men working in Llechwedd in that year,[101] only 125 were trade unionists, of whom 75 were fully paid up; this did not dampen the men's anger, however; on the contrary it had been the non-unionists who had been the most willing to strike, being persuaded not to do so only with some difficulty by the union members.[102]

The struggle in Llechwedd followed a pattern similar to that of the other disputes in the slate industry, breaking out as an angry protest against the ever-tightening grip of regulations at work and ending as a desperate attempt to prevent victimization. It is not clear why the Llechwedd men found the rules

[96] Though not with startlingly differing wage rates for, with some exceptions, these were generally agreed by the Ffestiniog and District Quarry Owners' Association. See, for example, *Quarry Owners' Assoc. Minute Book*, November 1895 (GAS, BJC/H/41). The association generally followed the example set by the Oakeley mine. This uniformity in rates did not, of course, mean, given the wages' structure of the industry, that men could not earn more in one quarry than in another.
[97] *Evidence to Departmental Committee upon Merionethshire Slate Mines*, 1895, no. 3091.
[98] N.W.Q.U., Minute Book, 25 June 1892.
[99] Ibid., 26 November 1892.
[100] Ibid.
[101] *Slate Trade Gazette*, Vol. VIII, p. 229. Llechwedd produced approximately 20,000 tons of slate a year.
[102] N.W.Q.U., Minute Book, 3 June 1893.

in force at their work more intolerable than did other quarry-men in the district. It may have been a consequence of the November settlement, which was not as well received by J. E. Greaves, part-owner with his brother, and general manager of the Llechwedd mine, as by other quarry-owners.[103] Regulations may have been tightened in an attempt to boost production in order to cover the cost of the rise in wages. Technical difficulties in the mine, particularly those resulting from the use of water-power for the machinery in the slate-dressing sheds, seem also to have aggravated the situation. Whatever the cause, Charles Warren Roberts, the resident manager of the Llechwedd quarry, complained in 1895 of the 'great deal of trouble' he had experienced in getting the men to accept quarry rules.[104]

The men complained bitterly about the strictness of many new regulations; 'it is hardly possible', they explained, 'to move either to the right or to the left without breaking some rule or other'.[105] In particular, they objected to the discontinu-ation of old customs, such as the right to take home a round piece of slate, or the walk to the top of the tip before the bell for the end of their shift rang; the right to take a day off to attend a funeral was also threatened.[106] Above all, the men objected to the stringent way the rules were being applied and to what they considered to be the severity of punishments meted out by the management.[107]

A further complication at the quarry was the shift system, adopted because of the shortage of water; this affected some categories of men. In other quarries these men worked two shifts: 4 a.m. to 12 and then 12 until 8 p.m. In Llechwedd, however, a form of split-shift system appears to have operated which meant that some men were forced to stay idle at the quarry for three and a half hours with strict rules to prevent them leaving.[108] This, and the other rules and regulations in

[103] The men's original claim had apparently been 'warmly' received by Dunlop of Oakeley Quarry but received a cold reception from Greaves (*Y Genedl Gymreig*, 1 June 1892).
[104] *Evidence of Departmental Committee upon Merionethshire Slate Mines*, 1895, no.3835.
[105] *Y Genedl Gymreig*, 23 May 1893.
[106] Ibid.
[107] Ibid. A group of men came up for lunch early and were stopped by a steward, W. Jones (Ffestinfab); while they were talking the bell rang but they were all suspended for the rest of the day. Another man was suspended for a week for leaving work nine minutes early.
[108] Ibid.

force, infuriated the men; they felt that 'working in the quarry has become almost intolerable' and that they were 'surrounded by . . . a thousand and more petty and useless rules'.[109]

The anger boiled over during an incident on 17 May, when Griffith Jones disagreed with the under-manager as to the time he was entitled to leave work. Having, as he thought, finished his shift, Jones refused to obey the manager's order to return.[110] During the ensuing argument a crowd of men gathered round and, when Jones was sent home, they walked out too, bringing the rest of the mine out with them.[111]

There is no doubt that this was a spontaneous gesture of frustration and anger by the men, a protest against the whole running of the quarry rather than simply at the case of Griffith Jones. One of the men's leaders, Councillor Ellis Hughes, made this quite clear at the mass-meeting following the walk-out. 'The storm has been coming for some time,' he said; 'this feeling has arisen because of the lack of trust in the officials. We are not asking for anything except that we be treated like men.'[112] It had been the cry of the Dinorwic men in 1885 and was to be the cry again of the Penrhyn men in 1900. And J. E. Greaves's reply was also familiar: 'By your actions you have taken the management into your own hands and by that you have made yourselves no longer workmen in the Llechwedd. . . There is no safety for a house if two lords govern it.'[113] The dispute had thus erupted over the perennially burning question in the slate quarries: what were the limits of the control to be exercised at work by men and by masters?

Following the walk-out, the men marched to hold a mass-meeting in Fourcrosses, where a strong delegation was elected to speak to the management concerning the unfair way Griffith Jones had been treated.[114] The delegation returned to inform

---

[109] Ibid., 30 May 1893.
[110] The merits of the case are not clear; Jones claimed to have worked $7\frac{1}{2}$ hours while his partners had only worked $5\frac{1}{2}$ hours. Men, in fact, worked considerably longer hours than these.
[111] *Y Genedl Gymreig*, 23 May 1893.
[112] Ibid.
[113] Ibid.
[114] The delegation consisted of D. G. Williams, a past president of the N.W.Q.U., John Hughes, Ellis Hughes, a local councillor, Morgan Roberts and Edward Jones (U.C.N.W. MS. 5911, Rhan o Gofnodion am Streic y Llechwedd Blaenau Ffestiniog, 17 May 1893).

the meeting that they had made no progress with Griffith Jones's case and that, moreover, the management was insisting that all the men must re-apply individually for work. The management had clearly understood very quickly the opportunity the dispute offered to exclude activists from its employ. The men rejected such a course and elected a strike committee of twenty-four.[115]

The committee soon arranged for the facts of the dispute to be publicised, and organised a meeting of quarrymen from all the local quarries at which a general committee to assist the strikers was elected.[116] Fund-raising was a major concern and the fund was able to give 10s. to each head of a family and 5s. to each single workman; N.W.Q.U. members were not to receive anything from the general fund because they were in receipt of benefit from the union.[117]

The men soon appreciated their weak position and agreed to suspend all grievances until they had returned to work; but they still would not accept any individual return. Greaves, however, would not yield on this point, and at a meeting on 3 July the men agreed overwhelmingly to a motion that 'we accept Messrs. Greaves' offer and will put it to the test, and if any of us are left out that we shall stop work'.

On the next morning, therefore, the men returned to the quarry and filed one by one through the quarry office to seek employment 'on Messrs. Greaves' terms'.[118] All went well until the management refused employment to some men, including some of the committee members. The applications for work promptly ceased and there was some disturbance in the quarry before all the men marched back down to the town and, in an angry spirit, condemned the Greaves brothers for their action.

J. E. Greaves offered no reason as to why some of the men were refused work, but a week later he sent a conciliatory note to the men explaining that the management 'were eager to meet our old workmen in every way possible, and are therefore prepared to give them permission to leave their tools here for the time being if they so wish'. But, he added, 'we take this

[115] Ibid.
[116] Ibid., 20 May 1893, 3 June 1893.
[117] Ibid., 13 June 1893.
[118] Ibid., 4 July 1893.

opportunity to state finally that we shall not move from the position we have taken'. The message was mis-timed, however, for the men's attitude had hardened and a mass-meeting voted to remove immediately all tools from the quarry.[119] New initiatives were undertaken to collect funds with two local ministers, the Revs. Cernyw Williams and John Williams, dispatched to various parts of the country. Ministers in Cricieth, Pwllheli, Nefyn and other places were also sent requests for support,[120] and circulars were dispatched to ministers of various denominations throughout Wales asking them to distribute them in their chapels.[121] Further chapels were circulated the following week. Other fund-raising schemes were also arranged: a group of quarrymen was sent on a musical tour through Anglesey, while a section of the Llan Ffestiniog silver band travelled through Montgomeryshire and then on to south Wales.[122] Money came from elsewhere: the Caernarfon branches of the printers unions organised a 'worker's meeting' in the town in July to help the Llechwedd men,[123] while the Caebraichycafn lodge of the N.W.Q.U. lent them £100 in August.[124] Fund-raising was successful 'beyond anything that they expected',[125] and the allowance to each man was raised in mid-August to £1 for a head of family and 10s. for a single man.[126]

At a meeting held towards the end of July, the men admitted that they had been somewhat impetuous in leaving their work on 17 May and assured Greaves that they had not previously planned a strike; they also apologised for the disturbances that had broken out when the quarry had briefly re-opened on 4 July and went on to set aside all grievances they may previously have held against the management.[127] All they asked for was that no one be excluded from the quarry. Greaves gave no assurances to this effect and on 7 August a meeting of the men

[119] Ibid., 9 July 1893.
[120] Ibid., 11 July 1893.
[121] Ibid., 26 July 1893.
[122] Ibid., 2 August 1893.
[123] Y Genedl Gymreig, 4 July, 1893.
[124] N.W.Q.U., Minute Book, 12 August 1893.
[125] Ibid., 22 June 1893.
[126] Rhan o Gofnodion, 14 August 1893.
[127] Ibid., 26 July 1893.

confirmed that 'we cannot see our way clear to accepting their terms and leaving our leaders behind'.[128]

The N.W.Q.U.'s executive committee had meanwhile been watching the dispute with interest. Resentment against the new rules was general throughout the industry and the Llechwedd dispute seemed to offer an opportunity for fighting the issue without too great a financial burden to the union. 'It would be a great advantage to us as quarrymen to fight this principle in the Llechwedd, where there are only 500 workers. The same thing is to be found everywhere', pointed out Thomas Parry to the N.W.Q.U. executive on 1 July, and toward the end of August the union accepted the strike committee's suggestion that an extraordinary conference of the union be convened early in September to discuss assistance to the Llechwedd men.

But in the meantime support for the struggle was crumbling amongst the Llechwedd men themselves, a process assisted by rumours that men from other quarries were seeking work in the idle mine.[129] The special N.W.Q.U. conference met in secret session at Caernarfon on Saturday, 2 September, but little came of it other than a resolution urging the men to go to arbitration. Arbitration had been sought earlier in the dispute but had not been pursued, since the chosen arbitrator, A. Osmond Williams of Castell Deudraeth, had refused to take part.[130] It was, in any case, highly unlikely that Greaves would accept any such scheme.

Aware of the inefficacy of the N.W.Q.U.'s suggestion, the strike committee met on the same day 'to make arrangements against the danger of the majority being for a return to work'.[131] The mass-meeting on Monday, 4 September, rejected a motion containing the N.W.Q.U.'s arbitration recommendation and voted instead, as the committee had feared, for a motion that they 'apply for their work back on Messrs. Greaves' terms'.[132] The committee met that afternoon to organise a fund to assist those of their number who would not be allowed back to work.

[128] Ibid., 7 August 1893.
[129] Ibid., 29 August 1893.
[130] Ibid., 19 June 1893.
[131] Ibid., 2 September 1893.
[132] Ibid., 4 September 1893.

After sixteen weeks the men returned to work without their leaders. There were, in the end, three Llechwedd 'martyrs', D. G. Williams, John Hughes and Ellis Hughes,[133] three of the most prominent and effective trade-union and radical leaders in the locality. Ellis Hughes had won a seat as councillor for the Teigl ward in March 1892, when he had stood as a 'labour and temperance' Liberal.[134] D. G. Williams[135] was also a prominent leader: considered a 'radical amongst Radicals', he had been active in the hours' struggle of 1882 in Ffestiniog[136] and he had chaired the committee that backed the independent Liberal candidate in 1885.[137] He represented the Ffestiniog lodge for many years on the executive committee of the N.W.Q.U. and in 1891 he had been elected annual president of the union; he also served as a vice-president in 1892 and 1893, and in February 1892 he stood unsuccessfully as a 'labour' candidate in a Liberal test ballot in the Fourcrosses ward.[138] The third victim, John Hughes, had worked at Llechwedd as a rockman for twenty-seven years and he also had stood unsuccessfully in the elections of March 1892 under a 'labour' label.[139] Two years after his victimization he was still without work, so it was with the voice of experience that he was able to explain to the committee of inquiry into Merionethshire slate mines in 1895 why quarrymen remained silent as to the true facts concerning safety in the mines and during inquests on men fatally injured at their work; men did not tell the truth, he explained, 'because they fear that if they told the truth it might cause them inconvenience in the

---

[133] N.W.Q.U., Minute Book, 30 September 1893.
[134] *Y Genedl Gymreig*, 9 March 1892.
[135] Ibid., 11 May 1892. Born the son of a quarryman in Dolwyddelan in 1837, D. G. Williams started work as a shepherd at the age of nine, before going to the Welsh Slate Company's mine when he was 16 where, though considered too old to master the craft, he became a skilled quarryman. Williams was a keen eisteddfodwr and an enthusiast for educational reform and temperance; a Congregationalist 'his religion and morality were a foundation to all his striving'.
[136] Ibid., 15 March 1893. He had then persuaded a mass meeting to reject the original proposals agreed by the men's representatives.
[137] *Cambrian News*, 21 August 1885. At the independent Liberal candidate's adoption meeting Williams had declared that 'as a Welshman he wished to see Wales governed by Welshmen . . . he should be very sorry to split a party, but he preferred principle to party'.
[138] *Y Genedl Gymreig*, 24 February 1892.
[139] Ibid., 9 March 1893. He had stood in the Cynfal ward.

quarry'.[140] And it must have been with a note of bitterness in his voice that he went on: 'there are in Ffestiniog and Caernarvonshire scores of men who have been deprived of their livelihood for speaking the truth'.[141]

Three of Blaenau's most prominent and respected radicals had paid the price of combination; a situation which gave some heart to the quarry-owners, whether Liberals or Tories. At the quarterly meeting of the Ffestiniog Quarry Owners' Association held in November 1893, Mr. Armstrong of Maenofferen moved that 'a hearty vote of thanks be given to Messrs. Greaves for the plucky way they had fought the battle in the matter of the strike'. The motion was carried unanimously and Mr. Greaves thanked his fellow proprietors for the assistance they had rendered him.[142]

Following the return to work, D. G. Williams explained the defeat in terms of a lack of trust by the men in the strike committee, though he also went on to add that while 'many of the workers would do the honourable thing . . . many others would need to be forced by a court of law before they would do their duty'.[143] The committee, however, appears to have been fairly efficient in its operations and open in its decisions; mass-meetings of the men were regularly held. What is surprising is not the final defeat of the struggle but the fact that the men held out for so long, for the difficulties they faced were immense from the start.

'We have been too cowardly in the past. What is needed is one little fight to show what was the situation of the two sides.' So spoke John Hughes early in the dispute.[144] But this aggressive tone was untypical, for in reality the men had been on the defensive from the very first day, when Greaves had made it clear that he was not prepared to allow them back to work as a body. From that moment onwards, the men's original grievances took second place, and it was clear that what was at stake was the threatened victimization of the leaders. The

---

[140] *Evidence of Departmental Committee of Inquiry*, 1895, para. 344, 345. J. E. Greaves was one of the committee's members.
[141] Ibid., para. 361.
[142] Quarry Owner's Association Minute Book, 21 November 1893 (GAS, BJC, Add. BJC/H/41).
[143] N.W.Q.U., Minute Book, 30 September 1893.
[144] *Y Genedl Gymreig*, 30 May 1893.

men were ill-prepared for such a struggle. Only a quarter of
them were union members and there were other problems as
well. The Llechwedd mine did not draw most of its labour
from the town of Blaenau Ffestiniog itself; the workers at the
mine were largely *pobl y ffordd bell* ('people from a distance'),
drawn from the surrounding villages of Llan Ffestiniog,
Talsarnau, Trawsfynydd, Penrhyndeudraeth, Dolwyddelan,
Llanfrothen, Betws-y-Coed, Llanrwst and others, all of them
travelling to work daily by rail.[145] The sense of a community
united in struggle, so characteristic of disputes in Bethesda and
Dinorwic, was thus largely absent, and there were considerable
problems in organising strikers scattered over such a wide
area.[146] This problem was compounded, moreover, by the fact
that all the other quarries in the area remained open, so the
strikers were in daily touch with men still at work and earning,
a situation which did not apply with the same force in the
virtually one-quarry community of Bethesda.

Given these considerations, the men's sixteen-week struggle
displayed considerable determination born of an outraged
sense of justice.[147] The quarry remained idle throughout, and
there were no reports of strikers secretly seeking to be re-
employed. Llechwedd's production for 1893 fell by a quarter
but this seems to have made little impression on the Greaves
brothers.[148] The family had owned the quarry since, in 1846,
it had struck the highly profitable 'Old Vein', and they
absorbed easily enough the disruption of production. The men
had realised this from the start and consequently put their trust
in the justice of their case and the honour of those concerned.
'The workers cannot stay out long without working', explained
John Hughes, 'and Mr. Greaves can afford to keep the quarry
closed for an extensive period.' 'But', he asked, 'would that be
an honourable thing for him to do?' especially, one could have

---

[145] *Y Genedl Gymreig*, 30 May 1893.

[146] On 14 July the strike committee had to send a deputation to Penrhyndeudraeth 'to keep the peace and ensure order' (Rhan o Gofnodion, 14 July 1893).

[147] And, for some, of a wider perspective: 'This is the battle of labour against
capital', stated Robert Pugh to a mass-meeting during the second week of the
dispute (*Y Genedl Gymreig*, 30 May 1893).

[148] Production in 1890 had been 21,324 tons; in 1893 it was 15,615 tons
(*Slate Trade Gazette*, Vol. VIII, p. 229; *Report* of Committee of Inquiry 1895,
Appendix V).

added, for a Liberal.[149] Greaves's sense of honour was not John Hughes's, and Hughes and his two comrades were to be sacrificed before Mr. Greaves's code of honour was to be satisfied.

---

[149] *Y Genedl Gymreig*, 30 May 1893.

VII

THE FIRST PENRHYN LOCK-OUT

I. THE EARLY 'NINETIES

Hyn sydd yn sicr, fod y gweithwyr yn unfarn bron, fod rhaid sefyll allan rhyw ddiwrnod, y gwahaniaeth yw, pa bryd?[1]

Following George Douglas Pennant's action in 1885 in withdrawing unilaterally from the 1874 Pennant Lloyd agreement and replacing his manager Wyatt shortly afterwards by E. A. Young, relations between management and men at the Penrhyn quarries had been bitter but contained.[2] They were contained in large part by that disunity amongst the men, caused by managerial promises and threats, but engendered also by a general disillusionment with the N.W.Q.U., which had allowed Pennant to introduce his fearsome changes.

The Caebraichycafn committee was not in a position to negotiate with the management for many years after 1885 and those years witnessed much heart-searching and recrimination. The lodge was actively involved in the attempts during these years to amend the rules of the union, and many differences of opinion as to the best structure for the union became apparent. Loud as ever were those voices calling for some kind of 'local' union in the quarry, and in 1889 a 'Local Fund' was in fact launched with the proviso that

> if we have reforms in the N.W.Q.U., and those meet our wishes, we shall fall in with it; if it does not do this, we shall continue as a local fund.[3]

In April 1889 the Penrhyn lodge had presented a gloomy report to the N.W.Q.U. council: 'we have at present been hit

---

[1] 'This much is certain, that the workers are almost unanimous that there will have to be a strike one day, the point is when?' *Y Genedl Gymreig*, 2 September 1891.

[2] Pennant's father, Lord Penrhyn, died the following year and Pennant inherited the title.

[3] GAS, N.W.Q.U. Bethesda Minute Book, 20 January 1890; the resolution had been passed on 26 August 1889.

by a wave of failure', explained the No. 2 lodge delegate; 'would it not be better to give up the union?'.[4] Three months later, in a reference to the split in the ranks caused by the Local Fund, the delegate's report was even more desperate: 'we must do something', he said, 'the union has been torn apart by a barefaced enemy—everyone feels that something must now be done. We have asked for the very least that we could ask for and we have been refused.'[5] In October their plight was the same; 'we live in wretchedness still in the Cae . . . great complaints, working only five days'.[6] The situation was changing, however. The slate market showed signs of stirring once again and in January 1890 the N.W.Q.U. itself accepted new rules which greatly enhanced the local autonomy of the lodges.[7] In May the union conference expressed its considered opinion that the time had arrived for a united push for an increase in wages.[8] And in the same month the Penrhyn delegate struck a note of restrained optimism by calling for a public meeting in Bethesda as 'it seems as if things will change there'.[9]

Following the changes in the N.W.Q.U. rules, negotiations started between the committees of the No. 2 lodge and of the Local Fund breakaway. Despite many difficulties and objections from the Fund leaders, the question of which body was to represent the Penrhyn men was put to a ballot in July; the result was an overwhelming vote of confidence in the union.[10]

By July 1890, therefore, the men were in a better position than they had been since 1885 to 'start up the union again'.[11] The lodge was quickly re-activated, grievances were discussed, and demands formulated. The men were restless for change and some chafed at the more considered pace of the lodge committee; in early September four galleries threatened to strike in protest at the management's interference with holiday customs.[12] The committee prevented the strike but protested

[4] N.W.Q.U., Minute Book, 27 April 1889.
[5] Ibid., 27 July 1889.
[6] Ibid., 26 October 1889.
[7] Ibid., 4 January 1890.
[8] Ibid., 17 May 1890.
[9] Ibid.
[10] W. J. Parry, *The Penrhyn Lock-Out*, 1901, p. 53. 296 voted for the Local Fund, 1,392 for the union.
[11] GAS, N.W.Q.U. Bethesda Minute Book, 18 July 1890.
[12] Ibid., 12 September 1890. The four galleries were Ponc Lord, Sinc Bach Twll No. 2., Ponc Smith, and Ffridd.

strongly against 'the way we are being treated' by the management.[13]

In October the lodge, now with over 1,600 members, pressed the N.W.Q.U. to hold an emergency conference to discuss united action on wages, hours and conditions.[14] The union council agreed and a conference was held in Caernarfon on 13 December with 81 delegates from eleven lodges present, each delegate representing 100 men. W. H. Williams of Bethesda addressed the conference on 'The State of the Quarryman': 'our situation as quarrymen', he said, 'is totally unsatisfactory; we are not receiving those advantages which we should from the enlivening of the market'. D. Williams of Ffestiniog, speaking about the level of wages, concurred but went further than W. H. Williams by proposing that a united move should be made to raise the standard of wages to 5s. a day for quarrymen; the planning of such a move, he proposed, should be left to the union council. His proposals for action were accepted.[15]

The conference's decisions were endorsed by a mass-meeting of the Penrhyn men in February 1891,[16] and several demands were formulated for presentation to the management.[17] The struggle was approached with seriousness (a request from Dinorwic quarry for a joint claim was turned down, it being thought that this would weaken their case); all the men signed a bond pledging them to the claim, and all those who did not sign were reported to the lodge.[18] A meeting of the lodge's negotiators with the works manager, D. Pritchard, bore no fruit, and neither did the meeting with the manager, E. A. Young, a fortnight later.[19]

The men therefore determined to take their demands to Lord Penrhyn himself, and many galleries threatened to strike until

[13] Ibid., 13 September 1890.
[14] Ibid., 11 October 1890.
[15] N.W.Q.U., Minute Book, 13 December 1890.
[16] GAS, N.W.Q.U. Bethesda Minute Book, 19 February 1890.
[17] Ibid., 13 March 1891. These demands were (1) that wages be 5s. a day for quarrymen, rybelwrs, miners, smiths and moulders; 4s. 9d. for sawyers; 4s. 6d. for bad-rockmen and loaders; 4s. for labourers; (2) that more liberty be allowed in the selection of partners and that rybelwrs be let monthly bargains; (3) that in cases where the men fail to reach the standard for two months in succession they be given a price in the third month to enable them to make this up; (4) that the custom of allowing the last Wednesday in the quarry month as a day off be restored.
[18] Ibid., 1 July 1891.
[19] Parry, op. cit., p. 53.

such a meeting took place.[20] On 20 August 1891 Lord Penrhyn met the deputation, but little discussion of the men's claims took place since much of the time was taken up by an accusation of dishonesty levelled at the committee's secretary, W. R. Evans. Evans was presented with a document of 'apology' which he had to sign or be sacked. Such an atmosphere was not conducive to any meaningful negotiations.[21]

The failure of the negotiations was reported back to the men and a strike seemed a very real possibility; the N.W.Q.U. had earlier warned sternly against any strike action in Penrhyn and had forbidden any meeting being held independently of the committee.[22] In the event, the men, under the committee's guidance, appear to have agreed that there was little they could do other than 'to take the present conditions we are in and present them before God in prayer'.[23]

A further deputation was organised to meet the management in April 1892;[24] they held a barren meeting with E. A. Young on 23 May.[25] In June the men voted by 1,567 to 327 in favour of strike action in the event of their negotiations failing to make headway, but this vote had been taken in the belief that all north Wales's quarrymen would strike together.[26] When it became apparent that the N.W.Q.U. was not about to organise an industry-wide stoppage, the Penrhyn men decided first for arbitration[27] and then to accept once again that 'the time has not arrived for us to strike'.[28]

The continuing rebuffs demoralised the lodge and it was with difficulty that a chairman was found for the committee when that post became vacant in December 1892.[29] But there was still considerable pressure for an increase, and in February 1893 a motion calling for a strike during the coming April was only headed off by a motion which called for the postponement

[20] N.W.Q.U. Bethesda Minute Book, 8 August 1891.
[21] Parry, op. cit., p. 54.
[22] N.W.Q.U., Minute Book, 8 August 1891.
[23] N.W.Q.U. Bethesda Minute Book, 26 August 1891.
[24] Ibid., 25, 26 April 1892.
[25] Ibid., 24 May 1892.
[26] N.W.Q.U., Minute Book, 25 June 1892.
[27] Ibid., 20 July 1892.
[28] Ibid., 13 September 1892.
[29] N.W.Q.U. Bethesda Minute Book, 8, 18 December 1892. Three of those approached refused the job and Robert Davies accepted only with great reluctance.

of such action until certain changes of rule had taken place in the N.W.Q.U.[30] Membership in the quarry increased with the growing scent of confrontation, but an attempt to introduce a strike motion in March was again averted, this time by a motion calling on the N.W.Q.U. council to concert action.[31] But leadership on this issue was not forthcoming and the stalling led to demoralisation; by May, twenty-seven galleries in Penrhyn were still eager to pursue their claim, but the men generally were not as united as they had been. This disunity it was felt, was caused by the setting agent's control of the wages' system leading to a tactical variation in the wage rates of different crews; 'the management has succeeded in dividing us', reported the Bethesda delegate to the N.W.Q.U.[32]

The opportunity for mobilisation had passed but the committee went on, to very little effect, to hold several meetings with E. A. Young and eventually met Lord Penrhyn on 30 June. The men's deputation appears to have been nonplussed by Penrhyn's aggressive manner during the meeting, and some contradictory statements regarding the 5s. standard were made. Penrhyn exploited these inconsistencies fully in a mocking report of the meeting which he sent to all his employees. His own position was made quite clear:

> you shall have a rise of wages whenever it is warranted by the state of the slate trade . . . there is no necessity for my being asked for a rise, I will always consider your interests.[33]

As evidence of this, he pointed to the two rises of 5 per cent he had made to certain classes of workmen since 1891, rises which did not coincide with any claim or demand made by the men.

Despite good organisation and support in the quarry since 1890, the lodge had failed to make any impression on Penrhyn's opposition to real negotiations with them; indeed they seem only to have aroused his spleen. With failure apparently the only fruit of their efforts, the lodge and the N.W.Q.U.

[30] Ibid., 27 February 1893.
[31] Ibid., 13 March 1893.
[32] N.W.Q.U., Minute Book, 13 May 1893.
[33] Parry, op. cit., pp. 69, 70. In his statement, he referred to 'some rather evasive answers (more particularly from John Roberts, who made a very bad impression on one by fencing with the truth and refusing repeatedly to answer me in a straightforward manner)'. This attack on an individual member of the delegation greatly angered the men.

generally entered another period of self-examination and doubt about the purpose of their existence.

There were fears that the membership fee would be too high to retain those members who remained through a lean period of little promise: 'better that many should pay 6d than a few 1/-', argued H. H. Davies in a lodge meeting in September 1893. W. H. Williams, however, had different perspectives, arguing that financial exigencies were not the main reason for loss of membership and that 1s. a month should therefore remain the membership fee; he must also have terrified some of the 6d.-a-month camp by suggesting that 2s. a week should be levied if any members were on strike. His argument was based on a belief that the men would return soon enough to membership, whatever the fee:

> we will not have to wait more than a year before we shall see the workers coming back again to be unionists. It is certain that our law-makers will make our places so hot and intolerable that the union will once again be our only refuge.[34]

Events were to make his time-scale appear optimistic, but they also confirmed his sense of the inevitable, impending crisis.

The years that followed the raised expectations and the dashed hopes of 1890–3 were as lean as those which had followed the defeat of 1885. In January 1894 a ballot of the men in the quarry showed 800 still willing to support the union, with 180 against; but the majority had not voted at all.[35] By May 1895 some were voicing the opinion that 'the best medicine would be to give up the union',[36] though by September of that year others felt that 'though no one could see a clear vision . . . a dawn was about to break and there was but need to wait a little to see it'.[37] The union during these three years seems only to have survived in the committee's limited activity and there was no attempt to mobilise the men or to negotiate with the management. The lodge complained about the appointment of slate inspectors,[38] protested about the rates of pay of the borough council's employees[39] and actively argued for the

[34] N.W.Q.U. Bethesda Minute Book, 9 September 1893.
[35] Ibid., 25 January 1894.
[36] Ibid., 25 May 1895.
[37] Ibid., 7 September 1895.
[38] Ibid., 11 August 1894.
[39] Ibid., 8 June 1895.

appointment of a full-time organiser for the union, a position filled by D. R. Daniel in January 1896.[40] In April 1894 the lodge had also condemned, without being in a position to do anything more, the spread of large contracts in the quarry. 'How long', it was asked, 'are we as trade unionists going to allow the "Big Contracts" to be taken without our protesting against them? According to the talk these days [contracts] are increasing in our midst and there is a danger that many will be thrown upon the tender mercies of the contractors.'[41]

As the dawn, prophesied in September 1895, began to break in the New Year of 1896, the issue of the 'big contracts', first raised by the lodge in 1894, was to be the angry sun that dispersed the clouds. By February 1896 the lodge was in a position to hold a mass-meeting in Bethesda;[42] on 15 March it received a letter from the general secretary of the N.W.Q.U., W. J. Williams, informing them that 1,600 men had joined the union in Dinorwic and enquiring how things were in Bethesda.[43] The answer to him was not long in coming.

II. THE RIGHT OF COMBINATION

Six months after he had been appointed full-time organiser for the N.W.Q.U. in January 1896, D. R. Daniel was asked by a member of the union's council whether he was 'ready to do battle with the masters on the principle of Union, whatever the consequences'.[44] The questioner was thinking of the tense situation then obtaining in the Penrhyn quarries, where a conflict between master and men was daily appearing more likely.

The crisis finally came to a head at the end of September 1896. On the 28th the men voted overwhelmingly to prepare for a strike in March 1897; that same afternoon 71 men, including all 57 members of the men's committee, were suspended from their employment as from the following

[40] Ibid., 11, 18 May 1894, 3 December 1894. The lodge organised a meeting in May 1894 to discuss the role of 'agents' in miners' unions.
[41] Ibid., 19 April 1894.
[42] Ibid., 15 February 1896.
[43] Ibid., 15 March 1896.
[44] N.W.Q.U., Minute Book, 27 June 1896.

evening. The men stopped work and at a mass-meeting on the
30th passed a resolution:

> That we, as workmen at Caebraichycafn, consider that we are
> today out of work on the all-important question of the right
> of workmen to unite together to act through a committee and
> deputation to secure their just and reasonable rights, and we
> trust that all working-men throughout the country will stand
> by us in the fight.[45]

They returned to work eleven months later on the 25 August
1897.

The early months of 1896 had witnessed a re-awakening of
union activity in the quarry and in April it had been decided
that the men should, as a body, attend the Labour Day
demonstration in Blaenau Ffestiniog on 4 May. The *Gŵyl Lafur*
(Labour Day) had been introduced by the union in 1891 to
coincide with the union's annual conference. It had originally
been intended that 1 May should be the date for the festival,
but in fact it took place during the first week of May.[46]

The first *Gŵyl Lafur*, held in Caernarfon in 1892, had been
a grand affair, with Sir John Gorst, a Conservative M.P., and
William Abraham M.P. (Mabon) as guests of honour: the men
'marched through the town, bands leading the sections from
the different lodges. No such procession has ever been seen in
Caernarfon, or indeed anything similar.'[47]

It is far from clear who took the decision to inform the
management that the Penrhyn men were to take the day off to
attend the Ffestiniog demonstration in 1896. Penrhyn was to
claim that it was organised by the committee and that members
of the committee went round the men with a book persuading
them 'to sign not to work on May 4th'.[48] The committee denied
this and argued that leave on the *Gŵyl Lafur* was an established
custom and that the men themselves were determined to attend.
Whatever the degree of union involvement in organising for
the *Gŵyl Lafur*—and it must have been considerable—it was
the committee itself that put in an application for leave on
behalf of the men rather than each man applying individually.

[45] Parry, op. cit., p. 105.
[46] N.W.Q.U. Minute Book, 15, 16 May 1891.
[47] *Y Genedl Gymreig*, 11 May 1892.
[48] Parry, op. cit., p. 109.

There was no mistaking the meaning of such a move: here was the principle of combination, of the committee acting on behalf of the men collectively, re-introducing itself into relations with the management. E. A. Young refused to accept the collective application for leave and demanded that each man apply individually. This was rejected by the men and a deputation visited the manager to inform him that the men were to attend the *Gŵyl Lafur*. On 4 May 2,500 men stayed away from work, though it is not clear how many of them in fact travelled to Blaenau Ffestiniog. When they returned to the quarry next day, they were informed that they were all suspended for two days. The men held a mass-meeting that afternoon, when they protested against the closure of the quarry; sensing the approach of battle, the meeting also urged 'all the workmen to join the Union as the only effective means to secure our just rights', and called upon 'the workmen at Caebraichycafn [to] bind themselves to keep united in whatever course is decided upon'.[49]

Feeling was running high following the *Gŵyl Lafur* incident; union membership grew rapidly and it was reported in mid-July that virtually all the workers in the quarry were union members.[50] The committee, sensing that support was growing amongst the men, carefully formulated a series of demands to put to the management. The initial demand was for a general increase in wages, with 5*s*. 6*d*. a day the standard wage for quarrymen, miners, etc., and 'to have, when they fail to reach the standard on the letting, 4/6 a day; and that other classes are to follow in the same ratio'. Particular demands were also made on behalf of *rybelwrs*, mill and yard workers, stonemasons and apprentices.[51]

These demands were presented to E. A. Young on 1 July and turned down by him on the 29th of that month, with the explanation that he was unable to grant a rise as 'the cost of production has risen'. Following this rejection, the committee determined to present their case to Lord Penrhyn himself and on 7 August a document listing grievances and demands was

[49] Ibid., p. 72.
[50] *Y(r) H(erald) C(ymraeg)*, 21 June 1896.
[51] Parry, op. cit., p. 72.

sent to him; the issue of the letting of large contracts in the quarry was the main complaint.[52]

There then followed a period of fruitless negotiation and of charge and counter-charge. A voluminous and hugely-detailed correspondence passed between the committee and Young regarding the particulars of grievances and the form of future negotiations. A deputation met Penrhyn on 17 August, when they were subjected to a lengthy reply to their demands before any discussion could take place. On 26 August the men dispatched another detailed document to Penrhyn, and it was clear that much would depend upon the nature of his reply, for the quarrymen were determined that this time they should be taken seriously. 'I am very much afraid that it is more than probable work will cease at the Penrhyn Quarries on Tuesday week',[53] wrote E. A Young on 22 August, and fifty-three of the quarry's districts had in fact voted to strike from the beginning of the following quarry month.[54] They were only dissuaded by a letter from Young promising that the claims made would be 'looked into carefully by his lordship', and by a request from the council of the N.W.Q.U. that they await Penrhyn's reply before striking.[55]

The length and detail of Penrhyn's document, released on 25 September, did not disguise his rejection of all the men's demands.[56] With the men already in a mood to 'get their demands whatever happens', confrontation now seemed inevitable.[57] The men had been further infuriated by the suspension of two of their comrades, Robert Owen and David Davies, who were to be disciplined for carrying out some unauthorised measuring in the quarry on behalf of the committee. They had been summoned to appear before the manager but had refused to do so on the principle that the management should discuss the matter with their representatives. They were suspended for disobedience on 14 September.[58]

[52] Ibid., p. 74.
[53] GAS, P(enrhyn) Q(uarry) L(etter) B(ook), 139: letter from E. A. Young to Mr. Patridge, 22 August 1896.
[54] Parry, op. cit., p. 89.
[55] Ibid.
[56] A section of it covers 11 printed pages in Parry, op. cit., pp. 91–102.
[57] Y.H.C., 25 August 1896.
[58] Parry, op. cit., p. 90.

The committee met on 26 September to discuss Penrhyn's rejection of their claims and on the 28th it presented three resolutions to all the galleries in the quarry. The first resolution stated that

> we believe that it is our duty as workmen to announce that it is our intention to strike in March next if we don't see in the meantime that the principal points in our demands and complaints as different classes in the works have been granted.

The second resolution called for the intervention of the Board of Trade under the terms of the Conciliation Act, 1896, and the third called for a strike ballot throughout north Wales in preparation for a March strike. The resolutions were approved by 33 districts, two were doubtful, and 13 were for an immediate strike.[59]

The committee clearly hoped that the matter could be resolved before March; the promise of a strike to come was the only way they could pacify those demanding immediate action. The resolutions had been taken to the districts rather than being presented to a mass meeting because the committee feared that the enthusiasm generated by such a meeting would cause caution to be thrown to the winds and an immediate strike to be declared.[60] But there were positive reasons for delay as well: William Williams of Ffestiniog, a delegate to the N.W.Q.U. council, had warned the Penrhyn men not to come out until March because they would not then have to suffer through the cold weather;[61] more important, the delay would give the N.W.Q.U. time to build up a strike fund which would have enabled the men better to withstand a long dispute. Perhaps most significant of all, they could come out, according to Lord Penrhyn,

> at a time when they . . . thought that the greatest amount of injury could be inflicted upon the employer with the least harm to themselves, but at the cost of the disorganisation of the slate trade and the many industries connected therewith, at the commencement of the busiest season of the year.[62]

[59] Ibid., p. 103.
[60] *Y.H.C.*, 29 September 1896.
[61] N.W.Q.U., Minute Book, 29 September 1896.
[62] Parry, op. cit., p. 110.

In the event, the committee's calculations came to naught, for when news of the men's decision, taken at lunchtime on Monday, 28 September, reached Young and Penrhyn they reacted swiftly. That same afternoon some 50 men were interviewed individually and, shortly before work finished for the day, 57 members of the committee and 17 other men had been handed a note which read:

> I have to inform you that you are hereby suspended until further notice as and from the end of this quarry month, viz Tuesday night, 29th inst, E. A. Young.[63]

The news 'spread like a thunderbolt through the quarry' and the quarrymen met for a mass-meeting in a field behind Bethania chapel. The 3,000 men burned copies of pro-Penrhyn newspapers and sang hymns[64] before they resolved that 'it is our duty as workmen to cease work until we have received an explanation' for the suspensions and 'that unless this explanation is given no-one is to take his bargain for next month'.[65]

The men went to the quarry on Tuesday morning to receive Penrhyn's explanation for the suspensions. None was forthcoming, and the month's bargains were not taken; in the afternoon Young circulated a terse note: 'that all the men who have refused to take their bargains to-day have to remove their tools, etc., this afternoon'. The men met again on Wednesday morning and declared themselves on strike 'on the all-important question of the right of workmen to unite together to act through a committee and deputation to secure their just and reasonable rights'.[66] W. Williams, Gerlan, one of the suspended seventy-one, warned that they 'may have to be out for a long time—possibly for years', while David Davies, Penybryn, who was also suspended, saw 'the Red Sea—the winter—in front of us and the Egyptians—capital—in pursuit'. Another speaker, John Williams, Brynmeurig, praised the young quarrymen: 'fair play to the boys', he said, 'if it had not been for the old men they would have been out years ago'.[67] And then the three thousand sang *O Fryniau Caersalem* ('From the hills of

[63] Ibid., p. 104.
[64] *Y.H.C.*, 29 September 1896.
[65] Parry, op. cit., p. 104.
[66] Ibid., p. 105.
[67] *Y.H.C.*, 6 October 1896.

Jerusalem') and *O Arglwydd Dduw, Rhagluniaeth* ('Lord God of Providence'):

> Yng ngwyneb pob caledi, y sydd neu eto ddaw,
> Dod gadarn gymorth imi i lechu yn Dy law.[68]

III. THE STRIKE

Within a week of the men coming out, two sergeants from the 23rd Division of the Royal Welsh Fusiliers visited Bethesda on a recruiting venture, but they apparently met with no success.[69] There was a demand for slate and many men immediately found work in neighbouring quarries and on local projects, such as the construction of the Snowdon Mountain Railway. Others travelled to Llŷn for work in the granite quarries and within a couple of days hundreds of men had also left for Merthyr Tydfil, Cardiff, Aberdare, Neath and Aberavon in south Wales and for Manchester, Liverpool and North Staffordshire; some made plans to emigrate to Western Australia and South Africa. No-one expected a speedy end to the dispute and only about one half of the labour force was left in Bethesda in second-best suits. The rest were labouring in strange quarries, in coal mines, docks and brickworks, throughout Wales and the north-west of England;[70] by November 1,340 of the men were working away from home.[71]

The financial state of the N.W.Q.U. was parlous, the coffers having remained empty after the crippling expense of the five-month Dinorwic lock-out ten years earlier;[72] a levy was not raised on the membership, but collections were organised in the other slate quarries. In the first two weeks of October large solidarity meetings were held in Blaenau Ffestiniog, Waunfawr, Talysarn, and Penrhyndeudraeth;[73] fund-raising concerts by local musicians were held in Llanberis and Nantlle, and a large meeting was organised in Llanberis in early November.[74]

---

[68] (In the face of all suffering, that is or is yet to come; give me staunch support to shelter in Thy hand.) Usually sung to the tune 'Pembroke'.
[69] *Y.H.C.*, 6 October 1896.
[70] Ibid.
[71] *Y.H.C.*, 10 November 1896.
[72] *Y.H.C.*, 6 October 1896.
[73] *Y.H.C.*, 20 October 1896.
[74] *Y.H.C.*, 10 November 1896.

Leaders of the Bethesda men addressed those and other meetings,[75] and a threepenny pamphlet explaining the men's case was being distributed by November.[76] £250 came from Llanberis, and £65 from Blaenau Ffestiniog, and the people of Blaenau were thanked in December for their 'ready kindness . . . to the quarrymen of Bethesda'.[77]

Despite this support from the quarrymen of other areas, however, the N.W.Q.U. noted in January 1897 that 'more money was coming from outside than from the quarrymen for Bethesda'.[78] A farmer from Llanfaglan gave the men a ton of potatoes, but above all support flooded in from the British trade-union movement: Manchester printers sent £10, coal miners from Rhosllannerchrugog £56[79] (in 1893 the Bethesda men had collected £46 for miners on strike in Rhosllannerchrugog and Coedpoeth),[80] Liverpool building workers levied their members to raise funds and Liverpool Trades Council lent their solidarity to the struggle in Bethesda.[81] £150 came from a teachers' conference in June 1897.[82] But it was the enthusiastic intervention of the *Daily Chronicle* that really made the cause of Caebraichycafn a national crusade: the fund they established swelled to over £7,500.[83]

Bethesda was divided into twenty-two districts for the purpose of distributing relief, and a local committee made up of quarrymen and tradesmen was established to oversee the collection and distribution of funds.[84] Tours by choirs from the strike-bound town raised £2,400, and a further £5,800 came from general subscriptions and collections; in all, £19,161 19s. 7d. was collected all over Britain to sustain the struggle in Bethesda.[85]

The Penrhyn quarries opened for work on four occasions—

[75] Meetings in Groeslon in October (*Y.H.C.*, 27 October 1896), Dolwyddelan and Trawsfynydd in November (*Y.H.C.*, 17 November 1896), and Llithfaen in December (*Y.H.C.*, 15 December 1896).
[76] *Y.H.C.*, 10 November 1896.
[77] *Y.H.C.*, 17 November 1896; 1 December 1896; 29 December 1896.
[78] N.W.Q.U., Minute Book, 2 January 1897.
[79] *Y.H.C.*, 15 December 1896; 29 December 1896.
[80] N.W.Q.U. Bethesda Minute Book, 13 September 1893, 7 December 1893; they also collected £21 for Hull strikers in that year (ibid., 12 June 1893).
[81] *Y.H.C.*, 10 November 1896; 1 December 1896.
[82] GAS, P.Q.L.B., 292 (15 June 1897).
[83] Parry, op. cit., p. 168.
[84] *Y.H.C.*, 13 October 1896; 20 October 1896.
[85] Parry, op. cit., p. 168.

24 November 1896, 13 January, 8 February and 2 April 1897; no one turned up for work and the threat of blackleg labour from outside was the least of the committee's worries. A few men had continued working after the start of the strike, but they were not quarrymen and their presence was no threat, though it did create some friction and there was at least one incident when a group of some sixty men and boys harried them on their way to the quarry.[86] There was also a threat of action from Bethesda's women early in the dispute, when there was a suspicion that loaders from Port Penrhyn were to come to remove slates from the quarry.

> Let them come, and if you men do not send them back quicker than they came, then we, the women, will do that instead of you, you will see.[87]

That was one woman's reported response. But incidents of this sort were not a feature of the dispute and when the allegation was made that strikers had placed rocks on the railway line between the quarry and Port Penrhyn, W. H. Williams's condemnation was swift and surprisingly absolute: 'The quarrymen of Bethesda are not ruffians', he declared, 'but men ready to give the same justice to their masters as they expect to receive themselves. If they refused to work themselves they should recognise the right of the masters to employ others . . . the quarry belonged to Lord Penrhyn and he had the right to do what he would do with it.' And, he added characteristically, 'it is better to lose the battle than to win through unfair means'.[88]

Such an attitude was possible because there was no threat of outside labour seriously affecting the course of the dispute; the rocks of Caebraichycafn could be worked effectively only by those who had learnt their secrets after many years of labour, that is, by the men who were on strike. Some blacklegs might come, a member of the committee thought in December,

> but as for them being people who could do the work of the quarryman, the hard-rockman and others, that is out of the question.[89]

[86] *Y.H.C.*, 13 October 1896. They were working in the Felin Fawr.
[87] *Y.H.C.*, 6 October 1896.
[88] *Y.H.C.*, 13 October 1896.
[89] *Y.H.C.*, 1 December 1896.

The quarrymen were protected by their particular craft—except, of course, against themselves. If they remained united they could also remain confident that the quarry would not work; but if they split under the strain, then the perspective would change completely.

Stressing the importance, and working for the maintenance, of unity thus became one of the committee's main tasks and a significant object of its rhetoric. 'The only danger is dissension within our ranks', stressed W. H. Williams. 'It would be possible to bring a divided Bethesda to destruction, but it would never be possible to destroy the quarrymen as an united body, there was no one else who could do the work. Let us therefore be united, faithful and determined.'[90] Dissension there may have been, but there was no split in the ranks and the men remained united throughout the eleven months.

While there was therefore no need for any picketing or other forceful activity to maintain the men's position, there were a few minor incidents in April and May 1897 which caused concern in some quarters. E. A. Young wrote to the chief constable, Colonel Ruck, pleading for mounted police to be drafted into the area as 'the aspect of affairs at Bethesda . . . is becoming more riotous'.[91] But his evidence for such a claim was somewhat impressionistic: on a bicycle trip he had noticed that 'some of the men near Bethesda were very sullen', while some strikers working in Llandudno Junction had seen fit to shout at him as he rode by; more alarmingly, he reported that when his name had been mentioned at a mass-meeting there had been calls of 'shoot him' and 'kill him', while a Welsh newspaper had printed the suggestion that his teeth be knocked out and a knife be stuck in his bowels. Despite Young's fears, however, actual acts of violence were few: workmen's cupboards in the quarry were interfered with, while the foreman's hut near the slate mill was smashed; and early in May Hugh Jones, a carpenter still at work in the quarry, was attacked by a group of young men, while Richard Hughes, a contractor, had been harassed and pestered in the streets of Bethesda. Following these incidents, a somewhat paranoiac Young had written begging

[90] *Y.H.C.*, 29 December 1896.
[91] GAS, P.Q.L.B., 260: E. A. Young to Col. Ruck, 7 April 1897.

Ruck to send police re-inforcements to the area.[92] But these were isolated cases: the men had no need of any campaign of intimidation.

IV. NEGOTIATIONS AND SETTLEMENT

The negotiations that took place during the course of the dispute were as tortuous and barren as those that had preceded the stoppage.[93] The men were hopeful that under the Conciliation Act's provision for the intervention of the Board of Trade in industrial disputes pressure could be exerted on Penrhyn to negotiate and settle. Early in October, Sir Courtenay Boyle, the secretary of the Board of Trade, wrote to Lord Penrhyn suggesting a meeting with a deputation of the men and a representative of the Board. An exhaustive three-cornered correspondence ensued in which Lord Penrhyn's adamantine though circumspectly-phrased opposition to any 'interference' by an outside body became the increasingly formidable obstacle. On 9 December he wrote to Boyle that

> with regard to the suggestion contained in the second resolution that a Board of Trade official should attend at the first interview whilst I thank you for having expressed your readiness to meet my convenience on the subject, I must in reply, with all due respect, beg to decline to comply with such a suggestion, as my acceptance of it would establish a precedent for outside interference with the management of my private affairs.[94]

To this an obviously angry and frustrated Boyle replied that

> the Board cannot admit that the settlement of a prolonged dispute affecting some thousands of men and their families can be rightly regarded as a matter of private interest only.[95]

Penrhyn and the Board of Trade clashed also over the definition of what meaningful negotiations entailed and over the question of supplying Penrhyn with copies of correspondence from the men. On 28 December Penrhyn made plain his 'absolute

[92] GAS, P.Q.L.B., 274: Young to Ruck, 15 May 1897.
[93] Twenty-six of the letters exchanged between men, master and the Board of Trade can be found in Parry, op. cit., pp. 117–29.
[94] Ibid., p. 121.
[95] Ibid., p. 122.

conviction that the dispute is more likely to be prolonged than curtailed by the continuance of negotiations with the Department', and the Board of Trade withdrew from the business defeated and powerless against Penrhyn's convictions:

> The Board of Trade made an endeavour to promote a friendly conference between yourself and your workmen . . . the conditions, however, upon which you insist make it useless for them to continue the endeavour.[96]

'Tear up your Conciliation Act', concluded the Liberals in Parliament, 'it is not worth the paper it is printed on.'[97]

In February a new initiative to bring the two sides together was launched, this time with the intervention of C. T. Ritchie, the President of the Board of Trade himself. Although Penrhyn rebuked him for suggesting that his intervention was in any way necessary,[98] this new initiative finally bore fruit in a meeting held on 18 March between, on the one hand, Lord Penrhyn, the Hon. E. S. Douglas-Pennant M.P., and E. A. Young, and, on the other, W. H. Williams, Robert Davies and Henry Jones.[99]

W. H. Williams argued the men's case forcefully and effectively during the meeting, but Penrhyn refused to admit the validity of his arguments over the right to combine effectively and the meeting ended with no agreement. 'We have held out for six months against this', Williams told Penrhyn, 'and we intend holding out again for some time . . . we have no inclination to give in for some time yet. We shall press still more, until we are even in want of bread, before we shall give in on the question of combination, and that is not likely to be accomplished for some months.'[100]

There were no further meetings between the two sides until the same deputation met E. A. Young on 13 May; as a result of this and further meetings, a set of proposals presented by Young was put to a meeting of the men on 29 May and unanimously

[96] Ibid., p. 128.
[97] *Hansard*, Sir William Harcourt (Monmouthshire West), 28 January 1897, 726.
[98] Parry, op. cit., p. 144.
[99] One of the reasons for the delay in arranging the meeting was a dispute over interpreters and shorthand writers.
[100] Parry, op. cit., p. 158. The transcript of the meeting is printed. Ibid., pp. 148–59.

rejected. The final settlement was reached in mysterious circumstances which left a pall of suspected betrayal over the struggle. W. J. Parry, in his otherwise meticulous description of the negotiations, gives hardly a sentence in explanation of the circumstances which led to a resumption of work, merely stating that

> early in August 1897 negotiations were again opened with Lord Penrhyn through Mr. Lloyd Carter, a member of the firm of solicitors acting for his lordship. Eventually, on the 18th of that month, the following terms were agreed upon and signed.[101]

There is no doubt that Parry and, perhaps more important, the general secretary of the N.W.Q.U., W. J. Williams, secretly manoeuvred the committee into the settlement. Williams unilaterally and secretly wrote to Lloyd Carter on 6 July without the committee's knowledge; according to the men's deputation (W. H. Williams, Robert Davies and Henry Jones) and D. R. Daniel, this left them in an impossible situation for, in their own strong and angry words,

> The evil of individual action of the kind undertaken in this case on his own initiative, and on his own responsibility by Mr. W. J. Williams without any consultation with or intimation to any of his colleagues, the men's authorised representatives, is now apparent, inasmuch as it produced in Lord Penrhyn's mind several erroneous impressions, every one of which was destructive to the men's hopes of securing satisfactory terms of settlement.[102]

Chief amongst the 'erroneous impressions' given by W. J. Williams was

> that the men felt their case to be so hopeless that they were on the point of surrendering at discretion, whereas, as a matter of fact, they were never more determined to insist upon the concession of the terms laid down by them after the last interview we had with Mr. Young in May.

[101] Ibid., p. 162.
[102] N.L.W., D. R. Daniel Collection, 2496: a typescript of 'a true and correct account of the circumstances attending the negotiations referred to in it signed by William H. Williams, Robert Davies, Henry Jones (Deputation); C. W. Brymer, Secretary Relief Fund; David R. Daniel, Organising Secretary Quarrymen's Union', p. 17.

Even in this difficult situation, the committee hesitated before agreeing terms for, according to the account of the negotiations given by Lloyd Carter, the men refused to accept the settlement for a week because they were going to London to see Tom Ellis M.P. and the T.U.C., presumably with the intention of discussing the possibility of continuing the dispute. W. J. Williams and Lloyd Carter 'thereupon decided to ask a number of local Liberals to write to Tom Ellis with the object of influencing Mr. Ellis to advise the leaders to bring the strike to a close'.[103] It was with some justification, therefore, that W. H. Williams and the other Bethesda men felt that the agreement had been reached behind their backs.

The terms of the settlement were these:

'1 (a) The grievances of any employee, crew, or class shall be submitted by him or them in the first instance to the Local Manager. If dissatisfied with the decision of the Local Manager, then the said grievances shall be submitted to the Chief Manager either personally or by deputation appointed in such manner as the workmen may deem advisable, but to consist of not more than five employees selected from the same class as the person or persons aggrieved who must be included in the deputation.

(b) Grievances in which the employees generally are interested or which they may adopt on behalf of an employee, crew, or class who have submitted their grievances under the preceding clause and are dissatisfied can again be submitted to the Chief Manager by a deputation consisting of not more than six employees appointed in such manner as the workmen may deem advisable.

(c) Finally in a similar manner in all cases of importance an appeal may be made to Lord Penrhyn either by the individual or by a deputation, against the decision of the Chief Manager, the grounds of such appeal shall in all cases be first submitted to his Lordship in writing.

---

[103] GAS, M/622/25, Penrhyn v. Parry, rider by Mr. H. Lloyd Carter.

2 Suitable Rybelwrs will be given Monthly Bargains without delay as soon as the Management find it practicable.

3 The letting of contracts to be left in the hands of the Management who engage all persons employed thereon and see that each employee received his just ratio of wage.

4 Previous to the cessation of work the average wage paid to the Quarrymen was 5/6d per day, other piece work classes being in proportion, (viz: Badrockmen 4/7d and Labourers 3/7d); when work is resumed this same basis will be continued so long as trade permits.

5 All the late employees who desire work in the Penrhyn Quarry will be readmitted in a body as far as it is practicable, and the remainder as soon as work can be arranged for them. Reasonable time being allowed to those who may now be employed at a distance.'

It is difficult not to concur with E. A. Young's judgement of this settlement as 'being a complete victory on every point'.[104] 'The terms now agreed upon', he wrote to J. Menzies,

> are precisely similar to the conditions in force not only immediately previous to the strike but for the whole of the last 12 years ever since Lord Penrhyn took charge of Quarry Affairs in May 1885.[105]

The terms were put before a mass-meeting of the men on 21 August and upon hearing an assurance from Mr. Lloyd Carter that 'there was to be no black-list', they were accepted.[106] The men returned to work on 25 August. William R. Evans, a member of the committee, exclaimed that 'we have fought such a battle as to make us deserve 40 years of peace henceforth'.[107] But E. A. Young was not wholly confident, despite his victory, 'I have no doubt', he wrote, ' . . . the result of such a beating will be a lesson to them to be content in future when they are well off, but unfortunately, they never seem to realise when they are well off.'[108]

[104] GAS, P.Q.L.B., 307: E. A. Young to J. G. Ashmore, 24 August 1897.
[105] GAS, P.Q.L.B., 306: Young to J. Menzies, 23 August 1897.
[106] Parry, op. cit., p. 163.
[107] N.W.Q.U., Minute Book, 28 August 1897.
[108] GAS, P.Q.L.B., 307: E. A. Young to J. Nellar (?), 24 August 1897.

V. THE AFTERMATH

The settlement arrived at in August 1897 had far-reaching effects both on internal affairs in the Penrhyn quarries and within the N.W.Q.U. Throughout the dispute the two most prominent spokesmen for the quarrymen had been W. H. Williams and D. R. Daniel, and for some years following 1897 they were to become the most powerful figures in the N.W.Q.U. itself. W. J. Williams's interference in the final settlement arrangements sealed his fate as a quarrymen's leader. He had never been popular and there had been consistent complaints about his behaviour for years;[109] now feelings against him hardened. A special congress of the union held in Caernarfon on 28 August, only a few days after the resumption of work in Penrhyn, witnessed a lengthy discussion of a scheme, proposed by the Ffestiniog Lodge, to do away with the new post of organiser (then held by D. R. Daniel), to merge the office with that of general secretary (then W. J. Williams), and to create a new post of financial secretary. The intention of the scheme was clear to everyone since it was not envisaged that Daniel would lose his position: 'there is here a plan to uproot an old official, let there be no mistake about that', said one speaker at the meeting.[110] Despite there being a majority for the proposals at the conference, the matter was finally postponed until 25 September, by which time delegates could sound out feelings in their respective quarries.

Caebraichycafn quarrymen were overwhelmingly in favour of the change, with 36 districts for and 9 against,[111] and the second conference accepted in principle the new rules despite W. J. Williams's statement that he was not prepared to work under a younger and less experienced man; 'if you want to get rid of me, it would be better if you said that openly', said Williams,[112] and at the next union council meeting the Bethesda delegates did bring the matter out into the open. Williams asked them how things stood between himself and the Caebraichycafn quarrymen's deputation; the deputation, he was

[109] See p. 137.
[110] N.W.Q.U., Minute Book, 28 August 1897.
[111] Ibid., 25 September 1897. Nine districts in Penrhyn had no opinion on the question.
[112] Ibid.

told, could not trust him and refused to work with him.[113]

Under the new rules accepted by the September conference, the post of financial secretary was created and nominations for this post closed on 11 December. There were three contestants: J. E. Williams from Llanberis, D. Ll. Humphreys from Blaenau Ffestiniog and W. H. Williams of Cacbraichycafn. In the ensuing ballot Williams won an overwhelming victory, receiving 3,065 of the 3,865 votes cast.[114] His victory was assured by the Caebraichycafn vote, for the lodge was now by far the biggest in the union, and he received 1,925 out of the 1,978 votes cast in his home quarry. But his popularity was high through all the quarries and he topped the poll in all but two of the union's thirteen lodges, even defeating Humphreys and J. E. Williams in their own lodges.[115]

Following W. J. Williams's departure from office, the union headquarters moved to new premises at 1 Turf Square, Caernarfon. The fact that W. J. Williams had run the union from the same rooms as his own chartered accountant's and estate agent's business had long been a source of discontent among union members;[116] after his departure more serious charges of financial irregularities were levelled against him and the summer months of 1898 were soured by bitter wrangling between the new N.W.Q.U. executive and the former general secretary. It became apparent that certain monies belonging to the union were in a special personal account in the ex-general secretary's name.[117] On 22 August Williams agreed, on certain conditions, to transfer this money to the union fund, but six weeks later D. R. Daniel wrote again asking 'in the kindest possible way' for Williams to return the money, since 'the Council would very much regret being forced to take any further steps to get you to transfer . . . all the money and books in your possession which belong to the Union'.[118] W. J. Williams did not have long to live and the union's reticence in pursuing

[113] Ibid., 30 October 1897.
[114] Ibid., 24 December 1897. J. E. Williams received 593 votes and D. Ll. Humphreys 207.
[115] Ibid., Nantlle and Glyn Uchaf gave more votes to J. E. Williams.
[116] Situated at 7 Market Street, Caernarfon.
[117] X.N.W.Q.U. / 278; W. J. Williams to the executive, 22 August 1898.
[118] GAS, X.N.W.Q.U. / 101 / 457; D. R. Daniel to W. J. Williams, 4 October 1898. See also ibid., 101 / 453.

the matter may have owed as much to their knowledge of his
ill-health as to their understandable desire to avoid damaging
publicity. The end of W. J. Williams's reign was followed very
shortly by W. J. Parry's severing of all formal relationships with
the union when he resigned his position as union 'mediator' in
July 1898.[119] He, too, had been a casualty of the 1897 settlement and it is clear that W. H. Williams and the other Bethesda
men were deeply suspicious of his behind-the-scenes role during
August 1897 and resented his eagerness in seeking a settlement
and for spreading in July the prophecy that it 'was certain our
ranks would be broken in pieces before a fortnight', a view
bitterly opposed by W. H. Williams.[120] Parry was already so
unpopular with the Bethesda committee that, according to
Lloyd Carter, he failed to secure a meeting between the men
and himself in 1897 'as the leaders would not have anything to
do with him'.[121] Lloyd Carter also alleged that Parry's conciliatory approach during the dispute was at least partly
motivated by a desire to win back 'the explosives monopoly
which he had held previous to the year 1892',[122] a wish which
E. A. Young did not grant.

W. J. Williams did not live long after the 1897 settlement.
W. J. Parry was later said to have remarked that he had 'not
the slightest doubt that the worry of the strike of 1896–7 and
the ungrateful treatment which Mr. W. J. Williams received
shortened his life'.[123] Parry's own relationship with the union
was, by that time, tenuous; nevertheless, his and Williams's
removal from all positions of influence within the union
signified a major change in the N.W.Q.U. and was a direct
result of the 1896–7 battle and of the way in which the settlement had been reached.

In 1898 the N.W.Q.U. had, for the first time ever, two
full-time officials who had no employment other than their
union work; one of them, moreover, was himself a quarryman
with his roots in the embittered conflicts of the Penrhyn
quarries. The union of which they found themselves in charge,

[119] N.W.Q.U., Minute Book, 9 July 1898.
[120] D. R. Daniel Collection, 2,496, p. 8.
[121] GAS, M/622/25, rider by H. Lloyd Carter.
[122] GAS, M/622/24, proof of H. Lloyd Carter.
[123] Ibid.

however, was weak and desperately depleted. In 1897 membership had been 6,611,[124] the highest for eighteen years: there were 1,844 members in Dinorwic, another 928 in Ffestiniog and 2,650 in Caebraichycafn.[125] The defeat of 1896–7 shattered this confident picture: in 1898 membership slumped to 1,654 and by July 1899 the union had only 822 members.[126]

Support fell drastically in Caebraichycafn, with half as many members in 1898 as in 1897, and only half that number in 1899. But the collapse was even more drastic in other lodges; contributions from Ffestiniog fell in 1899 to only one-fifth of the 1897 total, and only Alexandra and Moeltryfan maintained their membership. The most serious collapse took place in lodge No. 1., Dinorwic, which, boasting almost 2,000 members in 1897, seems to have had no members at all by 1900,[127] though this may have had as much to do with the quality of the local leadership as with the effects of the Penrhyn dispute. Thomas W. Thomas, the lodge's delegate to the union council, had complained in January 1897 that 'there is a need of new leaders for us in Dinorwic'.[128]

The agreement signed on 18 August 1897 specified that

> All the late employees who desire work in the Penrhyn Quarry will be re-admitted in a body as far as it is practicable, and the remainder as soon as work can be arranged for them . . .[129]

The rub was in the phrase 'as far as it is practicable', for though the seventy-one men suspended in September 1896 were, with one exception, allowed back, and David Davies and Robert Owen, whose suspension had led to the dispute, were also given work after Young had 'heard your expressions of regret for the great mistakes which you made',[130] twenty-five men were not allowed to re-start work. Only one, Azariah Roberts, a committee man representing the men working under contract, was a union activist;[131] the others were considered 'men of bad

[124] *Annual Report on Trade Unions*, 1897.
[125] GAS, X.N.W.Q.U. / 48, Cash Books.
[126] *Annual Report on Trade Unions*; N.W.Q.U., Minute Book, July 1899.
[127] GAS, X.N.W.Q.U. / 48, Cash Books.
[128] N.W.Q.U., Minute Book, 2 January 1897.
[129] Terms of Settlement, Clause 5.
[130] GAS, P.Q.L.B., 309; E. A. Young to D. Davies and R. Owen, 2 September 1897.
[131] Parry, op. cit., p. 167.

character or unsuitable workmen'.[132] These were men like David Parry of Llandegai, who was considered by the management to be 'a rambler and greatly addicted to drink' and who later worked on the Liverpool docks;[133] and William G. Williams, who was also excluded for drinking and was in trouble again in 1902 for being drunk at 8.15 a.m.[134]

Whatever the management's reasons for excluding these men, they were clearly driving home the advantage gained by Penrhyn's victory. If these men had been taken on and dismissed a week later, W. H. Williams argued, there would have been little complaint, but to refuse to take them back at all was a clear breach of the agreement and of the assurance given by Lloyd Carter, Lord Penrhyn's solicitor, that 'no one would be left out'.[135] But there was little the men could do except protest, and the management's uncompromising position boded ill for the future.

As union organisation in the quarry weakened, E. A. Young became increasingly aggressive in his tactics. By 1898 he had a Mr. Ellis, 'my new detective',[136] gathering information about the leaders in the quarry, and in May 1898 he felt strong enough to sack two prominent union activists, John Williams 'Rynys, and Peter Roberts, Carneddi, for a breach of safety regulations— a 'slight breach', according to W. J. Parry, ' . . . that no one was ever known to have been dismissed for before'.[137] Peter Roberts was 'the very man who some years ago was always crying out for a Government Inspector', so his dismissal on safety grounds supplied Young with a certain satisfaction, while it is clear that John Williams was dismissed for being 'one of the very bitterest and most mischievous men during the strike'.[138]

In December 1898 William R. Evans, the chairman of the men's committee, was, without any explicit reason, dismissed, despite the fact that Young held a low opinion of his powers as an agitator; he was, he wrote contemptuously 'about 62–65 of

[132] Ibid.
[133] GAS, P.Q. 100/42; D. D. Davies to H. Meares, 24 June 1902.
[134] Ibid., 12 April 1902.
[135] Parry, op. cit., p. 166.
[136] GAS, P.Q.L.B., 404–06; Young to Pennant, 2 June 1898.
[137] Parry, op. cit., p. 168.
[138] GAS, P.Q.L.B., 404–06.

rather poor physique and no apparent sign of intellectual power, in fact not in any way a man I should have expected others to elect for their chairman'.[139] To many in the quarry, however, he must have symbolised the union's steady and unceasing perseverance, for he had been associated with the union since its inception; he had served as an official of the lodge for the sixteen years since he became treasurer in 1882 and he had also been a delegate to the N.W.Q.U. council.[140]

In June 1899 Young picked off another unionist of importance, Robert Davies; again no reason was given. Like W. R. Evans, Davies had long been associated with the union in Caebraichycafn and he had been a member of the deputation that visited Penrhyn in 1897; he had also been prominent in the N.W.Q.U., serving as a vice-president in 1895 and 1896 and as president in 1897.[141] The union gave him £6 on the occasion of the loss of his livelihood.[142]

Young attacked on other fronts as well. In November 1899 he refused to accept a peace offering from the committee, who had presented a gift to Lord Penrhyn.[143] He also unilaterally issued an instruction changing the rules for blasting in the quarry and, more significantly, reducing the number of holidays enjoyed by the men, when he ordered the doing 'away entirely with what are called Bangor Fair Days'[144] and other privileges. Victory appeared to be his, but his actions were storing up as a reservoir, not only of fear, but also of hate and bitterness. The dam burst in November 1900, three years after the truce of 1897. And this time the battle was 'to be to the death';[145] compromise would be a word without meaning to either Penrhyn or Bethesda.

VI. THE NEW LEADERS

The two men who were to dominate the N.W.Q.U. in the years of struggle after 1897, D. R. Daniel and W. H. Williams, were possessed of very different personalities. Williams had risen to

[139] GAS, P.Q.L.B., 490, 2 December 1898.
[140] GAS, Cofnodydd Penderfyniadau Pwyllgor y Gwaith Caebraichycafn, 12 May 1882.
[141] N.W.Q.U., Minute Book, 6 May 1895, 2 May 1896, 1 May 1897.
[142] Ibid., 29 July 1899.
[143] GAS, P.Q.99/6, 22 November 1899.
[144] Ibid., private letter from E. A. Young to H. P. Meares, 24 November 1899.
[145] U.C.N.W. Coetmor MSS. 73, p. 258; W. J. Parry to Wm. George, 24 November 1900.

his position after a lifetime in the Penrhyn quarries and a
position of leadership during the 1896–7 dispute; Daniel's
connections with the quarrying industry previous to his
appointment were non-existent.

Before his election as organiser for the N.W.Q.U. in January
1896, when he defeated J. W. Thomas of Waunfawr by 752
votes to 267 in a low poll, there was little in Daniel's career to
suggest an interest in either slate-quarrying or trade-unionism.[146] He was born in 1859, the son of a tenant farmer, in the
rural area of Cefnddwysarn, Merionethshire.[147] In the next
farm, Tom Ellis, later to be M.P. for Merioneth and the hope
of Welsh radicalism, grew up as a close childhood friend.
Daniel attended the college in Bala, presumably with the aim
of training for the ministry. He visited the United States in
1885 and returned to Wales in 1887 as a propagandist for the
temperance crusader 'Plenydd'. He became a well-known
speaker for the U.K. Alliance and 'debated in favour of the
principle of the control of the [drink] market by the people
from hundreds of platforms'. He also became active in the
radical Liberal ferment of the time, 'delighting to sit at the
feet of the Italian teacher Mazzini'.[148] Having moved to Four
Crosses, near Chwilog, Caernarvonshire, Liberalism became
his stage and he was a confidant and friend of David Lloyd
George. In 1895 he was elected an alderman of Caernarvonshire
County Council.

How he came to stand for the post of organiser for the
N.W.Q.U. is far from clear, though it seems likely that his
many and influential friends in the Liberal Party in Caernarvonshire considered that his talents would be put to good
use there. Once elected, he displayed considerable energy and
he was soon deeply involved in arguing the Penrhyn men's
case; he clearly enjoyed the confidence of the local leaders in
Bethesda in a way that W. J. Parry and W. J. Williams no
longer did.

The years that followed were extremely difficult ones for the
union, but Daniel made many attempts at recruitment, using

[146] N.W.Q.U., Minute Book, 18 January 1896.
[147] David R. Daniel, 1859–1931. See K. W. Jones-Roberts, 'D. R. Daniel',
Journal of the Merioneth Historical and Record Society, Vol. V, pp. 58–78.
[148] U.C.N.W. Coetmor MSS. 44, pp. 73–74 (*Papur Pawb*, 15 June 1895).

his skills as a propagandist to prepare a series of pamphlets on the necessity of union organisation in the quarries.[149] During the battle of 1900–3 his oratory was a constant feature of the strike meetings and the press reports. In 1906 he left the union as abruptly as he had arrived, accepting a London-based post as second secretary of the Coast Erosion Committee. Lloyd George was, without question, in part responsible for bringing his old friend to Whitehall. Although estranged from Lloyd George during the first world war Daniel remained in London until his death in 1931.

Though he had earlier been a religious man, his radical, inquiring mind led him to doubt many of his earlier beliefs. Observing the religious revival of 1904–5, he remarked that he was 'thinking much of this revival. They seem to be in a different plane from my own',[150] and in his later London years he moved further away from orthodoxy and became active in Ethical and Positivist Societies. Standing in the shadow of his prominent friends, Daniel has been largely forgotten and the judgement of another famous compatriot is cruel indeed, Thomas Jones described him as belonging

> to the class described by the early Russian novelists as 'superfluous men', by French novelists as a 'cut out of cloth which had no thickness' of whom we have examples in Wales— brilliant talkers full of good impulses, devoid of will power, content to puff rings of smoke from cigarettes enchantées. With them to do a thing and to say they had done it was the same. They were poets of sorts. In his charming futility Daniel was in complete contrast to the energetic friends of his youth.[151]

Something of this aspect of his character does come through in his years with the N.W.Q.U., but on the whole his leadership, while not blessed with any particular success, was marked at least by enthusiasm, new ideas, and what appeared to be a

[149] Four of these pamphlets were printed by May 1900: 'Paham y dylwn fod yn Undebwr' (Why I Should be a Trade Unionist), 'Addysg a'r Chwarelwr' (Education and the Quarryman), 'Yr Awr Giniaw' (The Dinner Hour) and 'Undeb Undebau' (The unity of unions). N.W.Q.U., Minute Book, 7 May 1900.
[150] Jones-Roberts, op. cit., p. 76.
[151] Thomas Jones, *Welsh Broth* (London, 1951), pp. 38–39.

genuine enough commitment to the quarrymen's cause. During these years, moreover, Daniel came as close as he ever did actually to affect the course of significant events.

If Daniel's sharp mind and radical energies found only a partial outlet in the N.W.Q.U., W. H. Williams was a man ideally suited for his union position, and yet his rise to influence had been equally unpredictable. Williams's reputation as a quarrymen's leader has been somewhat dimmed by the careers of W. J. Parry, who had preceded him, and R. T. Jones, who was to follow; and yet he was in at least one way the quarry-men's most interesting leader because he expressed in his own personality so much that belonged to, and was unique to, the quarrymen and their culture. The Penrhyn battles are under-standable only in the light of the humane fury of the outraged consciences of Williams and of men like him.

William H. Williams was born to a deeply religious quarry-man's family in Llwybrmain, Mynydd Llandegai, near Bethesda, in 1848. Though generally known as 'W.H.', his neighbours knew him throughout his life as William Arafon, so called after the name of the house where he was born.[152] His formal education was minimal and he started work in the Penrhyn quarries when he was ten and apparently mastered the quarry craft while still young. His father died when he was fourteen, leaving his mother with ten children to raise.

Williams was steeped in the culture of the chapel and he read deeply in the field of theology; his English was fluent and he had studied Mazzini and Carlyle in that language;[153] he also gave simultaneous translations into Welsh of public readings of *The Times* held during the quarrymen's dinner hour. But Welsh was his chosen medium and he rarely spoke in English, even when conducting negotiations with a monoglot English management. He saw no reason to justify this: challenged by the chairman of Caernarvonshire County Council to speak in English, Williams replied in Welsh and then continued in the same language.[154]

He apparently took an active part in the 1874 dispute in the

---

[152] William H. Williams, 1848–1917. See E. M. Humphreys, 'W. H. Williams', *Gwŷr Enwog Gynt* (1950), pp. 113–23.
[153] *The Clarion*, 31 October 1896.
[154] Humphreys, op. cit., p. 123.

quarry[155] and may have been the William Williams from Llwybrmain who represented the Holywell and Tangarret districts on the lodge committee of that year.[156] But there is no record of his taking any prominent role again in quarry affairs until 1889, when he served as a vice-president of the N.W.Q.U.;[157] his name first appears in the minutes of the Caebraichycafn lodge in the same year, when he was chosen as a member of a local rules revision committee.[158] In 1890 he was a representative on the lodge's general committee of the Edward (Twll) district and in July of that year he was elected president of the lodge. For the next three years he was deeply involved in union affairs in the quarry; in July 1891 he was elected a member of a deputation of eight to represent the quarrymen in negotiations, and he was a member of a further deputation in April 1892. In the same month he represented the lodge on the N.W.Q.U. council and he was elected annual president of the union in May 1892.[159] In February 1893 he was a member of a further deputation to represent the men, and he was active throughout that year, supporting the conference that encouraged the Llechwedd quarrymen on strike in August and attending the special conference on union rules in October.[160]

He had therefore made his mark on the union both locally and centrally in the four years up to 1893, but he was not one of the long-standing stalwarts of the Bethesda lodge like William R. Evans or Hugh H. Davies; moreover, it is clear that the union thought more of his abilities and of the contribution he could make than he did himself, for he refused to appear as one of the N.W.Q.U.'s representatives to give evidence before the Royal Commission on Labour in 1891[161] and appears to have dropped out of union activity completely at the end of 1893.

[155] Ibid., p. 116.
[156] N.L.W., W. J. Parry MSS., 8,738B: Llyfr Penderfyniadau Perthynol i gangen Undeb Chwarelwyr Gogledd Cymru. Dosbarth Caebraichycafn, 1874.
[157] N.W.Q.U., Minute Book, 25 May 1889. It was a position of no great influence.
[158] Bethesda Minute Book, 15 November 1889.
[159] Ibid., 18 July 1890; 9 July 1891; 26 April 1892; 13 April 1892. N.W.Q.U., Minute Book, 7 May 1892.
[160] GAS, Llyfr Perthynol i Lodge No. 2, Caebraichycafn, 11 February 1893; 30 August 1893; 5 October 1893.
[161] N.W.Q.U., Minute Book, 20 June 1891.

There is no question, however, that Williams was one of the most influential men in Bethesda and the surrounding area, and his position certainly seems to have been well established by 1891 when a eulogistic portrait of him was victorious in a local eisteddfod.[162] The author of this essay, John Williams 'Rynys, who was himself a prominent and victimized leader of the Bethesda quarrymen, saw that Williams's standing in the community owed much to the considerable strength of his personality and to his deep involvement in the local Calvinistic Methodist chapels. He had been raised to be a deacon in Hermon (M.C.) chapel in 1876 and he had an impressive presence in chapel meetings:

> when conducting the means of grace in public, he submits himself on his knees, one hand on the seat, the other holding the lamp post.[163]

He was a strict father but an enlightened Sunday School teacher, encouraging his pupils to think about questions rather than to give the mechanical answers, learnt by rote, that were demanded by many teachers. He had a reputation as a cultured and learned man, his two best-read books being the Bible and Lewis Edwards's *Athrawiaeth yr Iawn*, ('The Doctrine of Atonement') though he had also read more widely.[164]

He was a formidable and insistent debater, and few adversaries in theological or political discussions escaped unscathed. Having a reputation as a deep thinker, he rarely changed his mind once he had committed himself, 'he does not bend to anyone or anything', noted John Williams, 'though it is possible to take that which is praiseworthy in him too far, and perhaps his weak spot comes to light here—too stubborn'.[165] A humorous man who delighted in that vein of Welsh humour which relates character-displaying stories and perceptive remarks, there was no mistaking the forcefulness and strength of his personality. 'You do not have to talk to him for long', recalled E. M. Humphreys, 'to see that beneath the humour, the tolerant

---

[162] John Williams 'Rynys, *Braslun Buddugol o William H. Williams Arafon* (Bethesda, 1896).
[163] Ibid., p. 13; John Williams complains that he had a tendency to pray for too long 'as if seeing a second light and growing more tenacious', p. 9.
[164] Ibid., p. 6, 9.
[165] Ibid., p. 7.

philosophy, the easy-going manner . . . there lay steel.'[166]

In 1891 John Williams considered him to be 'The "Paul" of our thinkers, the "Gamaliel" of our Sunday School, "John", the dear disciple of the Church and the "Moses" of the quarryman'. It was in this last role that he was to make a central contribution to the struggles of the Penrhyn quarrymen. He took little or no part in the committee's preparations for the dispute in 1896,[167] but once the struggle had started he gave his public and eloquent support to the cause and he was given a 'princely' welcome by the first mass-meeting of the men on 25 August 1896, when he warned of the invincible power of Lord Penrhyn.[168]

Leadership of the struggle was imposed upon him, however, and did not come of his own choosing. According to John Williams, in his 1896 addendum to his original portrait, he was more than once asked to take a leading role but had adamantly refused all entreaties.[169] One of Lord Penrhyn's conditions during the early attempts at negotiation was that any deputation that came to discuss with him should not contain any of the 71 men suspended in September 1896; since all the members of the men's committee were amongst the 71 the movement appeared to be effectively decapitated. W. H. Williams had not been a member of the committee, nor had he been one of the 71 suspended. From then on Lord Penrhyn had, by his own conditions, to negotiate with Williams, a mistake which was soon recognised by Penrhyn, who wrote to Sir Courtenay Boyle of the Board of Trade in December 1896 protesting at the inclusion of Williams in the delegation, for 'the tone of some of the recent speeches made by William H. Williams . . . is such as to give but little hope of his acting in a conciliatory spirit in the suggested negotiations'.[170]

Since entering the fray, W. H. Williams had poured all his intransigence and massive sense of principle into his speeches. John Williams witnessed the metamorphosis of the devout and modest dogmatist into the man of scalded conscience and hard

---

[166] Humphreys, op. cit., p. 113.
[167] He was not a member of the men's committee.
[168] *T.H.C.*, 25 September 1896.
[169] J. Williams, op. cit., p. 13.
[170] Parry, op. cit., p. 121.

head who was to inspire the men of Caebraichycafn to four years of sacrifice, on the evening of 14 November 1896 in the Market Hall, Bethesda. For then 'he ascended to the summit of eloquence and inspiration' and turned 'the aim of his revolver, the muzzle of his cannon' on the doubters.

> He was on that night like the fire that melts, the fervency of his eyes, the stance of his body, the clenched fists, the fury in his voice; the inhabitant inside had been disturbed, and yes! the chieftains of our land would have to bend to truth and to justice and alleviate the wrong done to the oppressed.[171]

He rapidly became the dominant figure in the dispute, speaking at many public meetings and conducting the negotiations virtually single-handed: during the meeting with Lord Penrhyn and E. A. Young on March 18 his two comrades in the deputation spoke only once during the three-and-a-half-hour meeting and then only to endorse his position.[172] By the May negotiations, Young discerned some differences among the deputation, for 'Robert Davies in particular, showed (I thought) considerable signs of uneasiness when Williams persisted that he did not think the men would accept these terms and on this occasion neither he nor H. Jones chimed in to agree as they usually do.'[173] But there was still no doubting who the authoritative figure was.

Williams was a respected leader of his community in the only two ways that mattered to that community—at work and in prayer. He took the moral certainty, the intimacy with the absolute of the calvinistic Hermons, Jerusalems and Bethesdas into an industrial struggle which he was shrewd enough to realise early on could hardly be won; but then, as he saw it, 'it was not the result that was the question but what was their duty'.[174] We shall assess later the importance of this attitude in the course of the Penrhyn disputes, but there is no question but that W. H. Williams in this respect expressed the feelings of a great many of the people of Bethesda.

[171] J. Williams, op. cit., pp. 15–16.
[172] Parry, op. cit., p. 159.
[173] GAS, P.Q.L.B., 279; E. A. Young to Lord Penrhyn, 20 May 1897.
[174] Y.H.C., 20 October 1896.

His leadership of the dispute of 1896–7, and his known dissatisfaction with the settlement, catapulted him into the new post of financial secretary of the N.W.Q.U. in December 1898, when he won the election to the post by a huge majority. He remained working with the union until his death in 1917, though in later years he was not to figure as prominently as once he had. A radical Liberal most of his life, he switched his allegiance to the Labour Party before his death, though his friend E. Morgan Humphreys doubted his understanding of socialism; his real allegiance, Humphreys felt, was to trade unionism and the sacred principle of the right of workers to combine.[175]

W. H. Williams and his fellow trade unionists in Cae-braichycafn were convinced that victory might have been possible in the 1896–7 dispute, had W. J. Williams and W. J. Parry not intervened with the management. It is impossible to know whether their judgement was correct; what is beyond doubt is that the slate market was improving towards the end of the 1890s and that the men were more likely to succeed in such favourable economic conditions than in the depressed conditions that were to follow. The slate market was still buoyant when the quarrymen next walked out of the Penrhyn quarries, in 1900, but a recession was imminent and victory unattainable. The late 1890s were probably the last time that the slate-quarrymen of Gwynedd were in a position to win a major victory. But in 1900 no one could be aware of that fact.

---

[175] Humphreys, op. cit., p. 122.

VIII

THE PENRHYN LOCK-OUT 1900–1903

I. Y STREIC FAWR

In May 1899 the North Wales Quarrymen's Union was one of forty-four unions to affiliate to the General Federation of Trade Unions, a body set up under the sponsorship of the T.U.C. to offer unions 'a scheme of mutual insurance against being involved in a dispute too protracted for their own funds'.[1] It was a wise move for a weak union whose total membership fluctuated at the time around 1,000 and with business to finish with a determined employer. The move must be seen as a precaution, however, and in no way as preparation by the union for another battle. Membership in Caebraichycafn had fallen drastically since 1897 and contributions from the quarry declined from £1,075 in 1897 to only £261 in 1899.[2] In the first quarter of 1900 there were only 369 union members in the quarry out of the 2,700 men at work.[3] The dismissal of union leaders rather than any defiance from the men marked these years and it seemed most unlikely that battle could be re-joined with Lord Penrhyn.

The management's hard line since 1897 seemed to be paying off and in April 1900 E. A. Young dealt what might have been a severe blow to the union—he forbade the collection of dues in the quarry. Because of the scattered homes of many of the men, the collecting of dues was thus made well-nigh impossible. But the move misfired for, faced with this threatened annihilation of their union, the men rallied; due-collecting centres in Bethesda became recruiting centres for the union; within the next six months 1,197 men joined the local lodge and by the end of the year it had almost 2,000 members.[4]

---

[1] E. H. Phelps Brown, *The Growth of British Industrial Relations* (London, 1960), p. 249.
[2] GAS, X.N.W.Q.U./48, *Cash Book.*
[3] GAS, X.N.W.Q.U./63, Caebraichycafn Lodge No. 2. Register of Members.
[4] Ibid. These accurate figures, though not the same as those given by A. P. Thompson, *Desolate Bethesda!* (1902) and quoted by J. Roose Williams in 'The Life and Work of William John Parry, Bethesda, with particular reference to

With the union strong once again in the quarry and the issues which had precipitated the 1896–7 conflict as hotly in dispute as ever, and with the quarrymen's resentment fuelled by the management's unremitting behaviour since 1897, the peace between men and master in Bethesda was precarious indeed. By the end of November 1900 war had once again been declared.

The Penrhyn lock-out had its immediate causes in a series of confusing incidents starting in mid-October 1900. The trouble began with a disagreement between fourteen men working on *Ponc Ffridd* and their overseeing underagent concerning the contract of two of the men. The fourteen refused to work on Saturday and were suspended for three days. A fortnight later the fourteen were told that they were no longer to work on the same gallery but that they were to be scattered through the quarry and their bargains let in one contract to a 'big contractor'. When that contractor appeared on the *Ponc*, however, he was threatened, assaulted and thrown out of the quarry. A week later a similar incident occurred elsewhere in the quarry and legal proceedings were started against twenty-six men.[5] Three hundred dragoons entered the area in case more serious trouble should break out.[6]

The twenty-six men were dismissed from the quarry before trial and, as most were thought to be innocent by the rest of the quarrymen, feeling ran very high. When the case came up in Bangor on 5 November the whole body of quarrymen marched to the town in their support. This insubordination earned the whole workforce a fortnight's suspension from work. Of the twenty-six tried, twenty were found not guilty.

When the suspensions ended on 19 November, the men returned to the quarry and bargains were let. It became apparent, however, that eight *ponciau* were not being let; on the 22nd 2,000 men refused to work until 800 fellow-quarrymen had also been let bargains. E. A. Young, the quarry manager, ordered them to 'either go on working or leave the quarry

his trade union activities among the slate quarrymen of North Wales'. (University of Wales M.A. thesis, 1953), p. 311, confirm the impression of rapid union growth in Caebraichycafn after April 1900.

[5] Parry, op. cit., pp. 170–75; *Yr Herald Cymraeg*, 30 October–27 November 1900.

[6] *Yr Herald Cymraeg*, 2 November 1900.

quietly'. By mid-day the quarry was deserted apart from the stewards and a small group of workers numbering eighty-five in all: the rest of the men, including every single skilled quarryman, had taken their tools and left. Of the 2,800 men who walked out of Lord Penrhyn's quarry on 22 November 1900, almost one thousand were not to return until after November 1903; another thousand were never to return.

In the ensuing three years both sides produced a mass of printed material to justify their stand and to expose their opponents; few negotiations can ever have been conducted so publicly and so fruitlessly.[7] The first negotiations, from 18 to 21 December 1900, took place in London through the intervention of Clement Edwards, then a journalist on the *Daily News*. The men's demands were:

1. The right freely to elect spokesmen from the ranks of the men in the quarry to discuss grievances with the management from time to time.
2. The right of the men during the dinner hour to discuss matters among themselves in the quarry.[8]
3. The reinstatement of certain victimised leaders.
4. The establishment of a minimum wage.
5. The punishment of unjustifiable conduct on the part of foremen and officials towards the men.
6. The introduction, experimentally, of a system of co-operative piecework in place of work hitherto done under contract.
7. The humanizing of the harsh rules of discipline, and the reduction of punishments for breaches of them.
8. The reintroduction of the annual holiday on 1 May.
9. More democratic control of the Quarry Sick Club.[9]

Nothing was agreed at the conference but the terms offered by Penrhyn were put to a secret ballot; they were rejected by 1,707 votes to 77.

By December a considerable number of men had left to work elsewhere, most of them to the coalfields of south Wales; altogether between 1,400 and 1,600 men left Bethesda during the dispute. Through the spring of 1901 things were relatively

---

[7] See bibliography for list of pamphlets produced by the two sides.
[8] I.e., to hold meetings in the quarry.
[9] Parry, op. cit., pp. 172–73.

quiet apart from a mass-meeting at Easter,[10] but in June excitement returned to the area as rumours intensified that the quarry was about to re-open.[11] On 11 June Penrhyn did open his quarry and some 500 men, including 242 quarrymen, went back to work. Demonstrations, meetings and violence followed. The anti-blackleg violence fell into a continuing pattern of threats and minor attacks. On Wednesday, 30 July, on the pretext that 300 youthful strikers were returning from South Wales, 200 infantry and sixty cavalry were moved into Bangor; on Saturday, 2 August, one hundred men of the East Yorkshire and South Staffordshire Infantry came into Bethesda itself, followed by thirty dragoons.[12] The trouble that followed was minimal and the troops left. Attacks and threatening behaviour toward the blacklegs continued, however, with arrests taking place regularly; at the beginning of September another twenty-six men came before the magistrates in Bangor.

On New Year's Eve 1901[13] more serious trouble flared in the town and one hundred police and a hundred and fifty soldiers came in and some twenty-seven arrests were made. In February 1902 the Caernarvonshire County Council intervened in an attempt to arbitrate. They held several meetings with the men's representatives and with E. A. Young, the quarry manager; in the face of Penrhyn's refusal to be interviewed, however, their peace moves failed.[14]

By June 1902 there were some seven hundred men back in the quarry and the weekly meetings became less well attended. Some antagonism toward the men's committee became apparent, but nevertheless over two thousand men were still out and violence could still flare up, as it did early in September. At the end of September Lord Penrhyn agreed to meet a deputation of the men if a 'quarry committee is not discussed'. When, however, he refused to talk about 'representation' at all, the deputation was called off.[15]

In December 1902 the Board of Trade was asked to intervene

[10] *Yr Herald Cymraeg*, 9 April 1901.
[11] Ibid., 4, 11, 18, 25 June 1901.
[12] Ibid., 6 August 1901.
[13] Ibid., 7 January 1902.
[14] See *Caernarvonshire County Council and the Penrhyn Dispute*.
[15] *Yr Herald Cymraeg*, 10 June 1902; 8 July 1902; 13 May 1902; 16 September 1902; 23 September 1902; 7 October 1902.

under the terms of the Conciliation Act, but, as in 1896–7, the Board refused to act on the grounds that Lord Penrhyn would not be bound by the act and that both parties had to ask for intervention.[16] In March 1903 Penrhyn instigated libel proceedings against W. J. Parry. Parry was forced to pay £500 damages, but as an aftermath to the Court proceedings Penrhyn's lawyer, Sir Edward Clarke, offered negotiations to the men's leaders. The negotiations were no more than an attempt at an organised return to work; no demands were made except that there be no victimisation. Substantial agreement was reached but, at the last moment, Penrhyn withdrew his confidence in Clarke.[17] Penrhyn wanted nothing less than unconditional surrender.

Also in March 1903 William Jones, M.P. for Caernarvonshire Arfon, brought the matter up in the House of Commons, moving an 'Adjournment of the House for the purpose of discussing a definite matter of urgent public importance'.[18] The debate attracted a dozen speakers, including Gerald Balfour and Lloyd George. On 2 April Campbell-Bannerman asked a question in the House on the dispute and the Liberals pressed for a full-scale debate on, as they saw it, the government's failure to implement the 1896 Conciliation Act.[19] On 27 April the Liberals proposed a vote of censure on the government:

> That in view of the grave social and public interests involved in the continuance of the industrial dispute at Bethesda, this House condemns the inaction of His Majesty's Government...[20]

The motion was proposed for the Opposition by Asquith and opposed by Gerald Balfour, president of the Board of Trade. In the long debate that followed, the prime minister, amongst others, showed that he was well briefed on the matter. The Tories treated the motion as

> merely a political manoeuvre of the most transparent character, designed partly to occupy a little time, and partly to catch a

[16] Ibid., 2 December 1902; 23 December 1902.
[17] See Asquith's speech in the House of Commons: *Hansard* Parliamentary Debates, vol. CXXI, fourth series, pp. 482–95.
[18] *Hansard*, vol. CXVIII, pp. 1649–80.
[19] For the 1896 Conciliation Act, see Clegg, Fox, Thompson, op. cit., pp. 213–14, 263.
[20] *Hansard*, vol. CXXI, p. 505.

few socialist votes for a party which stands sadly in need of them.[21]

This judgement might well have been correct, but whatever their intentions, the Liberals failed to move the government into any action and the situation in Bethesda remained the same.

In April 1903 the committee made a desperate plea for arbitration, inviting the prime minister, Lord Rosebery, Joseph Chamberlain, Lord James of Hereford, or anyone appointed by H.R.H. Prince of Wales or H.M. Government to intervene as arbitrator.[22] Penrhyn would hear nothing of it. The lock-out continued, somewhat aimlessly, with much recrimination and confusion; the men could see that they were not budging Penrhyn an inch. A growing number began to emigrate to the U.S.A.; many applied secretly for work.[23] In late September the General Federation of Trade Unions stopped its payments to the men; later in October the G.F.T.U. declared that as far as it was concerned 'the dispute is over'.[24] Early in November a small meeting in Bethesda voted narrowly to return to work.[25] One by one, and quite arbitrarily, some of them were taken back. By December the situation in Bethesda was 'no work, no union, no fund . . . every fountain has dried up'. The traditional Saturday market closed down; and as the year drew to a close, poverty intensified and fever shut the schools.[26] Men were allowed to trickle back into the quarry but a thousand men were never to return; in 1907, four years later, the work force in the quarry was still only 1,800,[27] and in 1910 the population of Bethesda was well below the 6,000 it had been in 1899.[28]

II. THE ISSUES

The issues which underlay the three-year confrontation in Penrhyn and which motivated the two sides were essentially the same as those which characterised the dispute of 1896–7;

[21] See the defence of Penrhyn in *Hansard*, vol. CXXI, pp. 539–48.
[22] *Yr Herald Cymraeg*, 14 April 1903.
[23] Ibid., 25 August 1903; 8, 15, 22 September 1903.
[24] Ibid., 29 September 1903; 27 October 1903.
[25] By 192 votes to 161 (ibid., 10 November 1903).
[26] Ibid., 1 December 1903; 8 December 1903.
[27] Roose Williams, op. cit., p. 276.
[28] *Bennetts Business Directory* (1899, 1910).

the two disputes will therefore be discussed together. The issues at stake were many, complicated and deeply rooted, not only in the Penrhyn quarries but also in the attitudes and beliefs of the parties involved. Behind the slogan of 'the right of combination', there lay claims concerning money, efficiency and control as well as of principle. 'This is not a quarrel', protested D. R. Daniel in May 1902, 'between master and workers concerning some halfpenny an hour more wages, it is a hard struggle for independence, for freedom, and for humanity.'[29] By 1902 his remarks rang true, for by then the sole issue in contention was the principle of representation. But money had been a most important ingredient in the recipe for the conflict, and its flavour was to be found on many of the 'principles' involved. In the months preceding the 1896–7 stoppage, the men's demand for an increase in wages had been central. In July 1896 the committee had submitted their demand for an increase in wages to Lord Penthyn:

> We have come to an unanimous decision to ask for 5/5 a day as standard wages for quarrymen, miners and sawyers in the mill and to have, when they fail to reach the standard on the letting, 4/6 a day; and that other classes are to follow in the same ratio.[30]

Claims were also made on behalf of *rybelwrs*, stonemasons, 'apprentices' and the men working in the mill and the yard. This was their first and basic set of demands, but the simple issue of increased wages was quickly complicated by a series of other, interlocking issues. The question of contracts, of *rybelwrs*, and disputes about efficiency, control and, above all, about freedom and combination, came to dominate the negotiations.

A month after their first demand was submitted, the men's committee received a note from E. A. Young refusing virtually all their requests; angered by this rebuff, the committee drew up a longer and more comprehensive list of complaints. Their major attack was on the 'system of letting contracts that has lately been introduced to the quarry'.[31] The system of letting

---

[29] *Yr Herald Cymraeg*, 20 May 1902.
[30] W. J. Parry, *The Penrhyn Lock-Out*, p. 72.
[31] Ibid., p. 74. The contracts varied in size from three bargains to nearly a whole gallery.

sections of the quarry in large contracts to sub-contractors, who would then employ the various classes of quarrymen, was a system deeply offensive to the men; one of the major complaints of 1896–7, this system caused the violent snapping of temper in November 1900 which precipitated the struggle of 1900–3.

The men argued that the contract system was exploitative, unjust and inefficient. It was exploitative because a middleman was introduced who creamed off the excess created by his quarrymen employees; this was the 'sweat shop principle' to which the men often referred. It was unjust because the contracts were not always let to 'practical quarrymen', resulting in 'many workmen of experience and ability' being kept 'in a state of dependency on inferior workmen to themselves'. It was inefficient because the inexperienced men at work on the contracts took, according to the men's committee, good slate rock 'over the tips' instead of making slates from it.[32]

Related to the contracts issue was that of the *rybelwrs*, those men and boys not in bargains, who 'freelanced' around the quarry and were often reduced to begging crews of quarrymen for work. The men demanded the end of this system and the regularising of the position of the *rybelwrs* by granting them monthly lettings on a poundage related to that of the quarrymen proper; they should be given bargains on the rock then being worked by the contractors.

These were significant enough demands in themselves and they had given rise to considerable resentment and a sense of injustice among the quarrymen. But they were also linked to the men's demands regarding the low level, and uncertainty, of wages. It is clear that the demand for the regularisation of the position of the *rybelwr*, resulting in part from the miserable standing of this class in the quarry, owed something also to the feeling among quarrymen that in many situations in the quarry the low-paid *rybelwr*, who received no poundage on blocks sent to the mill and whose poundage, tonnage, and yard prices were lower than the quarryman's, was used in preference to the more expensive labour of the quarryman.

In the question of contracts, the situation was even more

[32] Ibid.

clear and was nicely stated by Lord Penrhyn in his reply to the men during his meeting with the committee on 17 August 1896:

> it seems to me that your real objection to the contract system on a large scale is founded upon the feeling that the work now done by contract would be carried on at a greater profit to the quarrymen if it was sub-divided into single bargains.[33]

Lord Penrhyn had had some research carried out into the matter and he had ascertained that the working of 40 badrock bargains over thirteen quarry months had resulted in a cost per ton of slate of 2s. $6\frac{1}{4}d$. Worked under contract, the cost had been only a third of that sum per ton.

The men based their demand for an increase in wages on the generally improving state of the slate market in the late 1890s, a market which had compensated for the falling away of foreign sales by a vigorous boom in the building industry at home, which created a state of virtual slate famine. Quarries were re-opened in 1895 and 1896, men taken on and advances made in wages; five per cent extra was paid in both Penrhyn and Dinorwic in 1895, threepence a day in several Ffestiniog quarries. The five per cent in Penrhyn, however, was not added to the standard wage but was a percentage of the wages bill after costs had been deducted. Whenever a reduction was made, the men pointed out, it was a percentage of the standard 'and we cannot consider any advance satisfactory . . . if it is not done on the same principle'.[34]

Young and Penrhyn argued in reply that the men's references to a booming market were mistaken, since not only the price of slate but also 'the cost of production had risen, and continues to do so'.[35] It is difficult to understand on what premise this argument could be based, because profits were certainly booming at this time and production in 1899 finally topped the record year of 1877. One can only speculate that Penrhyn and his manager, E. A. Young, were determined to prevent the N.W.Q.U. from riding to success, membership, and higher wages on the crest of this boom as they had done on the boom

---

[33] Ibid., p. 80.
[34] Ibid., p. 75.
[35] Ibid., p. 73.

of the mid-'seventies. Their determination was fed by the realisation that the bargain system on which slate-quarrying was founded was a vastly more costly system, both in terms of money and of control, than the contract system which the management was clearly trying to introduce on a large scale.

Such straightforward accounting, resulting in a straightforward conflict, was not, however, the crux of the Penrhyn dispute, even though it provided the fundamental division of financial interest between men and master. Money provided the stage but the drama was played out with the actors mouthing other lines, and, as in any good play, the words were open to several interpretations.

Very rapidly the original locking of antlers over the question of wages and wages' systems gave way to what to many outside observers appeared to be no more than a meaningless and infuriating, if also entertaining, slaughter by semantics. Penrhyn counter-attacked not on economics but on ground much more remote but vital; he encircled the men's detailed demands, pouncing on loose ends and there he chose to fight, knowing full well that the loose ends led to the heart of the matter. He accused the members of the committee of being liars because they had stated that contracts were 'newly introduced' to the quarry; they were not, he pointed out, and moved on not to nail the lie but to accuse the 'liars' of spreading it. In a series of long documents, he countered the men's demands, point by point, with tightly and well-argued defences; he mounted his own attack on different terrain, on a question of 'principle', namely the principles of loyalty and obedience to the employer.

It could be argued that he chose this rhetorical ground because justice and logic supported the quarrymen's case. Probably so; but such an explanation is not sufficient, and the length of the struggle cannot be understood in such terms alone. Penrhyn was dedicated to the defeat of anything resembling effective trade unionism in his quarries, partly because of the possible threat to his profits, but far more because of its threat to his power and his standing. What he refused to countenance was not the men's demands but the fact that they had been submitted by a committee elected by the men which, however much that committee might deny it, clearly signified the presence in his quarry of the muscular arm of a trade union.

Lord Penrhyn and, even more, his manager, E. A. Young, were committed to the ideas of 'free labour' and became in time the heroes of the anti-trade union lobby in Britain, hailed as the vanguard of a new employers' offensive; it was a role they were clearly delighted to fill. Penrhyn's attitudes and behaviour, however, were also deeply rooted in the politics of north Wales.

George Sholto Gordon Douglas Pennant had just celebrated his sixtieth birthday when the first dispute broke in 1896, but he was by no means unaccustomed to being a public figure. The Penrhyn family had won the Caernarvonshire parliamentary seat in 1841 and Penrhyn's father, the first Baron Penrhyn, had been the member from that date to 1866, when he transferred the responsibility to his son. Penrhyn held the seat as a Conservative, for two years, before losing it in a historic and bitterly-fought election in 1868 to the Liberal, Thomas Love Jones-Parry. Six years later, Penrhyn fought the seat again and this time he re-captured it. He lost it for good in 1880 in an electoral contest which clearly made a deep impression upon him; he felt that he had been betrayed by the electors, who included, of course, some of 'his' quarrymen, and he made a venomous attack upon them which the Welsh press never allowed him to forget. 'Caernarvonshire', he railed,

> stands on top of the list, by this electoral struggle, as a lying county . . . 1,143 electors, by their deception, have tried to prove that there is no trust any longer to be placed in the word of a Welshman in this county.[36]

He did not absent himself from local politics as a result of this defeat, however, and he served as a justice of the peace and later as a Conservative county councillor for Llandegai.

A political activist, Penrhyn was also a very rich man with powerful friends. Educated at Eton and Christ Church, Oxford, he was a colonel of the Fourth Regiment, Royal Welsh Fusiliers. When he inherited the Penrhyn estate from his father in 1886 he found himself in possession of one of the largest landed estates in Wales, over 72,000 acres by 1896, worth an

[36] Frank Price Jones, 'Gwleidyddiaeth Sir Gaernarfon yn y 19eg Ganrif', *C.H.S.T.*, vol. 26 (1965), p. 98.

annual rental of £27,000,[37] and one of the most profitable concerns in the land, the Penrhyn quarry which, it was estimated, produced some £100,000 profit annually.[38] This was a direct income, quite apart from interest on investments, many thousand times greater than that of any of his quarrymen. He was often away from the family home of Penrhyn Castle and spent much time in his London house near Hyde Park Corner or on his other estate in Stoney Stratford.[39] During the first month of the 1896–7 dispute Penrhyn's guest at Penrhyn Castle was Sir Michael Hicks-Beach, the chancellor of the Exchequer.[40]

Penrhyn's political career had been interrupted by the newly-blossoming power of Welsh Liberalism. In an age of political transformation, he found himself, despite his wealth and his power, defending a crumbling order. He had refused to accept the verdict of 1868 and had, indeed, successfully turned back the tide in 1874, but only temporarily. Against him he saw ranged Welsh nonconformity, energetic middle-class radicals, land reformers and his own 'disloyal' quarrymen. He fought them all in turn. Above all, he was nervous of any political movement that actually threatened his economic standing—of land reform and trade unionism in particular. In 1886 he founded, and was chairman of, the North Wales Property Defence Association, a body set up to counter 'the incessant interference of outside agitators . . . and the open encouragement given by a large portion of the Welsh press to schemes practically of confiscation'. He gave evidence to the Royal Commission on Land in Wales in 1893 when he attacked, in particular, the virulent anti-landlordism of the radical Welsh press.[41]

Penrhyn placed his disputes with the quarrymen in the context of his general struggle against the forces of radicalism

---

[37] *R.C. on Land*, Appendix 10; this sum was from farms and cottages only and does not include leaseholds on ground rents. See p. 11.

[38] *Mining Journal*, 10 September 1859; *Carnarvon and Denbigh Herald*, 29 March 1845.

[39] His London home was Mortimer House, Halkin Street, S.W.1; his other property was Wicken Park, Stoney Stratford.

[40] *Yr Herald Cymraeg*, 29 September 1896.

[41] *R.C. on Land*, evidence of Lord Penrhyn 22,777–23,013. He also bemoaned the fact that the north Wales terrain was not suitable for fox-hunting: 'I am sure that if there were hounds in North Wales it would do a great deal of good, it would bring farmers and labourers together' (23,013).

surrounding him; that was one important reason for his willingness to suffer the huge losses involved in the closure of his quarries. His battle with the N.W.Q.U. was one more skirmish in a general war; to lose the skirmish was not a local defeat alone, restricted to the quarry, it was of far more general import.

Even when the split between W. J. Parry and the new leaders of the union became apparent in 1897 Penrhyn saw no significance in the dispute; as far as he was concerned, Parry and his ilk, energetic Welsh businessmen and radicals, were still the main enemy, the quarrymen no more than their stage army, and he hunted Parry remorselessly, with all the considerable legal power at his disposal, during his famous libel suit against him in 1902.[42]

Trade unionism, he had no doubt, was another insidious weapon in the armoury of radicalism, implanted in his works by those who wished to undermine his authority and, as he understood it, his right to run his own quarries as he wished. As we have seen earlier,[43] the power wielded by the union committee in Penrhyn should not be underestimated; if it might seem impressive to us it appeared outrageous to Penrhyn. It was outrageous not only because of its effects on wages and conditions of labour, but also because trade unionism disrupted the nature and hold of his own power system. The quarrymen of Bethesda had for long been divided between those who sought a collective and aggressive answer to their plight and those who sought instead to survive by ingratiating themselves with Penrhyn's agents. The grip of trade unionism explicitly challenged the latter path, denied the sovereignty of managerial authority and rejected the spoils of paternalism as sufficient compensation for their complaints.

Penrhyn's father had built and provided the quarry hospital; he himself contributed £200 annually towards the quarry club, widows of quarrymen killed at work were granted small pensions, as were some men who had grown old in his employment; those still capable of work were given light tasks in the quarry along with men who had received injury. Penrhyn's wealth

---

[42] Penrhyn sued Parry for remarks published in *The Clarion*; he was awarded £500 damages.
[43] See pp. 95–97.

and power allowed him to bestow many favours; these, and the 'loyalty' which was exhibited by those who wished to earn them, constituted the system upon which Penrhyn's control of his men had long relied.

When the quarrymen rebelled in disciplined formation they rejected not only the terms of employment but also the paternalistic power structure. In 1874 the men's leaders had made it clear to Penrhyn's father that they were 'perfectly willing that his lordship should keep his charities to himself—if those in any way interfere with him in his giving us proper wages'. But the roots of Penrhyn's power went deep and his paternalism maintained its controlling presence in the quarry. When the final rupture came in 1900, Penrhyn saw this as his opportunity to change the working system in the quarry and also to dismiss not merely the leaders, but all those who gave allegiance to any power system other than his own. The 'excluded-list' drawn up during the dispute makes it perfectly clear that all those not actively, or at least passively, loyal to Penrhyn and his management and his system were to be excluded from the quarry;[44] trade unionism was to be surgically removed in an operation which called for not only the cutting out of the diseased organs but also of all the surrounding tissue suspected of being infected. In this operation, there was a high risk of killing the patient; his permanent disability was guaranteed. For the Penrhyn lock-out not only shattered a community, it also dealt a crippling blow to the Welsh slate industry; with the world's largest slate-quarry either closed or producing at only a fraction of its capacity, buyers of slate looked elsewhere, particularly to the U.S.A. and, more ominously, to tiles for their roofing materials.[45] Penrhyn considered it a price worth paying.

In this ambitious project, to nurture a new generation of malleable quarrymen, Penrhyn was ably assisted by his hand-picked manager, Emilius Alexander Young. He was a London accountant dedicated to 'business methods', who provided the bourgeois cutting-edge to his lordship's aristocratic pretensions.

[44] See pp. 262–65.
[45] 'In 1896, owing to strikes in the Welsh quarries, the U.S. gained a foothold again in England and in the English colonies.' T. Nelson Dale, *Slate in the U.S.* (1st ed., 1906), p. 137.

Young was in day-to-day control of the quarry and the disputes, and he bore considerable responsibility for the course of events, particularly as Penrhyn himself was often absent from north Wales. Young's position was brutally simple:

> Neither you nor I can force men to work on Lord Penrhyn's terms—nor can the men force Lord Penrhyn to employ them upon those terms—nothing remains to be done. Those who prefer working elsewhere are free to do so, and on the contrary those who are willing to work for Lord Penrhyn are free to apply and *if approved* [Young's emphasis] can start at once. Our battle is for freedom.[46]

Young could not understand the reluctance of the quarrymen to accept the strict work discipline he imposed: 'the more I try and introduce business principles', he grieved, 'the more they rebel'.[47] He was also unsympathetic towards the Welsh in general, considering them 'childish and ignorant', easily irritated and making poor foreman material.[48]

A great many issues, therefore, stemmed from the men's demand in July 1896 for 5s. 6d. a day: issues of economics certainly, but issues also of control and principle. To break the patronage system and challenge the divine right of the employer, the men needed organisation; to negotiate for wage increases and to defend the bargain system, they needed organisation. The battle was fought therefore on the 'principle of combination'. Penrhyn claimed he had no objection to men joining a trade union as long as they did not expect him to negotiate with it; the men pointed out that that was the whole point.

On the men's side, too, deeper issues were involved and attitudes which were able to sustain the massive sacrifices they were willing to make. The men opposed Young's régime because it usurped their position as skilled quarrymen, curtailed what they considered to be their rights and promoted those whose skill lay not in handling the rocks but in flattery. Most of the arguments of the men in the first months of the 1900–3 stoppage concerned the 'attitudes of the management'.[49] One of the ten demands of 1900 called for the 'punishment of un-

[46] GAS, P.Q. 100/42: E. A. Young to ?, 17 May 1902.
[47] GAS, P.Q. 99/6, 7; Young to Webb, 11 December 1900.
[48] Ibid., 24 January 1900; 11 December 1900; 28 November 1900.
[49] *Yr Herald Cymraeg*, 4 December 1900.

justifiable conduct on the part of foremen and officials towards the men'. The quarrymen refused to take any more, refused any longer to 'suffer the vanity, harshness, arrogance and injustice of the under-agents'.[50]

The quarryman had a high regard for his own skills and a definite opinion as to the respect they deserved. By 1900 the attack on this craft pride had become intolerable, for not only was it being physically undermined by the extension of the contract system, but it was also being daily assaulted by the boorishness of Penrhyn's management.

It was not a change in temperament alone that the men called for; they also demanded 'the humanizing of the harsh rules of discipline' which had been considerably tightened in previous years. Some traditional customs had been forbidden, but more significantly there was an intensive effort to ensure that the men kept regular working hours, the most detested rule being the one which stated that a quarryman who was fifteen minutes late in the morning would lose two days' pay.[51] Strict rules as to hours interfered with a man's responsibilities and his independence: a father claimed he could not visit a dying son without being penalised; traditional events such as funerals, always attended by hundreds of men in quarry districts, were interfered with.[52]

Where the quarrymen did concur with Penrhyn was in the importance they attached to the struggle. It was not seen as a dispute which could be won or lost, but as *the* struggle which had to be won. The idea of a tactical defeat, to return and fight another day, did not occur to them, or, if it did, it was never seriously contemplated; this was 'life's battle' in which men staked their whole identity.[53] The prize was a 'human' life; defeat meant a loss of manhood, not in the act of defeat but in the conditions which would then have to be tolerated in life and at work. The quarrymen knew that the lives Lord Penrhyn expected them to live were not only hard and often miserable, they were also degrading. Their own industrial practice, bound

[50] Ibid., 5 February 1901.
[51] Ibid., 4 December 1900.
[52] Ibid., 1 January 1901. See also *Report of Quarry Committee of Inquiry*, p. 38.
[53] *Yr Herald Cymraeg*, 20 January 1903.

up with their definition of their craft, made them conscious of the loss of freedom implicit in 'business methods', in the constraints tightening around them at work; they knew well enough that the morning hooter and the insulting under-agent were the demands of an employer and not an immutable fact of life. To go back to Penrhyn's slate trap was to accept alienation's bribe and sell one's humanity.

Other than W. H. Williams the leading local leader was Henry Jones, a reflective, reliable and somewhat autocratic man who was, paradoxically, an Anglican.[54] He continued to attend church though 'the vicar passes my house to go to the house of others'.[55] Henry Jones was a member of the executive committee of the N.W.Q.U. and in May 1903 he became the union's vice-chairman;[56] he chaired all the mass-meetings in Bethesda, making lengthy addresses at each one.

The other prominent members of the men's committee were Owen Griffith (Gerlan), vice-chairman,[57] and Griffith Edwards, secretary;[58] Edwards was also on the general council of the N.W.Q.U.[59] Other members were R. G. Pritchard, who became an auditor of the N.W.Q.U. in 1902;[60] R. J. Jones; William Williams (William Aber), a vice-chairman of the N.W.Q.U.;[61] J. Williams 'Rynys, who was victimised in May 1898[62]; and John Roberts.[63]

With W. H. Williams and D. R. Daniel, these men provided the leadership of the struggle locally, often assisted by the eloquence of W. W. Jones, or 'Cyrus' as he was commonly known, the president of the N.W.Q.U. and an enigmatic figure, who though foremost in the struggle of labour was primarily

---

[54] The *Daily News* claimed that he was also a Conservative, but there is no other evidence for this unlikely claim.

[55] Standing Joint Police Committee, *Report* of the sub-committee to enquire into matters in Bethesda, 1903, evidence of Henry Jones.

[56] N.W.Q.U. Minute Book, 27 October 1900; 4 May 1903.

[57] *Yr Herald Cymraeg*, 7 January 1903.

[58] *Y Chwarelwr Cymreig*, 4 June 1901. See E. Roberts, *Bargen Bywyd Fy Nhaid* (Llandybie, 1963).

[59] N.W.Q.U. Minute Book, 25 July 1903.

[60] Ibid., 5 May 1902.

[61] Ibid., 6 May 1901.

[62] *Yr Herald Cymraeg*, 11 December 1900.

[63] He was also an Anglican. Emyr Hywel Owen, *Lleufer* (Summer 1963). A group photograph of the committee also shows Lewis Griffith but not John Williams.

dedicated to 'temperance, freedom and morality'.[64] 'Cyrus' was a Methodist deacon in his native Nantlle valley and his main pre-occupation was religion; yet in the debates during the lock-out he showed a remarkable political awareness, veering more than any of his comrades towards socialism.

'Cyrus', W. H. Williams and the others expressed the anger and frustration of the men; they also provided a stubborn and unrelenting leadership. They took the style and the language of religious fundamentalism into an industrial struggle which even at its inception held out little enough promise of success; but once the conflict had become inevitable it also became essential, if only because of all the indignities of the past. The sense of moral certainty which formed the hard core of so many servile appearances, and the vastly over-developed sense of principle—the more precious for its enforced contravention in the pursuit of survival within Penrhyn's power—these had been goaded so often, for too long screamed in silent outrage, submitted on bended knees in gloomy Hermons and Jerusalems, like W. H. Williams himself 'fallen on his knees one hand on the seat', to make surrender inconceivable.[65] The prophets of the Old Testament strode through these men's brains like awe-inspiring and recently-mourned ancestors; the cruel compulsion to act, when it came, demanded and received, a rush of allegiance. It was from this position of rewarding sacrifice and joyous defiance that the sail-trimming caution of W. J. Parry and W. J. Williams had appeared so squalid in 1897.

The *Daily News* commented in 1901 that

> They do not complain of their wages or of their hours. The burden of their complaint is the spirit of their treatment. 'Let us be treated like men' is the supreme form of their demand.[66]

The Penrhyn quarrymen certainly did complain of their wages and of their hours, and of a good deal besides, but the *Daily News* correspondent was nevertheless right in his emphasis. One of the men themselves, John D. Jones, Salem, explained:

---

[64] W. W. Jones, 1837-1903; he visited America in 1902 on a not very successful fund raising tour and died in August 1903 before the end of the dispute. See obituary in *Y Werin*, 3 September 1903.

[65] J. Williams, op. cit..

[66] *Daily News*, 8 January 1901.

A man must be respected as a man and as a worker by every squire and lord in this country. This present struggle has bred men in Bethesda that will never more bend to Baal. We have breathed the fresh air of freedom. The castles of oppression will come down one day.[67]

III. SOCIAL CONTROL

(a) *Pressure*

Despite the Penrhyn quarrymen's tradition of union organisation, the explosion of 1900 came not from any formally organised channels but from below, using methods which appear quite alien to those of British trade unionism in the twentieth century. When fourteen men, threatened with having their bargains replaced by contract work, reacted in November 1900, there was no effective union committee of any kind to turn to. The union, though at that time attracting a large membership, had no influence with the management at all; it was powerless to stop the contractors. The men therefore defended themselves in another way: they warned the contractors, Richard Hughes and Edward Williams, not to come near their bargains. Williams ignored their earlier warnings and the threats directed at him when he arrived at the quarry; consequently, he was attacked, chased round the galleries, assaulted and physically thrown out of the quarry.[68]

In the following week, events escalated. Richard Hughes, the other contractor, made the grievous error, in a newspaper interview, of calling the men 'loafers'. That night the following poster went up around the town:

> To the Loafers of Chwarel Y Penrhyn—take notice. Monday night, October 29th, there will be a procession starting at 10 o'clock from Adwy-y-Pant, Bethesda, to visit a certain place in the district when we shall pay our debts to the arch-loafer. It is hoped that all will be over at midnight. Everyone with an interest in the present disturbances is invited to attend with the appropriate weapons.[69]

[67] *Yr Herald Cymraeg*, 20 May 1902.
[68] *Yr Herald Cymraeg*, 30 October 1900.
[69] Ibid., 6 November 1900.

Hughes fled and escaped the planned attack; three days later, he returned to the quarry accompanied by his three sons. He was attacked and escorted, bleeding, back to Bethesda by a singing crowd of several hundreds. The crowd returned to the quarry to seek a supervisor, Thomas Price, who, found hiding in nearby woods, was given the same treatment as Hughes. He was being escorted in the direction of the river when he was saved from his fate by the local constabulary. The men then returned once more to the quarry to seek out two other officials, Messrs. Ellis and Pennant Roberts, but these had swallowed their bravado and flown.

The men's leaders came to speak critically of this outburst of violence, especially under pressure from the General Federation of Trade Unions, which considered that

> Whatever the grievances under which they were labouring may have been, physical force was no remedy, was opposed to Trade Union principles, and must be wholly condemned.[70]

But at the time of the incidents the quarrymen seem to have been overwhelming in their approval. A local Liberal paper commented rather incredulously: 'All the workers, the old, the middle aged and the young, are unanimous in their belief in the propriety of the strange course taken on Thursday.'[71]

An analysis of the nature of this 'strange course' might help us to understand why it took place. Its nature seems to point to a pre-trade union pattern of employees' self-assertion and defence. This is brought out clearly in the second poster to be circulated in the area. It read:

> Dear countrymen
> As we have sent the Archloafer away from the quarry as well as his two sons, I am greatly hoping that we shall give them a similar welcome if they dare come to the quarry again, that is, any one of the three *diawliaid* (devils). I am thinking that there are three more of the stewards who need to be treated in the same way, because of their behaviour in the past . . . namely *stiward ceg fawr* (big mouth steward) . . . marker, the one who was instrumental in suspending four of our fellow workers for four days when they had done

[70] G.F.T.U., *7th Quarterly Report*, March 1901.
[71] *Yr Herald Cymraeg*, 6 November 1900.

nothing wrong, for this and for several other reasons this is the time and the most promising moment to pay him back. And also . . . who, say the people working under him, has been a terrible oppressor.
I am,
One who has suffered.[72]

No social generalisation is apparent here. The violence was to be directed not against the management as such, or against the system of working, but rather against particular individuals singled out to be punished for their personal behaviour and their specific crimes.

Why did this violence take place and why did it take this form? The first question is the easier to answer. As the men's committee was quick to point out, this is the sort of thing that happens if you do not have proper union representation; grievances are allowed to build up, men are too scared to take their complaints individually to the management, and even if they were not they would find no redress; without an acceptable negotiating machinery men would continue working until the situation became intolerable and then they exploded. In truth, a committee would be 'a Local Board of Conciliation', restraining men from rebellion.[73]

The nature of the path taken, however, especially its somewhat ritualised aspects, needs further explanation. The posters, the threats, the selective use of violence, the march to the river, all remind one of early-nineteenth-century industrial activity and rural rebellion, rather than of a trade dispute in the 1900s.[74] Tom Ellis, M.P., who knew Wales well, thought nonconformity and industrialisation had not quite completed their transforming task:

> The old turbulence is gone, though exciting moments in the tithe war and coal strike showed that the hot Celtic blood still needs restraint.[75]

---

[72] *Yr Herald Cymraeg*, 6 November 1900. The names of the officials objected to were not published in the press.

[73] Parry, op. cit., pp. 177–78.

[74] Cf. the 'Scotch Cattle' outbreaks in the coalfield of South Wales; the intense hatred of contractors was an important factor then as it was in Bethesda. See D. Jones, *Before Rebecca* (London, 1973), pp. 86–116 and passim.

[75] Ed. A. J. Ellis, *Speeches and Addresses by Thomas E. Ellis* (Wrexham, 1912), from 'Social Life in Rural Wales' (1894), p. 134.

That was written in 1894; had he been alive six years later he might have added the incidents in Bethesda to his list. The wilder patterns of a rural, pre-nonconformist past could still break through when crises evoked them, especially perhaps if those patterns were not so remote as might be thought. Lord Penrhyn had had experience of anonymous letters before: 'Wales', he told the Land Commisioners in 1893, 'is a land where the people are particularly addicted to sending anonymous letters.'[76] Neither was he nor the community unaware of the uses of subversive direct action, for 'Lord Penrhyn admitted that considerable difficulty had arisen in his district owing to the fact that the pasturage of the tenants had been enclosed'. The difficulty arose when fences erected were torn down by 'persons . . . influenced by dislike of law and order'.[77] Rural unrest was endemic in Wales and its nature must have been evident to the quarrymen who identified and sympathised with such activity, and its value was not lost on them.

This behaviour, however, was not just copied; it was part of the quarryman's own reflexes. In the situation of November 1900, the ethic of respectability and trade unionism was insufficient to meet the crisis. Faced with the growing threat to their way of life, a threat which had already secured its chains on them, the men reacted with a different ethic: the *Herald Cymraeg*'s reporter noted that

> it is now argued by many that the time of patience and moderation and singing hymns in public meetings has proved incapable of bettering the situation of those who feel that they are being oppressed.[78]

The rusty ritualisation of their use of violence was drawn from their own experience. But the ethic was activated only by crisis and for the rest of the dispute it had to jostle with the immediate culture of Welsh nonconformity and the disturbing new concepts of class.

The concept of popular justice and control was maintained throughout as the quarrymen, having made their rebellious stand, sought to defend themselves both from the assaults of

---

[76] *R.C. on Land*, 22,836.
[77] J. E. Vincent, *The Land Question in North Wales* (London, 1896), pp. 258–59.
[78] *Yr Herald Cymraeg*, 6 November 1900.

the police, the courts and other suppressive institutions and, more important, from any breakdown in their own discipline and singleness of purpose. In sustaining both functions they found themselves clashing with 'legality'.

Though they were in an otherwise disadvantageous situation, facing an enemy who had abundant resources other than his quarry, the quarrymen had one strong bargaining point—their own skill. As we have seen earlier, quarrying was an occupation which demanded local knowledge as well as skill; imported blacklegs, therefore, would not be of much use, though they could of course do a limited amount of work. Even the bringing of an experienced quarryman from outside would not make up for the loss of the indigenous Penrhyn workman. The only way the quarry could begin to work properly again was if a section of the strikers themselves went back to work. The threat to the success of the struggle came not from 'scabs' from without, but from those within the body of workmen itself.

In the earlier months of the strike this was a source of strength and of comfort; betrayal was not then thought possible. Rumours of blacklegs arriving to take their jobs were discounted, 'for you must get quarrymen, strangers cannot work in the quarry'.[79] Even when the quarry had been re-opened the men were confident because 'only between 35 and 40 *practical, skilled* quarrymen are in the quarry'.[80] In this dispute therefore, more than in most others, internal control was of paramount importance. Solidarity had to be maintained for the only danger came from within.

The methods employed to impose the collective decision were diverse, drawing on all the sanctions the community knew. The main techniques were boycott, picketing, processions and demonstrations, forms of what might be classified as rough music, riot and a selective use of violence, including attacks on individuals and property. Other pressures, religious, educational and psychological, attempted to exclude totally the 'blacklegs' from the life of the community. Not only were these forms of social control adopted, but their rationale was at times clearly articulated.

---

[79] Ibid., 1 January 1901.
[80] N.W.Q.U. Minutes, 2 November 1901 (the secretary's underlining).

In the earlier stages of the dispute action was only necessary at the outset, to solidify the men in the first confusing weeks. Thus, there were two mass processions to Bangor to show solidarity with the arrested twenty-six. These were huge affairs in which almost the whole community marched the five miles to the court.[81] Bethesda's British and National schools were seriously affected as children took the day off, Bethesda Cefnfaes British School was closed on 13 November 1900, 'the teachers being anxious to go down to Bangor because of the trial of the quarrymen'.[82] These demonstrations must have united the whole community in its determination to stay together. Little else seems to have happened until June and only two mass-meetings were held in the first eight months.

The crisis came in June as rumours that Penrhyn was to open the quarry intensified.

> During March and April clergymen, curates and officials went about the neighbourhood to try to persuade timid people to allow them to send in their names to Mr. Young as prepared to resume work on his terms, and pressure and threats were brought to bear on some . . . it was mentioned that 1,500 and sometimes 1,300 and 1,100 and at other times 1,800 of old workmen had sent in their names to Mr. Young at the Port Office.[83]

In these suspicious months there were signs that the community was losing its solidarity and there was secret grumbling among the ranks.[84] There had been an earlier rumour that the quarry was to open in the third week of January; women had reacted then by filling their aprons with stones and stationing themselves 'ready as an army at the top of the road, waiting for any fly to appear'.[85] Women and children were again prominent early in June, when the rumours were at last confirmed and the stewards went back to the quarry; on their way they were hooted by a noisy crowd, some making rude noises by blowing through sea-shells. Though seven people

---

[81] *Yr Herald Cymraeg*, 13 November 1900. 100 students in caps and gowns greeted the marchers in Bangor.
[82] Bethesda Cefnfaes British School *Log Book*, 13 November 1900.
[83] Parry, op. cit., p. 174.
[84] See the editorial in *Yr Herald Cymraeg*, 19 April 1901.
[85] *Yr Herald Cymraeg*, 22 January 1901.

were arrested for obstruction and for making threatening remarks, it seems that

> there was nothing in the behaviour of the crowd which could be called threatening or anything to call for such a large number of policemen.[86]

The picketing and hooting against the stewards were a warning to those workmen who were thinking of returning. On 11 June the quarry re-opened for all classes of workmen; in the chapels on the previous evening the ministers counselled peace and, apart from a few scuffles, peace prevailed.[87] No one was sure how many had gone back; it was thought the number was four hundred, of whom one hundred were skilled quarrymen.[88] However much of a minority this may have been, it was a serious breach which called for urgent sanctions. Boycott was the most obvious weapon. D. R. Daniel urged the men not to talk to the blacklegs, to turn their faces away when they came near, to boycott the shops where they bought food. To be sure of identification and so that maximum pressure could be brought to bear, cards were issued to all strikers' homes bearing the slogan *Nid oes bradwr yn y tŷ hwn*, ('There is no traitor in this house'). Most of those cards were to hang in Bethesda windows for over two years; when one came down betrayal was thus easily identified. Houses were made to wear the badges of defiance or of submission. To make identification even easier, the radical Welsh papers *Y Werin* and *Yr Eco Cymraeg* published lists of blacklegs with their addresses.[89]

The boycott worked in various ways: barbers refused to shave 'traitors'; those who had cows could not sell their milk; those who weighed pigs could find no pigs to weigh; shopkeepers refused to serve them fearing a removal of custom by those who were still out; finally and significantly, blacklegs found it difficult to get served with beer in some of Bethesda's pubs.[90]

The last point is interesting because the line between pub and chapel was a clear mark of social differentiation in temper-

[86] Ibid., 4 June 1901.
[87] Ibid., 18 June 1901.
[88] Ibid.
[89] *Y Werin*, 13 June 1901; *Yr Eco Cymraeg*, 15 June 1901.
[90] Ibid., 22 June 1901.

ance, nonconformist Welsh villages. It seems to have been crossed by both sides during the lock-out, for although there is evidence to show that the blacklegs were more given to drink than the strikers, there is also evidence that alcohol was consumed by at least some of the strikers who made the Bethesda pubs their own and drove the blacklegs to drink at home or in Bangor.[91] Further pressure was exerted in the chapels as those returning to work withdrew from the embarrassing intimacy of the chapel meetings and were excluded from the social communion that accompanied them. Some seem to have forseen this difficulty and left chapel for church even before they went back to work.[92] Others were driven out: 'it was made so hot for some members of chapels, after they had gone back to work, that some of them had been driven into the church'.[93] One blackleg was hooted out of his chapel.[94] Some managed to accommodate themselves by forming separate groups within the chapels; a separate class for the children of those working was established by their parents at the Wesleyan Sunday School. Others remained in the fold but attended very irregularly. By December 1902, however, 'It is almost the rule . . . whoever goes to the quarry goes to Church'.[95]

Going back to the quarry meant expulsion from the community, even the community at its most Christian. The crime of those who returned was clear: they had broken the collective decision of the group. W. H. Williams explained the position in June 1901:

> they had agreed to be united, and none of them, individually, had the right to settle how things were to be between him and his master. This was the kernel of the argument.[96]

But it was not until August 1902, by which time more men had slipped back, that the case was fully argued. The theory was that

[91] Standing Joint Police Committee, *Report* of the sub-committee appointed to enquire into matters at Bethesda (January 1903), ff. 595, 719.
[92] *Yr Herald Cymraeg*, 11 June 1901.
[93] S.J.P.C., *Report*, ff. 721.
[94] *Yr Herald Cymraeg*, 20 January 1903.
[95] S.J.P.C. *Report*, p. 39, ff. 704.
[96] *Yr Herald Cymraeg*, 25 June 1901. Williams used the same argument to defend the first world war.

> any man who takes part in a discussion commits a crime
> against one of society's basic elements if he, in the end, does
> not give in to the majority.

Not to do so was considered

> one of the most disgraceful sins . . . trampling underfoot
> society's most important elements . . . let every man remember
> that after having stated his case he is bound to stand with the
> decision of the community.[97]

The community was imposing an extra-legal law, a law which
was not written in any statute book but was no less real for
that; as a speaker at the first mass-meeting after the 11 June
re-opening proclaimed:

> The men that returned to their work had broken a law, and
> the Bangor magistrates should know that.[98]

The law was a moral law and necessarily clashed with the law
of the land; a quarryman, Richard Wynne Pritchard, explained
in January 1903; 'there are many things which are bad in the
face of the law of the land and which are good in the face of
the moral law'.[99] This sentiment (as we shall see later) was
bolstered by the religious conviction and rhetoric of the men.

The main punishment for breaking the 'law' was expulsion
from the community; those who rejected the decisions of
society rejected their right to membership of that society.
Expulsion, as we have seen, meant expulsion from all the
institutions of the community, chapels, pubs, shops; those back
at work were absent even from the 1902 annual meeting of the
local Oddfellows Lodge.[100] Even the blacklegs' children could
find themselves excluded, for

> The strikers' children go mostly to the British school, and the
> others to the National school, generally speaking.[101]

Where the two groups did attend the same school there were
a few cases of children being persecuted; one child was allowed
to leave half an hour earlier than the rest for fear of being

[97] *Yr Herald Cymraeg*, 5 August 1902.
[98] Ibid., 25 June 1901.
[99] Ibid., 27 January 1903.
[100] *Yr Eco Cymraeg*, 4 January 1902.
[101] S.J.P.C., *Report*, ff. 765.

molested on the way home.[102] But some parents 'apprehend danger ere it comes, and remove their children' to the Church schools.[103] On the whole, however, with repeated warnings from their headmaster, 'the children of strikers and secessionists fraternize together'.[104]

Those who betrayed the community by going back to work were denied not only their citizenship but also their humanity. By accepting Penrhyn's twenty pieces of silver they lost their manhood.[105]

> There was not enough wealth in the whole quarry to re-pay to them that which they had lost, for they had sold their own selves.[106]

The traitors were not often called 'blacklegs', the common name for them was *cynffonnau*, whose literal Welsh translation is 'flatterers', but it also means 'tails'. With this term they were mercilessly lashed; those with tails were animals, not fit for human consideration. As a striker song of May 1903 put it,

> Ofer siarad am bersonau
> Baich y testun yw cynffonnau.[107]

This definition broke through any Christian belief one might have expected to find. Thomas Robert became the only man to be shouted down at one of the strikers' weekly meetings; his offence was to suggest that the men should 'love their enemies', that is, that they should adopt a Christian attitude toward the *cynffonnau*.[108] The popular sentiment, expressed in a quarryman's letter to the press, was that 'no man who betrays his fellow workers can belong at all to Christ's religion'.[109] This belief was made easier, perhaps, by the predominantly calvinist faith of the men; the enemies of the elect are the enemies also

---

[102] Ibid., p. 42.
[103] GAS, Carneddi British School, School Log Book, 2 September 1903.
[104] Ibid.
[105] The silver was paid as a bonus to all those going back to work on his terms. *Hansard*, vol. CXVIII, p. 1654 (4 March).
[106] W. H. Williams, as reported in *Yr Herald Cymraeg*, 2 June 1903.
[107] 'It's useless talking about persons/For our subject is cynffonnau.' N.W.Q.U., *Cynhadledd Bethesda*, 1 May 1903. The song was *Punt y Gynffon*, sung to the tune of *Y Mochyn Du*.
[108] *Yr Herald Cymraeg*, 12 May 1903.
[109] Ibid., 2 July 1901.

of God. A poem written by a quarryman ended thus:

> Pwy gara byth ond diafl mewn cnawd
> I fyw i fod yn fradwr,
> A bod i'r byd yn destun gwawd,
> A digio ei Greawdwr.[110]

Nonconformity, therefore, was recruited into the community's extra-legal armoury of control, but more traditional tactics were also employed. After June 1901 a constant harassment of strike-breakers began; it was mainly non-violent and consisted only of the making of animal noises by hooting crowds as the *cynffonnau* went home. Sometimes the tension of these situations gave rise to spontaneous fights; or other times the violence was more premeditated. Sometimes the community acted together, at other times in small groups.

The day after the re-opening of the quarry there was a large demonstration of 3,000 people; it ended with twenty people summoned for threatening behaviour.[111] Demonstrations and processions marching round the town became regular features during 1901. Some 1,500 took part in another march on the following Saturday, ending in a mass-meeting. Mass-meetings of the strikers also became a weekly feature of the dispute, right until the end.[112] The processions and the meetings were instruments for unifying those taking part; the marches were also a means of pressurising those tempted to return to the quarry into standing their ground. Outside blackleg homes the processions stopped for hooting and hissing and sometimes to smash a window. Women were prominent in these activities; for example, women accounted for a third of the procession on Saturday, 30 June; marching together in the rear they carried their own banner.[113] This emphasised the social nature of the struggle; it was not just an industrial matter, it was one for the whole community.

---

[110] 'Who but a devil in man's flesh would ever wish/To live to be a traitor/And be to the world a figure of contempt/And earn the wrath of his Creator.' Ibid., 24 June 1902.

[111] Ibid., 18 June 1901.

[112] Reported widely in the local press, they are the main source for the men's opinions.

[113] *Daily News*, 2 July 1901.

The summer months of 1901 were eventful ones: early in July a crowd of some 200 attacked the police as they were arresting two men;[114] and there were regular arrests for obstruction and insulting language.[115] At the end of the month the pubs were closed early on Saturday nights to prevent violence.[116] Early in August some three hundred of those working away returned home; fighting broke out as police escorted the *cynffonnau* from work and a policeman was injured by a rock.[117] The authorities retaliated massively, sending 200 infantry and 60 cavalry into Bangor and moving 100 South Staffordshire and East Yorkshire Infantry, accompanied by thirty dragoons, into Bethesda. The atmosphere was tense for the Saturday night mass-meeting; troops stood by and the magistrates were ready with the Riot Act. But the crowd of 4,000 filed quietly into the Market Hall to listen to their leaders and the guest speaker, Keir Hardie. There were some minor scuffles during the week and a few arrests were made, but there was no major trouble.

Minor incidents continued throughout August: on the 20th some fifty cavalry had moved in when strikers attacked a pub where two blacklegs were drinking; some stone-throwing and window-breaking followed. At the end of the month, twenty-six people came before the magistrates charged with disturbing the peace and obstruction; the next week two were charged with assault.[118] October passed in the same vein. A glimpse of the conditions prevalent can be caught from the daily list of their persecutions compiled by the *cynffonnau* for Penrhyn; the reports for two days, 14 and 15 October, show well the constant harassment suffered by those at work.[119] On 14 October a W. R. Hughes of Llwybrmain complained of a stone thrown at him and of men walking around his home late at night; R. Hughes and H. H. Thomas also complained of personal attacks and there were reports of crowds booing blackleg homes late on Saturday night. On the 15th there were reports of considerable shouting in Llandegai. John W. Roberts, who

[114] *Yr Eco Cymraeg*, 13 July 1901.
[115] *Yr Herald Cymraeg*, 23 July 1901.
[116] Ibid., 30 July 1901.
[117] Ibid., 6 August 1901.
[118] Ibid., 20 August 1901; 3 September 1901; 10 September 1901.
[119] GAS, M/622/38, 39.

lived some way from Bethesda, complained of damage to his property. A new recruit to the quarry was especially harassed: walking home, he had been met by a crowd which threw stones at him and his police escort and called him a traitor and a murderer; during the day his wife had been pestered by children who had thrown stones and a dead rat into the house. From Henbarc a workman complained of stones being thrown at his house, while Evan Evans from Coed y Parc complained that Samuel Jones, 'who looked very threatening' had scared his wife. From Bryntirion came the report that 'booing and shouting took place last evening as usual'.

In the last week of October four men were imprisoned for assault, two for two weeks, two for a month.[120] The next weekly meeting expressed its solidarity with them and when they were released from prison a huge procession went to greet them; 'all Bethesda apparently went to the station to expect them home'.[121] On the whole, the pressure was not violent; shouting and hooting and noises at night were the most that the black-legs had to suffer. Where violence did take place it was often against property rather than persons; window-breaking became a regular feature of Bethesda life. Where those attacked actually had farms, the traditional methods of rural revenge and sanction came into play: gates were broken down, resulting in animals straying;[122] more serious was at least one case of rick-burning, the victim being the under-manager of the quarry.[123]

Towards the end of December, a hundred men arrived home from south Wales; there were a few incidents on Christmas Day, but the major outburst came on New Year's Eve.[124] It was to be Bethesda's most violent week. Though denied vigorously, a semblance of planning might have been involved in the near-riot of New Year's Eve; more probably it grew spontaneously from the traditional gathering to greet the New Year. The (very sympathetic) correspondent of *Yr Herald Cymraeg* thought he recognised a plan, for at the stroke of midnight

[120] *Yr Herald Cymraeg*, 29 October 1901.
[121] GAS, Bethesda, Cefnfaes British School Log Book, 7 January 1901.
[122] GAS, M/622/39.
[123] *Yr Herald Cymraeg*, 5 November 1901.
[124] Ibid., 14 January 1902; 7 January 1902.

a secret sign was given to many and they started throwing stones in all directions . . . The disturbances arose in a second and windows in all directions were smashed. The police could not prevent it at all. The people flowed here and there, led in different sections to different places.[125]

The crowd broke up into several groups, thereby becoming uncontrollable by the police, and they went straight for their targets; despite the stones thrown 'in all directions', the crowds were very discriminating. As they rampaged through the streets, blackleg windows were smashed, one group broke all the windows in the Conservative Club, others attacked the Waterloo Inn and the Victoria Hotel, the lairs of pro-Penrhynites, and finally the crowd attacked the home of the unfortunate Richard Hughes, the first attack on whom had started the whole dispute; his windows were smashed and boulders crashed through his door. The following day the South Staffordshire Infantry and the 7th Hussars were brought into the district. On Thursday there was what seems to have been a serious attack on the *cynffonnau* as they were returning from work at 5 p.m. with their police escort; many were forced to flee across the river into the woods. During further incidents in the town two blacklegs were severely beaten and the police drew their truncheons; they were forced to seal off the blackleg streets to prevent attacks on them. At 10 p.m. the cavalry arrived and a large crowd gathered outside the police station. They were pacified by their leaders, however, and after being led by William Jones M.P. in the singing of *Hen Wlad fy Nhadau* (Land of my Fathers), they dispersed.

On Saturday afternoon 100 police and 150 soldiers escorted a hooting procession of some 600 around the town, but there was no trouble. In the mass-meeting that followed, the men's leaders and the local preachers pleaded for an end to violence. Breaking windows, as the Rev. T. Griffiths of Bethania pointed out, was not respectable. Only D. R. Daniel was equivocal in his judgement; he did not approve of the violence but it was the fashion of the times, it was what Chamberlain and Balfour believed in: 'don't follow the fashion too far but let freedom and justice continue to burn in your hearts until victory'. The

---

[125] Ibid.

other speakers protested that Chamberlain's example should never be followed.

Twenty-seven people appeared before Bangor magistrates following the disturbances; they were charged variously with stone-throwing, an offence under a bye-law, disturbing the peace, using threatening language and riotous behaviour. As a reward, perhaps, for their efforts, they won two converts from among the blacklegs, but the rest continued at work.[126]

Incidents continued throughout 1902 but at a lower level than before; certainly fewer incidents were reported in the press. In February there was a dangerous moment when strikers hooting outside a blackleg home were fired on with a revolver; on 18 March *Yr Herald Cymraeg* reported that the breaking of windows was continuing apace. By the end of March the cost of maintaining constant police patrols was beginning to tell and the Caernarvonshire Police Committee applied to have Bethesda made a special police area, paying for its own police protection, an idea hotly opposed by Bethesda's ratepayers. The Home Office also disapproved of such a change.[127]

The only major incidents took place when men returned home from south Wales. There was some fighting over Easter, following the return of 100–200 men.[128] Early in September trouble flared up again; this time it started at the *eisteddfod* in Bangor, where groups of men home for the event clashed with blacklegs.[129] The fighting continued sporadically on Saturday night when 80 police tried to control the situation; a serious attempt was also made by some 60 young men to prevent some of the blacklegs going into the quarry after the weekend, but it failed when mounted police intervened.

During the last year of the struggle, incidents of the kind common in 1901–2 became fewer and more isolated. There was some hooting in August 1903 and the last procession was in September, when a crowd of 100 greeted W. J. Parry returning from his trial in London and dragged his carriage through the town.

[126] Ibid., 14, 21 January 1902; 28 January 1902.
[127] Ibid., 25 March 1902; 1, 15 April 1902.
[128] Ibid., 1 April 1902.
[129] Ibid., 16 September 1902.

How serious were these disturbances and incidents? Inevitably, it is very difficult to judge because one side minimized their importance and the other maximized it. Certainly compared with disturbances during other industrial disputes they were not too serious; there was never any sustained fighting with police or military. During the dispute of 1896–7 John Burns had pointed out that

> if Lord Penrhyn's quarries had been in the Rhondda Valley . . . it is possible that his castle might have been pulled down about his ears . . . these men have been too conciliatory and peaceable, and have been singing hymns instead of learning how to box.[130]

This judgement, however true of 1896–7, was not quite true of 1901–2. In the period from 3 June 1901 to 24 December 1902, 852 incidents were reported to the chief constable by those working in the quarry.[131] This figure is undoubtedly inflated and includes many non-criminal incidents, but, as we have seen, much trouble did take place. From 30 September 1901 to 4 December 1902 the county paid £4,418 8s. 11d. for peace-keeping in Bethesda, and in that same period there were 125 prosecutions.[132] Lest these figures be taken as conclusive, one should also point out that the expense of law and order was considered to be 'most exorbitant' by the Standing Joint Police Committee and the number of police used thought to be far more than was necessary. Moreover, of the 125 men prosecuted, 39 were discharged, 13 charges were withdrawn, 2 men absconded and only 71 were convicted or committed for trial. It was a conviction rate of about 57½ per cent, which was 'considerably under the normal ratio'.[133]

Even with these significant qualifications, it is plain that something other than hymn singing was taking place in Bethesda at this time. The reason why the commotion was always contained was because it was meant to be so. The violence of the community was a judiciously used instrument, only one of a range of pressures and controls available. Hooting

---

[130] John Burns, *Hansard*, vol. XLV, pp. 735–36, 28 January 1897.
[131] C.S.J.C., *Report*. p. 2.
[132] Ibid., p. 5.
[133] Ibid., p. 6.

and shouting and making threatening noises in the night are not, in this context, examples of 'violence' but rather expressions of a traditional extra-legal, non-violent means of internal social control. Very often violence flared when those carrying out these practices were interfered with or provoked by blacklegs or police; in yet another incident concerning the contractor Richard Hughes, even the chief constable, A. A. Ruck, argued that Hughes 'behaved towards the crowd in an aggravating manner'.[134] Indeed, there is much evidence to show that the *cynffonnau* were themselves easily moved to violence.[135]

The activities of the strikers, though widespread and, at least for a year, daily in their persistence, were contained to fit a certain pattern of control. As W. H. Williams told the Standing Joint Police Committee,

> If there were any intentions on the part of the men to injure people they could blow them into atoms in spite of the police.[136]

Or, as John Williams tried to explain,

> If there were 100 policemen—the windows would have been broken just the same . . . It is something else and not the police, that induces people to keep the peace.[137]

In disciplining its own members, the community was acting within recognised bounds.

(b) *Law and Order*

While the 'moral law' of the community was thus being enforced, the law of the land was meeting with some resistance. In his annual report for 1902, the chief constable of the county of Caernarvon, A. A. Ruck, noted that

> a great strain has been laid upon this force for many months past, owing to a dispute between the owner of the slate quarries at Bethesda and quarrymen, and it has been a very anxious time for the chief constable.[138]

The problem lay in the inadequacy of the local police force to deal with any major incidents and to maintain a sustained

---

[134] GAS, M/622/30–32: A. A. Ruck letter to E. A. Young.
[135] E.g., see the evidence of strikers to S.J.P.C. *Report*, pp. 19, 40.
[136] Ibid., p. 10.
[137] Ibid., p. 37.
[138] *Police Reports*, for year ended 29 September 1902, county of Caernarvon.

presence. Faced with the events in Bethesda, Ruck concentrated as many of his men there as he possibly could; replying to a request for a policeman to attend to a call elsewhere in the county in June 1901, Ruck was

> sorry to say that so many of our men are on duty at Bethesda now that it is almost impossible to find a constable at present for any extra duty.

During the summer of 1901 the number of police kept in the Bethesda district varied between 25 and 50 per cent of the whole county force, incurring an extra expense of £1,300.[139] Before the dispute broke out Bethesda was a peaceable town policed by only one sergeant and four men, but during the dispute there was a continuous presence of 20 to 30 policemen in the district. The force was temporarily increased, with the sanction of the Home Office, by 20 men during the turbulent Christmas period of 1901, though they were discharged at the end of May.[140]

Ruck had to rely on outside police assistance at all times of stress; in August 1901 he wrote to the head constable of Liverpool asking for re-inforcements:

> as many as possible should be able to speak Welsh as I believe there are a considerable number of Welsh-speaking constables in the Liverpool force.[141]

And in January 1902 he borrowed 50 police from four neighbouring counties.[142] During 1902 police were borrowed, in the following numbers, from:

Derbyshire   —   1 inspector, 19 men;
Shropshire   —   1 superintendent, 4 sergeants, 36 men;
Lancashire   —   1 sergeant, 8 men;
Anglesey   —   4 constables;
Stockport   —   1 sergeant and 10 constables;
A total of two high-ranking officers, six sergeants and seventy-seven constables.[143]

---

[139] GAS, Constab. Add/7. Letter Book, A. A. Ruck to Mr. Wynn Griffith, 27 June 1901. *Report*, on special calls upon the police, 30 October 1901.
[140] Ibid., 29 September 1902.
[141] Ibid., Ruck to head constable, Liverpool, ? August 1901.
[142] Ibid., Ruck to Home Office, 5 January 1902.
[143] Ibid., *Report*, on special calls, 29 September 1902.

Despite the concentration of the county force in Bethesda and the availability of extra men from other forces, the police at times felt unable to cope with the situation. In the first week of November 1900 cavalry from York and infantry from Preston were moved into Bangor at the request of the chief constable. This was in response to the dramatic incidents which marked the beginning of the dispute and to the lack of any immediately available police re-inforcements. Their presence aroused considerable local protest though the Home Office thought that their presence was a 'good instance of the value of soldiery in preventing the outbreak of disorder'.[144] The troops were removed from the district on 23 November 1900.

In June 1901, in a letter to the army's Chester-based chief staff officer for the North-Western District, Ruck again foresaw a situation arising in Bethesda which, if the strikers were to mount a determined attack on those at work, 'would in all probability lead to a disturbance with which the Police alone would be unable to cope'.[145] The possibility of drafting troops into Bethesda was discussed throughout the eventful months of June and July, Ruck having been authorised by the Standing Joint Police Committee on 31 May

> to inform the officer commanding the Troops in the District that military aid might be required shortly and asking him to hold troops in readiness.[146]

It was later claimed that the chairman of the Standing Joint Committee, magistrate Henry Kershaw, was also authorised to sign the requisition for troops when such a requisition was deemed necessary.[147] By 18 July it was thought that the troops should no longer be held in readiness, but the mood changed rapidly.[148] By the last week of the month Ruck felt that he had definite information of the return of a large body of men from south Wales.[149] On 30 July he sent a telegram to Chester

[144] P.R.O. HO45 10263 X80592 (7).
[145] GAS, Constab. Letter Book, Ruck to chief staff officer, Chester, 19 June 1901.
[146] Ibid., Ruck to under-secretary of state, Home Office, 1 July 1901.
[147] Ibid.
[148] Ibid., Ruck to chief staff officer, 18 July 1901.
[149] Ibid., Ruck to E. A. Young, 26 July 1901. He had earlier written to the police in Mountain Ash, Glamorgan, asking for information as to whether a large body of men were going to come up 'for to drive the others out' (19 June 1901).

calling for troops 'at once as arranged'; later in the day the official requisition requiring Chester to 'send troops to Bangor, North Wales in aid of the Civil Power' was dispatched with Henry Kershaw's signature.[150]

The next day Ruck wrote to the Home Office justifying the decision to bring in troops by the claim that the police were no longer able to cope since some policemen had had to be returned to neighbouring forces.[151] The troops did little while in the area and it is doubtful whether their presence did anything other than further embitter the feelings of the strikers; the infantry were removed within a week, though the cavalry were to remain until the end of the month.[152]

When troops were next requisitioned, on 1 January 1902, there was somewhat more justification, though once again their value to the authorities was minimal. Ruck had reported to the Home Office in mid-December that 'mischief' was likely when men returned to the area for Christmas, though he had no definite information of this; all available men, about forty constables in all, were to be sent to Bethesda for the holiday, but troops, he felt, were not needed.[153]

The near-riot of New Year's Eve, however, when twenty-six houses were attacked, caught the police off-guard.[154] They were unable to do anything to prevent the disturbances and they were also,

> owing to its being a very dark night . . . unable to identify any of the persons who were taking an active part in the disorder.[155]

After surveying the night's damage on the following morning, Ruck sent a telegram to Chester requiring them to hold 100 infantry and a troop of cavalry in readiness pending a decision by the magistrates. By 6 p.m. the magistrates had met and authorised the requisition;[156] the infantry arrived in Bethesda at 4 a.m. the next day, the cavalry in the evening. They do not

---

[150] Ibid., telegrams to chief staff officer, 30 July 1901.
[151] Ibid., Ruck to under-secretary of state, Home Office, 31 July 1901.
[152] Ibid., 7 August 1901.
[153] Ibid., 16 February 1901.
[154] Ibid., 1 January 1902.
[155] Ibid., Ruck to magistrates, 1 January 1902.
[156] Ibid., Ruck to chief staff officer, 1 January 1902.

appear to have been present, however, when a column of those going to work with their police escort was attacked and scattered on 2 January. The strikers had then 'made a rush, which the police were unable to stop, for the workmen, who had to escape as best they could'.[157] The cavalry was used over the next few days to escort men, along with police and a magistrate, to and from the quarry; but when two special trains took many of the strikers away again on 6 January the area soon became much quieter and the infantry were withdrawn on the ninth. The cavalry, however, remained, stationed at Bangor and Bethesda, as the area continued tense with windows and other property being smashed. They did not leave until 28 January.[158]

Throughout the years of the dispute, A. A. Ruck was bombarded with requests and demands for increased protection and increased action against the strikers; they came from Lord Penrhyn, E. A. Young, and those who had gone back to work.[159] Before the re-opening of the quarry on 11 June 1901, Ruck had given a personal assurance to two of those due to return that

> protection will be afforded to you and the other workmen intending to return to work at the Penrhyn Quarries for as long as it appears to be called for.[160]

But the actions he and his men took were never considered adequate and the pressure upon him to step up anti-striker activities persisted throughout the dispute. 'I may say', he wrote to the under-secretary of state at the Home Office, on 1 July 1901, 'that hardly a day passes without my receiving complaints from the manager of the quarry as to the hostility shown by the people and the inadequacy of the Police protection in some place or another.'[161] The note of exasperation with the quarry management's complaints was clearly to be heard in a letter to H. P. Meares, an under-manager at the quarry, in December 1901: 'I am doing all that appears to one to be practicable and required by the exigencies of the moment . . . If this appears to you to be insufficient I can only suggest that you should

[157] Ibid., Ruck to Home Office, 3 January 1902.
[158] Ibid., 5 January 1902; 12 January 1902; 1 January 1902.
[159] Ibid., 28 January 1902.
[160] Ibid., Ruck to D. Roberts, W. Williams, 8 June 1901.
[161] Ibid., Ruck to the under-secretary of state, Home Office, 1 June 1901.

address yourself to the County Magistrates.'[162] Three weeks later he was having to make the same point to Lord Penrhyn himself in response to a letter complaining about the degree of protection extended to those at work.[163]

His disagreements with the quarry-owner and management were over two issues: the definition of what was actually 'illegal' behaviour and the quarry management's refusal to admit that those at work should modify their behaviour for the sake of peace. The first was a point which Ruck found considerable difficulty in getting the quarry management to recognise. They wanted immediate action against all those who embarrassed or insulted those at work. Lord Penrhyn wrote to Ruck on 26 June 1901 demanding action against the Saturday-evening demonstrations in Bethesda. Ruck replied that

> my duty as a Police Officer, as I understand it, is to consider whether they amount to what is known as an 'unlawful assembly'.

For the moment he did not think that they did, though

> whether they constitute 'intimidation' under the Conspiracy and Protection of Property Act 1875 is another matter. But as I have said from the first I do not think it is the duty of the Police to initiate proceedings under that act.

He also rejected Penrhyn's advice that he should 'warn' certain individuals.[164] A year later he was having to repeat very much the same point to Penrhyn, i.e., that while he could, and had, acted in any clear case of assault, when it came to the incidents of 'hooting' in the district there was 'very little we can do about it, however annoying'.[165]

The second point at issue between Ruck and the Penrhyn quarry management was the public behaviour of those who had returned to work. By the spring of 1902 it would appear that Ruck was becoming increasingly convinced that,

[162] Ibid., Ruck to H. P. Meares, 3 December 1901.
[163] Ibid., Ruck to Lord Penrhyn, 21 December 1901.
[164] Ibid., 27 June 1901; see also Penrhyn (?) to Ruck 10 May 1901 (GAS, P.Q.99/6).
[165] Ibid., 10 April 1902.

according to information I have received from the Police, the workmen themselves, by their conduct, were responsible for a disturbance which occurred recently.[166]

He had written to Lord Penrhyn in December 1901 asking that workmen and their wives avoid provocative places, quoting the example of the wives of two blacklegs who had gone shopping in Bethesda on Saturday night and had consequently been hooted.[167] He re-iterated the point to E. A. Young in May 1902:

> I should like again to point out that nearly all the more serious disturbances are caused by the appearance in the streets of Bethesda of workmen or their families at times when large numbers of the opposite party are about.[168]

This time he quoted the example of two blacklegs who had provocatively waved their hats and laughed outside a public house while strikers streamed to a meeting at the Market Hall.

A furious E. A. Young replied with his characteristic brand of logic, arguing that Ruck was wrong in charging that 'nearly all the more serious disturbances are caused by the appearance in the streets of Bethesda of my workmen or their families'. Surely the opposite was true, 'for if the strikers kept away from Bethesda all would be peaceful'. He was forced to admit, however, 'the possibility of some of the workmen being injudicious from time to time', but, he claimed, 'a great number of them are peaceful men'.[169]

In general, therefore, relations between the intransigent quarry management and the rather more moderate, if confused, chief constable were somewhat strained. 'There is no doubt whatever', wrote Young to his employer, 'that the police protection is insufficient.'[170] This prompted Young to encourage independent legal action by his workmen, with costs paid in many instances by the quarry, and generally to use his

---

[166] Ibid., Ruck to Henry Jones, 13 May 1902.
[167] Ibid., Ruck to Lord Penrhyn, 21 December 1901.
[168] Ibid., Ruck to E. A. Young, 13 May 1902.
[169] GAS, P.Q. 99/6, 99/7; E. A. Young to A. A. Ruck, 16 May 1902.
[170] Ibid., E. A. Young to Lord Penrhyn, 21 September 1901.

solicitors H. Lloyd Carter and H. Corbet Vincent and Jones of Bangor, to encourage prosecutions.[171] Thus, Mr. Vincent put pressure on the magistrates in November 1900 to issue warrants for the arrest of twenty 'of the ringleaders' rather than the summonses which the magistrates 'in such a state of terror of the mob' favoured.[172] And in May 1901, following the disturbances associated with the return of officials to the quarry, Vincent was stationed at his office to 'take the evidence of the constables with a view to prosecuting as many as he can get the names of'.[173]

In February 1901, when he was eager to re-open the quarry, Young went so far as to enquire from the Free Labour Protection Association (F.L.P.A.) whether they were in a position to supply him with special constables because protection for prospective blacklegs was 'not forthcoming from Ruck until there is another riot'.[174] When Millar of the F.L.P.A. replied with an offer of twenty such 'special police', Young hesitated in accepting them since '20 men would [not] be of the slightest use' except to push Ruck 'to do his duty'.[175]

If E. A. Young and those who had gone back to work considered police action in Bethesda ineffective and in-sufficiently tough, the majority of the population of the district saw them as biased and over-zealous and found their presence offensive. There were too many of them and their function was plain. A striker's song, 'Song of the Traitor', explained:

---

[171] Every man returning to work was sent a copy, in Welsh, of the Conspiracy and Protection Act, 1875 (GAS, P.Q. 100/85). Vincent certainly acted for blacklegs in dispute. When another of 'our men' was summonsed for being involved in a disturbance in Bangor in September 1902, it was suggested by the management that Vincent take up his defence along with that of another man then at work. (GAS, P.Q. 100/42, 18 September 1902). The size of the solicitors' bills to the quarry would suggest considerable scope to their activities: in May 1901 they presented a bill for £450, in April 1903 a bill for £1,467 plus a further £176, and in September of the same year they received a cheque for £700. (GAS, P.Q. 99/6, 7, 1 May 1901, 20 April 1903, 9 September 1903). In July 1902 the quarry paid £11 15s. 6d. expenses for men at Caernarfon re. quarry riots. (GAS, P.Q. 13/2, General Cash Book, 10 July 1902).

[172] GAS, P.Q. 100/40, 4 November 1900.

[173] GAS, P.Q. 99/6, 7: E. A. Young to Lord Penrhyn, 31 May 1901.

[174] Ibid., Young to Millar, 1 February 1901.

[175] Ibid., 5 February 1901. Young was interested in the idea, however, and enquired again of the F.L.P.A. about mounted ex-police, ibid., 8 February 1901.

Mae lluoedd o heddgeidwaid
I'w gweld yn britho'n gwlad,
Dan nawdd yr awdurdodau,
Er mwyn amddiffyn Brad.[176]

The people of Bethesda had no confidence in the police;

they now consider that to add to the number of policemen is nothing more than to add to the number of Lord Penrhyn's supporters in the district.[177]

Their complaints fell under four headings:
(a) Want of tact on the part of the police;
(b) Acts of cruelty and improper language by the police;
(c) False evidence by the police;
(d) Want of impartiality on the part of the police.

The evidence in support of these complaints, as presented to the Standing Joint Commission committee inquiry, is convincing. This sub-committee of the Caernarvonshire Standing Joint Police Committee was set up to 'enquire into matters at Bethesda' and it carried out its investigations in November and December 1902, hearing dozens of witnesses from the strikers' ranks and from the police. The majority report, signed by five of the seven members, was severely critical of the police and supported many of the complaints of the men. It recommended:

(a) that the number of police stationed at Bethesda should be as soon as possible reduced to normal, inasmuch as the presence of a large force of policemen tends to irritate the people,

(b) that the Superintendent in charge in Bangor be removed to another division and that 'Sgt. Owen, now in charge of the Bethesda District,' who was severely criticized by the strikers, should be transferred to another district despite having done his work well, as 'further prolonged hard work and mental strain could not fail to injuriously affect his health'.[178]

---

[176] *Yr Eco Cymraeg*, 6 July 1901. (There are hordes of policemen/To be seen speckling the land/Under the patronage of the authorities/So they may defend Betrayal.)

[177] S.J.P.C., *Report* evidence of Rev. Th. Griffiths.

[178] Another historian writing on the role of the police in the dispute quotes the Minority Report of the S.J.P.C., signed by only two of the seven members of the sub-committee, as being the conclusion of the whole investigation. He completely ignores the Majority Report. J. Owain Jones, *The History of the Caernarvonshire Constabulary, 1856-1950* (Caerns. Hist. Soc., 1963), Chapter vi.

The presence of extra police and particularly of the military in Bethesda resulted in widespread protests both locally and nationally. Several awkward questions were asked in the House of Commons by Lloyd George, Keir Hardie, D. A. Thomas and William Jones, and there was an attempt to adjourn the House over the issue.[179] Protests from local authorities were even more strident and the Caernarvonshire County Council, the Bethesda Urban District Council, the Bangor Borough Council, the Rhyl Urban District Council, the Prestatyn Urban District Council and other bodies wrote to the home secretary in protest at the decision.[180] The Caernarvonshire County Council motion was particularly effective since it raised the difficult question of the authorisation of military aid. The motion, passed overwhelmingly by the council with only three councillors voting against and three, including Lord Penrhyn, abstaining, unequivocally condemned the movement of troops and police into the area. Their presence was seen as 'not only unnecessary, but a slander upon the character of the men of Caernarvonshire, and a standing menace to the rights and liberties of the people'.

More significant even than this condemnatory and radical rhetoric was the way the motion questioned the decision-making process involved in bringing in the troops:

> the Caernarvon County Council place on record an expression of its strong and unqualified disapproval of the action of the person or authority responsible for invoking military aid . . . and consider it an unwarrantable interference with the liberties of the people to import troops into the county without the sanction of the Standing Joint Committee, as the duly constituted authority appointed to deal with questions of Police administration and good government of the county.[181]

The unprecedented problem in Caernarvonshire was that presented by a situation in which an elected local authority, including its 'police' committee, disagreed entirely with a decision of the local magistrates. The problem was compounded

[179] *The Times*, 3 August 1901.
[180] Public Record Office, Home Office Papers (hereafter P.R.O. H.O.) 45/ 10263 x 80592, 9, 13, 16 and *passim*.
[181] GAS, Caernarvonshire County Council Minutes, 8 November 1900.

by the fact that the requisition order was signed by the Chairman of the Bangor magistrates, on behalf of, but not following a special meeting of, the magistrates.

The Home Office privately admitted that this was 'a curious state of things' with which it was not entirely happy; but it could not evade the implications of the 1888 Justices Act which had left the responsibility of requisitioning troops 'in aid of the civil power' with the magistrates.[182] The doubtful procedure whereby the requisition had actually been made, and the way it was justified by the chief constable also led to some mild criticism from the Home Office especially as it had resulted in the secretary of state making 'misleading comment in Parliament'.[183]

The whole episode was characterised by confusion and conflicting evidence and the Home Office was clearly reluctant to defend the sending in of troops particularly in the light of criticisms also from the military.[184] Major General L. V. Swaine, the G.O.C. of the North Western District, wrote critically to the Home Office in June 1901:

> Of course the Civil authorities on the spot are the best judges, but from reports that have reached me, I am inclined to think that matters are not being well managed there . . . I believe in this case a large force of Police would do all that is required.[185]

And later during the same summer the home secretary Ritchie sent a telegram regarding the troops in Bethesda to Sir K. Digby which read:

> I doubt whether they were wanted at all but they should certainly be withdrawn as soon as they safely can.[186]

The Home Office was under constant pressure to improve the protection for those who had decided to go back to work, but following the political difficulties which had followed the intervention of the military in November 1900 and in July 1901

---

[182] P.R.O. H.O. 45/10263 x 80592, 13.
[183] Ibid., 49.
[184] It was not entirely clear at the time where the War Office's responsibilities ended and the Home Office's began. See P.R.O. H.O. 45/10263 x 80592, 24.
[185] Ibid., 22.
[186] Ibid., 37.

it was reluctant to sanction any more interference. The ferocity of the events on New Year's Eve 1901 caught the authorities unawares but the Home Office position did not change. In reply to a dramatic telegram from E. A. Young which talked of 'stones falling upon women and children in their beds' and an imperious one from Lord Penrhyn requesting 'efficient protection for my people' the Home Office replied by telegram that 'responsibility for preservation of peace in Bethesda rests with local authorities'. The magistrates thought differently and again called in the troops.[187]

The home secretary was perturbed and wrote to the clerk of the justices on 8 January with the recommendation that the summoning of military aid be avoided in the future, if at all possible, and suggesting that the swearing-in of special constables be investigated.[188] The Home Office was becoming increasingly suspicious of the motives of the magistrates in calling in the troops and saw that their presence was more of a financial convenience than a necessity for maintaining law and order. But the home secretary was also made aware of the political and psychological importance of the military presence for the minority which had chosen to return to work. The beleaguered isolation of these men was well expressed by a spokesman on their behalf, almost certainly Rev. W. Morgan, the Vicar of St. Ann's Bethesda, who, in a letter forwarded to the Home Office, having made the significant point that most of the men who had gone back to work were Conservatives, went on not unrealistically to compare their plight to 'the horrors of the Loyalists of Ireland'.[189]

The authorities involved, therefore, including the magistrates, the County Council, the Home Office and the police, were all operating under a degree of political pressure. The police and Home Office attempted to an important extent to avoid this pressure and they both displayed considerable scepticism in their dealings with Penrhyn Castle but, largely because of the power of the local magistrates, the troops nevertheless did enter the district on three occasions, and each time in opposition to the overwhelming weight of local opinion and contrary to the

---

[187] P.R.O. H.O. 45/10264 x 80592, 69, 71, 72.
[188] Ibid., 89.
[189] Ibid., 90.

wishes of every elected Member of Parliament, County Council and Urban Council in the area.

(c) *Effects*

The effectiveness of all the pressure—the 'unseen tyranny', as Young called it—exerted by those refusing Penrhyn's terms is not readily gauged.[190] The solidarity of the community during the first months certainly seemed unbreachable, an impression confirmed by the ballot of December 1900 which had rejected Penrhyn's terms by 1,707 votes to 77. The management clearly underestimated this solidarity; Young was confident that the men would be only too glad to return to work when he re-opened the quarry on 19 November, particularly in view of 'the over-awing presence of the military'.[191] This was an opinion of which he was to be rudely disabused.

By the end of January, Young was again hopeful that he could 'shortly . . . restart work' and in February he was claiming that men were applying for work at the rate of five or six a day.[192] Active in recruiting for him at this time was the Rev. W. Morgan of St. Ann's Church and by the end of February Young was thanking him, for his

> efforts by way of speaking quietly to some of the men is bearing fruit, for, after a cessation of applications for work several fresh ones came in yesterday and no less than ten this morning.[193]

By mid-April Penrhyn was writing to Ruck intimating that he could soon be 'naming a date for the return of several hundred men to their work'. The thirteenth of May was suggested by Young as a re-starting date, but this was postponed by a month to 11 June, by which time all the complicated precautions necessary would have been completed. On 6 June Young was reassuring a worried prospective blackleg from Pentir that he would be able to come by train, that there would be police on the train, that there would be extra police as an escort from

[190] GAS, P.Q. 99/6, 7: 'I regret to note your threat of social disadvantage to the minority. Is not that unseen tyranny?' E. A. Young to Rev. T. Isfryn Hughes, Bethesda, 9 June 1901.

[191] GAS, P.Q. 99/6, 7: Young to Pennant, 17 November 1900.

[192] Ibid., Young to Ruck, 21 January 1901; Young to Millar, 1 February 1901.

[193] Ibid., Young to Rev. W. Morgan, 27 February 1901. The men often accused the Anglican vicar of recruiting for the quarry; this letter proves that their accusation had substance.

Pentir to Felin Hen, and that some fifteen of his neighbours were also giving up the struggle and returning to work and that it would be advisable for them all to travel together.[194]

It is not clear exactly how many men returned on 11 June; Young claimed a figure of 500 and this would seem to be accurate.[195] Those who had lacked courage in June followed during the summer, and by September Young was claiming that 'the Quarry is now in full swing with about 650 workmen'.[196] Out of a total work force of over 2,500, this was by no means the rebellion of the loyal that Young and Penrhyn had hoped for, but it was, nevertheless, a serious breach in the solidarity of the quarrymen. The knife had missed the jugular but it had inflicted its wound and the bleeding, however slow, could not now be staunched.

In the following months the blood dribbled very slowly and the number who joined the original blacklegs was minimal. At the end of November Young was complaining about a press report, 'put in with no friendly intent', which had suggested a mass return to work on the previous Monday; in the event, only one new man came in on that date. Young estimated that during the previous quarry-month six slate-makers and a dozen labourers had returned.[197]

There is no evidence to suggest that the rate of the return increased at all significantly during the remaining months of 1901 or throughout the whole of 1902. It was not until the spring of 1903 that the flow quickened appreciably: thirty-three men, of whom nineteen were slate-makers, were taken on during the quarry-month ending on 12 May 1903. The following week nine men came in. But this was still far from a flood; that did not take place until the autumn of 1903, when all was lost and could clearly be seen to be lost. One hundred and one men re-started in October and in the first week of November applications were being received at the rate of ten a day. On 3 November, a few days before the three-year

[194] Ibid., Penrhyn to Ruck, 15 April 1901; Young to Penrhyn, 22 April 1901. Young to J. M. Lloyd, 6 June 1901.
[195] Each man who returned on 11 June received a gold sovereign; 650 had been withdrawn from Lord Penrhyn's current account in readiness but only 533 were paid out, suggesting that that was the number to return. GAS, P.Q. 13/2, General Cash Book, 11 June 1901.
[196] GAS, P.Q. 99/6, 7: Young to J. Samuelson, 17 September 1901.
[197] Ibid., Young to ? , 20 November 1901.

struggle was formally abandoned, Young reported that '5 more started work this morning, making an addition of 25 for the first week of this Quarry month'. There were 1,565 at work seven weeks later on 30 December.[198] Given an estimated 500 who had returned to work during the late autumn, this would suggest that as late as the end of September 1903 there were not many more than 1,000 at work in the quarry, considerably less than half the original work force.[199]

Many of these men, moreover, were 'new' men who had not been amongst those who had walked out in November 1900. It is not clear how many 'new' men entered Lord Penrhyn's employment during the dispute; he himself stated in January 1903 that 'since work was resumed at the Quarry in June 1901 a number of new hands besides nearly 100 boys have been taken on', and Young referred several times to 'the newcomers' or 'the new men' in the quarry.[200] Some came from a distance, others came from the locality and of this group several were ex-employees, i.e., men who had in the past worked in Penrhyn but had not been at work in November 1900.

A group of Italians, working at the time in a lead mine near Aberystwyth, offered their services in March 1902;[201] several men came from Penmachno in September 1902; others came straight out of the army, one from service in the Boer War; the churchwarden of Dolwyddelan parish was employed in July 1903.[202]

---

[198] Ibid., Young to Pennant, 13 May 1903; Young to Penrhyn, 15 May 1903; 31 October 1903; 3 November 1903; 30 December 1903.

[199] This is guesswork. 101 returned in the four weeks up to 31 October 1903, 96 in the first fortnight of November, a rate which presumably increased further following the 'official' ending of the dispute; by December it would appear that as many as twenty a day were returning. It would not, therefore, appear unreasonable to estimate that at least 500 men returned between 1 October and 30 December. In May 1902, however, Young was already claiming that there were 900 'now working happily': GAS, P.Q. 100/42: Young to ?, 17 May 1902.

[200] GAS, P.Q. 99/6, 7: Lord Penrhyn to Rev. Howell Roberts, Clynnog, 12 January 1903; Young to Penrhyn, 31 October 1903; Young to Wynne Jones, 9 December 1901.

[201] 'The Italians are a very good set of workmen six are miners and very good they are. We had never any trouble with them, no tinkers or noisy men and willing to work every hour day or night overtime on Saturday afternoon and Sunday', wrote A. C. Heire, Frongoch Mine, Devils Bridge, Cardiganshire, to Young, 5 March 1902 (GAS, P.Q. 100/42).

[202] Ibid., Davies to Young, 4 September 1902; H. Hughes, Glasinfryn to Young, 3 October 1902. He was three weeks out of the army. William Owen had been a private in the Liverpool Regiment, ibid., 17 September 1902; J. Davies to Young, 17 June 1902, 21 July 1902. He had originally been refused entry.

A good number of the local men taken on, who had not been in the quarry in 1900, had either failed to get work in the quarry previously or had been dismissed from their employment there, usually for drinking; some of these were re-employed while others were considered to be too incorrigible and were refused; of those who were re-employed, some soon found themselves in trouble again.[203]

In part of a letter to the *Liverpool Daily Post* which he was later to delete, Young admitted that

> the number of labourers employed each month varies and those found unfit for the work are gradually weeded out.[204]

It is clear from his correspondence files that a goodly proportion of those who found employment after 11 June were men who would not have been employed in normal times; some of them were so unfit that they had be to dismissed. Given the one hundred boys and the number of 'new' men employed at the quarry, the exact size of this group cannot be assessed, but the evidence suggests that they formed a not insubstantial section. The number of quarrymen originally employed in the quarry in 1900 and again returning to work before the autumn of 1903 would appear to be decidedly fewer than the 1,000 estimated earlier.

To that extent, therefore, the community's solidarity, and the pressures brought to bear to maintain it, were remarkably effective. The management, of course, was in no doubt that the hooting, the demonstrating, and the boycotting were keeping men away from the quarry; that was why it maintained such constant pressure on the chief constable to take action

---

[203] Ibid., Jones to Young, 10 January 1902. H. O. Jones originally came from Bethesda, had moved to Crewe to work after he had failed to get into the quarry in 1891, was a fireman on the L.N.W.R. but was now given work in the slate mill. D. D. Davies to H. P. Meares, 24 June 1902, re. David Parry of Mynydd Llandegai, who was taken on after a severe warning despite having been dismissed in 1896 and being 'a rambler and greatly addicted to drink'. Davies to Meares, 18 August 1902, G. O. Griffiths of Tregarth, who had been suspended five years earlier 'for being on the spree for a few days', was refused work because he was considered 'a confirmed drunkard . . . one of the most besotted men in the neighbourhood'. Davies to Young, 16 October 1902, re. Moses Jones, Sling, who had been dismissed in 1897 and then re-employed in November 1901; being found drunk at his work for the fourth time, he was discharged as 'incorrigible'. Ibid., 12 April 1902, re. William Griffith Williams who, dismissed for drink in 1897, had been re-employed after 11 June and had been suspended after being found drunk at work at 8.15 a.m.

[204] Ibid., Young to editor, *Liverpool Daily Post*, 29 January 1902.

against all sorts of 'harassment'. 'More men would have applied for work', local manager D. D. Davies told Young in July 1902, 'had not the strikers been so successful with their intimidation.'[205] A few months earlier, Young himself had fulminated about those who applied for work, received a 'ticket', and then failed to turn up because 'their fear of working . . . drives them to South Wales instead of into temporary lodgings on the Tregarth site until things become quieter'.[206]

Another worry for the management was to ensure that the new recruits were properly skilled men. Evidence is hard to come by here, but some of it at least would suggest that labourers were rather easier to recruit than skilled quarrymen. There is little to suggest that many skilled men came from other quarrying districts, for there was a general feeling throughout the quarrying area that men should not seek work in Penrhyn and 'take another man's living'.[207] What is certainly true is that the men were quite convinced that the real threat to them came not from a mixed, unskilled work force of men previously sacked or recently having left the army, however many of them there were; the danger to their cause increased significantly only when a skilled slate-maker or rockman (i.e., 'quarrymen') returned to work. Thus, it was reported in December 1901 that

> we have had [no] case of persecution in any shape or form against new men taken on. It is against the old hands returning to work that the chief attack is made.[208]

The men may have overestimated the importance of skill in the new production schemes being operated in the quarry, but there is no doubt that what Young wanted was 'respectable, qualified quarrymen' and that all the men's efforts were designed to prevent him getting them.[209]

---

[205] Ibid., Davies to Young, 23 July 1902.

[206] GAS, P.Q. 99/6, 7; Young to Trench, 17 April 1902. Thirty-three of those who applied for work in June 1901 failed to attend; one gave his 'ticket' to the strike committee and accepted a railway fare to south Wales; ibid., P.Q. 100/42 D. D. Davies to Young, 12 August 1902.

[207] Ibid., P.Q. 100/42: Thomas Jones to Young, 20 June 1902; Jones, from Talysarn, wanted to take a contract in Penrhyn but not a bargain, because 'people at Nantlle and other places would speak about him and say that he has gone to Penrhyn to take another man's living'.

[208] GAS, P.Q. 99/6, 7: Young to Wynne Jones, 9 December 1901.

[209] GAS, P.Q. 99/6, 7: Young to Wynne Jones, 9 December 1901. Firm evidence could, of course, be offered by production figures for the periods before

Perhaps nothing speaks so eloquently of the workers' solidarity in Bethesda as the geographical basis of 'blacklegging'. The men who returned to work came overwhelmingly from the villages of Tregarth and Sling, or were forced to move there or to Bangor when they removed their card from their houses in Bethesda itself or in the villages of Cacrllwyngrydd, Gerlan or Mynydd Llandegai.[210] Tregarth was considered the 'nesting place of *cynffoneiddiaeth*' ('blackleggery')[211] and there is evidence to support this accusation: on a list of thirteen men who returned to work on 11 June, seven had addresses in Tregarth, while only two came from Bethesda; of the sixteen men working in Shed J, eleven were from Tregarth and only four from Bethesda. Others who chose to go back to work found that life was impossible in the streets of Bethesda and chose rather to leave the town and move to Bangor; Bethesda itself remained virtually solid until the end.[212]

The relatively small number of men to return was not purely the result of solidarity, however, for a considerable number applied for work only to receive a curt note from the manager informing them that he had 'no need for their services at present'.[213] For the management had no intention of allowing back to work anyone who had been involved in the disturbances or in the N.W.Q.U.; they wanted only 'loyal' men. Penrhyn made his position clear in a private letter in January 1903:

> I do not wish to have men in my employment who have no confidence in myself or in the officials who are appointed by me and nothing is further from my intentions than to again invite the leaders of mischief to re-enter my service.

The intake of 'new' men and boys, and

> the additional fact that there were far too many men engaged in the quarry previous to the strike will necessitate the exclusion

and during the strike but the evidence here, though plentiful, defies accurate interpretation; see GAS, P.Q. 47/5 Slates brought from Quarry 1891–1905, GAS, P.Q. 36/2 Quarry Slate Books, GAS, P.Q. 100/144.

[210] *Daily News*, 2 July 1901, p. 7.
[211] *Yr Herald Cymraeg*, 25 June 1901.
[212] GAS, P.Q. 173; GAS, P.Q. 265. 'Some of the late employees who are desirous of resuming work contemplate removing from the worst districts . . . into lodgings at Bangor.' Young to Editor, *Liverpool Daily Post*, 29 January 1902; GAS, P.Q. 100/42. See also Young to Penrhyn, 27 March 1902 (P.Q. 99/6, 7), and Appendix VI below.
[213] GAS, P.Q. 100/42: Young to W. J. Pritchard, 24 September 1902.

of some hundreds of the former employees who severed their connection with my Quarry over two years ago.[214]

The message is unmistakable: this was to be no victimisation of 'ringleaders', nor the sacking of the seventy-one as in 1896. Penrhyn's object was completely to re-fashion his work force, to cut out all those who recognised any authority other than his own. 'I believe that a large number of men will remain out for years to come', wrote Young in May 1902; ' . . . we have maintained the right to manage the quarry without the dictation of the trades union interference.'[215]

In order to realize this ambitious project, a system to garner information had to be constructed which would vet every man applying for work. Those failing to measure up to scrutiny had their names registered on what the management variously called 'the Black list' and 'the excluded list'.[216] The assiduous keeper of this list and the man in charge of collecting information on the people of Bethesda was D. D. Davies, who was appointed local manager in March 1902. He reported to Young on every applicant for work and on every applicant for a tenancy or pension. His reports classified men according to a gauge running from 'very loyal' through 'loyal' to 'passively disloyal' and 'actively disloyal'. His reports, of which there were scores, were sometimes lengthy and often written with a wry sharpness.[217]

The information was gathered from those at work, from officials in the quarry and from a paid informant. Spying was in the air in Bethesda; another interpretation of the term *cynffonnwr* is 'tale-teller'. Gossip, stories, slander, petty quarrels as well as hard information must have poured into D. D. Davies's compendious files. Telling tales, it was claimed by the strikers, was a sure way of ingratiating oneself with the managers of the Penrhyn quarries.

---

[214] GAS, P.Q. 99/6, 7: Lord Penrhyn to Rev. H. Roberts, 12 January 1903.
[215] GAS, P.Q. 100/42: Young to ? , 20 May 1902.
[216] 'I have his name on the Black List', wrote Davies to Young about Edward Davies, 16 June 1902, (GAS, P.Q. 100/42). Richard Wynne Pritchard, according to Davies, was 'one of the first we put on the Excluded List': ibid., Davies to Young, 17 June 1903. There was also reference to a 'bad list' in ibid., 30 January 1902.
[217] See Appendix VI.

The business was rather more serious than the mere collection of personal details, unsavoury though that might be, for there was always a fear and a suspicion that confidential union decisions were reaching the ears of Young and Penrhyn.[218] When Penrhyn required the minutes of the quarry committee up to 1885 for his libel case against W. J. Parry, he was able to lay hands on them easily enough. In May 1902 there is reference in a letter from the solicitor Vincent to a copy of the quarry committee minutes provided by a Mr. John Evans; these were probably pre-1885 minutes, though they could, of course, have been from a later period.[219]

Leaks were always possible, and not always from obvious sources: John Jones of Tregarth, for example, an official who had quarrelled with the Penrhyn management in 1900, wrote in November to the manager of the nearby Dinorwic quarry, W. W. Vivian, informing him that, although himself a non-unionist who had not joined in any disturbances, he was 'in a position to be able to attend their secret Cabinet and get to know all if desired'. One cannot be sure how much credence to give to this claim; Jones, an intelligent enough commentator on Penrhyn, was desperately trying to get himself appointed in Dinorwic, but if information had flowed from him, or from others in similar positions, then it would undoubtedly have found its way finally to Young.[220]

Young certainly received regular reports from the men's mass-meetings and though these were usually reported in the local press, it obviously helped to have his own man, who was presumably not known as a Penrhyn man, present. Thus, in late October 1903, when there were rumours of a major clash amongst the strikers, Young informed Penrhyn that he was, 'therefore, sending a special reporter and if there is any special news I will advise you tonight'.[221]

The final component of this structure was a paid informant, Mr. T. Ellis. Ellis appears to have been taken on as early as

---

[218] R. G. Pritchard, a member of the strike committee, firmly believed that there was a spy close to the decision-making. (Information given privately by his grandson in June 1970).
[219] GAS, P.Q. 99/6, 7: Vincent to D. Pritchard, 18 May 1902.
[220] GAS, D.Q. 2045: John Jones to W. W. Vivian, n.d.; see also ibid., 2036: Jones to Vivian, 3 November 1900.
[221] GAS, P.Q. 99/6, 7: Young to Lord Penrhyn, 31 October 1903.

1898, when Young refers to him as 'my new detective'. It is not clear what exactly his duties were, though he may well have been the 'T' who had prepared a report on Glasinfryn men for Davies.[222] Under the heading 'Quarry Riots 1900', he was given nearly £40 between November 1900 and January 1901, and in November 1903, after the strike was over, under the heading of 'Quarry Sundries (strike)', he was given £10 'as a present to pay expenses of removal'.[223]

The purpose of all this information gathering was to prepare the 'excluded list' of those who were not to be allowed back into the quarry or to receive any of Penrhyn's pensions or tenancies. The control of housing had seemed to have been a strong card in Young's hand: writing to Mr. Trench, the manager of the Penrhyn estate who was in charge of tenancies, in November 1900, Young asked him that,

> in view of the fact that many of the men are absolutely disloyal I should be glad of an opportunity of making enquiries about any would-be tenant before you give any definite permission.

It is clear from the lists of men applying for houses that a definite bias existed henceforward in favour of the 'loyal'.[224] But the system was by no means water-tight and Trench regularly ignored Young's reports, probably out of a professional desire to find good tenants, a fact which drove Davies to comment angrily that

> the men cannot understand, and really it is difficult to understand, why cannot the Estate Office give the same loyal support to the quarrymen who are fighting Lord Penrhyn's battle as well as their own, as the Port Office [where the quarry management was] is giving them.[225]

If the Estate Office failed to enter completely into the spirit of things, the quarry management stuck resolutely and ruthlessly to its 'excluded list'. Of the applications for work

---

[222] GAS, P.Q.L.B., 404–06: Young to Pennant, 2 June 1898. See also Appendix VI.

[223] GAS, P.Q. 13/2, General Cash Book, 15 November 1900, 12 December 1900, 14 December 1900, 15 January 1900, 2 November 1903.

[224] GAS, P.Q. 99/6, 7: Young to Trench, 29 November 1900. See also the list of applicants for 12 Tregarth Houses; GAS, P.Q. 100/43, 13 May 1903. All twelve applicants were 'loyal' to some degree.

[225] GAS, P.Q. 100/42: Davies to Young, 5 April 1902.

coming in at the rate of ten a day in late October 1903, Young commented that 'about half are acceptable'; of the fifty-three men who applied during the first week-end in November 1903, 'fully half are not acceptable'. On the morning of 29 December, seven weeks after the dispute had ended, Young 'spent over four hours going through reports on the character of a great number of applicants and accepted thirty-five'.[226]

Two months after the end of the dispute, John Buckley of Glasinfryn wrote despairingly for work; his previous letter in September had brought no reply. Fifty-six years old, he had worked for thirty-eight years for the Penrhyn family; he claimed that, 'I always attend to my work and during the strike I have kept perfectly quiet and never attended any meetings.' Opposite his name on the excluded list, however, was 'T' 's six-word denunciation that was to seal his fate: 'very bitter to those he knows'.[227]

The blacklist, the 'over-awing presence of the military', and all the power and patronage of the Penrhyns were therefore thrown against the hooting and the boycotting. For three years the community's weaponry, and its sense of justice, proved adequate. Of those who returned, exchanging their membership of a society for work, few—and then hesitant—generalisations can be made. Little is known of their spokesmen.[228] They lived as a caste, paid every month but spurned and humiliated, sustained often by family ties and by the society of their own streets. They had a tendency to be Anglicans, and returning to work certainly 'converted' many to the Church of England; they had, possibly, a tendency to drink more often than their enemies; some were from families who had long been thought of as *cynffonwyr*; a few had been active strikers in November 1900; many must have gone back in poverty and despair. One gets the impression that, on the whole, they were men who were in any case not in the mainstream of Bethesda society: Anglicans, drifters, drinkers, not community-minded, men willing to accept Penrhyn's authority,

<hr>

[226] GAS, P.Q. 99/6, 7: Young to Penrhyn, 31 October 1903; 3 November 1903; 30 December 1903.

[227] GAS, P.Q. 100/44: J. Buckley to Young, 6 January 1904; GAS, P.Q. 100/43, n.d. See Appendix VI.

[228] The two most prominent were Melancthon Williams and David Pritchard, both of Tregarth.

and his money, rather than the authority of the community's own deaconry, an already established out-group. But one should hasten to add that amongst the ranks on both sides there were many exceptions to these generalisations.[229]

In March 1902 two strikers touring south Wales to raise money told an audience of workmen near Cardiff that even if a settlement were to be reached the problems raised by the dispute would not be solved, for

> the great drawback . . . is to find some peaceful means between both parties for the future because those who are out say that they can never look upon, nor do anything for those now working. They will never give a helping hand in event of a sledge having derailed or something similar.[230]

The hatred that grew between strikers and *cynffonwyr* was searing and absolute. In those cases where it did soften it did so only after many years, and many families in Bethesda three-quarters of a century later knew full well from which camp they were descended.[231]

---

[229] 'They' were Anglicans—so was Henry Jones, chairman of the strike committee; 'they' ran in families—in November 1901 the nephew of Griffith Edwards, treasurer of the strike committee, went back; 'they' lived in the same streets—Henry Jones's next-door neighbour went back in February 1903.

[230] GAS, PQ. 100/42: 'Henry', Aberdare, to his parents, 20 March 1902.

[231] There is still a street known locally in Bethesda as 'Tell-tale street'. The word *bradwr* (traitor) can still crop up in playground disputes. (Information given by the headmaster of a school in the Bethesda district, August 1970).

IX

REPERCUSSIONS

I. THE NATIONAL DIMENSION

The disputes at the Penrhyn quarries in 1896–7 and 1900–3 were of national importance, seen by both the trade-union movement and by the anti-union, 'free labour', lobby as being of crucial significance. These were years of notable defeats for the labour movement, above all of the crushing of the engineers in 1898. Here in Bethesda was a struggle for the rights of trade unionism which could, and did, catch the imagination.

The trade-union movement rallied impressively to the defence of the quarrymen, the obstinate and imperious Lord Penrhyn being an obvious target for any labour orator, and his lordship's wealth and cruelty were castigated on many a platform up and down the country. In 1902 the Trades Union Congress at its London congress passed unanimously a motion proposed by John Ward of the Navvies and General Labourers Union, and seconded by Hugh Boyle of the Northumberland Miners, which expressed congress's 'utmost contempt at the continued obstinacy of Lord Penrhyn' and pledged the delegates 'to render assistance, both by money and Parliamentary agitation to enable the men to carry their struggle against arbitrary feudalism and landlordism to a successful conclusion'.[1]

In the discussion, D. R. Daniel spoke of the 'unbroken spirit and determination to continue the struggle' of his union's members; Pete Curran of the National Union of Gasworkers and General Labourers told congress how he had visited Bethesda four times in the previous twelve months, and William Abraham (*Mabon*) appealed to the trade unionists of the country to 'come to the rescue at this juncture and do something tangible to make defeat impossible'.[2]

In the following year's congress the president referred to the Penrhyn struggle as

[1] *Report*, T.U.C. London Congress, 1902, p. 64.
[2] Ibid.

unique in the history of trade union fights at least here in England [sic]. It ought not to be in the power of one man to place the lives and interests of so many thousands in jeopardy.

And the Parliamentary Committee reported on its efforts to achieve support for the Penrhyn men.[3]

Early in 1901, the N.W.Q.U. launched an appeal 'To the Trades Unions' and emphasised that any moneys donated would be distributed to union members only and would not go toward alleviating the 'general destitution of the locality'.[4] £20,518 was collected in this way, with contributions coming from hundreds of trade union branches throughout the country.[5] In May 1901 alone there were 155 trade union donations totalling £1,278 5s. 5d. Some of the donations received were massive: £1,000, in two instalments, came from the Operative Bricklayers' Society, London; £400, in three instalments, from the South Wales Miners' Federation, with a great deal more contributed by individual lodges and districts. Many others made smaller donations, such as the 30s. sent by the Aberavon branch of the National Association of Shop Assistants in December 1902. And it was not only official donations by branch committees which swelled the fund: collections, the pennies of individual workmen, accounted for £2 from the Chatham docks; £6 7s. 0d. and £6 3s. 6d. from the Great Mountain, Tumble, and Onllwyn, Dulais Valley, collieries respectively; miners in Rhosllannerchrugog imposed a levy of threepence a week on all union members in February 1901. The list of donations, month by month, reads like a catalogue of the British trade-union movement. Donations came from overseas as well: £17 from the General Slaters' Union of Pennsylvania in May 1901, with £167 in all from the United States.[6]

[3] *Report*, T.U.C. Leicester Congress, 1903, p. 40, p. 44.
[4] N.W.Q.U., *An Appeal to the Trades Unions* (February 1901).
[5] N.W.Q.U., *The Penrhyn Quarry Dispute* (1904).
[6] X.N.W.Q.U., 281, Ledger: contributions towards the Penrhyn dispute, 1901; see also X.N.W.Q.U., 282, 10 September 1902 and pp. 170–77. The S.W.M.F. gave £200 on 9 December 1902, £100 on 20 January 1903, and £100 on 20 June 1903; the Aberdare district donated £150 in 13 contributions, the Rhondda No. 1 District £445 in 14 contributions; many individual lodges also contributed (e.g., Pembre £10 on 13 May 1902, Maerdy £10 on 5 May 1902, Primrose Colliery, Pontardawe, £18 8s. 0d.). Also *Yr Herald Cymraeg*, 19 February 1901.

The men's case was taken up vigorously and early by the *Daily News* and was energetically and ably argued by Clement Edwards, a contributor to that paper; the London Central Committee, set up by the *Daily News*, collected over £3,600, much of it in street collections and meetings.[7] In the East End

> the poor responded splendidly . . . In Bethnal Green, a district that raised over £300 for the men, £25 was subscribed in farthings.

It was remarkable testimony to how deeply the Penrhyn question moved British workers.[8]

Innumerable meetings and demonstrations were held up and down the country: there was a mass-meeting in the Memorial Hall, London, in May 1901; in November 1902 there was a series of meetings and parades in support of the Penrhyn quarrymen 'under the auspices of the various East London trade union and Temperance organisations'. Support came from stevedores, cabdrivers, carpenters, carmen, waiters and the Phoenix Society.[9]

The Penrhyn dispute was a great working-class issue, seen as a battle of upright workers against a dictatorial and 'noble' employer for basic trade union rights. Bethesda itself became an essential town for prominent trade unionists and socialists to visit: George Barnes, Pete Curran, Allen Gee, Isaac Mitchell, Ben Tillett, Robert Blatchford, Keir Hardie and *Mabon* all came to display their solidarity, many of them to speak at mass-meetings. A host of less renowned working-class organisers also made their appearance, amongst them Bellcher, a London socialist, Brewer of the General Workers' Union, Kirkham of the Bolton Labour Church, Riley of the Huddersfield I.L.P. and A. M. Thompson, the *Clarion*'s 'Dangle'.

Other newspapers—the *Northern Weekly*, the *Morning Leader*, and the *Clarion*—followed the *Daily News*'s example in setting up funds in support of the struggle, though the £5,600 they collected was sent to the Penrhyn Relief Fund rather than to the N.W.Q.U. Fund.[10] The Penrhyn Relief Fund, the chairman

[7] N.W.Q.U., *The Penrhyn Quarry Dispute* (1904).
[8] *London Central Committee Report* (1904). 24,000 people, contributing a farthing each, would have donated £25.
[9] *Daily News*, 24 November 1902.
[10] Penrhyn Relief Fund, 1904, *Statement of Accounts*.

of which was W. J. Parry, the secretary Rev. W. W. Lloyd, was a charitable fund the aim of which was to alleviate the general distress.[11] Bethesda was divided into fourteen districts each with a sub-committee; applications for aid were investigated by the sub-committee, discussed by the general committee and then met in kind or by tickets. The ticket system was designed to help not only those in distress but also the shopkeepers by ensuring that those receiving aid bought their goods in Bethesda shops. The fund's main source of income was the three choirs from Bethesda, who toured the country to great acclamation and who between them collected almost £33,000.[12] The N.W.Q.U. fund and the Penrhyn Relief Fund together collected a massive £88,122 between the beginning of 1901 and the summer of 1903.

If the widespread popular support for the men was impressive the national support for Lord Penrhyn was no less significant. While the dispute of 1896–7 was still in progress, Frederick Millar's *The Liberty Review*, a waspish right-wing monthly, warned that any fund set up to defend the right of combination in Penrhyn

> should be met by another fund to defend the right of an employer to manage his business free from the dictation of Trade Union bosses and the impertinent interference of a Government department. Lord Penrhyn deserves the best thanks of every capitalist and employer in the United Kingdom . . .[13]

Lord Penrhyn, as it happens, had no need of outside funds, but he had plenty of friends nationally who were eager and willing to argue the case of an employer putting up a 'plucky single-handed fight with the disreputable and besmirched labour-union gang'.[14] For if the Penrhyn lock-out was a cause for the trade-union movement, it was a cause also for all those who argued for an employers' offensive against trade-union 'interference'.

---

[11] Penrhyn Relief Fund, *Bethesda* (Altrincham, 1902).
[12] Two male voice and one ladies choir. *Statement of Accounts*, op. cit.
[13] *The Liberty Review*, 15 January 1897. Not all Tories were pro-Penrhyn. In Liverpool the maverick but powerful Archibald Salvidge supported the strikers. S. Salvidge, *Salvidge of Liverpool* (London, 1934), p. 42.
[14] *The Liberty Review*, 15 August 1901.

William Collison's National Free Labour Association, the Liberty and Property Defence League, and Frederick Millar's Employers' Parliamentary Committee were all vocal and influential supporters of Penrhyn's stand. The National Free Labour Association, an organisation the stated aims of which were employers' unity, counteracting the abuses of trade unionism, actively opposing picketing and supplying 'free labour' during disputes, was more than a mere vociferous front and claimed in 1902 to have 'defeated upwards of over 500 senseless strikes . . . organised the Great Revolt of intelligent workmen against the tyranny of Trade-unionism and . . . enrolled 351,000 under the Banner of Free Labour'.[15] In his journal *Free Labour*, Collison argued that 'the Penrhyn quarries of North Wales . . . bid fair to prove epoch-making in the industrial annals of the country'.[16]

Both *Free Labour* and *The Liberty Review* delighted in attacking the quarrymen. During the 1896–7 dispute, *Free Labour* commented that the men of Bethesda had

> discovered that it is much more agreeable to send round the hat and divide the proceeds in idleness than to go back to the quarries, and so long as the milch-cow of the Unions holds out you may depend upon it the Welsh quarrymen will stick tenaciously to the udder.

The men's leaders were portrayed as 'a cabal of fire-eating and ranting stump orators aided and abetted by a process of violence and outrage upon non-unionists'.[17]

In similar vein, *The Liberty Review* explained how

> the quarrymen are doing the Christmas carol business at suburban chapels with pleasure and profit to all concerned, it is easier work than splitting slates.

And a note of English exasperation with the radical Welsh often crept in: 'a gang of little Bethelite preachers and Radical rowdies'; in 1897 it was said that the men would all have gone back but for fear of being stoned to death by the 'gentle,

---

[15] The N.F.L.A. had earlier been known as the Free Labour Protection Association. See *The Liberty Review*, 15 October 1897, p. 292; *Free Labour Press (and Industrial Review)*, 4 January 1902.

[16] Ibid., 15 May 1897; he also thought the dispute in the Pallion Forge in Sunderland 'epoch-making'.

[17] *Free Labour*, 15 June 1897; 14 November 1903.

cultured, submissive mountain folk, perhaps by the Bethesda choir'; in 1900 there were 'cowardly and brutal assaults committed by the simple, pious, overfed slate quarrymen', the 'Bethesda hooligans'.[18]

Lord Penrhyn also had a somewhat less raucous ally in *The Times*, but his own relations with the organised anti-union lobby were close; particularly after his refusal to allow Ritchie at the Board of Trade to intervene in the dispute under the terms of the 1896 Conciliation Act, he became the hero of that lobby. George Livesey of the Southern Metropolitan Gas Co., himself a scourge of trade unions, wrote admiringly in December 1900 that 'the tyranny of Trades Unions would never have attained such a power if more of the employers were of the same stamp as Lord Penrhyn'.[19]

These, of course, were Young's sentiments, and his and Lord Penrhyn's allegiance to the notions of 'free labour' was unquestionable. In the first month of the years of crisis, September 1896, Young explained that

> the crisis which we have now arrived at will in the long run be a great benefit to all Quarry proprietors and in fact many other employers of labour also.[20]

Young and Penrhyn saw themselves in the vanguard of a national employers' offensive against trade unionism, and their stand was appreciated as such by others. In an article on Penrhyn, *The Liberty Review* called upon 'employers . . . whenever possible [to] repudiate this so-called collective bargaining, which is injurious to everybody but the trade union bosses who thrive on labour disputes'. Penrhyn's role in the general campaign was greatly valued; he was considered to be 'the one man in the realm who has done most for the freedom of labour', for

> it is indubitable that Lord Penrhyn's courageous fight for the mastership of his own quarry was very largely responsible for the great triumph of the rights of employers against labour-union oppression which resulted from the engineering dispute

---

[18] *The Liberty Review*, 15 February 1897; 15 November 1896; 15 September 1897; 15 November 1900.
[19] GAS, P.Q. 99/6, 7: Livesey to Young, 31 December 1900.
[20] GAS, P.Q.L.B. 165: Young to Capt. Gower Bancath, 30 September 1896.

of 1897–8. Lord Penrhyn's success was of the utmost encouragement to the winning side in that long fight.[21]

Significant praise indeed! And it was praise echoed by many individual employers.[22]

The suggestion that the whole business was a socialist plot, first made by the *Cambrian News* and later popularised in the pamphlet *Tilletism at Bethesda*, was also one that greatly delighted anti-labour organisations.[23] In 1901 the Free Labour Congress noted that the strikers were prompted,

> by the desire on the part of socialist leaders to control the Quarries at Bethesda for the spread of socialism and its anti-economic and subversive theories.

They had earlier made an even more startling reference to 'the raid on the slate quarries of Lord Penrhyn by the I.L.P. for the purpose of experimenting in Marxian Socialism'.[24]

Young and Penrhyn shared *Free Labour*'s paranoiac distaste for trade unionists and socialists and were eager supporters of its campaigns: in October 1897 Young donated £50 to the National Free Labour Association and a further £100 'towards the initial expenses connected with the establishment' of the organisation, which sum, he presumed, would 'enable you to place the names of both Lord Penrhyn and myself on the list of members'. Donations were also made to the Employers' Parliamentary Council and further donations to the N.F.L.A.[25]

Even more important than this formal membership of the N.F.L.A. was the N.F.L.A.'s direct relationship with the slate

---

[21] *The Liberty Review*, 15 July 1897, 15 May 1902; see also GAS, P.Q. 100/42: Employers' Parliamentary Council to Young, 29 May 1902.

[22] Many employers wrote to Young offering solidarity and admiration: W. Smith of South Tottenham wrote begging to thank Lord Penrhyn 'for the gallant stand he has made so long against Working-Class Tyranny', a few more like him and Britain would not be 'beaten in most of the world's markets abroad'; J. Harris of Harris Cooke and Co. Shoe Manufacturers, Stafford, admired his courage in 'not submitting to the presumptious dictation of those paid agitators'; Thomas Ruscham of Northwich saw them as 'fighting a good fight', GAS, P.Q. 100/42, 8 September 1902, 23 April 1902, 11 December 1902.

[23] *Cambrian News*, 19 April 1901.

[24] *Free Labour Press*, 12 October 1901 (GAS, P.Q. 100/85); 1 June 1901.

[25] Young appears to have been somewhat confused as to who ran which organisation, mistaking Collison for Millar (GAS, P.Q.L.B. 311, 11 October 1897; P.Q.L.B. 312, 13 October 1897). See also GAS, P.Q. 99/6, 7, 26 January 1900, 14 August 1900.

industry in the figure of W. W. Vivian. Vivian, manager of the Dinorwic quarries, was a member of the Association's ten-man executive committee. Vivian's role in Penrhyn's troubles is unclear, he was certainly in close consultation with Young at the onset of the dispute in September 1896, and Young was mindful of the fact that he would lend him 'aid at any moment, if called upon'.[26]

In November 1900 collusion between the two managers seems to have been closer, with Vivian offering Young advice which, in its intransigence, he was faithfully to carry out. Close the quarry, Vivian advised, for it was 'the only course . . . open to you consistent with your duty', and furthermore, 'be firm and do not think now of taking back those you have decided not to re-employ'. Vivian spoke the language of Collison and Millar. 'Beyond doubt', he told Young,

> if you wish peace in the future, you must obtain this discipline even if the soldiers have to be called out, for if you give way in the very least, I am confident graver troubles will arise in the near future, so I urge you on no account to give way one tittle over this question of discipline.[27]

Vivian was free also with detailed advice as to the practical course Young should follow, and it appears as if he might even have drafted some of the notices put out by Young in November 1900.[28] There is no evidence of Vivian's guiding hand in the affairs of Penrhyn after this date, but the degree of his involvement in November 1900 would suggest that it was not altogether missing. What is certainly clear is that the strident politics of 'free labour' must be seen in the forefront of the Penrhyn attack, even if Collison was not directly to supply the quarry with his 'free' workers.[29] The Penrhyn quarry may have been remote and its workers isolated, but the issues raised by the dispute were at the centre of a crucial national debate on the 'rights' of trade unions and employers, and both sides in that debate inscribed the struggle on their respective banners.

[26] GAS, P.Q. 100/85. Free Labour Protection Association Report, 1897; ibid., P.Q.L.B. 154: Young to Vivian, 15 September 1896.
[27] GAS, D.Q. 20, Transcript of telephone conversation between Vivian and Young, 20 November 1900.

II. '. . . IN A KNOT ONE WITH THE OTHER'

'Man', it was generally accepted in Bethesda, 'does not live by bread alone.'[30] But sustenance had to be found by these strikers as by any others. The main source of the community's income during the period of the dispute was the work of its absent sons. Most of these worked in the coal mines of south Wales, but some were scattered throughout the country, Liverpool being the other main centre. Scores left immediately the quarry closed on 22 November 1900. Within three weeks it was claimed that some 1,800 had left, though the figure given in December 1902 seems more reasonable; it was then estimated that there were some 1,300 working away, 100 working in Bethesda's small but friendly Pantdreiniog quarry, 100 travelling the country with the Penrhyn choirs and some 700 living in Bethesda.[31] The importance of this large number living and working away from Bethesda was two-fold: it meant that most of the strikers were self-supporting and that in Bethesda itself the two rival sections were more equally divided than they would otherwise have been if all the men had been present locally. This would explain why major trouble was dependent on the periodic return of the men working away, and it might also explain why the *cynffonwyr* were able to defy the pressures put on them.

Despite the working quarrymen, there was severe hardship. For those who stayed there was no work; those who went away could find only unskilled jobs; slate quarrymen took time to learn how to become coal miners. Moreover, there was the difficulty of maintaining two homes, one for the man near his workplace, the other for his family in Bethesda; others found their new jobs intolerable and drifted back to Bethesda.[32] 'The

---

[28] GAS, D.Q. 2038, 2050, 2054.

[29] Though the workmen in the quarry did display some allegiance to the Free Labour Congress: GAS, P.Q. 100/85: W. Collison to Melancthon Williams, 11 October 1901. Collison would appear to have interfered with an earlier dispute in north Wales, a 13-week strike at Little Ormes Head quarry, Llandudno; when the strike failed 'the places of the strikers all being filled up': ibid., N.F.L.A., Advance Press Copy, 9 October 1899.

[30] *Daily News*, 8 January 1901.

[31] *Yr Herald Cymraeg*, 27 November 1900; 11 December 1900; 16 December 1902.

[32] *Y Werin*, 27 June 1901.

suffering', as Lloyd George exclaimed, 'is intense . . . These men have endured hardships that I cannot depict.'[33]

To ease the suffering there were only two major sources of funds: the trade-union movement, and the Penrhyn Relief Fund. There is no evidence of striker families applying for poor relief.[34] The North Wales Quarrymen's Union was a member, in the lowest section, of the General Federation of Trade Unions and as such was entitled to 2s. 6d. per member as lock-out pay.[35] This, however, only applied to financial members, i.e., men who had been union members for over one year; in the Penrhyn lodge there were 560 such members out of a total of 1,750 members. N.W.Q.U. strike pay also depended on length of membership; those who were members for up to 13 months received 6s. per week; up to 2 years, 7s. 6d; 3 years, 10s; 5 years, 12s. 6d. The majority of the men, therefore, received only 6s. a week as official N.W.Q.U. strike pay.[36]

Money came from the N.W.Q.U. fund and the Penrhyn Relief Fund, the latter relying heavily on the money collected by the three choirs from Bethesda which toured the country. As we have seen the labour movement mobilised impressively to sustain the struggle financially, and the aid from this quarter seemed all the more generous in comparison with the lack of response from the quarrymen's traditional allies, the non-conformist Liberal establishment. The response was also disappointing from other north Wales quarrymen.

The Bethesda men thus had a telling lesson in solidarity and could see clearly who their friends were. The effects of this lesson became increasingly apparent as the months passed. The *Herald Cymraeg* noted in an editorial of May 1901 that the shipbuilders of Sunderland and the engineers of Manchester were helping the men of Penrhyn more than the quarrymen of Caernarvonshire and Merioneth. In July another editorial asked whose fault was it that the north Wales quarrymen were doing so little? The same complaint was raised again in October

[33] D. Lloyd George, 'Trusts and Monopolies', *Better Times* (London, 1910), p. 11. Speech originally delivered in Newcastle, 4 April 1903.
[34] There is nothing in the records of the Bangor and Beaumaris Poor Law Union to suggest an increase in applications for poor relief in the Bethesda district.
[35] D. R. Daniel, Dinorwic Lodge Minute Book, 14 February 1902.
[36] N.W.Q.U. *Minute Book*, 31 January 1903.

1902, and the inactivity of north Wales quarrymen was condemned by one of the strikers in November of that year:

> the awful thing is that our fellow quarrymen in North Wales can sit down and smoke, and watch Bethesda's quarrymen fighting the battle while all England's workers are enraged.[37]

North Wales quarrymen were not quite as apathetic as this criticism might suggest. Demonstrations and meetings in support of the Penrhyn men were held in other quarrying districts, in Penygroes and Blaenau Ffestiniog, for example, in the summer of 1901. Speakers from other quarries carried their support to the mass-meetings; sometimes they took part in the disturbances, as when men from Llanberis broke some contractors' windows in Bethesda.[38] But these were isolated cases. The Penrhyn men had the support of militants from other quarries but they failed to get any active support from the mass of north Wales quarrymen.

To an important extent this was a failure of mobilisation. The N.W.Q.U., at the G.F.T.U.'s bidding, circulated 10,000 leaflets in November 1901 calling on all quarrymen to join the union and the results seem to have been encouraging.[39] But the crucial issue was the levy. In May 1902 the union executive sent to the lodges a request for comments on the suggestion that a toll be levied for three months to make up the union's depleted finances. In August the lodges replied: nine were for some kind of levy, two were undecided, and one was against. After a lengthy discussion, however, it was decided to refer the question back again to the lodges, with the suggestion that they accept a levy of 6d. per member per month for three months. At the next meeting on 29 August, a decision was postponed for another month; by October the lodges appear not to have replied. There the matter rested until July 1903, when the G.F.T.U. demanded a levy of 1s. a month on all members as a condition of further funds; this was accepted at a general meeting of the union. But a month later the G.F.T.U. insisted on a levy of 1s. per week. This was rejected as being

[37] *Yr Herald Cymraeg*, 7 May 1901, 2 July 1901, 18 October 1902.
[38] Ibid., 2 July 1901, 19 May 1903, 18 June 1901; *Y Werin*, 6 June 1901.
[39] N.W.Q.U. *Minute Book*, 30 November 1901, 25 January 1902.

totally impracticable . . . we believe that the result of this would be to lay a bigger burden on our Union than it can bear, and create a loss rather than an increase.[40]

Even though a majority of quarrymen had voted for a levy, the union knew that many, if not most, had not voted at all: in Dinorwic, for example, where there had been a vote of 332 to 38 in favour of a levy, 647 members had not voted.[41] An imposed levy was therefore seen as a real threat to the union and quarrymen's contributions remained largely voluntary; in its fear of alienating the mass of the membership, the union failed effectively to mobilise the hundreds of quarry trade unionists who were willing to offer active solidarity.

In equally sharp contrast to the activity of the Labour movement was the relative inactivity of Welsh Liberalism. It has been suggested that Welsh Liberalism's response to the Penrhyn strike, compared with the 1898 coal stoppage in southWales, was one of 'immediate interest and sympathy'.[42] But William Jones, the Liberal M.P. for Arfon, his silver-tongued eloquence apart, did no more than the minimum expected from a constituency M.P.; and while it is true that Lloyd George made many references to Penrhyn[43]—in truth he could hardly fail not to—it was not until 1903 that he really stressed the issue, that is, not until the Liberal Party leadership had noted its parliamentary and electoral significance. It was not until April 1903 that, at a meeting in London, Lloyd George and William Jones set up a committee to organise a Welsh movement in support of the quarrymen, a movement which does not seem to have grown any further from its inception.[44] The 'Welsh party' came under bitter attack for its indifference: in the *Daily News*, Lloyd George and William Jones were personally reprimanded and it was noted that, disillusioned with Liberal parliamentarians, 'an attempt will be made from Bethesda to force the matter on the attention of the House, through the agency of the Labour

[40] Ibid., 31 May 1902, 2 September 1902, 25 October 1902, 25 July 1903, 15 September 1903.
[41] GAS, Dinorwic Lodge Minute Book, 1 August 1902.
[42] Kenneth O. Morgan, *Wales in British Politics*, (Cardiff, 3rd edn., 1980), p. 212.
[43] E.g. the Newcastle speech 4 April 1903; he also attended delegations to the T.U.C. on behalf of the quarrymen.
[44] *Yr Herald Cymraeg*, 14 April 1903.

members'.[45] Keir Hardie made the point in 1903 that 'for three years the I.L.P. has been giving practical help and support to those men at Bethesda' whilst the Liberal Party waited for three years until 'it made a pretence of coming to their rescue'.[46]

The lesson was being learnt, that the middle class, Welsh, nonconformist and radical as it might be, was not to be trusted. The position was made very clear in a fiery speech by W. H. Williams in August 1901:

> For half a century the workers of Wales have been used to push up the middle class; but how is that middle class treating the workers today? . . . We have lived too long on the charity of people like this, but now the workers are fighting their own cause, and that is their hope . . . Let the worker take care of his own welfare first, and be in a knot one with the other. The workers of England have shaken off the middle class; and have taken the workers of Wales into that knot with them.[47]

The point was repeated a fortnight later by D. R. Daniel.[48] If the N.W.Q.U. leaders were later to reject direct Labour representation and 'argue convincingly for sectionalism within the existing party structure',[49] during 1901–2 some of them were also arguing for what sounds very much like independent labour representation. The president of the union, W. W. Jones, was the most persistent advocate of labourism; in October 1901 he lamented that there were not more labour representatives in Parliament, but looked forward confidently to a 'pretty strong Labour party before long, strong enough to rule the other two parties'.[50] He repeated the point again in April 1902, insisting that 'the oppression they suffer will not be moved until they get the reins of the government of the country into the hands of workers' representatives'. 'Parliament', he cried, 'should be transformed not into a workshop of oppression but into a home of freedom.'[51] His opinions were echoed among

---

[45] *Daily News*, 24 November 1902.
[46] Cyril Parry, 'The Independent Labour Party and Gwynedd Politics, 1900–20', p. 51.
[47] *Yr Herald Cymraeg*, 13 August 1901.
[48] Ibid., 27 August 1901.
[49] Cyril Parry, op. cit., p. 46.
[50] *Yr Herald Cymraeg*, 22 October 1901.
[51] Ibid., 15 April 1902.

the quarrymen. William Williams, Frondeg, a member of an earlier Penrhyn strike committee, argued that 'the duty of the workers was to send to Parliament a strong united body of labour representatives'.[52] Owen Griffith, vice-chairman of the 1900–3 strike committee, called in May 1903 for more Labour M.P.s, pointing out that though 'they already had men who loved labour's cause . . . they, as a class, had no power over them'.[53]

These sentiments found expression in a resolution passed at the May 1903 conference of the N.W.Q.U., which announced 'That it would be in our interest as trade unionists to have a paid member to look after our welfare in Parliament',[54] and though William Jones was regarded as being reasonably sensitive to the demands of Arfon's quarrymen, there were attempts to remove Osmond Williams from his seat in Merioneth.[55]

Not only did Labourism therefore become a strong feature of the men's consciousness in 1901–3, but socialism also made an appearance, though it was not cogently argued and remained a vague and ill-defined doctrine. Thus, D. R. Daniel argued that

> Unionism is something temporary and a day will come when it will not be needed for then there will be no master and no worker, but everyone will be both master and worker.[56]

Only W. W. Jones seems to have had a theoretical grasp of socialism:

> it is obvious that the whole life of the world stems completely from two sources . . . materials in the earth and the ability in the worker's arm . . . ownership or capital are secondary things.[57]

In February 1902 he pointed out that

> Lord Penrhyn and his officials, after all, are only the smallest teeth in the cogs of the great wheel of society. If they were

---

[52] Ibid., 10 September 1901.
[53] Ibid., 12 May 1903.
[54] N.W.Q.U. *Minute Book*, 4 May 1903.
[55] *Yr Herald Cymraeg*, 6 October 1903, 1 December 1903.
[56] Ibid., 25 February 1902.
[57] Ibid., 21 October 1902.

knocked out the machine would not slow down, but the wheel could not turn at all without the workers.[58]

That he was not alone—and the N.W.Q.U. executive generally must have been sympathetic towards socialism, at least a Fabian version of it—is shown by the union's unprecedented step in November 1901 of buying and distributing 1,000 copies of Rev. J. Clifford's Fabian Tract, translated into Welsh, *Socialism and Christ's Teaching*,[59] in which it was stated that

> we seek, like the early Christians, with a fiery enthusiasm to make Society a materialisation of the co-ownership principle rather than the individual principle.[60]

Independent socialist or labourist organisations, however, did not immediately appear; not until 1908 was Bethesda to have an I.L.P. branch.[61] Even W. W. Jones's socialism led him to advocate not the nationalisation of the means of production but the nationalisation of the land. And most of the appeals for labour representation seem to have been made within a Lib-Lab rather than an independent Labour context; *Mabon* was as popular as Keir Hardie with the men of Bethesda.

This confusion of political expression and articulation, however, should not hide the underlying changes in consciousness: they were fighting now as workers, not as Welshmen or nonconformists; they were fighting 'the battle of all the workers in the kingdom'.[62] They had, indeed, as W. H. Williams had advocated, 'shaken off the middle-class'. W. J. Parry, Bethesda's most prominent radical bourgeois, was still active, but in organising charity not in leading the union. The Welsh Liberal establishment was opposing the Education Bill, the Boer War and the beer, all issues the quarrymen, too, felt strongly about; but in their crucial struggle they found themselves alone, for 'now the workers are fighting their own cause'. Even the very radical local Welsh press was proving unsatisfactory: at the 1903 May conference of the N.W.Q.U., the Bethesda lodge

[58] Ibid., 18 February 1902. Owen Griffith made substantially the same point in May 1903: *Yr Herald Cymraeg*, 12 May 1903.
[59] N.W.Q.U. Minute Book, 2 October 1901.
[60] Rev. J. Clifford, *Sosialaeth a Dysgeidiaeth Crist* (Tract no. 87, Fabian Society, 1899, 1908).
[61] See E. H. Owen, 'Cyn y Chwalfa ac wedyn', *Lleufer*, summer 1963, pp. 55-60.
[62] *Yr Herald Cymraeg*, 20 January 1903.

proposed that 'we have ... a newspaper for the workers'.[63] The cautious steps into politics did not show a fiery labour independence, but rather a new suspicion of their old allies, the radical middle-class Liberals. At the first executive meeting of the N.W.Q.U. following the collapse of the struggle in November 1903, Henry Jones raised the matter of workers' representation on the county councils and it was later agreed that a close investigation be made 'into the beliefs and feelings of every candidate to the various councils to determine whether the rights of Labour claim his greatest attention'.[64]

These were indeed the techniques of sectionalism, but they pointed to the breakdown of the Liberal hegemony, to splits in that Welsh nonconformist radical tradition which had dominated north Wales since 1868. A class consciousness was appearing out of the Liberal identity.

The development of this consciousness, however, was uneven and stunted. The past and the exigencies of events dragged heavily and offered other answers. Nationalism, despite the generosity of the English, was still a force; Lord Penrhyn, after all, was considered to be an Englishman and he was an Anglican, and though W. W. Jones did not wish

> to say a word against the freedom of Englishmen to come to Wales . . . if they come here to oppress and to lay the yoke of oppression on the shoulders of the workers until their patience run out, then they must take the responsibility for the consequences.[65]

The battle being fought was, he said, 'the battle for nationalism', and it was seen as such by many. A telegram from strikers working in Porth exclaimed that

> We exalt Snowdonia, our culture, ourselves, our country, our race, and our Welsh pulpit by keeping our oath and standing like men. Better death than betrayal.[66]

The old question of the land was also grasped as a solution. There were rumblings about the expropriation of Penrhyn in March and April 1903 and claims were made that the

[63] N.W.Q.U. Minute Book, 4 May 1903.
[64] Ibid., 28 November 1903, 19 December 1903.
[65] Yr Herald Cymraeg, 18 February 1902.
[66] Ibid., 20 May 1902.

mountain which the quarry was slowly removing had 'within the memory of those now alive been common land under the Crown'.[67] But these demands seem to have come more from the radical press and politicians than from the quarrymen themselves.[68]

Another projected solution was a co-operative quarry. This was not a new idea; the N.W.Q.U. had invested £2,000 in a co-operative quarry in 1881, and the initiative seems to have come in 1903, as it did in 1881, from W. J. Parry.[69] In July 1903 the North Wales Quarries Ltd. was established and was followed by the setting up later of the National Co-op. Quarries.[70] The co-operative venture was supported by Liberal newspapers and Lib-Lab politicians, but the whole project was out of the hands of the quarrymen themselves.[71] A small quarry was procured, but the attempt to make it a real source of alternative employment to the Penrhyn quarry was a signal failure. That this was an attempt firmly outside the quarrymen's control was forcefully shown when there were complaints by workmen of 'Penrhynism' at the 'co-op' quarry and representations were made to the N.W.Q.U. to take action against North Wales Quarries Ltd.[72]

The culture which collided with Lord Penrhyn in November 1900 did not, as we have seen, involve the quarryman alone. The complex mixture of religious conviction, middle-class radicalism and trade unionism was put under a severe strain which revealed clearly enough the tensions and antagonisms inherent in it. In particular, the local Welsh middle class found itself out of step; fighting, as usual, the power of English landlordism but no longer leading that fight, it was overwhelmed by the quarrymen acting on their own behalf. The quarries had created a new class, property-less and industrial and active, but the quarrymen were acting in a social and political context frozen by the battles of previous generations, complicated by the still incomplete victory of the nonconformist Welsh bourgeoisie over landlordism. As well as its own battle, trade

[67] Ibid., 31 March 1903.
[68] Ibid., 21 April 1903 (see the editorial).
[69] G. Ellis, op. cit., p. 109.
[70] Ibid., p. 108.
[71] *Daily News*, 1 June 1903.
[72] Roose Williams, op. cit., p. 276.

unionism was having to fight the battle which Welsh middle-class radicalism had still not won.

In the end, the alliance held despite betrayal and indifference for, though the quarryman came to act on his own behalf, and to speak with his own voice, the words were often those of middle-class radicalism. Yet, while the quarrymen had earlier been mobilised by the radicals for service in their struggle against landlordism and Anglicanism, in 1900 the Bethesda quarrymen mobilised themselves for action in their own cause: they certainly fought as Welshmen and as non-conformists, but they also fought consciously as workers. Failing to control this movement the radicals either involved themselves in charitable action or fell into a sulky and sullen sympathy; the quarrymen came to shiver from the keen chill of their support. A new consciousness, a new identity, was being forged, struggling within and away from the claims and patterns of the past. The language of class did not come easily but the nature of the struggle forced out the words, articulated the clumsy syllables.

III. 'A POOL WHICH IS CALLED IN HEBREW, BETHESDA . . . '[73]

The people of Bethesda took their religion very seriously; for many of them the chapel was an obsessive preoccupation consuming all their spare time. It is not suprising, therefore, that the rhetoric of the pulpit was constantly used during mass-meetings or that salvationist religious positions were put forward from the beginning of the struggle. What is significant is the way in which such a fundamentalist position, from being the solution proposed by a minority of zealots came, by the end of 1903, to be an important and generally-accepted definition of the struggle.

The quarrymen's rhetoric and imagery were from the beginning Biblical, the commonest image being that of the tribes of Israel in the wilderness:

> If the quarrymen . . . return from the wilderness into the land of captivity there, without doubt, they will stay for gener-

---

[73] John 5, viii; 'there is in Jerusalem by the sheep gate a pool, which is called in Hebrew Bethesda, having five porches. In these lay a multitude of them that were sick, blind, withered.'

ations . . . But the faces of the tribes are turned to the land that is seen; and they are determined to travel toward the Jordan, even if they fail to reach the promised land.[74]

After each mass-meeting the men sang the hymn, '*Rwy'n gweld o bell y dydd yn dod*' ('I see from afar the day that is coming').[75] The chapels played a full part in the struggle, the ministers being solid with the men, helping with relief and other tasks. The only noticeable effect of their intervention on policy was their efforts to maintain peace.[76] The chapel hierarchy was, in fact, linked with that of the union, the strike committee was made up of 'the leading men of the district, leaders of religion'.[77] The vice-chairman, Owen Griffith, was himself a deacon of Gerlan Chapel; William Williams, another prominent member of the committee, was a deacon of Carneddi Chapel.[78]

The fundamentalist chapel view had been posed early to the mass-meetings: R. R. Jones in June 1901 urged them to leave the issue in God's hands and make it a matter of prayer; then they could be sure that all would work out.[79] In November 1902 the men were again urged to 'be submissive before God and leave everything in His hands'.[80] The reply to these religious exhortations was simply that 'The Kingdom of God will not come by waiting'.[81] W. H. Williams went so far as to suggest that as Christians 'They can contribute toward the ministry if they wish; but that is not necessary', but they must care for the poor.[82]

---

[74] *Yr Herald Cymraeg*, 9 April 1901.
[75] The second verse was particularly apt; roughly translated, it reads:
  'The beautiful light of the dawn,
  From land to land now proclaims,
  That daybreak is at hand;
  The tops of the hills rejoice,
  As they see the sun draw nearer,
  And the night retreat away.'
[76] *Yr Herald Cymraeg*, 7 January 1902.
[77] Ibid., 16 December 1902.
[78] There might well have been others but in dealing with Welsh names without their addresses it is dangerous to assume that the same name appearing several times in different contexts is the same person; the chances are that they are several people with the same name.
[79] *Yr Herald Cymraeg*, 25 June 1901.
[80] Ibid., 18 November 1902.
[81] W. W. Jones, ibid., 28 January 1902.
[82] Ibid., 13 August 1901.

It was not in its purely salvationist, other-worldly aspect that fundamentalism was to become important during the dispute, but rather in its emphasis on sacrifice and suffering. Writing before the struggle started, W. J. Parry noted that the religious history of the community, the struggle to maintain nonconformity in the face of a hostile, Anglican landlord, had made them 'more eager to sacrifice on the altar of service'.[83] This element of sacrifice and a consciousness of its assumed beneficial effects was present throughout the dispute. W. H. Williams in November 1900 talked of those 'who had brought the sins of the people on to their shoulders'; such sacrifice, he claimed, 'would not fall dead to the ground'.[84] A year later he drew attention to the fact that 'all who try to follow His paths by attempting to raise the lowest class' must always be persecuted.[85] But it was not until 1903 that this attitude came to the fore.

On New Year's Eve 1902 the press and police were prepared for a revival of the violence which had exploded into a near-riot when that year had been born. All, however, passed quietly; there was no riot, for

> one could hardly conceive that this sad crowd had sufficient spirit left to indulge in anything of the kind.[86]

The reporter went on to explain that

> the gnawing heartache caused by hopelessness and the scars of more than two years of struggle and anxiety had broken the spirits, but not the determination . . . Hope seemed to have fled, and desolation reigned supreme.

The struggle had become hopeless; Penrhyn was immovable. Voices of loyal strikers had come to be raised in criticism of the committee's leadership.[87] A note of despair crept into the meetings; in January a striker complained that the committee did nothing but

---

[83] W. J. Parry, *Cyfrol y Jiwbili, Eglwys Bethania Arfon* (Dolgellau, 1900), p. 5.
[84] *Yr Herald Cymraeg*, 13 November 1900.
[85] Ibid., 12 November 1901.
[86] *Penrhyn Dispute* (reprint of *London Daily Chronicle* articles, 9 January 1903), p. 4.
[87] *Yr Herald Cymraeg*, 26 October 1902.

urge us to stand out until the windows of Heaven open, or some other windows which, at the moment, no-one knows about.[88]

A letter to the *Herald Cymraeg* urged a full conference to settle the matter, for

what reason is there for us to stay out like this, without saying or doing anything but waiting for something that we do not know what it is, nor where it will come from, if indeed it comes from anywhere.[89]

The criticism was understandable. The point had been reached when defeat could have been admitted. The local leaders of the quarrymen, however, had by now come to see their struggle in a different light; it was no longer a trade dispute for a change in the work situation, but a religious experience, a salvationist crusade, above all, a test.

The theory of suffering had been clearly enunciated by the Congregationalists of Bethania Chapel who, in their annual report for 1902, explained that

terrible times have overtaken us . . . they are Trials poured like the flood on to us to test our fidelity to God, to each other, and to the principles. And we believe we shall be better men for God and society as a result of these tragedies. The path to Canaan, in all ages, leads through desert, chaos and pain.[90]

The lock-out became a test; to go back to work was to fall into 'temptation'.[91] Attention was drawn to Ridley and Latimer, 'Who died gloriously despite being burnt', and to John Penri, Wales's own 'young martyr'.[92] D. R. Daniel explained that

a little suffering in the desert for another season would be more of a blessing . . . than the pleasures of Egypt.[93]

In June, W. H. Williams, in a rousing speech, re-defined the purpose of the battle:

[88] Ibid., 27 January 1903.
[89] Ibid.
[90] *Adroddiad Eglwys a Chynulleidfa Bethania* (1902).
[91] *Yr Herald Cymraeg*, 25 July 1901.
[92] Ibid., 3 March 1903.
[93] Ibid., 14 April 1903.

one of the great aims of this struggle was to make better men
of us when we came out of the furnace, and if we succeed
in getting only 200 purified, the battle will not have been
in vain.[94]

The aim of the struggle had become the purification of those
involved. This was emphasised by Henry Jones, chairman of
the committee and the leading speaker at all the meetings
since 1900; five weeks before the end, he testified that he was

ready to fight on—yes even if our number is no more than
300, and it would be a privilege for that 300 to be sacrificed
for the principles they fought over.[95]

The last weeks of the struggle, therefore, were sustained by a
religious energy, no word was 'heard in the public meetings
of victory . . . the days of the great certainty' were gone.[96]

The committee's only strategy was emigration and a number
of men left for the quarries of the U.S.A.[97] The only aim was
to suffer. The men cracked, and during September increasing
numbers applied for work.[98] Meetings were held to determine
whether to stay out or to give in; in Bethesda 452 defiantly
voted to continue and 76 for a return to work. From four
meetings of exiles in other parts of Wales came the same
reply: Rhaeadr voted 13–2 to continue, Tredegar and the
Rhondda were unanimous for the same course, Merthyr
pledged to 'stay out till death'.[99] But famine increasingly
became the alternative to submission and men were forced to
apply for work.[100] In a bitter meeting at the beginning of
November, acrimonious accusations were thrown around the
hall, and men publicly announced that they were applying to
the quarry manager. The next week Bethesda voted by 192
votes to 161 to give up. Henry Jones bitterly addressed his
'fellow traitors'.[101] The men in the south did not comment.
Bethesda had fallen. When the movement collapsed the men
lay still, all energy spent.

[94] Ibid., 2 June 1903.
[95] Ibid., 27 September 1903.
[96] Ibid., 7 July 1903.
[97] Ibid., 22 September 1903, 5 September 1903.
[98] Ibid., 6 October 1903.
[99] Ibid., 13 October 1903.
[100] Ibid., 29 September 1903.
[101] Ibid., 17 November 1903.

Not only was their community shattered and on the verge of famine, but they had also failed in their impossible struggle for purification. Defeat was total, and the repercussions spread right through the community, including its religious life. For in their struggle for survival the religious energy of the community had run dry; they had staked not only their material belongings but also their God on the success of the battle. It was not God who had failed them: far worse, it was they who had failed Him.

The effect of the disaster can be traced in the annual reports of the chapels.[102] The figures dealt with are, of course, very small, but in such a previously stable and integrated community changes in chapel membership, even small changes, do hold some significance.

The figures for Jerusalem Methodist Church show a decline in 1900, a steadying out during 1901 and 1902 and a further decline in 1903.[103] What is interesting is the 1903 slide, for by that year most of those who were to leave had already left: a good many, perhaps aware that they would never return to Bethesda, might have transferred their chapel membership to chapels nearer their new homes, but others would have lapsed for different reasons.

Perhaps a more sensitive guide to attitudes to the chapels are congregation figures rather than membership. Capel Gerlan, where these are available, shows a slightly different pattern from Jerusalem: there is a membership decline in 1901 but the congregation remains stable; in 1902 the trends are reversed and the congregation slumps while the membership is static.[104] During 1903 both decline but, significantly, the sharp decline comes in 1904, after the total defeat of the lock-out. Changes in membership figures, as has been suggested earlier, could depend on those away deciding to stay away; the drop in actual attendance, however, means that, unless there was a significant exodus from the town in 1904, some of those going to Gerlan Chapel in 1903 were not doing so in the following year. There is, in fact, no evidence to suggest an

[102] The reports of four chapels have been consulted, Bethania and Bethesda (Congregationalist), Gerlan and Jerusalem (Methodist), at the N.L.W.

[103] *Adroddiad* Eglwys a Chynulleidfa Jerusalem M.C. Bethesda, 1900–5.

[104] *Adroddiad* o Sefyllfa a thanysgrifiadau Eglwys a Chynullcidfa, Gerlan Bethesda, 1900–3.

exodus in 1904; on the contrary, many of those working away would have returned as the quarry slowly took back several hundred more men. Some other cause dissuaded them from worshipping.

The primary reason was the bitterness and personal unpleasantness which marked the last stages of the dispute,[105] as those loyal almost to the end fell one by one into 'temptation'. Certainly the chapels were worried about their ex-members in Bethesda who no longer worshipped. Indeed, one chapel report implied that those personally alienated formed the main group of absentees:

> It can be said that what has taken place in this working area has scattered the Church, and caused a great loss in membership, greater than in any other period of her history. We feel that it would be better for this year not to go into details, hoping that during the coming year many for whom we now feel concern will be restored to health.[106]

Their hope was finally fulfilled in 1905, when membership rose from 345 to 423. This undoubtedly was a result of the great religious revival that was sweeping Wales in 1904–5. What is interesting is that in at least two chapels, Gerlan and Bethania, the revival seems to have had little effect. Membership and congregation in Gerlan declined during 1904, and though there was a rise in membership in 1905, the congregation increased only very slightly. Bethania gained only ten members during 1905 and the total membership still remained below the 1902 level. And this at a time when the chapels of Wales were overflowing with ecstatic converts.

The revival certainly affected Bethesda during the winter of 1904–5, and with a particular ferocity; but its effects were not what they were elsewhere. The memory of the struggle of 1900–3 was an insuperable barrier running through the community, unassailable even by the Holy Spirit. The revival of 1904–5 originated in the small village of Newquay in Cardiganshire in October 1904. It is difficult to follow the

---

[105] See J. Owen, 'Sylwadau y Sylwedydd', *Y Goleuad*, 29 January 1947. Writing a review of T. Rowland Hughes's *Chwalfa*, he recalled the days of the lock-out when he was a minister in Bethesda and when 'Angry emotion clawed its way over the handrail of an occasional *Sêt Fawr*'.

[106] *Adroddiad* Eglwys Gynulleidfaol Bethesda Arfon, 1900–4.

spread of the revival, but it first lit up south-west Wales before exploding into the Glamorgan coalfield early in November, when the name of the mysterious 'revivalist', Evan Roberts, came to be associated with the movement.[107] Within two months the whole of Wales was shaking in a paroxysm of salvationist joy. By April 1905, 25 per cent of the patients entering the Denbigh asylum were 'religious cases'.[108] When the wave subsided in the summer of 1905 it left behind, according to one sceptical observer, some 80,000 converts in the four larger nonconformist denominations; convictions for drunkenness in Wales dropped from 10,282 in 1904 to 5,490 in 1906.[109]

The revival hit Bethesda in the last week of November, when the local Wesleyan evangelist, Rev. Hugh Hughes, preached on Monday, Tuesday, Wednesday and Thursday evenings to huge congregations in Jerusalem chapel.[110] The most striking feature of the first weeks was the effect on the women of the village: five hundred of them met daily in the afternoons for prayer meetings. An observer described one typical meeting where,

> some two dozen unnamed women took an active part. It is not really possible to describe what they did. The meeting was supposed to be a prayer meeting: but it was everything—it was a fellowship meeting [seiat], a singing meeting, a preaching meeting as well. But the spirit of prayer was in everything and some strange happiness frequented the place . . . many sweet tears were cried by almost every one of the five hundred sisters present.[111]

Young people were also deeply affected and held their own meetings, lasting, on at least one occasion, from 2.30 in the afternoon until past midnight.[112]

The involvement of women and young people was a feature of the revival throughout Wales, as was the spontaneous nature

[107] One of the more interesting discussions of the 1904–5 revival is C. R. Williams, 'The Welsh Religious Revival, 1904–5', *British Journal of Sociology* vol. iii (1952), pp. 242–59.
[108] *Yr Herald Cymraeg*, 25 April 1905.
[109] J. V. Morgan, *The Welsh Religious Revival, 1904–5*. (1909), pp. 247–48.
[110] *Y Genedl Gymreig*, 29 November 1904.
[111] Ibid.
[112] Ibid., 6 December 1904.

of meetings, with preachers and established local religious leaders often silenced by the insistent stridency of those who had for long been quiet recipients of their dogmas. In January, for example, a Sunday school examination in Jerusalem was abandoned when the congregation burst out singing and praying, eventually forcing the examiner to retreat.[113]

Some of the meetings in Bethesda rivalled those anywhere in Wales in their intensity and hysteria. Thus,

> Thursday night's meeting was the most awesome . . . so far . . . The tone of the whole area has become quiet after this strange meeting. The feelings were so violent and intense that we feared seeing some going mad under their influence. Mr. Jenkins preached very powerfully. After that Miss Maud Davies sang '*Cofia ddweud*' (Remember to say) magnificently. As she was finishing someone on the edge of the gallery recited with great feeling Hugh Derfel's hymn '*Y Gŵr a fu gynt o dan hoelion*' (The Man who was under the nails) and it was then sung so that many said 'If heaven was no better than this, who would not be ready to do anything to get there? . . .' How many times was it re-sung? When was such singing ever heard before?

Later in the evening, in the young people's meeting, 'the Dam burst':

> several were praying together. Two sisters and one brother on their knees praying their best in the pew and another brother on his feet in the singing pew praying with all his energy. At one point I could also hear the voice of another sister praying by the door. She raised her arms and shouted . . . another girl broke down into loud prayer.[114]

At another meeting a divine presence was discerned: half way through the meeting, uneventful except for a 'comforting savour on the whole service', a man rose to pray and

> there came a sound like a sound from heaven, and it fell as a heavy shower on the congregation. Those who were present can only describe it as a shower falling on everybody in the place until the place was boiling. Some weeping, some groaning,

---

[113] Ibid., 3 January 1905.
[114] Ibid.

others shouting '*Amen*', '*O diolch*', '*Bendigedig*', '*Dyma Ef wedi dod*' (Amen, O Thanks, Blessed, He has come). And everyone praying. This scene lasted for some quarter of an hour.[115]

Despite the euphoria engendered by these well-attended meetings, the revival in Bethesda was not altogether successful. It was estimated in mid-February 1905 that some 120 souls had been 'saved' in Bethesda in the preceding months, a figure that did not compare very favourably with the 600 'saved' in Blaenau Ffestiniog or the 500 in the Nantlle valley.[116] This failure to win sinners from 'the world' in Bethesda was a fact bemoaned throughout the months of the revival;[117] describing a meeting in January 1905, the *Genedl Gymreig* noted that it was 'a surprise and a disappointment that after such a meeting no-one new stayed behind'.[118] The problem was only too apparent:

> before we can honestly expect religious revival in Bethesda as in every other place . . . it certainly will not do for you to treat each other as brothers and sisters in the chapel, and then pass those same brothers and sisters on the street the next day with a scowl and hostility.[119]

It was reported in February 1905 that it was generally felt that in Bethesda it was not

> any obvious and rash sins . . . that stand in the way of the success of the Holy Spirit . . . but the devilish sins the apostle talks of—wrath, anger and betrayal.[120]

In January and early February 1905 there were signs that these obstacles were beginning to be overcome; in one revival meeting some strikers and blacklegs openly embraced one another and prayed for each other, and it was reported in mid-January that 'the two parties are slowly beginning to melt into one another'.[121] By early February one reporter was

---

[115] Ibid., 27 December 1904.
[116] Ibid., 14 February 1905.
[117] Ibid., 29 November 1904; 6 December 1904; 13 December 1904; 14 February 1905, etc.
[118] Ibid., 24 January 1905.
[119] Ibid., 29 November 1904.
[120] Ibid., 14 February 1905.
[121] Ibid., 3 January 1905; 17 January 1905.

greatly hoping that industrial questions will never again become a stumbling block . . . to the churches as they have been like a nightmare in the past.[122]

But the revival's influence, powerful and all-embracing as it was, could not solder together the split community. A minor incident outside Penrhyn quarry in mid-February 1905 resulted, according to one report, in inciting

the most bitter feelings between religious brothers, and this, it is feared, has generally overcome the conciliatory spirit that had begun to take hold of the local people.[123]

The revival, therefore, certainly affected the religious life of Bethesda, but it left the chapels with their flocks hardly increased. In the revival meetings there was obviously a tremendous straining after reconciliations: 'Save this district, Lord, the *whole* district', prayed a local youth; 'I have felt for some time that there was something in the way, whatever it is. The English call it a stumbling block. We feel it all the time.'[124] The stumbling-block was the inheritance of hatred bequeathed by the community's three-year struggle. What energy remained could not, despite prayer, devotion and divine intervention, overcome that stumbling-block.

Writing at the end of 1903, the deacons of Jerusalem had sorrowed, for they feared that, in their religious work, 'there are signs that we are failing from exhaustion'.[125] When the revival, with all its insistent, ecstatic demands, its spiritual challenge and promise came boiling from chapel to chapel, the people of Bethesda could not fully respond: they strained to open their hearts to Christ but they could not overcome themselves and allow the kneeling *cynffonwyr* into their hearts as well.

---

[122] Ibid., 7 February 1905.
[123] Ibid., 14 February 1905.
[124] J. V. Morgan, op. cit., p. 37.
[125] *Adroddiad* . . . Jerusalem, op. cit.

Part 3
Aftermath

X

THE UNION 1900–1922

The nineteenth century brought rapid expansion and also depression to the slate industry; the twentieth century brought calamity. The profitable but partial recovery of the late 1890s gave way to a depression which spiralled downwards to the First World War, when the industry suffered a virtual collapse. The union's fortunes initially mirrored this decline, particularly as it coincided with, and was in part caused by, the disastrous aftermath of the Penrhyn dispute. But as the century progressed, and attitudes toward labour changed, the union paradoxically found itself growing in strength and importance as the industry itself crumbled. In 1918 the slate industry had rarely been in such a parlous state and the N.W.Q.U. had never before been so powerful. In this chapter we shall be concerned with the causes of this growth in trade-union influence.

The twentieth-century depression in the slate industry had several causes, the most important being the decline in demand consequent upon a depressed building trade and the competition for a shrinking market from tiles and foreign-produced slates. The effects of this depression on the quarrying districts were deep and painful. Unemployment and emigration became constant features of the slate communities; distress was widespread. In the quarries there was short-time working, closures and reductions in earnings. Between 1906 and 1913 the number of men at work in the quarries in the Ffestiniog district shrank by 28 per cent, in Dyffryn Nantlle the number at work fell even more dramatically, by 38 per cent.[1] Many of the redundant left to seek work in Liverpool, south Wales or the United States.[2] The depression lifted somewhat in 1910 but

[1] Owen Parry, *Undeb y Chwarelwyr, 1908–1929* (Caernarfon, 1930), p. 6.

[2] As, for example, did workers from the closed Braichgoch, Corris, quarry in July 1906. *Yr Herald Cymraeg*, 26 July 1906.

only temporarily and modestly; the gloom persisted until after the end of the First World War.

Total surrender in Penrhyn and a sudden and deepening economic crisis came close to liquidating the union. By 1905 membership had fallen to only 1,200. But the union, by now hardened to adversity and perhaps even somewhat complacent because of it, soldiered fitfully on with D. R. Daniel and W. H. Williams remaining at the helm. At this low ebb in the union's fortunes there were only 200 trade union members in Nantlle and 150 in Ffestiniog; in 1907 there were a hundred or so in Penrhyn and only sixty-seven in Dinorwic.[3] The union had to expand or disappear. At the annual conference held in Caernarfon in 1907 Isaac Mitchell, of the General Federation of Trade Unions, who had been closely involved with the union during the Penrhyn dispute, spoke harshly and bluntly of the N.W.Q.U.'s record. He claimed that the union, by its failure since Penrhyn, had let down those English trade unionists who had made sacrifices to aid the men of Bethesda. He castigated the weaknesses in the union's organisation, and in particular its lack of discipline over its members; the disputes which had sporadically broken out since 1903 he saw as 'not the result of organisation but rather of disorganisation'.[4] In the conference hall was a delegate from Blaenau Ffestiniog called R. T. Jones, who was soon to change all that.[5]

Mitchell's strictures were largely justified. The following year the president of the annual conference, O. Ellis Jones of Nebo, grieved that

> it was regrettable that after fighting against autocracy and capitalism on the one hand and treason and derision on the other, the Quarrymen's Union at present did not embrace one half of the quarrymen of North Wales.[6]

The picture painted by W. H. Williams at the same conference was even more depressing. Over the previous ten years, he

---

[3] Three years earlier in 1902 there had been 6,700 union members. Owen Parry, op. cit., p. 7.
[4] *Caernarvon and Denbigh Herald (C. and D. Herald)*, May 1907.
[5] Robert Thomas Jones 1874–1940. Born in Blaenau Ffestiniog, secretary of the N.W.Q.U. 1908–33, M.P. 1922–23, member of T.U.C. General Council 1921–32.
[6] *C. and D. Herald*, May 1908.

estimated, membership had averaged around 2–3,000. As many as 8,500 men 'had trifled with the union by becoming members and retiring in a short period'. In ten years the monthly subscriptions had totalled £14,391 while members had received £41,000 in strike and lock-out benefits.

Apart from the Penrhyn dispute, and despite the low union membership, the industry witnessed a rash of disputes in this period, particularly in the Dyffryn Nantlle district. The issue at stake was normally a reduction in wages, achieved in a variety of forms. In July 1905 there was a serious dispute in Dyffryn Nantlle when the effective minimum was cut from 4s. 6d. a day to 4s. 3d. a day. The stoppage is interesting because it affected many quarries in the one district rather than just a single quarry. By mid-July the strike had spread to Talysarn, Gloddfa'r Coed, Blaenycae, Tanrallt, Galltyfedw, Coedmadog, and South Dorothea, and by the end of the month only Galltyfedw and Coedmadog had returned to work.[7]

In 1906 there was a similar, though longer, dispute in Moeltryfan; by this time the proposal was for a further reduction to 3s. 9d. a day. It is clear that during this dispute the men were at least as much concerned about redundancy as they were about the reduction: in November 1905 they had decided to work four days a week instead of the customary six in order to prevent some of their number being thrown out of work. In June 1906, however, the management demanded a reduction in wages and a return to six-day working; they agreed with the men that this would mean more redundancies, but pointed out that those at work would be better off under the new arrangement. The men, however, refused to accept the proposals and walked out.[8]

A recurring feature of these disputes, and one which caused the union much concern, was the fact that union members were often only a small minority of those involved. The president of the annual conference for 1906, Henry Cunnington

[7] *Yr Herald Cymraeg*, 20 July 1905, 27 July 1905.

[8] Ibid., 5 June 1906, 12 July 1906. Other disputes in these pre-war years were at Glyn Uchaf, Coedmadog, 1908; Penrhyn, Alexandra, Dorothea, Talysarn, 1910; Dinorwic, 1911; Talysarn, Pen-yr-orsedd, Cilgwyn, Nantlle, Alexandra, 1912. C. Parry *The Radical Tradition in Welsh Politics: a Study of Liberal and Labour Politics in Gwynedd, 1900–1920* (University of Hull Occasional Papers in Economic and Social History, No. 2, 1970), p. 38.

of Blaenau Ffestiniog, criticised the role played by trade unionists in a dispute with the North Wales Quarries Co., during which they had acted as spokesmen for the non-unionist majority.[9] The following year the new annual president, Morris D. Jones of Clwtybont, voiced the same criticism, pointing out that

> it was hardly reasonable that the union should be called upon to make contributions to members when the union had no voice in the dispute or in deciding the terms upon which work was to be resumed. This . . . was the result of being in the minority.[10]

The problems were the old ones of lack of central control of the lodges and a failure really to impress upon the majority of quarrymen the benefits of trade unionism, problems to which R. T. Jones was to apply himself with some energy in the years after 1908.

W. H. Williams's health broke down and in August 1907 he gave the executive committee notice of his intention to resign from his position as financial secretary of the union.[11] His resignation was not, however, accepted for a further year when, in August 1908, R. T. Jones became financial secretary in his place. Three nominations for the position were announced to the annual conference of 1908 for submission to a ballot of the members. The three were O. Ellis Jones of Nebo, who was that year's annual president, R. T. Jones of Blaenau Ffestiniog and H. M. Williams of Waunfawr. In the first ballot in May 1908 R. T. Jones, who was fighting an energetic and well-publicised campaign, was just ahead of O. E. Jones, with Williams trailing.[12] A second ballot between the two leading contenders was ordered and it would appear that Williams's votes went by two to one to R. T. Jones, who won with 1,164 votes to O. E. Jones's 969. R. T. Jones became the new financial secretary of the union on 1 August 1908. At the same time, that enigmatic character D. R. Daniel, the union's organiser, decided it was time to move on to a post in London; no

[9] *C. & D. Herald*, 11 May 1906.
[10] Ibid., 10 May 1907.
[11] Owen Parry, op. cit., p. 5.
[12] *C. & D. Herald*, 11 May 1908. The figures were: R. T. Jones 901, O.E. Jones 849, H. M. Williams 309. N.W.Q.U. Minutes, 30 May 1908.

successor was appointed and so R. T. Jones became the union's sole officer, with W. H. Williams remaining to advise and assist him.[13] At the next annual conference held in Caernarfon in 1909, the new organisational structure was approved with W. H. Williams agreeing to become the union's treasurer while R. T. Jones was confirmed as general secretary.[14] From then on it becomes impossible to differentiate between the history of the N.W.Q.U. and the career of this man.

At the time when he became an official of the N.W.Q.U., Robert Thomas Jones, born in Blaenau Ffestiniog and working in the slate quarries there since he was thirteen, was president of the Ffestiniog lodge of the union, having previously been vice-president; he was also vice-president of the newly-formed Ffestiniog branch of the Independent Labour Party and had recently become a labour member of the Ffestiniog Urban District Council.[15] R. T. Jones was *'un o "ddynion ieuanc" Silyn yn y Blaenau'*,[16] one of a small group of young quarrymen in Blaenau Ffestiniog who had come under the influence of the poet and I.L.P. propagandist, Rev. R. Silyn Roberts, then a minister in nearby Tanygrisiau. He had been a bright school-child who had not lost his interest in learning when he had gone into the quarries: a devotee of evening classes, he had studied mathematics and book-keeping and had become proficient in the use of the English language.[17] His library had been cited as a remarkable example of the cultured quarryman's reading habits in evidence to the Royal Commission on the Church of England in Wales.[18] He was also a Sunday School teacher and a strong advocate of temperance.

R. T. Jones's salary was £2 a week, but the executive committee also decided to offer him a bonus of £1 for every £100 of members' annual subscriptions over the first £1,000, plus his expenses.[19] Jones was an energetic and ambitious man and he probably did not need the additional financial incentive,

---

[13] Ibid., 27 July 1908, 1 August 1908.
[14] Owen Parry, op. cit., p. 6.
[15] *Daily Herald*, 26 February 1927, see also GAS, X.N.W.Q.U. (R. T. Jones scrapbook), letters from T. J. Evans and R. Silyn Roberts.
[16] David Thomas, *Silyn* (Liverpool, 1956), p. 69. (One of Silyn's young men in Blaenau).
[17] GAS, X.N.W.Q.U., letter from John Cadwaladr.
[18] Ibid., letter from R. Silyn Roberts.
[19] N.W.Q.U. minutes, 27 February 1909.

but his presence as the union's leading figure soon had a cheering effect on membership figures. R. T. Jones was the union's first career trade-union official, its first 'labour movement' functionary; W. J. Parry had always had his outside business and political interests, as indeed had W. J. Williams. W. H. Williams had come late to union prominence, while D. R. Daniel's interest in trade unionism was academic and fitful. Jones was to spend his life as a trade-union official, involved in countless committees, becoming briefly a Labour Member of Parliament, and sitting for years on the General Council of the T.U.C. He exercised caution and restraint, nursing the union's funds, but he also demanded organisation and discipline; within a decade of his appointment the union had virtually 100 per cent membership in the quarries.

His first achievement was to centralise the union and bring the headstrong lodges and their expensive stoppages under the executive committee's (and his own) control. He refused to authorise lock-out or strike payments to members unless they were fully in compliance, and unless the dispute in which they were involved was fully in accord with union rules. Fully paid-up members tended to be exceptional and disputes very often took place with no reference to the union's executive committee or to union rules, especially in those quarries where union members were in a minority. Jones's new policy, therefore, caused considerable bad feeling and the union members involved in a stoppage in Coedmadog early in 1909 complained bitterly when the executive refused to authorise payments to them.[20] A similar dispute between the executive and striking members took place in Chwarel-y-Braich the following year.[21] The intention was clear: the years of the lax application of the rules by indifferent officials were over; under Jones's stewardship the rules were to be applied and regular payment of subscriptions insisted upon.

In 1909 and 1910 new rules were discussed and introduced, but the real difference lay not so much in the rules themselves as in the new spirit in which they were now to be administered. In 1911 Jones tightened the centre's control of the lodges by demanding monthly, instead of quarterly, financial returns;

[20] Ibid.
[21] O. Parry, op. cit., p. 10.

in 1912, in the wake of proposed plans to amalgamate certain small lodges, it was agreed that the list of members should henceforth be kept in the central office, while the lodges had to send in their subscription returns monthly. The lodges objected to the latter demand and it was dropped; but in the following year, 1913, it was agreed that all the expenses of the lodges would be met centrally and all the lodge funds, other than those relating to certain benefits, were incorporated in the central fund.[22] Within five years Jones had created a centralised trade union from what had been, in effect, no more than a loose federation of virtually autonomous lodges.

This process was made easier by the union's success in other directions: growth in membership, recognition as a responsible body under the 1911 National Insurance Act and the drawing up of a single programme of demands for all quarrymen—the Quarryman's Charter. Membership had begun to grow in 1906 and increased again in 1907; during Jones's first two years as secretary this growth was maintained,[23] and between 1910 and 1914 membership more than doubled.[24] This was partly the result of an energetic membership drive with many well-produced leaflets, but it also reflected the growing seriousness, and therefore attractiveness, of the union.

The compilation of the Quarryman's Charter, and its printing and general distribution, was one of the spurs to membership. It had always been a problem for the N.W.Q.U. that the relative autonomy of the lodges reflected a very real degree of variation in work practice and wages between the different quarrying districts and, indeed, between different quarries in the same district; there was nothing approaching a unified wages' structure for the industry. The formulation of a programme which would unite quarrymen working in different districts with differing rates, working times, and customs, was therefore a difficult matter but an essential pre-requisite for the building of a united union.

The charter, which was finally adopted by the annual conference of 1912, was the result of some four years of discussion and

---

[22] Ibid.

[23] C. & D. Herald, 10 May 1907, 8 May 1908, 7 May 1909; Yr Herald Cymraeg, 2 May 1911.

[24] O. Parry, op. cit., p. 18. Membership rose from 2,100 in 1910 to 4,800 in 1914, but still less than half the potential membership.

debate. It contained twelve points relating to the standardisation of hours of labour, holidays, regularity of payment of
wages and, most important, a proposed minimum wage (of
4s. a day for quarrymen proper) and a proposed apprenticeship
scheme for youngsters (of five years' duration).[25] The charter
expressed what had always been the main concern of trade
unionists in the quarries: the attempt to inject into the
bargaining system a degree of standardisation which would
give the quarrymen some protection from the vagaries of
stewards and setting agents, let alone of the slate rock. A partial
sliding-scale was also included, though the minimum wage was
to remain constant whatever the selling price of slates might be.

The charter, of course, was only a set of demands with little
chance of being accepted by the employers given the depressed
state of the market, but it was more than merely an ambitious
piece of paper; for the first time it offered a set of aims which
could unite all the quarrymen and which many of them
thought sufficiently attractive to justify their joining the union.
The charter was presented to the Ffestiniog area owners but
their response was distinctly chilly,[26] and the union, indeed,
did little seriously to attempt to force the charter on the
employers; this procrastination brought an impatient motion
from the Nantlle lodge to the conference of 1913.[27]

Another factor which enhanced the union's prestige was its
recognition as a 'responsible body' under the terms of the 1911
National Insurance Act. R. T. Jones was a member of the
national advisory board on the workings of the Act and a plan
was worked out for payments of unemployment and sickness
benefit to be made through the union.[28] The union was thus
recognised by the state before it had been recogised by any of
the major employers in the industry, a considerable boost to
a union in such an unenviable position.

This growth in the size and importance of the union is the
more remarkable given the state of the slate industry at this
time. Depression is not normally a recruiting agent for trade
unionism and, apart from a few months in 1911–12, the slate

[25] See appendix IV for full text of the Charter.
[26] O. Parry, op. cit., p. 13.
[27] Yr Herald Cymraeg, 6 May 1913.
[28] O. Parry, op. cit., p. 11.

industry was deeply depressed with, as we have seen, high unemployment and massive emigration. In his address to the union's conference in 1910 the annual president, Mr. W. R. Williams from Llanllyfni in the Nantlle district, the worst-hit of the slate-quarrying areas, commented that

> The conditions under which the quarryman had lived had created a serious doubt as to the recuperative powers of the industry and as to whether the day of the slate as a marketable product had not altogether gone by.[29]

He was being somewhat over-pessimistic, but there was little in the situation to discourage such pessimism.

Faced with such an acute depression, however, many quarrymen, particularly in the Nantlle and Blaenau Ffestiniog districts, turned to a collective response for the first time. In part this can be attributed to the renaissance in the union's organisational powers, but it must also be viewed in the context of the national upsurge in trade-union activity during these years and as part of the pre-war 'labour unrest', particularly in the years 1910–14. There is no evidence of syndicalism or even of so-called 'proto-syndicalism' in the area; but the new energy which coursed through the working-class movement throughout Britain undoubtedly affected the quarrymen.[30] It reflected itself in a growing commitment to labour politics and it also expressed itself in a growth of trade-union and class consciousness amongst the quarrymen. As early as 1907 the annual president for that year, Mr. Morris D. Jones of Clwtybont, had made the point that

> Hitherto it was mainly due to the efforts of the well-organised and united workmen of England that the quarrymen were indebted for what they now enjoyed. They must be convinced of the futility of trying to secure justice by relying upon the good will or kindness of the employer however admirable that might be . . . the quarryman ought not to be content with looking from a distance upon the great struggles which were going on between their fellow workers and their opponents in other parts of the kingdom.[31]

[29] C. & D. Herald, 6 May 1910.
[30] See Bob Holton, Syndicalism in Britain (Pluto Press, 1977).
[31] C. & D. Herald, 10 May 1907.

Similar sentiments were frequently voiced in subsequent years, even if the union's practice, under R. T. Jones's guidance, tended toward conciliation.[32]

The most serious dispute of the pre-war years was that in the Alexandra quarry on the Crown lands above the Nantlle valley. The union had deep roots in this quarry and in the neighbouring Moeltryfan quarry, and the history of disputes in these two quarries would suggest a particularly resilient trade-union tradition in this quarry-cottager area.[33] The Alexandra stoppage, though involving only a small number of men, is noteworthy for its length (it lasted from November 1913 to March 1914) but more particularly for the fact that it was the first stoppage in the industry to follow what might be called 'normal' trade-union procedures. As we have seen, all the great disputes had boiled over from the immediate anger of a particular quarry, with little organisation or planning beforehand and with no official approval from the union's executive committee. The first strike called by the union executive itself was in Chwarel-y-Rhos in Capel Curig in 1877; the second was in Alexandra in 1913. Alexandra was the first test of R. T. Jones's new centralised policies and the remit was, in the short term, satisfyingly successful for him.

The situation in Alexandra first came to the attention of the executive in October 1913, when it was reported that the setting standard for the following month was to be severely cut. The executive advised the lodge that

> they protest against the terms but go to their work in accordance with the union's Rules until such a time as the union can deal with the matter.[34]

R. T. Jones was dispatched to negotiate with the manager, A. W. Kay Menzies, and all the subsequent negotiations were between these two, trade-union official and quarry-manager, a situation which would have been unthinkable during the Penrhyn disputes. Menzies pleaded that financial constraints made the cut inevitable and the men in the quarry were

---

[32] See, for example, ibid., 8 May 1908.
[33] There were disputes in Moeltryfan in 1892, 1896, 1899, and 1906, in Alexandra in 1879, 1910 and 1912.
[34] N.W.Q.U. Minutes, 11 October 1913.

balloted on the question of strike action; the result was clear-cut, with 161 men voting for strike action and 20 against. The union's executive therefore authorised the stoppage and sent a notice to Menzies that this quarry would stop work at the end of the quarry month.[35]

There were several unsuccessful negotiations during the ensuing months with the Board of Trade and with Sir G. R. Askwith, the chief industrial commissioner, who was brought in at various stages. In March an agreement was finally reached which, while conceding a certain cut in the standard, was generally seen as a conclusive victory for the men and the union.[36] Work re-started in April but by June the quarry was only working four days a week and the following month it closed. Like all the disputes in the industry, the Alexandra strike displayed a bitter determination on the part of the men 'when the discontent brewing for some time in the quarries finally came to a head',[37] but unlike most disputes it also displayed union-controlled actions with no problem presented by non-unionists and with the general secretary of the union playing a decisive role.

Encouraged by this development, the union applied for recognition agreements with several managements in the summer of 1914, and in September the Oakeley mines in Blaenau Ffestiniog agreed to recognise the union for negotiating purposes. By the end of the war most quarries had followed suit.

II. THE FIRST WORLD WAR

The First World War came close to destroying the slate industry; it also ensured the short-term stability and success of the N.W.Q.U. The war brought paralysis to the building industry and cut off slate's remaining export markets. The effects were felt immediately: within a month of the outbreak of war those quarries which had not stopped all production were on short time; by the end of September 1914 there were 1,170 unemployed quarrymen in Dyffryn Nantlle; in 1917

[35] Ibid., 21 October 1913.
[36] Ibid., 15 November 1913, 5 December 1913, 23 January 1914, 31 January 1914, 16 March 1914.
[37] O. Parry, op. cit., p. 8.

the slate industry was declared a non-essential industry; by the end of the war scarcely one-third of the original work-force remained in the quarries.[38]

In common with much of the labour movement, the union's attitude toward the war itself involved a certain sceptical support which was in large part opportunistic. Thus, while the chairman of the 1915 annual conference maintained that Britain was in the war 'with an honest mind', he was wary of praising the government overmuch lest that be misinterpreted as support for the 'secret diplomacy' which he deplored. As early as this it was apparent to him that the war presented certain opportunities for trade unionists: in the first place, 'as a result of the crisis the Government had been obliged to turn to socialism for advice and assistance, and the voice of the people demanded that they should proceed further on the same lines'; secondly, it was already apparent to him that the men who would return from the front 'would not be satisfied with the old order'.[39] The war was being seen as a forcing-house for social change.

On the question of recruitment to the armed forces, the union executive tried to cling to the pacifism of the Welsh radical tradition and initially refused to support a recruiting campaign in the quarrying districts.[40] Even in October 1915 the executive turned down a government request that they encourage recruitment to the colours, maintaining that enlistment was a personal decision and that the union could do nothing officially to support it.[41] R. T. Jones, however, did not share his executive's misgivings and he was active in supporting various recruitment drives from the start of the war.

The distress being caused in the slate-quarrying villages did not encourage support for the government's policies and there was a great deal of muttering about the 'Prussianism' that was to be found closer to home than Germany.[42] The distress committees which were set up to alleviate some of the problems caused by the collapse of the industry, and on which the union

---

[38] Ibid., pp. 18–19.
[39] *C. & D. Herald*, 7 May 1915.
[40] C. Parry, op. cit., p. 49.
[41] O. Parry, op. cit., p. 20.
[42] See, for example, N.W.Q.U. annual conference report 1916, *C. & D. Herald*, 5 May 1916.

was represented, were severely criticised by the 1915 annual conference because 'of their treatment of workmen who for adequate reasons were compelled to remain at home and were destitute'; the union objected to the pauperisation of 'honest and persevering workmen'.[43]

The union pressed, among other things, for a government-supported building programme and for the use of the giant quarry sheds as sites for war industries; but all to no avail. Even the loyalist R. T. Jones went so far as to declare to the 1916 conference that 'no industry in the country had received so much injustice at the hands of the Government as the slate trade'.[44] His conviction must have been deepened when the industry was declared 'non-essential' in 1917.

Faced with the unemployment crisis in the districts, the union could do little but encourage transfer to other industries and lobby for the industry's future. By February 1915 it was reported that close to 500 union members had been transferred to other industries and other unions. The N.W.Q.U. did not wish to see these members lapse and so it was agreed that the transferred quarrymen could retain their N.W.Q.U. membership while at the same time becoming members of their appropriate union. In one case the union even negotiated a pay rise for some of its members working on the railways.[45] The same procedure applied to members who joined the armed forces; they were able to retain their membership at a reduced subscription, and some seven or eight hundred union members had joined up by 1916.[46]

The war witnessed an unprecedented integration of the trade unions in the administrative machinery of the state. The N.W.Q.U. was no exception and by the end of the war the union was represented on official distress committees, pensions committees and tribunals, while its general secretary

---

[43] C. & D. Herald, 7 May 1915.
[44] Ibid., 5 May 1916.
[45] O. Parry, op. cit., pp. 21–22.
[46] The monthly subscription was cut to 6d. a month in the early years of the war because of the distress amongst the members; in 1916 it had to be raised to 1s. a month again but it remained at the lower rate for members in the armed forces. O. Parry, op. cit., p. 21. Both during and after the war there was some criticism of the quarrymen for not enlisting in greater numbers, particularly in the light of the high unemployment in the industry. The union, however, vigorously denied the charge.

was also for a while the deputy-controller of foods for north Wales.[47] After the war the union was represented on a committee for the re-structuring of the quarrying industry which in time became the National Joint Committee on the Quarrying Industry.[48]

On this and other committees, the union found itself joining forces with the employers in pleading desperately for the future of the industry. The aggravation of the crisis brought about by the war forced the employers into recognising the union as an ally in the battle for the slate industry. The alliance was facilitated by the establishment in 1917, following pressure from the Ministry of Labour, of a North Wales Slate Quarries Association; for the first time in the industry's history the owners could now speak with one voice and the previous destructive competition and distrust (particularly between Penrhyn and Dinorwic, on the one hand, and the smaller concerns, on the other) came under some control.

The co-operation between union and employers finally found expression in the establishment of a Board of Arbitration and in a series of agreements with the major quarries. The pattern was set, ironically, by an agreement signed by the union and the management of the Penrhyn quarries that

> the management agree to meet representatives of the men relating to terms of employment of the workmen as a whole, or any particular class of workmen and failing agreement to submit the claims in question to the decision of an arbitration acceptable by both parties. Representatives of the men to consist of three workmen from the Quarry representative of the classes concerned in any particular point at issue and the Secretary of the North Wales Quarrymens Union.[49]

In May 1918 the new mood was cemented by an agreement on wages and on apprenticeship in the quarry which enshrined the main points of the 'Charter' of 1912. The sufferings of 1896–7 and 1900–3 must have appeared at least partly vindicated, but in truth the circumstances had changed so drastically

---

[47] Having earlier turned down the post of 'area Substitution Officer' for North Wales: O. Parry, op. cit., p. 21.
[48] Ibid., p. 32.
[49] GAS, X.N.W.Q.U. 253: Agreements signed with Penrhyn Quarry, 9 August 1917, 22 May 1918, etc.

in the meantime as to make comparisons with the earlier period unhelpful and unfruitful.[50] In the succeeding months the agreement with Penrhyn was followed by similar agreements with Dinorwic and the Blaenau Ffestiniog quarries.[51]

The war, therefore, saw the coming of age of the N.W.Q.U. as a trade union which could freely negotiate on behalf of its members with the employers in the industry. From being an arena for a central confrontation between capital and labour, the slate industry became a cause for conciliation and compromise as its continuation as a viable concern became problematic; to form a defensive bloc against the ruthlessness of a predatory market the union's fullest co-operation was needed, and it was recognised and consulted for that purpose. In 1918, following the local agreements negotiated by the union, came the first general agreement, covering all quarries, between union and employers.[52] It guaranteed 4s. 6d. a day as a minumim wage for quarrymen, a central plank of the 1912 charter, and also established a sliding-scale whereby the setting price could be established.

The revolution in the union's fortunes seemed complete; after almost half a century the N.W.Q.U. had arrived as a modern trade union, recognised by the employers and employing a regular staff of professional full-time officials.[53] In 1905 the union had organised some 15 per cent of the slate quarrymen; by July 1919 it felt strong enough to send a printed letter to the few remaining non-unionists in the industry requiring them to join the union or else be forced out of employment. Union members were to refuse to work alongside

[50] As one historian has correctly noted: 'No doubt some trade unionists felt that recognition justified the long campaign waged since 1874; most of them, however, realized that this was a compromise that arose from exhaustion and that the union, though now accepted by employers, would henceforth be tied to the techniques of rearguard action as the industry faced a period of steady decline.' C. Parry, op. cit., p. 48.

[51] X.N.W.Q.U. 253: Agreements with Dinorwic; 3 December 1917, 15 April 1918, 3 January 1919, 9 June 1919; Oakeley, 18 October 1918; Llechwedd, 14 December 1918; Graigddu, 4 March 1918; Manod, Votty & Bowydd, 4 January 1918; Maenofferen, 8 January 1918; Parc and Croesor, 30 January 1919.

[52] Nantlle was the only district where the employers voted against such an agreement: O. Parry, op. cit., p. 30.

[53] In 1918 Joseph Williams was appointed full-time organiser for the Blaenau Ffestiniog district; he was followed in 1919 by R. W. Williams, the first quarryman to attend Ruskin College and who became organiser for Nantlle; and in 1923 by J. H. Jones, who became the Llanberis organiser: O. Parry, op. cit., p. 33.

non-unionists. Several hundred non-unionists joined as a result
and henceforward the N.W.Q.U. was, for the first time, to
represent virtually all the quarrymen in the scattered slate
industry.[54] This dramatic change in the union's fortunes has
often been attributed to the increasingly conciliatory policies
of the N.W.Q.U., but in truth the official union had rarely
been anything other than conciliatory. The difference was that
the employers now recognised that trade unionism could be
an ally in the battle for the industry.[55] The growing seriousness
and professionalism of the union's administration under R. T.
Jones also encouraged growth as did the increasing absorption
of the union into war-time organisations. This was a development which affected most British trade unions; the only major
difference between the N.W.Q.U. and some other growth
unions during the war was that the slate industry, unlike many
others, did not suffer from labour shortages.

The history of the union during the immediate post-war
years mirrors even more closely the fortunes of trade unionism
nationally, with boom followed by depression and amalgamation. The post-war boom in the industry was dramatic and by
July 1920 the price of slates was treble that of war time;
output rose from 164,098 tons in 1919 to 237,350 tons in 1921,
while the number of men employed grew from 6,604 to 9,520
in the same period.[56] The recovery was not complete, however,
and the industry never regained its pre-war dimensions; in
particular, it had lost its export markets and was consequently
to become almost wholly reliant on the fortunes of the domestic
economy and, in particular, on the domestic building industry.

Following the pattern of the economy as a whole, the industry
and the union flourished briefly until the winter of 1920–1 and
then it entered a long period of stagnation and crisis.[57] The
agreement signed by the union and the employers in 1918
remained in force until mid-1919, when the union made a

---

[54] *C. & D. Herald*, 9 May 1919. See also O. Parry, op. cit., p. 33. The actual
membership figures were: 1916, 2,650; 1918, 4,000; 1919, 6,500; 1925, 9,000.
[55] See, particularly, O. Parry, op. cit., p. 27. In fact, the union may have been
conciliatory, but it was certainly not slavish during the war; there was considerable unrest during 1915 and there was a strike in Penyrorsedd in 1917.
[56] Jean Lindsay, op. cit., pp. 284–85.
[57] O. Parry, op. cit., pp. 34–39.

series of new demands, most of which were granted, including
a comprehensive wages' scale for apprentices, an increase to
8s. 3d. in the minimum wage and a shortening of hours to an
average of 46 hours a week. In the autumn of 1919 a further
demand for an increase was made; the employers refused to
concede but agreed, under the terms of the 1918 agreement,
to go to arbitration. The arbitration award increased the
minimum to 10s. 6d. a day. In May 1920, with slate prices still
rising, the union made a demand for a further increase to 15s.
a day; once again the issue went to arbitration, but the decision
pleased neither side and employers and union finally agreed
on a rise to 12s. 6d. a day. Wages were now three or four times
greater than they had been in 1914, but the boom was already
cracking.

In December 1920 the first signs of a new atmosphere became
discernible when the employers informed the union that they
would not in future agree to compulsory arbitration. In the
spring of 1921 the employers made their intentions clearer by
giving notice that they were to contract out of the 1920 agreement; the union insisted on six months' notice and it was not
until September that the owners published their new terms,
which involved monthly agreements and a cut in the minimum
and the day wage; the union resisted any cut in the minimum
wage but finally agreed to a cut of 2s. 3d. in the day wage; this
took wages back to their June 1920 level.

In 1922 there was a souring of relations between owners and
union, with the union claiming that while wages had fallen by
18 per cent, the selling price of slate had fallen only by 10 per
cent. The owners disputed these figures and replied that
productivity had fallen with the shortening of hours. After
much negotiation, the two sides agreed on a standard for a
sliding-scale of wages, but the owners insisted that the minimum
wage be no more than two-thirds of the day wage as determined
under the sliding-scale, in other words, it was a sliding minimum. The owners introduced their new terms on 12 June 1922,
but the union rejected them and, in the first industry-wide
stoppage ever, the quarrymen struck work. After a fortnight,
however, the union's resistance collapsed and the executive
committee conceded the owners' demands; the day wage fell
to 9s. 1d., the minimum to two-thirds of that plus 6d. a day.

Wages were henceforth to be on a sliding scale and the slide was to be downwards.

In the spring of 1921 the union had been hopeful of a prosperous future and the annual president reported to the N.W.Q.U. conference that 'the reforms already secured showed that the standard of living among quarrymen had improved beyond their most sanguine expectations'.[58] The minimum was then 12s. 6d. a day; within a year it had fallen to 6s. 6d., the union had lost its first trial of strength with the employers under the new conditions, and it could congratulate itself in the 1922 conference on little more than the sliding-scale, the willingness of the employers at least to talk to them, and the fact that despite the wage cuts 'the men nevertheless loyally followed the council's advice not to adopt extreme measures'.[59] The union had negotiated the precarious transition from boom to stagnation skilfully and, while winning nothing for its members but low wages, it had ensured its own survival unscathed. It was to prolong this survival that in 1922 the union amalgamated with the Transport and General Workers' Union.

III. AMALGAMATION

The possibility of amalgamation had been present in the mind of many N.W.Q.U. members since the early 1890s, when a surprisingly high number of them had voted to join with an unspecified union,[60] but it was not until the twentieth century that it became a serious option.

There were many reasons why amalgamation with a larger union or a number of unions seemed an attractive proposition. The most important was the small size of the slate industry, which meant that whatever percentage of quarrymen was organised the union would remain small and therefore incapable of providing costly benefits, professional and expensive advice, etc. for the members; in the aftermath of the Penrhyn dispute, the constraints on the union's resources were only too obvious. The other major reason was the union's lack of industrial muscle, in particular, its inability to control the movement of

---

[58] *C. & D. Herald*, 6 May 1921.
[59] Ibid., 5 May 1922.
[60] See p. 129.

stockpiled slates during the course of a dispute. This was a problem which affected many other industries and which had concerned many activists during the pre-war 'labour unrest', particularly in the light of syndicalist and industrial unionist criticisms of existing union structures.[61]

The N.W.Q.U.'s first approach in the direction of greater trade-union unity was in 1913, when representatives from the Settmakers' Union and the National Union of Quarrymen met the leaders of the N.W.Q.U. to discuss the possibility of forming one national union for quarrymen. Nothing came of these discussions, though the unions remained in contact with one another.[62] Furthermore, in 1913 the union came into conflict with James Sexton's Liverpool-based Dockers' Union: in that year the N.W.Q.U. complained to Sexton that local branches of his union were poaching their members.[63] The cause of the problem was probably the fact that the Dockers' Union had recruited dockers in the slate ports (who had once been N.W.Q.U. members) and was extending its influence from the railheads at the ports to the quarries themselves. The complaint was repeated in 1916 by the Bethesda lodge, but by this time it appears that relations between the two unions were friendlier and although R. T. Jones discounted any possibility of an amalgamation between the two organisations, 'because of the peculiar nature of the quarryman's calling', he saw no reason why they should not come to some mutually advantageous agreement.[64]

The union had explored another possibility in 1915 when it had sought a closer relationship with unions in the building industry.[65] These unions would be in a position to control the use as well as the distribution of slate, and common cause could be made with them in pleading for an expansion of the housing market and thereby of slate production.

By 1917 the union was continuing to think seriously about the possibility of amalgamation with the dockers and it was reported to the annual conference of that year that 'the difficulty was to draft a scheme which would secure the common interests

[61] This concern led to the setting up of the Triple Alliance in 1915.
[62] O. Parry, op. cit., p. 11; C. Parry, op. cit., p. 51.
[63] N.Q.W.U. Minutes, 11 October 1913.
[64] C. & D. Herald, 5 May 1916.
[65] Ibid., 8 May 1914.

and at the same time the identity of the Quarrymen's Union'.[66] When the April 1919 claim was sent to the employers, it was the result of joint consultation between the two unions and during the ensuing months a scheme of amalgamation was drawn up. In early 1920, however, that scheme was heavily defeated in a ballot of the membership.[67]

Following the founding of the Transport and General Workers' Union in 1922 and the unifying of the two dockers' unions, negotiations were once again re-opened and this time the members voted overwhelmingly in favour of amalgamation. In May 1923 Henry Cunnington, the annual president, opened the sixtieth annual conference of the N.W.Q.U. with the remark that

> they met that day at least for a period for the last time as the North Wales Quarrymen's Union for they had become amalgamated with the Transport and General Workers' Union.[68]

The agreement was an extremely favourable one for the N.W.Q.U., for it granted it all the benefits of membership of a large organisation whilst allowing it to retain a very large measure of control over its own policies and organisation. The first clause of the joint agreement made this quite explicit by guaranteeing 'That complete autonomy be granted to the North Wales Quarrymen's Union in its internal affairs'. The union did not by any means submerge its identity into that of the T.G.W.U. by becoming the Quarrying National Trade Group of the larger organisation. The N.W.Q.U. had to withdraw its independent membership of the General Federation of Trade Unions, but it was allowed to continue its affiliation to the TUC 'as a separate entity in the mining and quarrying group'. Little wonder that when the agreement came to be reviewed five years later in 1927, R. T. Jones described the existing arrangement as 'as clear and definite

---

[66] Ibid., 11 May 1917.
[67] O. Parry, op. cit., p. 43.
[68] C. & D. Herald, 11 May 1923. The agreement between the T.G.W.U. and the N.W.Q.U. was arrived at in August 1922; the membership voted in a ballot in October 1922 but the N.W.Q.U. did not formally cease to exist until the annual conference of May 1923. See Appendix V for the text of the agreement between the two unions.

an alliance as can be arranged, short of a complete amalgamation'.[69] The only real sacrifice made by the union was the change from its own unemployment benefit scheme to the accident benefit of the T.G.W.U., if that can be considered to have been a sacrifice, and the loss of its former autonomous financial control. As Owen Parry commented in 1930, 'the terms of the amalgamation secured completely the independence of the Union and the Transport Workers consider that it is an union for financial and economic reasons'.[70]

The 'amalgamation' marked the end of the North Wales Quarrymen's Union's independent existence, but it is perhaps more interesting as a comment on Ernest Bevin's union-building methods than as a milestone in the history of the quarrymen. It is easy to see what R. T. Jones gained from the move but, apart from a few thousand awkward members in a declining industry, it is not as easy to see what real benefits the agreement brought the T.G.W.U. In 1922 and 1923 Bevin had overseen the amalgamation of twenty-two separate organisations, several of them small and regional;[71] it is difficult to see why the N.W.Q.U. should have been granted such favours unless Bevin saw its entry into the T.G.W.U., along with the North Wales Craftsmen and General Workers' Union, as guaranteeing him the domination of trade-union organisation in one geographical area and a voice in the councils of the quarrying and mining industries.[72]

IV. THE RISE OF LABOUR

During this period some of the labour and socialist tendencies which appeared during the Penrhyn lock-out acquired organisational form and a public, controversial presence. Labour 'rose' as surely in Gwynedd as anywhere else in Britain,

[69] GAS., X.N.W.Q.U.; letter from R. T. Jones to Messrs. Gosling, Bevin and Hirst, 3 August 1927.
[70] O. Parry, op. cit., p. 43.
[71] Such as the Belfast Breadservers' Association and the Greenock Sugar Porters' Association.
[72] The North Wales Craftsmen and General Workers' Union organised some craftsmen in the north Wales coalfield and on at least one occasion jointly negotiated entry into the T.G.W.U. with the N.W.Q.U. See GAS, X.N.W.Q.U.: R. T. Jones to Stanley Hirst, 21 July 1922; J. W. Williams to R. T. Jones, 8 August 1922; R. T. Jones failed in his initial bid to make the North Wales Area of the T.G.W.U. synonymous with the N.W.Q.U. He did, however, quickly

culminating in 1922 in the election of R. T. Jones as Labour
M.P. for Caernarvonshire; but the rise was gradual and its
victory temporary and incomplete.[73]

The N.W.Q.U. did not affiliate to the Labour Party until
1920, following a debate within its ranks which had lasted in
a confused way since the closing years of the nineteenth century.
The changing allegiance from Liberal to Labour and the
consequent affiliation to a political party was a prolonged and
difficult process in which quite different positions, many of them
contradictory, were taken up by different lodges and individuals.
From the early-twentieth century, particularly following the
experience of the Penrhyn lock-out, a changed vocabulary
became commonplace in union meetings and a great deal of
sympathy for some form of 'labour representation' becomes
noticeable. At the 1903 conference a motion from Glyn Uchaf
was passed which proposed that local trade unionists should
have a paid representative in Parliament; later in the same
year, the N.W.Q.U. executive agreed that all candidates for
political office should be questioned about their attitudes to
the rights of labour.[74]

The question of Labour representation was debated in some
form in almost every annual conference until 1920, but progress
was slow. In 1905 D. R. Daniel, still an official of the union,
looked forward to a change of government and 'the strength-
ening of Labour representation in the House of Commons'.[75]
When this came about the following year the union expressed
its satisfaction at the increase in Labour members; Henry
Cunnington, the annual president, even went so far as to declare
that

> no effective legislation for the benefit of the worker could be
> expected until the Labour party was powerful enough to defeat
> the political parties in Parliament. The only hope of Labour

establish himself as the north Wales secretary of the T.G.W.U. It was later
often alleged that R. T. Jones's continuing presence on the General Council of
the T.U.C. as a representative in the mining and quarrying group was a
manoeuvre to prevent more mining, and left-wing, representation.

[73] For a full and interesting account of the emergence of Labour in Gwynedd,
see C. Parry, op. cit.

[74] N.W.Q.U. Minutes, 4 May 1903, 19 December 1903.

[75] C. & D. Herald, 5 May 1905.

lay in an independent, direct and socialistic Parliamentary representation.[76]

The conference cheered this section of his speech, but breaking with liberalism was to demand more than ringing declarations.

At the 1908 conference the annual president, O. Ellis Jones of Nebo, commented warmly on the 'distinct political and social awakening which was now taking place' in the slate districts and, as if to echo this claim, the delegates were later to listen to D. R. Daniel arguing that it was

> the duty of Welsh workmen to see how they could adapt their demands to those of the Socialistic party in England without sacrificing essentially Welsh interests.

and to the Rev. R. Silyn Roberts advocating the nationalisation of land, mountains and the means of the transmission of merchandise.[77]

All this, however, was mere rhetoric, however valuable it might be in changing attitudes. The real ambivalence of the union toward the question of affiliation was made clear in 1909 when the then annual president declared himself to be unhesitatingly in favour of Labour representation; he even saw it in some respects as a preferable alternative to industrial struggle, but, he asserted, 'the quarrymen could not commit a greater mistake than to associate themselves with any party'.[78]

The problem for the union was threefold: in the first place, their support for local Liberal M.P.s, particularly those in Caernarvonshire, had not yet been totally destroyed (and it has to be remembered that the towering figure in Gwynedd politics at this time was David Lloyd George, still wielding his radical sword threateningly before the citadels of landed interest).[79] Secondly, the quarrymen were conscious of the fact that were they to support a Labour candidate it was most unlikely that he would get elected in a constituency like Merioneth which, though it included substantial quarrying villages, was still a largely rural constituency. Thirdly, and

[76] Ibid., 11 May 1906.
[77] Ibid., 8 May 1908.
[78] Ibid., 7 May 1909.
[79] R. T. Jones told the 1910 Conference that the Caernarvonshire Liberal M.P.s 'were as Radical as any who could be found'.

perhaps most important, they were conscious of the fact that were they to offer a Labour challenge to Liberal dominance the result might well be a Conservative M.P., a thought intolerable to most quarrymen.

Both the 1910 and 1911 conferences were the scene of passionate debates on the question of affiliation and it is clear that a substantial number of delegates were enthusiastic for the idea. R. T. Jones, however, used all his skill and influence to defeat the motions. Jones's attitude is not easy to understand since, when he was elected to union office in 1908, he was one of only a small band of I.L.P. members in the area and he must have won the votes and carried the hopes of many of those who supported affiliation. They were to be disappointed, however, and Jones probably became the single greatest influence working against the union's affiliation to the Labour Party. Had he not been the union's leader during these years then affiliation might have come a decade—certainly two years —earlier than it did. He intervened decisively in the debates both in 1910 and 1911, and his 1911 contribution seems to have been particularly influential since he argued that affiliation to the Labour Party was illegal under the law of the land, a judgement which drew protests from the Nantlle lodge which had moved the motion to affiliate.[80] In 1912 Nantlle tried a different tactic, arguing that the union should ballot its members on the question of affiliation in order to avoid any legal obstacles, but this too was voted down.

At a local level, however, the union, and R. T. Jones in particular, was active in supporting initiatives for Labour representation. Jones was the most influential signatory of a letter sent out in 1912 to unions in Gwynedd inviting them to a meeting in Caernarfon to 'consider seriously the advisability of electing Labour Members to represent them on the County Council and the Local Administrative Bodies'.[81] This initiative

[80] C. & D. Herald, 2 May 1911.
[81] The other signatories were D. Jones, secretary of the Caernarfon Branch of the Typographical Association; G. H. Williams, Bangor Branch, Amalgamated Society of Railway Servants; T. A. Abrams, secretary, Bangor Branch, Shop Assistants' Union; William Williams, secretary, Portdinorwic Branch, I.L.P.; W. T. Jones, secretary, Caernarfon Branch, Postmen's Federation; John O. Roberts, secretary, Nevin Branch, Settmakers' Union; Owen Davies, secretary Trefor Branch, National Quarrymen's Union; David Thomas, I.L.P. and convenor for the planned meeting.

was to lead to the establishment of the Caernarfon Labour Council, in which the N.W.Q.U. was by far the biggest union. Putting up 'Labour' candidates and affiliating to the Labour Party were thus seen as being two quite separate issues.

By 1914 the union took a further step towards political intervention when the members were balloted on the advisability of establishing a political fund as authorised by the 1913 Trades Union Act. The members showed their enthusiasm by voting 2,488 votes to 709 in favour of the proposal.[82] Even R. T. Jones went so far as to declare to the 1914 conference that

> there was no doubt that the union received very little support from any of the recognised political parties—it was time to emphasise the special needs of quarrymen as a class apart from their common citizenship.[83]

One crucial factor in the growing disenchantment with the Liberals, apart from the constant arguments of the socialists and the I.L.P., was the failure of the Quarries and Slate Mining Bill, introduced in August 1913 and intended to establish a legally enforceable minimum wage, to reach even a second reading in the House of Commons. The N.W.Q.U., not for the first time, felt that local Liberal M.P.s could have been more enthusiastic in their support of a Bill designed to benefit the quarrymen. The final rupture with the Liberals, however, came two years later when a by-election in Arfon witnessed a humiliating rejection by the Liberals of the N.W.Q.U.'s nominee for the candidacy.

The stage was set during the union's 1915 conference, when the union gave notice of

> its claim and intention to nominate a Parliamentary candidate whenever the opportunity presents itself for one of those seats where a large proportion of the electors are quarrymen.[84]

Within a few days William Jones, M.P. for Arfon, was dead and the union had the opportunity to put its determination to the test. They approached the Arfon Liberal Association with the suggestion that R. T. Jones should stand as a Lib-Lab

[82] GAS, X.N.W.Q.U. 256, 2 September 1914.
[83] C. & D. Herald, 8 May 1914.
[84] Ibid., 7 May 1915.

candidate. The suggestion received short and, the union felt, contemptuous shrift; the executive felt insulted by the rebuff and some were eager for an electoral contest with the Liberals. In the event, they withdrew from the battle, and G. Caradoc Rees (Liberal) was returned unopposed. But their relationship with the Liberals was never to be the same again. In 1918 R. T. Jones stood in the new Caernarvonshire constituency as a labour and nationalist candidate. He polled 8,145 votes to the Coalition Liberal's 10,488 and beat E. W. Davies, the dissenting Liberal, into third place.[85]

Even in 1918, however, Jones did not stand as a Labour Party candidate, and at the union's annual conference of that year he continued to oppose affiliation to the Labour Party despite what seems to have been the almost unanimous support of the lodges for affiliation. The 1918 conference debated two resolutions on the question, one from Dinorwic advocating affiliation to the Labour Party, and the other from the radical Nantlle lodge advocating affiliation to the I.L.P.. R. T. Jones's reply was devious: he agreed that despite the fact that the majority of the lodges were in favour of affiliation he was opposed to the recommendation since it might mean interference from outside in the choice of a Labour candidate. He was, he claimed, worried lest

> the I.L.P. thrust upon them a candidate like Mr. Arthur Ponsonby, as was done in Scotland, whose only qualification was that he was a peace-at-any-price-man.[86]

This argument might well have been the result of Jones's fear of the local political influence of men like David Thomas of the I.L.P. (and later Labour Party organiser for Caernarvonshire), who had opposed the war whereas Jones had supported it; it may also be a sign of his determination that if anyone was to be an official Labour candidate in the area it should be himself.[87]

---

[85] The issues involved in the 1918 election were complicated; for a full account, see C. Parry, op. cit., pp. 58–70. The two Caernarvonshire county constituencies were merged into one in the 1918 redistribution.

[86] *C. & D. Herald*, 10 May 1918.

[87] Jones himself had been party to a plan in 1909 to bring Howell J. Williams, a London-Welsh builder and L.C.C. councillor, to Merioneth to fight on the Lib-Lab ticket. GAS, X.N.W.Q.U.: Letter from R. Silyn Roberts to R. T. Jones, 6 August 1909.

The 1918 result was encouraging and by 1920 Jones could see no reason for staying outside the Labour fold any longer; in that year the union finally affiliated to the Labour Party. In the general election of 1922 Jones stood again in Caernarvonshire, this time in a straight fight with a National Liberal; he won by 14,016 votes to 12,407. In Merioneth another Labour candidate, the lawyer J. Jones Roberts, polled 7,181 votes to the Liberal's 11,085. R. T. Jones was to lose his seat the following year, but Labour had finally arrived as a crucial element in the Gwynedd political scene, and as the vehicle for the political aspirations of more than one generation of quarrymen.

XI

'POLITICS OBTAIN HERE'

For a few weeks immediately before the general election of
May 1979, and for the first time for almost eighty years, the
slate-quarrymen of Caernarvonshire and Merioneth again
became nationally newsworthy as the political parties bargained
over compensation for their slate-dust-ravaged lungs. The
differences between the issues raised by the quarrymen in 1979
and those of 1900 could hardly be more startling. In between,
lay three-quarters of the twentieth century during which the
population of Gwynedd, and particularly that section which
worked in the slate industry, had experienced almost unrelieved
economic depression, high unemployment, low wages and ill
health.[1] The battles of the turn of the century involved clashes
between workers in an industry that was still important, pos-
sessing a self-confident culture, and a powerful and famous
slate-quarry proprietor and landowner. The issues raised in
1979 involved the chronic illnesses of men whose working lives
had already been spent in a declining industry and whose
employers had gone bankrupt, sold out or flown. In a quite
literal sense the debates of 1979 marked the end of an
experience. The money and the machinery gone, only holes in
the ground and the casualties remained.

The issues for which the quarrymen fought are not dead[2]
and some of the quarries are still alive. The Penrhyn quarries,
under new owners, are a not insignificant element in the local
economy. Several other quarries and mines continue on a more
modest scale; some thrive as tourist attractions.[3] But there are

[1] With over 11 per cent unemployed and a low-wage area, Gwynedd remains,
in the 1970s, one of the most economically-depressed areas in Britain.
[2] The Grunwick dispute of 1977–8, which witnessed an anti-trade union
employer, supported by 'Free Labour' organisations defying both the 'intervention' of the state's conciliation machinery and mass-picketing bears a startling
resemblance to the Penrhyn lock-outs.
[3] The Penrhyn quarries are now owned by the international Marchwiel
Holdings Ltd., associated with the name of Sir Alfred McAlpine. The Dinorwic
quarries, now closed, are the site for a massive Central Electricity Generating

no communities now that are dominated by quarrymen and by the concerns of the quarries, though in places like Blaenau Ffestiniog and Talysarn, the conversation of those over sixty is still dominated by argument about quarries now flooded and managers and quarrymen long dead.

The period covered by the independent existence of the North Wales Quarrymen's Union, 1874 to 1922, witnessed the transformation not only of a trade union, but also of the quarrymen and their communities. What changed was not simply the economic base of an industry but also the capacity of men to act: the Penrhyn lock-out witnessed Gwynedd's last independent working-class action of any significance; struggles were to follow but they drew upon partial and restricted experiences and elicited only partial and restricted responses.

The Penrhyn defeat, with its cruel affirmation of an anachronistic power-structure, was a victory for economic power over democracy, a victory won with a sneer and at the expense of a community and a hope. Since then the possibility of action has been effectively removed. In order to attach to the quarrymen's history the respect it deserves one must be honest about the extent of their failure. It is a depressing experience for the story-teller, rather like being a guest at a funeral. But it has justified the searching and the telling if only because it celebrates a group of Welsh workers who, whatever their shortcomings and whatever the sharp constraints upon them, were capable of unity, organisation, and action.

Three main reasons account for the increasing debility that characterised the twentieth century—the collapse of the industry and the ensuing depression; the Penrhyn defeat; and an historical change in the quarryman's culture and its reserves. All of these points have been touched on already in the course of the narrative, but it is useful to reiterate them explicitly.

As we have seen, the first two decades of the twentieth century witnessed a flight of men from the slate industry.[4] In such a situation only compromise was possible and the union that emerged from this period was a union of compromise and

---

Board hydro-electric power station and a museum. The Llechwedd and Oakeley slate mines in Blaenau Ffestiniog attract hundreds of thousands of tourists annually. The quarries are therefore as locked into the British economy as they ever were.

[4] The author's grandfather, Griffith Roberts, left Croesor quarry in Llanfrothen in 1912 to work on the prairies of Iowa.

caution, a policy expressed in the character of R. T. Jones himself. This is not the place to discuss Gwynedd's experience of the inter-war depression, nor to describe the area's exclusion from many of the benefits of the post-second-world-war boom; but it is worth emphasizing that the depression in Gwynedd started twenty years earlier than elsewhere. This prolonged gloom in the fortunes of the slate industry makes it difficult to reconstruct the halcyon days of mid-Victorian expansion when Gwynedd prided itself on being the world's largest producer of an essential commodity. In those years of growth and relative prosperity, a self-confidence and community were created which could sustain trials like the Penrhyn lock-outs. They could sustain them but not survive them, for if the quarrymen could offer confidence and solidarity, their opponents and masters could exert power, and power triumphed. The quarry-men were defeated, and defeat left them wounded, with their will to struggle enfeebled and damaged.

This may seem a curious argument to put forward given the changes in consciousness associated with the rise of Labour. Surely the quarrymen developed 'progressive' ideas and moved to a different level of struggle? In 1922, after all, Caernarvon-shire had R. T. Jones, general secretary of the N.W.Q.U., as its Labour member of parliament. Yet, the rise of Labour was not necessarily simply an extension and a development of the tradition of radicalism. On the contrary, it may be seen as marking a sharp disjuncture with the radical culture of the late-nineteenth century. As we have seen, the notions of class, and of a strategy for a British working class, were new and difficult ones for the quarrymen to adopt. Those who accepted them acquired a new vocabulary and new attitudes; they struggled for twenty years to win the N.W.Q.U. for the Labour Party; they broke the radical consensus as defined by the middle class.

In the particular, if not unique, circumstances of early-twentieth-century Gwynedd, this 'modernisation' of attitudes and of organisation, far from equipping the quarrymen for struggle, was to act as a further factor in stifling action as a realistic possibility. For the rise of Labour in Gwynedd took place in the shadow of defeat; to a significant extent, indeed, it arose out of that defeat. The Penrhyn lock-out was a test for the national trade-union movement: Isaac Mitchell and his comrades recovered rapidly enough from the defeat; the quarrymen did not. The fear of more defeats paralysed further action. The suffering and sacrifice of defeat became the quarrymen's badges. The fundamental and (in industrial terms) aggressive demands which had led to struggle, the refusal to accept the 'normalcy' of factory discipline—these could not be re-enacted. Determination and confidence became a bitter stubbornness and a reflex of immediate caution; no more contractors were to be beaten up and chased out of the quarries.

R. T. Jones's policies of control and conciliation also brought about a previously-absent institutionalization of conflict. The struggles of the last quarter of the nineteenth century involved whole men; they were battles into which were thrown all the resources available; they involved colliding cultures. Following R. T. Jones's intervention in the Alexandra dispute of 1913–14, conflict became institutionalized and professionalized. R. T. Jones succeeded where W. J. Parry had failed; he became a mediator, he acted with the security of the union and the overall interests of the industry foremost in his mind, not with the furious commitment of the men labouring daily in the quarries who had, themselves, caused and controlled the earlier battles.

The N.W.Q.U. was born in 1874 during a period of trade-union expansion which affected the whole of Britain. It had been formed at the same time, in the same fashion, and in response to the same economic boom, as many other trade-union organisations.[5] Unlike many of those organisations, however, it endured economic depression and despite the trials and defeats of the 1880s survived to enjoy some of the ripples from the widespread but brief enthusiasm for organisation associated with the development of new unionism, 1889–91. Further, it became, itself, one of the most important targets of the national anti-trade union offensive of the late nineties, most dramatically expressed in the lock-out of the Amalgamated

[5] This period of trade-union history has been much neglected by historians but between 1871 and 1875 'unions were established by agricultural labourers, dockers, gas-stokers, car-men, cab and omnibus drivers, railwaymen, sailors, firemen, brick- and tile-makers, box-makers, builders' labourers and coal trimmers'. D. Kynaston, *King Labour: the British Working Class 1850–1914* (London, 1976), p. 52.

Society of Engineers in 1897 and culminating in the Taff Vale judgment of 1902. In the twentieth century the union's history follows closely national developments: its own amalgamation with the Transport and General Workers' Union being part of a whole reorganisation in trade-union structure which produced not only the T.G.W.U. but also the General and Municipal Workers' Union and other amalgamated unions.

In an important sense, therefore, the history of the north Wales quarrymen reflected national developments, and their history must be placed in the context of British labour as a whole. In that perspective, much of their behaviour appears unremarkable. The degree to which the history of the N.W.Q.U parallels so closely developments elsewhere must temper any claim for the uniqueness of their experience and their contribution. The quarrymen were part of a British working class. In many respects they were, with their bowler hats, their poor diets and their Liberalism, archetypes of the Victorian working-man.[6] Their consciousness of a status as independent workmen with rights and privileges, and the lengths to which they went in defence of that status, were also typical of much of the skilled and 'semi-skilled' British working class. In crude comparison with an ideal-type factory proletariat they might appear backward and isolationist; but they fit easily enough into the real working class of Britain in the late-nineteenth century.[7] The quarrymen, therefore, must not be viewed in isolation. Their history must be seen in the context of national change and development.

In the context of Welsh politics and society and, in particular, in the peculiar context of Gwynedd outlined in Chapter I, however, the implications of the quarrymen's behaviour as unremarkable, 'independent', workmen became far-reaching. This was particularly true of the Penrhyn quarrymen and would probably have also been true of the Dinorwic workers had they not been so decisively defeated in 1885. The Penrhyn quarrymen, most especially in the lock-outs of 1896–7 and 1900–3, acted out a level of struggle which was not to be

---

[6] For the quarrymen's diet see pp. 31–33, for a comparison see D. Oddy, D. Miller, *The Making of the modern British diet*, (London, 1976).

[7] For a re-assessment of the British worker in extractive industries see R. Harrison ed., *Independent Collier* (Hassocks, 1978), R. Samuel, 'Mineral Workers' in *Miners, Quarrymen and Saltworkers* (London, 1976), pp. 3–97.

witnessed elsewhere in the area and to a degree therefore their experiences made them untypical of the other slate quarrymen. Their actions, however, had the deepest possible repercussions, not only for the N.W.Q.U. but for all the slate quarrymen and indeed for the whole of Gwynedd. Even those who did not share the struggle and the suffering with them could not avoid the implications of their actions.

The quarrymen were combatants in a ferocious political battle between Tory landlordism and nonconformist Welsh Liberalism. The exercising of their moderate, Victorian trade unionism in this context held considerable implications. In this setting the questions of cultural and political identity became merged. An industrial dispute, involving all the issues and conflicts of industrial relations, became something very much more significant. To this extent, therefore, the slate quarrymen must not only be seen in the context of the nineteenth-century British working class but must also be placed in the particular class configuration and complicated class tensions of Wales and Gwynedd. The crucial tension here is that between rival sections of the property-owning classes: the entrenched interests of landlordism and the aspirant clamourings of a nonconformist middle class which was acutely conscious both of its nonconformity and of its relative economic weakness. The quarrymen, troops in the nonconformist army, introduced a new challenge which nevertheless elicited old echoes. The conflict between working class and employer, based in the relations of production, most certainly obtained in Gwynedd at this time, but in a society as culturally and politically divided as late-nineteenth-century Wales, that conflict was transmogrified into a rare occurrence in British history: a series of industrial disputes which both raised fundamental issues about the relations of workers and employers and also involved two hostile cultures, each trying to displace the other. In this context the moderate trade unionism of the slate quarrymen, the demand for the right of combination, became, if only in a local arena, a force which was interpreted by its opponents as a revolutionary threat. The quarrymen as surely attempted to impose their view of the world on the Penrhyn quarry as Lord Penrhyn did on them. The quarrymen, their families and allies had their own morality, their own collective self-discipline, their own decision-making structures, their own allegiances, their own religion and their own language. Lord Penrhyn and his family and class had different and separate loyalties, beliefs and language. The attempt to 'calvinise' the quarries, to remove them from one culture to another, was real enough. It was an element in the history of the slate quarrymen which allowed them, in one great quarry and for some few years, to mount a unique challenge to the order of things. It was not a revolutionary challenge, for, as has been pointed out, many of its articulated demands were common enough, and reflected little desire to overturn the whole national economy, but it was a challenge which was perceived by those to whom it was offered as demanding a fundamental displacement of their power. The interest of the episode resides in the fact that men with a non-revolutionary and far from clear class-consciousness, with hardly a fixed trade-union consciousness, were nevertheless able, in a particular place and time, to conduct a struggle which in a very real sense raised fundamental issues of control and power. It was not merely skill in dramatic declamation which accounted for the quarrymen's persistent claim that their struggles involved their whole status as men, and that their suffering and solidarity were directed to a fundamentally important purpose.

On the other side the issues were perceived in a similar fashion. In March 1902 a 'reliable source' (almost certainly the Rev. W. Morgan of St. Ann's Anglican Church, Bethesda) wrote a detailed and confidential report on the political situation in north Wales for Conservative Central Office.[8] His document eloquently sums up the panic of the minority Conservative and Anglican section of the local population.

> Freedom has disappeared and that under a Conservative Government. Radical M.P.s come down and seem all-powerful. Mr. W. Jones (the local M.P.) interferes with the police and military, and speaks at public meetings as though the Conservative Home Secretary were his servant. All this is having a very bad effect, for the Radicals are jubilant and our people are dejected for they see no escape from their misery.

[8] This report was forwarded to the Home Secretary. PRO HO45/10264 X 80592 (90).

Morgan spoke for that minority which saw the Welsh, nonconformist and radical tide engulfing it: 'Radical party hereabouts is in the majority in the County and other Councils . . . the English press is almost entirely in their hands'.[9] Lord Penrhyn and his quarry not only earned the allegiance of this besieged minority; they also offered it its only hope. 'The Conservative minority has no more chance in a Court of Law than they would have in the Quarry if the Radicals got the upper hand.' The Rev. W. Morgan knew well enough what was at stake. 'Politics obtain here everywhere', he explained to Central Office, and that was the crux of the matter. The Penrhyn lockouts were not only industrial disputes; they were also indisputably and explicitly political, inextricably bound up in the struggle for power in a deeply-divided society.

The extensive and rapid social changes associated with the twentieth century's economic cycle of depression and boom, and with the effects of two world wars, removed many of the features of late-nineteenth-century Gwynedd society. The collapse of the slate industry weakened the significance of the actions of both men and masters; the rapid growth of bilingualism smoothed the grinding cultural edges, the rise of Labour offered other strategies, located new and bigger enemies for the quarrymen.[10] The late-nineteenth-century chasm between the two societies in Gwynedd, the sectarian and all-embracing nature of the conflict between them, these were fragmented and transformed. The bitterness remained but not the energy.

[9] PRO HO45/10264 X 80592 (93). The paranoia of the minority sometimes led to exaggerated fears but this should not detract from the reality of the paranoia.

[10] Remarkably little historical attention has been given to the growth of bilingualism in Wales as opposed to the growth of monoglot English speaking. And yet the decline in the numbers of people who were monoglot Welsh speakers, and their release therefore into an English-dominated world, was certainly of equal historical importance.

APPENDIX 1

MEMBERSHIP OF THE NORTH WALES QUARRYMEN'S UNION 1874 – 1925

APPENDIX II

THE PENNANT LLOYD AGREEMENT 1874

1. Prices for working slates increased.

2. Fixed maximum scale of wages of quarrymen abolished.

3. Wages of masons fixed at from 3s. 6d. to 4s. a day, according to merit; and up to 4s. 6d. if those wages were granted at Dinorwic Quarries.

4. Platelayers' wages to be from 15s. to 18s. per week, according to merit; and up to 21s. if those wages were granted at Dinorwic Quarries.

5. Wages to be paid every 4 weeks.

6. A supreme manager and umpire be appointed with powers to decide all disputes.

7. That a committee be appointed to manage the Penrhyn Quarries Sick Benefit Club, to consist of Lord Penrhyn as president; the supreme manager as vice-president; a treasurer, a secretary, and one workman from each district in the quarry.

8. Power to turn men out of the works to be in the hands of the supreme manager.

9. The power to take men into the works to be in the hands of the supreme manager.

10. The right to stop men until their case is inquired into by the supreme manager to be in the hands of the chief working manager.

11. The workmen who are working on rocks at 10s. in the £ are to be taken into bargains as circumstances will permit; and that the places that are now being worked by them, and which can be so let, be let as regular bargains.

12. That the same terms be allowed to rubble men as are allowed at the Dinorwic Quarries.

13. That one month be allowed all workmen to return to their places in the quarry.

14. That when necessary partners be allowed to name their new partner to be placed before the chief working manager and if refused by him that the name be placed before the supreme manager, whose decision will be final.

15. That if a quarryman by extra work makes 35s. a week, the agent is not to reduce his price if the rock is of the same quality next month.

16. That the bad-rockmen be similarly placed at 24s. 6d. a week.

17. That all complaints about letting be first referred to a committee appointed by the workmen; and if considered by them to be a proper case, that it be placed before the supreme manager for his decision.

18. That in the event of a quarryman failing to earn 27s. 6d. a week for two consecutive months, he is entitled to lay his case before the committee and through them before the supreme manager for his decision.

APPENDIX III

SOME CONTRIBUTIONS TO THE N.W.Q.U. FUND, MAY 1901

	£	s.	d.
Cigar Sorters and Bundlers Mutual Assoc., London	1	0	0
Great Mountain Colliery, Tumble, Llanelli (collection)	6	7	0
Manchester Portmanteau Makers Society		10	0
Amalgamated Society of Tailors West End Branch, London	5	0	0
National Amalgamated Labourer's Union of G.B. and Ireland, Swansea Branch	5	0	0
Onllwyn Colliery (workmen's collection)	6	3	6
I.L.P. West Birmingham Branch	1	0	0
Northumberland Miners Mutual Confident Association	20	0	0
Compositors 'Daily Chronicle', London		15	0
Bolton & District Hairdressers Assoc.		10	0
Derby Co-op Provident Society	100	0	0
Burnley Weavers' Association	10	0	0
Amalgamated Society of Railway Servants, Leeds City Branch		10	0
West Ham & District Trades & Labour Council	1	0	0
Chatham Dockyard (collection)	2	0	0
Birmingham Operative Tin Plate Workers Society	10	0	0
Amalgamated Society of Engineers, Barnes Branch	20	0	0
British Steel Smelters Assoc., Manchester	5	0	0
London Saddle & Harness Makers Trade Protection Society	5	0	0
Rhos Ruabon Miners	20	0	0
Seven Sisters Calvinistic Methodist Church		10	0
Durham Miners' Association	50	0	0
General Slaters Union, Pennsylvania, U.S.A.	17	0	0
Operative Bricklayers Society, London	500	0	0
Dock Wharf & General Workers Union	10	0	0
Cigar Box Makers & Paperers Trade Union, London	10	0	0
Leeds National Union of Life Assurance Agents	1	0	0

APPENDIX IV

THE QUARRYMEN'S CHARTER, 1912

1.—**Hours of Labour.**

February 14th to October 23rd:—
From 7 a.m. to 5.30 p.m.
October 24th to February 13th:—
From 7.30 a.m. to 4.30 p.m., with the exception of December, when the hours will be 8 a.m. to 4 p.m.
Leave off at 12 noon on Saturday all the year.
An hour for dinner, 12 to 1.
One half day, on the first day of the quarry month, to be a General Holiday, reckoned and paid for in favour of the men.

2.—**General Holidays as follows:—**

Easter Monday, Labour Day, Whit Monday, First Monday in August, Thanksgiving Day, Christmas Day; other holidays to be granted to any workman who applies for the same for and at any reasonable time.

3.—**A Minimum Wage to be paid:—**

Quarrymen, Rockmen, and other skilled workmen, such as Blacksmiths, Masons, &c.	..	..	4s.	per day.
Miners	..	..	.. 3s. 9d.	,,
Rock Labourers	..	..	.. 3s. 6d.	,,
Labourers	..	..	.. 3s. 4d.	,,

In addition to the Minimum, that the amount per yard and price per ton be paid to Miners, Rock Labourers, and Labourers, and Bounty to the Quarrymen on the value of the Slates produced, but the Quarrymen are not to receive the price of the Slates in their wages as well.

4.—The Bounty, Price per Yard, and Price per Ton to depend on the condition and circumstances of the Bargain, or agreed upon between the Setter and Taker.

5.—The following to be paid when working on Day Wage:—

Quarrymen & Rockmen	..	..	4s. 6d.	per day.
Miners	..	..	.. 4s. 4d.	,,
Rock Labourers	..	..	.. 4s. 2d.	,,
Labourers	..	..	.. 4s.	,,

6.—The following standard to be established:—

Quarrymen, Rockmen, and other skilled workmen, such as Masons, Blacksmiths, &c.	..	..	5s.	per day.
Miners	..	..	.. 4s. 9d.	,,
Rock Labourers	..	..	.. 4s. 6d.	,,
Labourers	..	..	.. 4s. 4d.	,,

7.—The Minimum to be paid weekly, on the Saturday, and the Bonuses earned as Bounty, Amount per Yard, and Price per Ton, to be paid together with the Minimum on the Fourth Week. Only one week minimum to be held in hand.

8.—No deduction of any kind, under any circumstances, to be made from the Minimum, with the exception of for loss of time.

9.—No Rubbling to be allowed, except to Apprentices, and men who may have been incapacitated by accident or other reasons from taking the responsibility of a Bargain or Day Work.

10.—When the Bargain fails to keep the workmen in the shed or mill fully employed, that the outside men should go inside to work until sufficient material can be got to keep them fully employed outside.

11.—Apprenticeship.

That Boys be apprenticed as Quarrymen for five years, with two years at least of the five to be spent on the rock.

(a) Party or Parties of Apprentices to be taught by a practical Quarryman, the wages of whom shall be paid by the Employer.

(b) 5s. a week to be paid to each Apprentice for the 1st year of his apprenticeship.

10s.	,,	,,	,,	2nd	,,
15s.	,,	,,	,,	3rd	,,
20s.	,,	,,	,,	4th	,,
24s.	,,	,,	,,	5th	,,

12.—The Standard and Day Wage to be increased or decreased for every increase or decrease that takes place in the price of Slates, but the Minimum to be stationary.

The above terms are based on the market price of Slates for the year 1911.

Signed on behalf of the North Wales Quarrymen's Union,

R. T. JONES,

Secretary.

APPENDIX V

TERMS OF AMALGAMATION, N.W.Q.U. AND T.G.W.U., 1922

1. That complete autonomy be granted to the North Wales Quarrymen's Union in its internal affairs, and the Branches thereof to continue to function as at present, subject to the Rules of the Transport and General Workers' Union.

2. That the North Wales Quarrymen's Union shall be formed into a National Trade Group.

3. That the present full-time Officials of the North Wales Quarrymen's Union shall continue to function for the Quarrymen of North Wales.

4. That the existing Legal Benefit of the North Wales Quarrymen's Union shall be continued as under present arrangements.

5. That the present Unemployment Benefit of the North Wales Quarrymen's Union be continued unless the members decide by Ballot vote in favour of the alternative Accident Benefit of the Transport and General Workers' Union, as per Scale A, Schedule 5.

6. That all contributions, levies and other receipts shall be paid by the branches to the Quarrying National Trade Group, from which fund all expenses of administration and benefits relating to the Group shall be paid as heretofore from the Headquarters at Caernarvon and all such payments and receipts to be subject to audit by the Central Office in London, and a Quarterly statement of accounts to be forwarded to the Central Office at London with a remittance of the Balance in hand, less an amount to be held in reserve in Caernarvon.

7. That a National Trade Group Committee shall be elected by the Branches to function in accordance with Rule 6 Clause 4 of the Rules of the Transport and General Workers' Union.

8. That the North Wales Quarrymen's Union shall withdraw from the General Federation of Trade Unions, but shall continue its affiliation to the Trade Union Congress as an independent union in the Mining and Quarrying Group, and as such shall be entitled to Nominate Delegates to Congress and for membership on the General Council of the Trade Union Congress. Affiliation fee to be paid out of the Funds (reserve) of the North Wales Quarrymen's Union.

9. That the Transport and General Workers' Union at a date to be agreed upon shall take over all the Financial obligations of the North Wales Quarrymens' Union Politically and Industrially. The North Wales Quarrymen's Union shall pay over to the Transport and General Workers' Union the sum of £5,000 to secure immediate Benefits in full for all its members.

10. That the annual Conference of the North Wales Quarrymen's Union to be held the First Monday in May 1923 shall be held as already arranged.

11. That North Wales be formed into an area as per Rule 7, to be deferred for future consideration.

12. That the Quarrying Trade Group if it so desires shall out of any additional income beyond the –/6d a week contribution, and –/6d Quarterage, be entitled to grant additional Benefits subject to Clause 9 Rule 6.

13. That remuneration of Local Officials to remain as at present until June 1923, when the position of same will be considered in conjunction with all Local Officials of the Transport and General Workers' Union.

14. That a synopsis of the Rules of the Transport and General Workers' Union should be printed in Welsh, at some future date.

APPENDIX VI

PROFILES

Information about the following people, involved in the Penrhyn struggle, comes partly from their own correspondence with the Penrhyn management but largely from the reports on them prepared, with the help of many informers, by D. D. Davies, 'Local Manager' of the Penrhyn quarries from March 1902. (GAS, PQ 100/41, 42, 43, Correspondence Files of the Penrhyn quarry.)

Hugh Hughes of 99 Carneddi Road, Bethesda, applied in October 1902 for 'the small pension given to old and incapacitated workmen' as he had worked in the quarry for 55 years with never a complaint as to his behaviour. A quiet man, he was, according to Davies, 'rather indifferent as to religion, politics etc., though he would probably call himself a Methodist Liberal and a member of the Quarrymen's Union'. He was not disloyal to Lord Penrhyn but his daughter was married to John Griffiths, the organising secretary of the strikers' choir in north Wales.

Robert Pritchard, aged 82, applied for a quarry pension in July 1902. He had worked for the first eight months of the strike but he was 'known as being a passively disloyal old man. His sympathies entirely with the strikers.' He lived with his daughter, Mrs. Elizabeth Williams, who was convicted of intimidating Messrs. John Evans and R. R. Davies on 30 May 1901.

Richard Pritchard Jones applied for work in the quarry on 19 April 1902, his two sons being already at work. He had been on the executive committee of the ill-fated strike in the quarry in 1865 and had soon afterwards left for America; he returned in 1875 and in 1879 he and his sons were transferred into the badrockmen class, 'like most of those who had been admitted as quarrymen after the strike of 1874'. This may have been the experience that soured his feelings toward the union for he refused to accept the demotion and left the quarry to work on the Llandegai parish roads. He became 'very loyal to Lord Penrhyn' but his application for work was refused on the grounds of his 'age and infirmity'.

R. O. Jones, a young quarryman of 25 years of age, had, according to Davies, 'been taking very active part in disturbances in the neighbourhood' since the quarry had re-opened; 'I have his name on the list of those to be excluded'. He applied for work on the Great Western Railway in Newport, Monmouthshire, in October 1902.

Owen Jones, of 49 Penybryn, Bethesda, had spent 50 of his 75 years in the employ of Lord Penrhyn when he applied for his relief not to be discontinued in August 1902. Davies reported that 'during the strike of 1896–7 this old man was most disloyal to the management. Although a member of the same chapel as Mr. Pritchard (an under-manager) there was nothing that he would not have done against Mr. Pritchard. I have no doubt that he is even more disloyal at present though he has not been able to show it.' One of the points against his application was that his son, J. O. Jones, who had once worked in the quarry and who had since moved on to become a Methodist Minister and a teacher in the Bala Theological College, had also given 'all his influence against the management during the 1896–7 strike'. Jones's application for relief was refused.

Richard Humphreys, 10 Penybryn, Bethesda, was at work in slate quarries in the Nantlle valley in October 1902 when his wife, Mrs. H. Humphreys, wrote to the Penrhyn quarries asking that he be employed there as this would encourage her son, who was already at work in the quarry, to return home. He was at the time 'compelled to lodge in the Parish of Llandegai . . . on account of the strikers' threatening aspect', the whole family being hooted and booed when he was at home. Davies, however, thought that the longer Richard Humphreys stayed in

Nantlle the better and that his son was better-off away from home. Richard Humphreys had had an eventful life for a quarryman, having been jailed for nine months for attempting to defraud his employers while working at Fodlas quarry, Betws-y-Coed, during the 1896–7 stoppage; he had, moreover, been 'all through his life a great poacher' who had been heavily fined for assaulting a police sergeant in a poaching affray.

Jollie Thomas was an Englishwoman who had married a Penrhyn quarryman and, as a result of the strike, found herself in New Tredegar, Monmouthshire. She wrote to Young in May 1902 protesting her own loyalty to Lord Penrhyn and explaining that her husband would have been the first to recommence work 'but his family relations are to him stronger than his own strength to stand . . . and myself, his wife, have fought the fight alone here in the South till I am quite boycotted by those of the North who are working here with their hearts at home'. If the management were to concede a little, she thought, then at least five men, whose names she enclosed and 'who were born on the grand hills around and consider that they want a little freedom', would return willingly to work. Of the five she mentioned, Davies could discover little that was objectionable in three of them; Robert Griffiths, originally of Braich, Tregarth, however, was a quarryman 'on excluded list', having been on the committee in 1896–7 and he was still speaking at meetings; he was, moreover, suspected of having taken part in the New Year's Eve 1901 riot. Thomas Jones, Rhiwlas, was also on the excluded list for taking part in disturbances at Rhiwlas and for molesting Robert Daniel Jones, a quarryman.

Robert Moses Roberts, of Hermon Road, Llandegai, was not considered to be a good workman and he took an active part in some of the disturbances arising out of the dispute. He had been one of a crowd that had manhandled Mr. Thomas Price in 1900 and though he had applied for work in the spring of 1901 he had then withdrawn his name; on 31 July 1901 he and three other young men were convicted at Bangor Police Court and fined 20s. with costs for obstructing the street opposite the Victoria Hotel, Bethesda, on 20 July when a crowd of 300–400 had gathered there. Since then he had been charged for being drunk and disorderly though the case against him was dismissed, partly because P.C.66 had already given him a 'very severe thrashing'. For all of those reasons his name had been put 'down on the list of those to be excluded'. Under 30 years old and married, he applied for work again in May 1902 explaining his earlier behaviour in terms of his having 'been very foolish to be persuaded so much by other people'. His father and brother had been at work since the quarry had re-opened on 11 June 1901, and Davies considered that his main fault was that 'when he gets drunk he is an excitable little chap'. E. A. Young gave him the benefit of the doubt 'for his wife's sake' and he was re-admitted to the quarry.

Edward Davies, of Penygroes, applied for work in June 1902 while working in south Wales. D. R. Davies gave him the following report: 'I have his name on the Black List . . . one of the wildest before the strike. He was every day taking active part in the disturbances in the quarry. Also one of the defendants in the Richard Hughes & Sons case. Not convicted but R. Hughes still declares that this young man was one of the most cruel of those who attacked him and that he kicked him most unmercifully. Apart from his connection with the disturbances he is quite undesirable, he was always discontented and unsettled while in the quarry.'

Rees J. Tyrner, of Bethesda, re-started work at the quarry when it re-opened in June 1901 but left on 21 January 1902 to work on the London & North Western Railway because 'he said his neighbours molested him because he was at work here while most of the late employees were on strike'.

When he applied for work in May 1902 Lewis Lewis Owen of Caergors, Llanllechid claimed that he had been too ill to start work earlier. Davies confirmed that Owen suffered from asthma and some infection of the lungs but added that he had 'been very disloyal, his wife extremely so . . . They have a boy also who has been continually annoying the Caellwyngrydd men.'

Owen Lewis was anxious that his mother should become the tenant of the family home when his father died in 1902. Davies reported that he was 'a sullen man' who 'is on the bad list' though there was nothing definite against him other than that he was apparently 'under the influence of Robert Roberts, Tynlan . . . one of the strikers' leaders in that neighbourhood'.

Catherine Davies wrote in April 1902 pleading that her son be appointed a machiner in the quarry. Davies reported that she had had three sons in the quarry before the strike, none had applied for work, two were on the excluded list, one 'a wild young man', the other 'stupid and obstinate', both having been involved in disturbances.

James Jones, of Mill Street, Bethesda, defied his father in February 1902 when he applied to re-start work. His grandfather and two uncles were working but not his father—'I can't help my father', he wrote. His father, according to Davies, was 'a great striker . . . taking active part in molesting our men' and with his 'name on Excluded list'. James Jones himself was refused employment after a medical examination showed that he had a tubercular knee and was unfit for work.

When William Hugh Roberts's brother left the quarry in June 1903 William Roberts was suspected of having persuaded him to leave despite the fact that he himself also worked at the quarry. It was later reported, however, that Richard Wynne Pritchard may have been the man responsible for persuading Roberts's brother to leave. Living in Glasinfryn, Pritchard was described by Davies as 'all through this trouble . . . one of the wildest and most bitter among the strikers in that locality. He has been speaking in the mass meetings on several occasions and he has been one of the most spiteful in his language. I have no doubt that he has done all in his power to prolong the dispute and I think he thoroughly deserves to be left out—the name was one of the first we put on the Excluded List.'

Toward the end of 1902 the quarry management wrote to women in the district asking them to lodge men working in the quarry; two replied, both refusing. Mary Hughes, of Slate Mill Cottages, Coed Park, quite agreed that the cottage in which she lived was a workman's house, but, she added, 'it has been a home to me too, Mr. Davies, for over twenty-two years and many things have happened here'. Miss Ellen Thomas, also of Slate Mill Cottages, replied to the quarry's letter and though Davies 'could not make much of her story', he was in 'no doubt but that she is in sympathy with the strikers and does not like to take men who are at work in the quarry and therefore is ready to make any excuse for refusing'.

In July 1903 Thomas Evans, aged 70, wrote to the Rt. Hon. Lady Penrhyn asking her ladyship to allow him a free ticket to a rest home in Rhyl, a gift normally granted to unwell quarrymen. In this case a quarry surgeon had informed the applicant that a change of air would do him a great deal of good. Davies reported that Evans had been employed most of his life in the quarry and later as a labourer in the quarry workshops but that he had been pensioned off eighteen months earlier 'when the staff at the workshops was reduced . . . because he was a lazy workman continually sitting down to talk and gossip. He was beside a disloyal man with all his sympathies with the strikers.' He was not given a ticket to go to Rhyl.

Richard P. Pritchard, a *rybelwr* in the quarry, aged over 60, applied for a Rhyl ticket a few weeks later and was granted one; he was, according to Davies, 'steady and loyal and resumed work, 11 June 1901 together with three of his wife's sons'.

Williams R. Williams, of Yr Afr Aur, High Street, Bethesda, had left the Penrhyn quarries in 1891 as a result of total deafness which made it dangerous for him to continue in employment; he started a coal business which later collapsed. In August 1903 he applied for work at the quarry though it is not clear with what result. Davies reported that he was 'an efficient workman in the sheds but owing to his deafness he had become very distrustful and subject to fits of bad-temper and stubbornness that made him quite unmanageable at times even his brother could not control him . . . he was a man of socialistic ideas and would devour any literature of that kind that would come to his hands. Nothing is known of him in connection with the present trouble.'

In January 1903 three men applied for the tenancy of a house in Braichmelyn. Davies reported: the first had been in the quarry since 1901 as a jobbing mason and lived in an old classroom in Tyntwr school; he was a member of St. Ann's Church; William Parry of Braichmelyn, a young married man, was considered 'a very disloyal man. His name is on the Excluded List for having taken part in the disturbances which brought on the strike in the quarry'; he had been found guilty of intimidating Mr. Thomas Price on 1 November 1900 and had been fined 40s. with costs by the Bangor bench; John Owen Williams of Penybryn, Bethesda, a fitter aged about 30, needed a house nearer the quarry as he had to work nights. He had worked in the Pantdreiniog quarry during the 1896–7 stoppage but had 'been undoubtedly loyal all through the present trouble' and was an 'obedient man and a very good worker'; a 'Methodist before the present trouble', his one fault would appear to have been that he was 'rather too fond of drink'.

In 1903 several men applied for the tenancy of a house in Caerberllan. D. D. Davies reported on the applicants:

1. David Davies, aged 35, of Cilgeraint, had been apprenticed as a fitter in the quarry and worked there until August 1900. He left to seek his fortune in England; he soon returned disillusioned, however, and re-started work on 1 November 1900, 'a good, steady and obedient workman'. He was injured in an accident and one of his feet had to be amputated. He was out of sympathy with his family since his father, brother and all his near relatives, except for David Davies, Penrhiw, were 'among the irreconcilable strikers'; his family were also Methodists and members of Jerusalem Chapel but David Davies himself, along with his wife and children, attended St. Ann's Church where he was a member of the choir.

2. O. Thomas Morgan, of Glanrafon, Tregarth, had both his father and brother at work in the quarry with him, he himself having started back in September 1901. A quarryman, aged 25, married with one child, he was, however, 'a very poor workman' and, moreover, 'after he resumed work he was recognised by some of our men as one who had been very active during the disturbances in the quarry. He had been under the influence of men who are . . . amongst the most irreconcilable of the strikers at Tregarth.'

3. Griffith Williams came originally from Bethesda but lived in Upper Bangor; he had worked as a *rybelwr* in the quarry until 1877, when he had gone to America; on returning he wandered from one place to another in north Wales and came back to the Penrhyn quarry from Cricieth in February 1902. He had a wife and one son, considered 'a worthless young man', and he himself was a 'very inferior workman' though 'quiet and loyal' as far as Davies could tell.

4. Elias Parry, contractor No. 547 in the quarry, was 34 and married with one child. He was considerd excellent in every way and he regularly attended Glanogwen Church.

5. Owen Parry, Goronwy Street, Gerlan, was 38 and worked in the quarry with the eldest of his four children; an average worker, he was steady, respectable and quite loyal though he had not started work until February 1903. This was put down to the fact that he owned a house and lived next door but one to Henry Jones, the committee chairman. Since re-starting work he had 'suffered much molestation' and he had sued a neighbour before the local magistrates, the case being dismissed. He was a member of Siloam Wesleyan Chapel, Bethesda.

6. Hugh Roberts, of 9 Ogwen Street, Bethesda, was a 'very quiet and loyal' engine-driver in the quarry; both he and his wife were members of the same Congregationalist chapel as W. J. Parry.

7. Thomas Williams, a 'strong and very active' badrockman of 23, had started work on 3 March 1903 and, a quiet and obedient workman, he was anxious to bring his wife and children over from Bodorgan, Anglesey.

In March 1903 John R. Jones, of 42 Callepa, Bangor, applied for a house in Bethesda. He was originally from Rhiwlas, but after starting work in August 1902 he had been forced to 'shatter a comfortable home and many other comforts'. He, his son and his son-in-law had originally applied for, and received, work in the spring of 1901 but they had then written to the men's committee saying that they had allowed themselves to be persuaded to apply for work but that they would not go in, and they did not for another year.

In April 1902 D. D. Davies wrote the following report to E. A. Young concerning Edward Parry, Gwernydd: 'He is a young married man about 25 years of age and worked before the strike as a quarryman in No. 310 Twllwndwr Right. He was a fairly good workman, but a wild ignorant and socialistic person. I am told he was among the foremost in instigating the disturbance which led to the present strike; and overlookers 1, 2, 4, inform me that he was among the wildest at the time of the 1896–7 strike. Edwin Davies, his partner in the quarry, reports about his conduct just before the beginning of the strike. When Mr. H. P. Roberts had stopped setting on the Right Side, Edwin Davies and another man were sent to ask when would the setting be resumed. On their return to tell the men that setting would be resumed as soon as the men who had already taken their bargains would settle down to work, this young man tried to instigate the men to go down to the lower galleries to prevent the men who had taken their bargains working; and he said that he wished he had a gun and dum-dum bullets to shoot Lord Penrhyn. He would have then pulled the bullets out of his body and shoot them into Mr. Young's. He was certain, he added, he should go to heaven for doing it. Another workman, Hugh H. Edwards, Treflys, has told me that he noticed Ed. Parry among the most threatening and turbulent on the Right Side before the strike and at the time they left the quarry. Ed. Parry has been away working during part of the strike but he has been seen occasionally in the crowds in the village and associating with the wildest and most turbulent young men in the neighbourhood but not doing anything. His wife is an adopted daughter of John Lewis (Gwernydd his wife's niece) who recently obtained the tenancy of the Taincoed Farm, Llanllechid, he being at the time a striker, member of the Relief Committee and having a son also among the strikers.'

Morris Davies came to the Penrhyn quarry from Pantdreiniog quarry where he had, for several months previously, acted as slate examiner and kept the slates account of the quarrymen. He left Pantdreiniog when Richard Griffith Pritchard, 'one of the strike leaders', took his place as slate examiner.

Griffith Daniel Jones, aged 50, was refused re-admission to the Penrhyn quarries in July 1901 as he was considered 'passively disloyal' and had also been seen in various crowds; he had, at one time, been overheard by Griffith Williams, then working, saying that he would 'kill one of the traitors if he had the chance'.

David Owens of Tanyrhiw, Tregarth, applied for work in September 1901 on writing paper embellished with a suitably 'loyal' picture of Bangor cathedral. He was 'on the Excluded List'.

David Morris, 64 Hill Street, Upper Bangor, was a quarryman aged 45 who resumed work on 1 April 1902. Considered a 'very quiet and loyal man and a very good workman', he would have applied for work earlier only 'he was afraid'. Before the strike he lived at Bryntirion, Bethesda, and had been a member of Jerusalem Methodist Chapel.

Richard Thomas, a contractor of 30 years of age, considered generally steady, hardworking and very loyal, 'suffered a great deal of intimidation and persecution' which forced him to move to Bangor. He had resumed work on 11 June and was an Anglican.

John Williams, Gordon Terrace, Bethesda, aged 35, had resumed work on 10 January 1902. An average worker, he was always 'fairly loyal'; he and his family were Church people.

Hugh Parry, aged 34, was a 'steady man' and an average badrockman who before the strike had lived at Llidiart Gwenyn, Carneddi Road. He was 'not a very pleasant man to deal with in the quarry rather inclined to grumble and nurse a grievance' but he was a nephew of Percival Jones and considered loyal. He and his wife and three children had 'suffered as much annoyance and molestation from the strikers as any . . . until they were compelled to remove to Bangor'. He and his family adhered to the Congregationalist denomination.

Henry Parry of Douglas Terrace, Bethesda, was a 58-year-old quarryman who had resumed work on 11 June 1901. He was a good workman, despite being deaf. He had ten children, three of whom also worked in the quarry; born and brought up in and around Tregarth, they were Church people and considered loyal. Not all the children appear to have been 'well behaved', however, and Edward, in particular, was very fond of drink, having been fined at Bangor Magistrates' Court for drunkenness in 1903.

Robert Roberts of Cefn Royal Oak, Rachub, was a quarryman with four or five children who resumed work in April 1902. 'A sober and very hard worker', his loyalty, however, was considered to be a 'matter of expediency'. He was a member of the Carmel Congregationalist Chapel.

David Morris, a 42-year-old quarryman, resumed work in April 1902. Considered a 'very good workman, very steady and loyal', he had lived at Bryntirion, Bethesda, after he had got married (he himself being a native of Gelli, Tregarth) but had moved to 64 Hill Street, Bangor, since re-starting work. A Churchman before his marriage, he had then attended Jerusalem Methodist Chapel.

John Morris Jones, of Vron Rhiw, Tregarth, was a 35-year-old quarryman who had gone back to the quarry in April 1902. Considered a good, steady, and loyal worker, he was married to the daughter of John Griffith, Pandy Farm, who was also the niece of Richard Griffith, Talgae, and of the late William Williams 'Counter', Port Penrhyn. A Wesleyan with no children, he worked in the quarry with Melancthon Williams, one of the leading spokesmen of those who went back to work.

Owen E. Jones of Tanrhiw, Tregarth, was a 32-year-old badrockman, good, steady and very loyal, who had resumed work on 11 June. The son of David Jones, butcher, Tregarth, he was a Wesleyan, though his wife was a Churchwoman.

Richard Thomas, aged 30, was a very hard-working 'very quiet and very loyal' badrockman contractor who used to live at Coetmor Mount, Bethesda, but he and his family were 'frightened out of the place by the strikers', their house being one of those attacked on the 'memorable' New Year's Eve of 1901, and he had since moved to 18 Friars Road, Bangor. He was a Churchman.

Henry Pritchard, a quarryman aged 30, of Hafodty, Tregarth, was one of a family of father and four sons who were at work. Considered very good, steady and loyal he had gone back on 11 June 1901, and his father, William Pritchard, had been one of the six men who had met E. A. Young at the pay office before the quarry had re-opened.

Thomas Williams, a badrockman from Penygroes, aged 30, had resumed work on 11 June and, although considered to be only a 'fair workman', he was 'quiet and very loyal'.

The following short reports on men from Glasinfryn were prepared in 1903 by one of D. D. Davies's informants known only as 'T'.

1. Samuel Griffiths (first house from the school) has been away all the time not interfered with any one.

2. Jno. Jones, son or adopted son of David Williams who is working in the quarry as a dayman and is home ill.

3. Richard Wynne Pritchard, labourer, has addressed meeting at Market Hall, Bethesda.

4. Richard Hughes, Tai House, nothing against him. (Accepted)

5. William Hughes, labourer, quiet but wife has been very bad.

6. William Pritchard, Quarryman (129), fairly quiet but very sneaky, actively hostile. (Refused)

7. O. J. Davies, W. B. Davies, brothers, latter a boy. Mother receiving £5 a year as husband was killed in the Quarry. She is bad. OJD is in South Wales. Have lost sight of the boy for a month or two.

8. R. Roberts, W. Roberts. Both quiet but former is lazy.

9. R. O. Hughes (Dick Blue) has been away in South Wales all the time.

10. Buckley—very bitter to those he knows.

11. H. M. Roberts, quarryman (129), now living in Bangor, but he has left a little furniture and keeps both houses going; a mouthpiece—bad. (Refused)

12. T. Hughes & son: gone out relief during last strike but not this time—has been away, son was in a weighing machine. (Accepted)

13. Benny Williams (21 years of age) spat in the face of I. Lewis who has been working in Quarry since 11 June.

14. W. J. Hughes (207), large family, regretted the strike, has been quiet all the time.

Jno. Williams (son of Eos Infryn) has been away all the time.

W. Roberts (Tenorydd Infryn) has worked on the line has not interfered with any one.

BIBLIOGRAPHY

I. SOURCES

The following lists are selective in that on the whole only sources actually referred to in the text are listed.

(a) PARLIAMENTARY REPORTS, OFFICIAL PUBLICATIONS

Census Returns.
Hansard, Parliamentary Debates.
Judicial Statistics (Police, Criminal Proceedings).
Report of Caernarvonshire Standing Joint Committee to enquire into matters at Bethesda, 1903.
Report of the Royal Commission on the Church of England and other Religious Bodies in Wales and Monmouthshire, 1910.
Report and Abstract of Labour Statistics (Mineral Production) 1897.
Report of the Royal Commission on Labour, 1891–4.
Report of the Royal Commission on Land in Wales and Monmouthshire, 1896.
Report of the Departmental Committee upon Merionethshire Slate Mines, 1895.
Reports of H.M. Inspector of Mines for the North Wales and Isle of Man District.
Report by the Quarry Committee of Inquiry, 1893.
Reports on Strikes and Lock-Outs.
Return of Rates of Wages in Mines and Quarries, 1890–91.
Statistical Tables and Reports on Trade Unions.

(b) MANUSCRIPTS

(i) *Gwynedd Archive Service* (Caernarfon, Dolgellau, Llangefni)
Penrhyn.
Dinorwic.
Dorothea.
Votty and Bowydd.
North Wales Quarrymen's Union.
Penyrorsedd.
J. W. Greaves.
Police.
Tanybwlch.
Oakeley.
Merioneth Constabulary.
Blaenyddol.
Ioan Brothen.
Caernarvonshire Constabulary.
Standing Joint Police Committee.
Penrhyn Strike.
Breese Jones and Casson.
Caernarvonshire County Council.
Bethesda Urban District Council.
Bangor and Beaumaris Poor-Law Union.
Miscellaneous.
Transport and General Workers' Union.

(ii) *University College of North Wales, Bangor*
Coetmor MSS.
Rhan o Gofnodion am Streic y Llechwedd.
Llyfr Cownt John Edwards.
Penrhyn Estate.
Llyfr Cofnodion Sink y Mynydd.

(iii) *National Library of Wales, Aberystwyth*
D. R. Daniel.
W. J. Parry.
(iv) *Public Record Office*
Home Office

(c) NEWSPAPERS AND PERIODICALS
National:
Clarion
Daily Chronicle
Daily News
Fortnightly Review
Free Labour Gazette
Justice
Liberty Review
Mining Journal
Our Gazette
The Quarry
Quarry Managers' Journal
Settmakers and Stoneworkers' Journal
Slate Trade Gazette
Times

Welsh:
Cambrian News
Caernarvon & Denbigh Herald
Y Celt
Y Chwarelwr Cymreig
Yr Eco Cymraeg
Yr Efrydydd
Y Genedl Gymreig
Y Geninen
Y Glorian
Y Gweithiwr
Y Gwyliwr
Yr Herald Cymraeg
Y Llenor
North Wales Chronicle
North Wales Gazette
Papur Pawb
Y Protestant
The Red Dragon
Y Rhedegydd
Y Traethodydd
Wales
Y Werin
Western Mail

(d) JOURNALS
Anglesey Antiquarian Society and Field Club Transactions
British Journal of Sociology
Caernarvonshire Historical Society Transactions
Flintshire Historical Society Publications
History Workshop
Llafur
Lleufer
Merionethshire Historical and Record Society Journal
Morgannwg
National Library of Wales Journal
Past and Present
Welsh History Review

(e) THESES

1. Gweirydd Ellis, 'A history of the slate quarryman in Caernarvonshire in the nineteenth century', University of Wales M.A., 1931.
2. Cyril Parry, 'Socialism in Gwynedd 1900–20', University of Wales Ph.D., 1967.
3. D. Dylan Pritchard, 'The Slate Industry of North Wales: a study of the changes in economic organization from 1780 to the present day', University of Wales M.A., 1935.
4. John Roose Williams, 'The life and work of William John Parry, Bethesda, with particular reference to his trade union activities among the slate quarrymen of North Wales', University of Wales M.A., 1953.

(f) PAMPHLETS

N.W.Q.U., *The Penrhyn Quarry Dispute*

N.W.Q.U., *The Penrhyn Quarry Dispute, 1900–03. A summary of events with list of contributions and General Balance Sheet* (Caernarfon, 1903).

N.W.Q.U., *Penrhyn Quarry Dispute. An Appeal to the Trades Unions*, 25 February 1901.

N.W.Q.U., *An Appeal to the Trades Unions.*

N.W.Q.U., *Cynhadledd, Bethesda, 6 May 1901, adroddiad D. R. Daniel.*

N.W.Q.U., *Cynhadledd, 1 May 1903.*

N.W.Q.U. & G.F.T.U., *At y Chwarelwyr yng ngogledd Cymru nad ydynt yn Undebwyr.*

N.W.Q.U., D. R. Daniel, *Y Chwarelwyr a'u sefyllfa yn bresennol*, 1904.

N.W.Q.U., *Rule Book.*

London Central Committee, Penrhyn Quarrymen's Fund, *Report and Balance Sheet, October 1902—June 1904.*

Penrhyn Relief Fund—*Statement of Accounts and Balance Sheet, Report of the Auditors, 1900–04.*

Bethesda Relief Committee, *Bethesda (illustrated), Special Trade Union Issue* (Altrincham, 1902).

Bethesda Distress Fund—*An appeal, 7 December 1903.*

Penrhyn Dispute (Reprint of London *Daily Chronicle* Articles), 9 January 1903.

Lord Penrhyn's Methods (The Press Gag, and How it was Burst), Extracts from *Daily News.*

Penrhyn Quarry Dispute—Mr. E. A. Young's reply to Mr. Herbert Bridge, 26 September 1901.

H. Jones, *Penrhyn Dispute—The Penrhyn Quarrymen and the alleged demand for Three Month's Holidays* (Caernarfon).

N.W.Q.U., *Penrhyn Quarry Dispute—Sir Edward Clarke's Negotiations, March 1903* (21 April 1903).

N.W.Q.U., *Penrhyn Quarry Dispute—Correspondence between the men and Lord Penrhyn, August—October 1903* (London, 25 October 1902).

Caernarvonshire County Council and the Penrhyn Dispute (1902).

Parch. John Clifford, *Sosialaeth a Dysgeidiaeth Crist* (Fabian Society, 1899, Tract No. 87).

Adroddiad o sefyllfa a thanysgrifiadau Eglwys a Chynulleidfa, Gerlan, Bethesda, 1900, 1901, 1902, 1903, 1904, 1905.

Adroddiad Eglwys a Chynulleidfa, Bethania, 1902, 1905.

Adroddiad Eglwys Gynulleidfaol Bethesda, Arfon, 1900–04, 1905.

Adroddiad Eglwys a Chynulleidfa, Jerusalem M.C., Bethesda, 1900, 1901, 1902, 1903.

II. WORKS OF REFERENCE

BATEMAN, J. *The Great Landowners of Great Britain and Ireland* (London, 4th ed., 1883).

BELLAMY, J., SAVILLE, J. (eds.) *Dictionary of Labour Biography*, 4 vols. (London, 1972–77).

British Labour Statistics, Historical Abstract 1886–1968 (London, 1971).

Y Bywgraffiadur Cymreig (London, 1953).
CRAIG, F. W. S. *British Parliamentary Election Results 1918–49* (Glasgow, 1969).
Idem, *British Parliamentary Election Results 1885–1918* (London, 1974).
Dictionary of National Biography (London, 1900).
Gore's Directory of Liverpool (Liverpool, 1850).
HARRISON, R., WOOLREN, G. R., DUNCAN, R. *The Warwick Guide to British Labour Periodicals* (Hassocks, 1977).
JENKINS, R. T., REES, W. *A Bibliography of the History of Wales* (Cardiff, 2nd ed., 1962).
North Wales and Chester Official Year Book (Liverpool, 1911).
REES, D. Ben *Cymry Adnabyddus 1952–1972* (Liverpool, 1978).
Slater's Directory of North Wales, Cheshire and Shropshire with Liverpool (Manchester, 1883).
Slater's Directory of North and Mid Wales (Manchester, 1895).
THOMAS, R. J. (ed.) *Geiriadur Prifysgol Cymru* (Cardiff, 1967).
Who's Who (London, 1902).

III. OTHER WORKS

AP NICHOLAS, I. *R. J. Derfel* (London, n.d.).
ASKWITH, Lord. *Industrial Problems and Disputes* (London, 1920).
AWSTIN *The Religious Revival in Wales* (Cardiff, 1904).
BEAZLEY, E. *Madocks and the Wonder of Wales* (London, 1967).
BOWEN, E. G. (ed.) *Wales: A Physical, Historical and Regional Geography* (Cardiff, 1941).
BRADLEY, A. G. *Highways and Byways in North Wales* (London, 1919).
BROTHEN, I. *Llinell neu Ddwy* (Blaenau Ffestiniog, 1941).
BROWN, E. H. Phelps *The Growth of British Industrial Relations* (London, 1960).
BROWN, K. D. (ed.) *Essays in Anti-Labour History* (London, 1978).
BURN, M. *The Age of Slate* (Blaenau Ffestiniog, 1972).
CEREDIG, *Y Dosbarth Gweithiol yng Nghymru* (Carmarthen, 1866).
CHAPPELL, E. (ed.) *The Welsh Housing and Development Year Book* (Cardiff, 1918).
CHAUMEIL, L. *L'Industrie Ardoisière de Basse-Bretagne* (Lorient, 1938).
CLEGG, H. A., FOX, A., THOMPSON, A. F. *A History of British Trade Unions since 1889, Vol. 1, 1889–1910* (Oxford, 1964).
DALE, T. N. et al., *Slate in the United States* (Washington, 1896; 2nd. ed., 1914).
DAVIES, D. C. *A Treatise on Slate and Slate Quarrying, Scientific, Practical and Commercial* (London, 1880).
DAVIES, E. *Hanes Porthmadog, Ei Chrefydd a'i Henwogion* (Caernarfon, 1913).
DAVIES, E. *Calvinistic Methodism in Wales* (London, 1870).
DAVIES, E. T. *Religion in the Industrial Revolution in South Wales* (Cardiff, 1965).
DAVIES, P. *Atgofion Dyn Papur Newydd* (Liverpool, 1962).
DODD, A. H. *The Industrial Revolution in North Wales* (Cardiff, 2nd ed., 1951).
Idem, *A History of Caernarvonshire 1284–1900* (Denbigh, 1968).
ELLIS, A. J. (ed.) *Thomas E. Ellis M.P.: Speeches and Addresses* (Wrexham, 1912).
EVANS, J. D. *Myfyrion Hen Chwarelwr* (Caernarfon, 1978).
GEORGE, D. Lloyd *Better Times* (London, 1910).
GEORGE, W. *Cymru Fydd: Hanes y Mudiad Cenedlaethol Cyntaf* (Liverpool, 1945).
GOULD, S. B. *A Book of North Wales* (London, 1903).
GRIFFITH, J. *Chwarelau Dyffryn Nantlle a chymdogaeth Moeltryfan* (Conway, 1934).
GRIFFITH, J. O. *Traethawd Ymarferol ar Lechfeini Sir Gaernarfon* (Tremadoc, 1883).
GRUFFUDD, W. J. *Hen Atgofion* (Aberystwyth, 1942).
HARRISON, R. (ed.) *Independent Collier. The Coal Miner as Archetypal Proletarian Reconsidered* (Hassocks, 1978).
HECHTER, M. *Internal Colonialism: the Celtic Fringe in British national development, 1536–1966* (London, 1975).
HINTON, James *The First Shop Stewards' Movement* (London, 1973).

HOLLAND, S. *The Memoirs of Samuel Holland* (Dolgellau, 1952).
HOLTON, Bob *British Syndicalism 1900–1914* (London, 1976).
HOWELL, D. W. *Land and People in nineteenth-century Wales* (London, 1977).
HUGHES, H. D. *Y Chwarel a'i Phobl* (Llandybie, 1960).
HUGHES, H. D. *Hynafiaethau Llandegai a Llanllechid* (Bethesda, 1866).
HUGHES, T. Rowland *Y Chwalfa* (Aberystwyth, 1942).
Idem, *O Law i Law* (London, 1943).
Idem, *William Jones* (Aberystwyth, 1944).
HUMPHREYS, E. M. *Gwŷr Enwog Gynt* (Llandysul, 1950).
Idem, *Y Wasg Gymraeg* (Liverpool, 1945).

ISHERWOOD, J. G. *Candles to Caplamps. The story of Gloddfa Ganol* (n.d.).

JENKINS, D. *The Agricultural Community in South West Wales at the turn of the Twentieth Century* (Cardiff, 1971).
JENKINS, D. E. *Bedd Gelert: Its Facts, Fairies and Folk-lore* (Portmadoc, 1899).
JONES, D. *Before Rebecca* (London, 1973).
JONES, D. G. *Detholiad o Ryddiaith Gymraeg R. J. Derfel* (2 vols., Denbigh, 1945).
JONES, D. R. *Diffygion y Cymeriad Cymreig* (Blaenau Ffestiniog, 1902).
JONES, E. *Canrif y Chwarelwr* (Denbigh, 1964).
JONES, E. *Senedd Stiniog: Hanes Cyngor Dinesig Ffestiniog 1895–1974* (Blaenau Ffestiniog, n.d.).
JONES, E. *Pan Oes Gofion* (Bala, 1910?).
JONES, H. *Dinasyddiaeth Bur* (Caernarfon, 1911).
JONES, J. Owain *The History of the Caernarvonshire Constabulary, 1856–1950* (Caernarfon, 1950).
JONES, J. Owen *Cofiant a Gweithiau y Parch. Robert Ellis* (Caernarfon, 1883).
JONES, J. W. *Y Fainc 'Sglodion* (Blaenau Ffestiniog, 1953).
JONES, R. A. *The Land Question and a Land Bill* (Wrexham, 1887).
JONES, T. *Welsh Broth* (London, 1951).
JONES, W. *An Essay on the Character of the Welsh as a Nation in the Present Age* (London, Caernarfon, 1841).

K. K. *Wales and its People* (Wrexham, 1869).
KELLOW, J. *The Slate Trade in North Wales* (London, 1868).
KYNASTON, D. *King Labour: The British Working Class 1850–1914* (London, 1976).

LEWIS, H. Elvet *With Christ Among the Miners* (London, 1906).
LEWIS, M. J. T. *Llechi/Slate* (Caernarfon, 1976).
Idem, DENTON, J. H. *Rhosydd Slate Quarry* (Shrewsbury, 1974).
LEWIS, W. J. *Lead Mining in Wales* (Cardiff, 1967).
LINDSAY, J. *A History of the North Wales Slate Industry* (Newton Abbot, 1974).
LINDSAY, J., PARRY, C., ARIS, M. *Chwareli a Chwarelwyr* (Caernarfon, 1974).
LLOYD, H. *Hunangofiant Rybelwr* (Caernarfon, 1926).
LLOYD, J. E. *Caernarvonshire* (Cambridge, 1911).
LLYWELYN-WILLIAMS, A. *Crwydro Arfon* (Llandybie, 1959).

MASTERMAN, N. *The Forerunner: the Dilemmas of Tom Ellis* (Llandybie, 1972).
MORGAN, J. V. *The Welsh Religious Revival 1904–05: a retrospect and a criticism* (London, 1909).
MORGAN, Kenneth O. *Wales in British Politics 1868–1922* (Cardiff, 3rd edn., 1980).
MORRISON, T. A. *Goldmining in Western Merioneth* (Llandysul, 1975).

NORTH, F. J. *The Slates of Wales* (Cardiff, 1925).
Idem, CAMPBELL, B., SCOTT, R. *Snowdonia: The National Park of North Wales* (London, 1949).

OWEN, F. *Tempestuous Journey: Lloyd George and His Times* (London, 1954).

PARRY, C. *The Radical Tradition in Welsh Politics—a study of Liberal and Labour politics in Gwynedd 1900–1920* (Hull, 1970).
PARRY, G. T. *Llanberis—Ei Hanes, Ei Phobl, Ei Phethau* (Caernarfon, 1908).
PARRY, W. J. *Caebraichycafn: Yr Ymdrafodaeth* (Bangor, 1875).

Idem, *Chwareli a Chwarelwyr* (Caernarfon, 1897).
Idem, *Cyfrol y Jiwbili, Eglwys Bethesda Arfon* (Dolgellau, 1900).
Idem, *The Penrhyn Lock-Out, Statement and Appeal* (London, 1901).
Idem, *The Cry of the People* (Caernarfon, 1906).
PHILLIPS, T. *Bro Deiniol* (Bala, 1936).
POPEREN, M. *Un Siècle de Luttes au Pays de l'Ardoise 1814–1914* (Anjou, 1972).
PRICHARD, C. *Un nos ola leuad* (Denbigh, 1961).
PRITCHARD, D. Dylan *The Slate Industry of North Wales, Statement of the Case for a Plan* (1946).

REES, E. *Cofiant T. Rowland Hughes* (Llandysul, 1968).
REES, D. Morgan *North Wales Quarrying Museum, Dinorwic* (Cardiff, 1974).
REES, T. *Miscellaneous Papers on subjects relating to Wales* (London, 1867).
RICHARD, H. *Letters and Essays on Wales* (London, 1884).
RICHARDS, M. *Slate Quarrying and how to make it profitable* (Bangor, 1876?).
ROBERTS, E. *Bargen Bywyd fy Nhaid* (Llandybie, 1963).
ROBERTS, K. *Traed mewn cyffion* (Aberystwyth, 1936).
RODERICK, A. J. (ed.) *Wales Through the Ages* vol. II, (Llandybie, 1960).

SALVIDGE, S. *Salvidge of Liverpool. Behind the political scene, 1890–1928* (London, 1934).
SAMUEL, R. (ed.) *Miners, Quarrymen and Saltworkers* (London, 1976).
SAVOY, E. *Ardoisier du Bassin d'Herbeumont Belgique* (Paris, 1905).
STAMP, J. C. *British Incomes and Property* (London, 1916).
STEAD, W. T. *The Revival in the West* (London, 1905).

THOMAS, B. Bowen (ed.) *Harlech Studies* (Cardiff, 1938).
Idem, *Lleufer y Werin. Cyfrol Deyrnged i David Thomas* (Abercynon, 1965).
THOMAS, E. G. *Bethesda* (Cheltenham, 1936).
THOMAS, D. *Y Werin a'i Theyrnas* (Caernarfon, 1909).
Idem, *Silyn* (Liverpool, 1956).
Idem, *Diolch am Gael Byw* (Liverpool, 1963).
THOMAS, D. Ll. *Welsh Land Commission: a Digest of its Report* (London, 1896).
Idem, *Labour Unions in Wales* (Swansea, 1901).

VINCENT, J. E. *Letters from Wales* (London, 1889).
Idem, *The Land Question in North Wales* (London, 1896).

WILLIAMS, D. *A History of Modern Wales* (London, 1950).
WILLIAMS, D. J. *The Borough Guide to Bethesda* (Bethesda, 1911?).
WILLIAMS, G. *Religion, Language and Nationality in Wales* (Cardiff, 1979).
WILLIAMS, J. *Braslun Buddugol o W. H. Williams Arfon* (Bethesda, 1896).
WILLIAMS, J. *Hynt Gwerinwr* (Liverpool, 1943).
WILLIAMS, J. Roose *Quarryman's Champion, the Life and Activities of William John Parry of Coetmor* (Denbigh, 1978).
WILLIAMS, R. H. *Straeon y Chwarel* (Caernarfon, n.d.).
WILLIAMS, W. *Hynafiaethau a Thraddodiadau Plwyf Llanberis a'r Amgylchoedd* (Llanberis, 1892).
WILLIAMS, W. G. *Chwarel a Chapel: Chwarel y Cilgwyn yn ei pherthynas ag Ymneilltuaeth y fro* (Caernarfon, 1930?).
WRIGLEY, C. J. *David Lloyd George and the British Labour Movement* (Hassocks, 1976).

INDEX

Aberavon, 187, 268
Aberdare, 187
Aberdeen, 115
Abergynolwyn, 21, 23, 26, 111
Aberllefenni, 80
Aberystwyth, 66, 258
Abraham, William, *see* Mabon
Agricultural Labourers, 8
Agriculture, 8, 20-5
Amalgamated Society of Engineers, 326
Alexandra quarry, 113, 129, 199, 304, 305, 325
America, North, *see* United States of America
Anarchism, 106
Anger, 1n., 106
Anglesey, 1, 6, 7, 10, 14, 21, 23, 25, 30, 66, 117, 142, 169, 245
Anglicanism, 63, 70, 71, 104, 139, 159, 226, 265, 282, 284, 328, 329
Anjou, 1n., 106
Ardennes, 1n.
Arfon, Ioan, *see* Griffith, John O.
Argyllshire, 59
Armstrong, Mr., 172
Askwith, Sir G. R., 305
Asquith, H. H., 214
Assheton-Smith family, 3, 9, 12, 40, 61, 64, 108, 109, 120
Assheton-Smith, George William Duff, 142–62, *passim*
Assheton-Smith, Thomas, 142
Australia, 187

Badrockmen, 73
Bala, 202
Balfour, A. J., 241
Balfour, Gerald, 214
Ballachulish Slate Quarry, 107
Bands, 17, 43, 154, 169
Bangor, 3, 14, 46, 51, 53, 54, 201, 239, 242, 253, 261
Bargain system, 81–5, chapter IV, *passim*, 119, 150
Barnes, George, 269
Barracks, 28, 29, 30, 117, 142
Basse-Bretagne, 1n., 106

Bassin d'Herbeumont, 1n., 106
Beddgelert, 5, 22n., 16
Belgium, 106
Bellcher, Mr., 269
Bethania chapel, 287, 290
Bethel, 18, 63, 137
Bethesda, ix, 11, 18, 20, 25, 27, 41, 44, 46, 51, 52, 56, 60, 62, 63, 64, 111, 112, 114, 116, 117, 122, 123, 126, 137, 152, 163, 173, Chapters VII, VIII, IX, *passim*
Bethesda lodge (N.W.Q.U.), 313
Bethesda Urban District Council, 54, 253
Bethnal Green, 269
Betws Garmon, 84, 112, 132
Betws-y-Coed, 173
Bevin, Ernest, 315
Blacklegs, *see also* Cynffonnwyr, 71, 84
Blaenau Ffestiniog (*see also* Ffestiniog), 3, 4, 18, 19, 20, 23, 24, 26, 27, 28, 30, 31, 32, 35, 37, 39, 40, 46, 48, 54, 65, 69, 72, 114, 116, 117, 118, 120, 121, 124, 162–74, 182, 187, 183, 197, 277, 293, 296, 298, 299, 303, 305, 309, 323
Blaenycae quarry, 297
Blatchford, Robert, 269
Board of Guardians, 68
Board of Trade, 185, 191, 192, 207, 213, 272, 305
Boer War, 258, 281
Bolton, 269
Boyle, Sir Courtenay, 191, 207
Boyle, Hugh, 267
Braich quarry, 113, 300
Brecon, 10
Brewer, Mr., 269
Brittany, 106
Brothen, Ioan, 20n., 21
Bryneglwys quarry, 26, 114
Brynhafodywern quarry, 117
Brynsiencyn, 30
Bryntirion, 240
Buckley, John, 265
Building societies, 27, 123
Burns, John, 243

Burt, Thomas, M.P., 128
Bute, Marquess of, 11

Caban, 57, 58, 78, 79, 164
Caebraichycafn, *see* Penrhyn quarries, Penrhyn lodge
Caerllwyngrydd, 261
Caerllwyngrydd Lending Society, 123
Caernarfon (town), 3, 14, 46, 53, 60, 68, 84, 109, 115, 122, 135, 137, 152, 169, 170, 182, 196, 197, 296, 318
Caernarfon Labour Council, 319
Caernarvon and Denbigh Herald, 89
Caernarvon Boroughs, 53
Caernarvonshire, 1, 6, 7, 8, 9, 10, 23, 24, 25, 40, 44, 63, 75, 115, 142, 202, 214, 220, 276, 317, 318, 320, 321, 324
Caernarvonshire County Council, 54, 202, 204, 220, 252, 253
Calvinistic Methodism, 46, 62, 206
Cambrian Coast line, *see* Railways
Cambrian News, 66–8, *passim*, 273
Campbell-Bannerman, H., 214
Capel Curig, 84, 112, 117, 133, 304
Cardiff, 187, 266
Cardiganshire, 10, 45, 290
Carlyle, Thomas, 204
Carmarthenshire, 7, 8, 10
Carmel, 63
Carneddi, 285
Carter, H. Lloyd, 193, 194, 195, 198, 200, 251
Casson, Thomas, 3
Casson, William, 3
Castell Deudraeth, 170
Cawdor, earl of, 11
Cefnddwysarn, 202
Cefn Du quarry, 113
Cefnfaes Estate, 26
Cesarea, 63
Ceunant, 136, 139n., 105
Chamberlain, J., 215, 241, 242
Chancellor of the Exchequer, 221
Chatham, 268
Choirs, 270, 275
Church of England, *see* Anglicanism
Chwarelwr Cymraeg, Y, 59
Chwilog, 202
Cilgwyn, 15, 15n., 17, 113
Clarion, 269
Clarke, Sir Edward, 214

Clifford, Rev. J., 281
Clwtybont, 298
Coast Erosion Committee, 203
Cockburn, Lord Chief Justice, 45
Coedmadog quarry, 297, 300
Coedpoeth, 188
Collinson, William, 271, 274
Conciliation Act, 1896, x n., 185, 191, 192, 214, 272
Congregationalists, 44, 63, 287
Conservative Central Office, 328, 329
Conservative Club, 241
Conservative Party, 49, 50, 53, 54, 67, 122, 163, 220, 318, 3279
Contracts, 85, 86, 216, 217, 218
Conwy, 53
Cook and Ddol quarry, 113
Co-operative quarries, 103, 283
Copper mining, 7, 23
Cornishmen, 84
Cornwall, 59
Corris, 24, 111, 112, 114
Craft consciousness, 74, 75, 76, 118, 224, 225, 232
Cragg, Wallace, 109
Cricieth, 14, 24, 53, 169
Crime, 46, 47
Croesor, 19n., 30
Crown lands, 2, 15, 283
Cumberland, 4, 59
Cunnington, Henry, 297, 314, 316
Curran, P., 267, 269
Cwmeiddew quarry, 112
Cwmorthin, 30
Cwmorthin mine, 116, 121, 164
Cymdeithas Undebol Chwarelwyr Cymru, ix, 50, 59
Cymru Fydd, 65, 70
Cynffonwyr, 92, 237, 238, Chapter VIII, *passim*, 275, 294

Daily Chronicle, 188
Daily News, 212, 227, 269, 278
Daniel, D. R., 181, 193, 196, 197, 201–4, 216, 226, 234, 241, 267, 279, 280, 287, 296, 298, 300, 316, 317
Darbishire, William, 4, 61, 122
Davies, David, 184, 186, 199
Davies, D. D., 260, 262, 264
Davies, H. H., 37, 180, 205
Davies, John, 77, 142–62, *passim*
Davies, Robert, 192, 193, 201

Davitt, Michael, 65, 163
Deiniolen, *see* Ebenezer
Denbigh, 291
Depression, *see* Slate industry
Derbyshire, 245
Derfel, R. J., 69
Digby, Sir K., 254
Dinorwic Benefit Club, 145
Dinorwic lock-out, 81, 83, 90, 97, 102, 104, 105, 107, 142–62, 167, 187, 326
Dinorwic lodge (N.W.Q.U.), 114, 116, 119, 125, 141, 152, 177, 199, 278, 296
Dinorwic quarries, 3, 9, 15, 21, 24, 30, 32, 40, 68, 81, 93, 101, 103, 111, 112, 116, 117, 121, 127, 128, 129, 130, 133, 136–9, 142–62, 163, 164, 173, 263, 274, 308, 309
Dinorwic quarries hospital, 36, 39, 40, 72, 77
Disestablishment, 63, 64, 70
Dockers' Union, 313
Dolerite quarries, *see* Settsworks
Dolgellau, 13
Dolwyddelan, 24, 111, 173, 258
Domestic servants, 8
Douglas-Pennant, Edward Sholto, 192
Drink, *see* Temperance
Drunkenness, 16
Drws-y-Coed, 23
Drysorfa, Y, 59
Dulais valley, 268
Dunlop, A. M., 163
Dyffryn Ardudwy, 24
Dysgedydd, Y, 59

Ebenezer (Deiniolen), 18, 44, 63
Eco Cymraeg, Yr, 59, 234
Education Bill, 281
Edwards, Clement, 212, 269
Edwards, Griffith, 226
Edwards, John, 123
Edwards, Lewis, 206
Eisteddfodau, 57, 60, 242
Ellis, Rev. Robert, 46
Ellis, T., 200, 263
Ellis, T. E., M.P., 49, 67, 68, 194, 202, 230
Ellis, Winifred A., 42
Emigration, 123
Employers' Associations, 9, 172
Employers' Liability Act, 145

Employers' Parliamentary Committee, 271, 273
England, 10, 11, 56
English Language, 47
Eton, 220
Europe, 5
Evans, Evan, 240
Evans, John, 263
Evans, Dr. R. D., 31, 34
Evans, T. F., *see also* Inspector of Mines, 37
Evans, W. R., 178, 195, 200, 205

Fabian Society, 69
Factory Acts, 38
Felinheli, *see* Port Dinorwic
Ffestiniog, *see also* Blaenau Ffestiniog, 25, 34, 56, 61, 66, 67, 69, 75, 77, 86, 111, 112, 114, 123, 124, 125, 129, 135, 137, 162–74, 185, 196, 199, 295, 296, 299, 302
Ffestiniog Friendly Society, 39
Ffestiniog Quarry Owners' Association, 172
Ffestiniog Railway, *see* Railways
Ffestiniog Urban District Council, 163, 299
First World War, 9, 203, 295, 296, 305–12
Football Clubs, 17, 43, 45, 46
Foster, C. Le Neve, *see also* Inspector of Mines, 163
Fourcrosses, 167
France, 1n., 106
Francis, J., 94
Free Labour, 271, 273
Free Labour Protection Association, *see also* National Free Labour Association, 251
Friendly Societies, 39, 123

Galltyfedw quarry, 297
Gee, Allan, 269
Genedl, Y, 59
Genedl Gymreig, Y, 150, 151, 293
General and Municipal Workers' Union, 326
General Federation of Trade Unions, 107, 210, 215, 229, 276, 277, 296, 314
General Slaters' Union, 268
General Workers' Union, 269
Geninen, Y, 59

George, David Lloyd, 13, 27, 50, 53, 67, 69, 202, 203, 214, 253, 276, 278, 317
Gerlan, 261, 285, 289
Germany, 306
Gladstone, W. E., M.P., 134
Glamorgan, 7, 8, 10, 291
Glasinfryn, 264, 265
Gloddfa'r Coed quarry, 297
Glynllifon, 12
Glynrhonwy, 31, 109, 113
Glyn Uchaf, 316
Goleuad, Y., 59
Goodman and Cambrian quarries, 113
Gorst, Sir John, M.P., 128, 182
Graig Ddu quarry, 164
Greaves, J. E. and R. M., 3, 61, 162–74, passim
Griffith, John O. (Ioan Arfon), 61, 126, 135
Griffith, Owen, 226, 280, 285
Griffith, Thomas Hugh, 32, 37
Griffiths, Griffith, 152
Griffiths, Rev. T., 241
Gruffydd, W. J., 18, 18n., 22
Gwalia, 59
Gŵyl Lafur, 182, 183
Gwynedd, x, Chapter 1, passim, 23, 49, 52–4, 56, 108, 209, 317, 321

Hafod Y Wern quarry, 84, 112, 132
Hardie, Keir, 239, 253, 269, 279, 281
Harlech, 14, 66
Hay-Harvest, 19
Herald Cymraeg, Yr, 52, 59, 231, 240, 242, 276, 287
Hicks-Beach, Sir M., 221
Holland, Samuel, M.P., 3, 4n., 9, 61
Holyhead, 5, 13
Home Office, 242, 245–256
Hopper, Thomas, 11
House of Commons, 88, 214, 253
House of Lords, 134
Huddersfield, 269
Hughes, Dr. (Dinorwic), 39
Hughes, Dr. (Waunfawr), 35
Hughes, Cllr. Ellis, 167, 171
Hughes, Rev. H., 291
Hughes, J. J., 135
Hughes, John, 171, 173, 174
Hughes, R., 239
Hughes, Richard, 190, 228, 229, 241, 244

Hughes, T. Rowland, 42
Hughes, W. R., 239
Humphreys, D. Ll., 197
Humphreys, E. Morgan, 64, 206, 209
Hyndman, H. H., 143

Immigration, 15, 22, 23, 53, 60
Independent Labour Party, 269, 273, 279, 281, 299, 318, 319, 320
Independent Order of Oddfellows, 123, 236
Inspector of Mines, 23, 27, 29, 37, 38, 42, 88
Ireland, 2, 4, 5, 15, 65
Italians, 258

James, Lord, 215
Jerusalem chapel, Bethesda, 289, 291, 294
Jones, Dr., 31, 33
Jones, David, 78
Jones, Rev. Ellis James, 44
Jones, Griffith, 167, 168
Jones, Henry Alexandra, 91
Jones, Henry, (Bethesda), 192, 193, 226, 282, 288
Jones, Hugh, 190
Jones, John, 263
Jones, John D., 227
Jones, John Lloyd, 135
Jones, Michael D., 67
Jones, Morris D., 298, 303
Jones, O. Ellis, 296, 298, 317
Jones, O. P., 94
Jones, Owen, 155
Jones, R., 103
Jones, Dr. Richard, 34, 35
Jones, R. J., 226
Jones, R. R., 285
Jones, R. T., 69, 204, Chapter X, passim, 324, 325
Jones, S., 240
Jones, Thomas, 203
Jones, William, M.P., 53, 88, 214, 241, 253, 278, 280, 319
Jones, W. W. ('Cyrus'), 69, 226, 227, 279, 280, 281, 282
Jones-Parry, Thomas Love, M.P., 51, 220
Journeymen, 74, 88
Justice, 143
Justices Act, 254
Justices of the Peace, see Magistrates

Kellow, Joseph, 87
Kellow, Moses, 4, 48n.
Kershaw, Henry, 246, 247
Kirkham, Mr., 269

Labour Church, 269
Labour Day, see Gwŷl Lafur
Labourers, 74, 117, 142
Labour Party, 136, 209, 278, 300, 315-21, 324
Labour Representation, 68, 69, 171, 279, 280, 281, 282, 315-21
Lancashire, 1, 2, 3, 4, 245
Lancashire Miners' Federation, 130
Landownership, 10, 64
Leasehold, 26, 64
Liberalism, 16, 49-54 passim, 55, 65, 66-8, 122, 126, 137, 139, 140, 163, 171, 174, 192, 202, 209, 214, 220, 276, 278, 279, 283, 317, 319, 320, 326, 327
Liberal Party, see Liberalism
Liberty and Property Defence League, 271
Liberty Review, The, 270, 271, 272
Liverpool, 3, 5, 62, 124, 153, 187, 188, 200, 245, 275, 295
Liverpool Daily Post, 259
Livesey, George, 272
Llanberis, 18, 24, 25, 26, 34, 46, 48, 109, 111, 114, 116, 129, 142-62, 163, 187, 188, 277
Llanddulas, 143, 156
Llandegai, 17, 220, 239
Llandudno, 5, 14, 14n., 120
Llandudno Junction, 190
Llandwrog, 23
Llanfaglan, 188
Llanfihangel-y-Pennant, 20
Llanfrothen, 19n., 30, 117, 173
Llangefni, 14
Llanllyfni, 46, 303
Llanrwst, 173
Llechwedd Dispute, 162-74
Llechwedd slate mine, 39, 58, 62, 107, 118, 121, 124, 129, 133, 205
Llithfaen, 8
Lloyd, Morgan, 66-9 passim
Lloyd, Pennant, 93
Lloyd, Rev. W. W., 270
Lloyd George, David, see George, David Lloyd
Llwybrmain, 204, 205, 239

Llŷn, 5, 25, 187
Local Board, 25, 28
Local Fund, 175, 176
London, 4, 143, 203, 221, 267, 268, 269
London and North Western, see Railways
London Central Committee, 269

Mabon, 182, 267, 269, 281
Madocks, William A., 6, 6n.
Maenofferen mine, 163, 172
Maentwrog, 111n.
Magistrates, 54, 134, 239, 242, 246-56
Management, 60, 62, 77, 79, 88, 89, 93
Manchester, 187, 188, 276
Mazzini, Giuseppe, 202, 204
Meares, H. P., 248
Mediterranean, 5
Menai Suspension Bridge, 4
Menzies, A. W. Kay, 304
Menzies, J., 195
Merioneth, 1, 6, 7, 10, 13, 18, 21, 23, 24, 40, 74, 88, 111, 115, 143, 162, 202, 276, 280, 317; election, 1885, 65-8
Merioneth County Council, 49
Merthyr Tydfil, 107, 288
Metalliferous Mines Regulations Acts, 38, 115
Middle-class, 13, 53, 54, 55, 70, 104, 135, 136, 281, 283
Military, 156, 211, 213, 239, 241, 246-56
Millar, Frederick, 251, 270, 274
Mining Journal, 76, 88, 121, 122
Ministry of Labour, 308
Mitchell, Isaac, 269, 296, 325
Mobility, 97, 165
Moeltryfan, 111, 117, 199, 297, 304
Moelwynion, 117
Moel-y-Don, 30
Montgomeryshire, 169
Morgan, Rev. W., 256, 328, 329
Morning Leader, 269
Morris, R., 94
Mynydd Llandegai, 204, 261

Nantlle, 23, 187, 296
Nantlle lodge (N.W.Q.U.), 302, 318
Nantlle valley, 3, 4, 15, 18, 19, 19n., 32, 46, 62, 84, 103, 111, 112, 114, 118, 122, 124, 125, 126, 132, 135, 152, 159, 293, 295, 297, 303, 305

National Association of Shop Assistants, 268
National Co-op Quarries, 283
National Free Labour Association, 271, 273, 274
National Insurance Act, 1911, 301, 302
Nationalism, 55–71, 282
National Joint Committee on the Quarrying Industry, 308
National Union of Gasworkers and General Labourers, 267
National Union of Quarrymen, 313
Navvies and General Labourers Union, 267
Nazareth, 63
Neath, 187
Nebo, 63
Nefyn, 53, 169
Newborough, Lord, 12
Newquay, 290
New Welsh Slate Company, 19, 75, 116, 165
Nonconformity, 16, 17, 43–4, 55, 62, 63, 124, 206, 208, 227, 235, 284–94
Non-Unionists Association, 159
Normal College, Bangor, 137
Northern Weekly, 269
Northumberland miners, 267
North Wales Craftsmen and General Workers' Union, 315
North Wales Observer and Express, 161
North Wales Property Defence Association, 65, 221
North Wales Quarries Ltd., 283, 298
North Wales Slate Quarries Association, 308
North Wales Quarrymen's Union, 15, 26, 53, 60, 61, 64, 65, 66, 69, 74, 77, 84, 91, 92, 95, 100, 102, 103, 143, 156, 164, 168, 169, 170, 175, 199, 201–5, 209, 276–83, Chapters V, VIII, IX, X, XI *passim*
  Amalgamation, 312–15
  Benefits, 126, 127
  Founding, 108–10
  Funds, 268–70, 276–7
  Leadership, 135–41, 201–9
  Lodges, 111n., 114, 125, 199
  Membership, 106–7, 199, 210, 296

Oakeley family, 12, 163, 164
Oakeley slate mine, 29, 39, 72, 106, 116, 120, 163, 164, 305

Ogwen Benefit Society, 123
Onllwyn, 268
Operative Bricklayers' Society, 268
Ormesby-Gore family, 12
Owen, Robert, 184, 199
Owen, T. H., 93
Owen, John, 114
Oxford, 220

Pacifism, 306
Pall Mall Gazette, 74, 83
Pantdreiniog quarry, 112, 113, 132, 275
Parliamentary Committee, 268
Parliamentary elections, 49, 51, 52, 53, 65–8, 220, 221, 316, 318, 320, 321, 322
Parliament for Wales, 65, 68
Parry, David, 200
Parry, Rev. G. T., 26
Parry, Owen, 315
Parry, Robert, (Ceunant), 78, 92, 131, 132, 136, 138, 139, 139n.
Parry, Robert, 86, 136, **138**
Parry, R. Williams, 57
Parry, Thomas, 162, 170
Parry, William John, 69, 112, 113, 131, 135n., 193, 198, 200, 202, 204, 209, 214, 222, 227, 242, 263, 270, 281, 283, 286, 300, 325
  Union, 133–40
  Dinorwic, 156–7, 160
Paternalism, 120, 121
Pembrokeshire, 59
Penmachno, 103, 111n., 258
Penmaenmawr, 8
Pennant family, 9
Pennant, Caroline Douglas, 11n.
Pennant, Eva Douglas, 11n.
Pennant, George Hay Dawkins, 2n., 11
Pennant, George Sholto Douglas, *see* Penrhyn, second baron
Pennant, Kathleen Douglas, 11n.
Pennant, Richard, 2, 6
Pennant Lloyd Agreement, 96, 110, 113, 119, 175
Penrhyn Castle, 2n., 9, 11, 50, 52, 53, 100, 221
Penrhyndeudraeth, 18, 24, 48, 111n., 125, 173, 187
Penrhyn, Edward Gordon Douglas, *see* Penrhyn, First Baron
Penrhyn estate, 10, 20, 26, 220, 221, 264

Penrhyn, First Baron of Llandegai, 2n., 11, 12, 51, 61, 63, 64, 93, 109, 110, 145, 163, 220

Penrhyn lock-out, 1896–7, ix, x, 86, 107, 121, 133, 138, 143, 308, 326, 329, Chapter VII *passim*

Penrhyn lock-out, 1900–03, ix, x, 54, 69, 86, 107, 120, 133, 143, 167, 295, 308, 313, 315, 316, 323, 326, 329, Chapters VIII, IX, *passim*

Penrhyn lodge, 114, 116, 119, 125, 136, 148, 169, 280, 296, Chapters VII, VIII, *passim*

Penrhyn, Lord, *see* Penrhyn, First Baron; Penrhyn, Second Baron

Penrhyn quarries, 26, 62, 72, 74, 80, 116, 121, 124, 127, 128, 136, 142, 146, 161, 164, 308, 309, Chapters VII, VIII, *passim*
  1825, ixn.
  1865, 82
  1874, 93–4, 108–10
  contracts, 85, 88
  early history, 2
  local economy, 9, 322
  recruitment, 97
  redundancies, 98

Penrhyn Quarries Hospital, 31, 39, 222

Penrhyn Quarry Committee, 85, 94–7, 113, 130, 137, 138, Chapters VII, VIII, *passim*

Penrhyn quarrymen, 50, 51, 84, 86, 90, 92, 100, 106, 119, 132, 139, Chapters VII, VIII, *passim*

Penrhyn, Second Baron of Llandegai, 2n., 12, 51, 53, 54, 65, 81, 96, 100, 102, 120–2, 175, 220–5, 327–9, Chapters VII, VIII, IX, *passim*

Penrhyn Relief Fund, 269, 270, 276

Penri, John, 287

Pentir, 256, 257

Penygroes, 18, 28, 31, 33, 42, 46, 277

Penyrorsedd quarry, 32, 37, 113, 112

Peris, Dewi, 60

Phillips, Thomas, 48

Phoenix Society, 269

Plenydd, 202

Police, 46, 54, 84, 242, 244–56

Political Union of the Welsh Nation, 67, 69

Population, 6, 7

Port Dinorwic, 3, 111, 119, 162

Porth, 282

Portmadoc, 3, 5, 6, 14, 24, 46, 152

Port Penrhyn, 2, 119, 189

Prestatyn, 253

Price, Thomas, 229

Print workers, 169, 188

Pritchard, D., 177

Pritchard, David, 265n.

Pritchard, R. G., 226

Pritchard, R. W., 236

Productivity, 146, 218

Profits, 8, 9, 121, 122, 142

Public houses, 46

Pugh, Hugh, 135

Pwllheli, 53, 169

Quarries and Slate Mining Bill, 319

Quarry Committee of Inquiry, 19

Quarrying National Trade Group, 314

Quarryman's Charter, 301, 302

Quarrymen, *see* Slate quarrymen

Queen's Hotel, Caernarfon, 109

Railways, 3, 5, 5n., 173
  Cambrian coast, 5
  Ffestiniog, 3, 30
  London and North Western, 5

Rees, G. Caradoc, 320

Reform Bill, 1884, 66, 133

Religious Revival, 63, 203, 284–94

Respiratory diseases, 34

Rhaeadr, 288

Rhiw quarry, 112

Rhiwbryfdir slate mine, 4

Rhondda, 288

Rhos quarry, 84, 111, 112, 117, 133, 304

Rhosllannerchrugog, 188, 268

Rhostryfan, 113

Rhosydd slate mine, 29, 117, 164

Rhyl, 253

Richards, Morgan, 76, 86, 97, 111, 123, 135n.

Riley, Mr., 269

Ritchie, C. F., 192, 254, 272

Roberts, Azariah, 199

Roberts, Charles Warren, 166

Roberts, Dr. E., 28, 32, 33, 42

Roberts, Evan, 63, 291

Roberts, J. Jones, 321

Roberts, John, 226

Roberts, Dr. John, 36

Roberts, J. W., 239

Roberts, Kate, 57

Roberts Peter, 200
Roberts, Robert, 165
Roberts, Dr. R. H. Mills, 32, 36, 40
Roberts, Rev. R. Silyn, 299, 317
Robertson, Henry, 65–8
Robinson, John, 4, 122, 128, 159
Rockmen, 74, 76
Roseberry, Lord, 215
Rothschild, Nathan Meyer, 4
Royal Cambrian Company, 4
Royal Commission on the Church of
    England and other religious bodies
    in Wales and Monmouthshire, 44,
    59, 299
Royal Commission on Labour, 1891,
    19, 22, 205
Royal Commission on Land in Wales
    and Monmouthshire, 20, 221, 231
Royal Hotel, Caernarfon, 122
Royal Welsh Fusiliers, 187, 220
Rubbishmen, 73
Ruck, Colonel, A. A., 190, 191, 244–56,
    passim
Rybelwr, 73, 88, 118, 183, 216, 217

St. Ann's church, Bethesda, 256
Schools, 233
Settmakers' Union, 115, 313
Settsworks, 8, 187
Sexton, James, 313
Shipping, 8
Shropshire, 245
Sick clubs, 17, 39, 40, 123
Slate industry, 1, 7, 8, 13
    Depression, 112–14, 295
    Boom, 310
Slate Mines (Gunpowder) Act, 38
Slate quarrymen,
    Accidents, 37–8
    Barracks, 28–30
    Creation of, 14–15
    Diet, 31–3
    Dress, 33
    Health, 34–6, 39–41
    Housing, 25–31
    Land, 19, 20–5, 64–5
    Language, 56–61
    Militancy, 106
    Numbers, 17
    Politics, 66–70
    Skill, 73
Sling, 261
Snowdonia, 20, 61

Snowdon Mountain Railway, 187
Social Democratic Federation, 69, 143
South Africa, 187
Southern Metropolitan Gas Company,
    272
South Wales, 45, 169, 187, 266, 275,
    294
South Wales Miners' Federation, 268
Staffordshire, 187
Standing Joint Police Committee, 54,
    244, 252
Stephen, Rev. Edward, 52
Stockport, 245
Stoney Stratford, 221
Sunday Closing Act, 65
Sunderland, 276
Swaine, Maj. Gen. L. V., 254
Swansea, 7
Syndicalism, 303

Taff Vale, 326
Talsarnau, 173
Talysarn, 18, 128, 159, 187, 323
Talysarn quarry, 297
Tanrallt quarry, 297
Tanygrisiau, 17, 121, 164
Tax returns, 7, 8
Temperance, 46, 65, 202, 234, 235, 265,
    299
Thomas, D. A., 253
Thomas, David, 320
Thomas, David (Surgeon), 135
Thomas, D. Lleufer, 22
Thomas, H. H., 239
Thomas, J. W., 202
Thompson, A. M., 269
Thompson, E. P., 12
Tidswell, Mr., 154
Tillett, Ben, 269
Times, The, 204, 272
Tories, see Conservative Party
Tourism, 5, 18
Trades Union Act, 1913, 319
Trades Union Congress, 211, 267, 300,
    314
Traeth Mawr, 6
Transport, 4, 5, 8, 30
Transport and General Workers'
    Union, 312, 314, 315, 326
Trawsfynydd, 24, 111n., 173
Tredegar, 288
Tredegar, Lord, 11
Trefor, 8

Tregarth, 19, 260, 261, 263
Tremadoc, 6
Trench, Mr., 264
True Ivorites, 123
Tumble, 268
Turner, F., 31
Turner, William, 3

United Society of Welsh Quarrymen, ix
Udgorn Rhyddid, 69
U.K. Alliance, 202
United States of America, In., 5, 202, 215, 223, 268, 288, 295

Vaynol estate, *see also* Assheton-Smith, 12, 52–3, 142, 161, 163
Victoria Hotel, Bethesda, 241
Vincent, H. C., 251, 263
Vivian, W. W., 40, 77, 81, 100, 128, 142–62, 263, 274
Votty and Bowydd mine, 163, 164

Wages, *see also* Bargain system, 91, 94, 113, 119, 129, 143, 183, 195, 216, 217, 218, 309, 311, 312
Wales, 1, 23, 24, 56, 63, 65
Wales, Prince of, 215
Warburton, Anna Susannah, 2
Ward, John, 267
Waterloo Inn, Bethesda, 241
Waunfawr, 35, 111, 113, 137, 187
Welsh language, 15, 47, 50, 54, 55, 56–60 *passim*, 67, 204
Welsh press, 51, 52, 55, 59, 161, 221, 281
Welsh Slate and Copper Mining Company, 4
Welsh Slate Company, 38, 112
Werin, Y, 59, 153, 234
West Indies, 3, 11
Whitehall, 203
William, Dr. John, 31, 36

Williams, A. Osmond, 170, 280
Williams, Rev. Cernyw, 169
Williams, D., 177
Williams, D. G., 26, 66, 69, 124, 171, 172
Williams, Edward, 228
Williams, H. M., 298
Williams, J. E., 197
Williams, John, 78
Williams, John, 244
Williams, John (Brynmeurig), 186
Williams, John (Rynys), 200, 206, 207, 226
Williams, Rev. John, 169
Williams, Melancthon, 265n.
Williams, Owen, 162
Williams, Sir Robert, 2
Williams, W. (Gerlan), 186
Williams, W. E., 135
Williams, W. H., 138, 177, 180, 189, 190, 192, 193, 194, 196, 198, 200, 226, 227, 235, 244, 279, 281, 285, 286, 287, 296, 298, 299, 300, Chapters VII, VIII, *passim*
Williams, William, 185
Williams, William, 226, 285
Williams, William, 280
Williams, William Cadwaladar, 20
Williams, William G., 200
Williams, William Gadlys, 35
Williams, W. J., 126, 135, 137, 138, 140, 161, 181, 193, 194, 196, 197, 198, 202, 209, 227, 301
Williams, W. R., 303
Williams-Wynn, Sir Watkin, 11, 12
Women, 41–43, 189
Working-hours, 72, 89, 111, 112, 164
Wyatt, Col., 144

Young, Emilius Alexander, 20n., 62, 81, 96, 161, 223–5, Chapters VII, VIII, *passim*